The Interface between Competition Law, Patents and Technical Standards

International Competition Law Series

VOLUME 59

Editor-in-Chief

Alastair Sutton,

Visiting Fellow at the Centre of European Law at King's College, London

The titles published in this series are listed at the end of this volume.

The Interface between Competition Law, Patents and Technical Standards

David Telyas

Wolters Kluwer
Law & Business

Published by:
Kluwer Law International
PO Box 316
2400 AH Alphen aan den Rijn
The Netherlands
Website: www.kluwerlaw.com

Sold and distributed in North, Central and South America by:
Aspen Publishers, Inc.
7201 McKinney Circle
Frederick, MD 21704
United States of America
Email: customer.service@aspenpublishers.com

Sold and distributed in all other countries by:
Turpin Distribution Services Ltd
Stratton Business Park
Pegasus Drive, Biggleswade
Bedfordshire SG18 8TQ
United Kingdom
Email: kluwerlaw@turpin-distribution.com

Printed on acid-free paper.

ISBN 978-90-411-5418-7

Printed and Bound by CPI Group (UK) Ltd, Croydon, CR0 4YY.

"Allowing companies to sit around a table and agree technical developments for their industry is not something that the competition rules would usually allow. So when it is allowed we have to look carefully at how it is done."

Neelie Kroes, former European Commissioner for Competition Policy, speaking about standards (SPEECH/08/317)

Table of Contents

Preface

This book is the outcome of a three-year industrial PhD project carried out in cooperation with Aarhus University, Denmark and the Danish law firm Gorrissen Federspiel.[1] Its content has been updated to reflect EU case law and legislation as of 30 May 2014.

My work on the project has provided me with an in-depth understanding of the competition law issues related to standardisation, and I am grateful to all who have supported me in the process.

Special thanks go to my supervisor, Associate Professor Hanne Kirk Deichmann, for her support and expert feedback during the course of the project. I would also like to thank Associate Professor Matthew Elsmore and Karsten Engsig Søren for always keeping their door open and for providing me with valuable input on the issues dealt with in this book.

As an employee of Gorrissen Federspiel I have gained valuable experience on the practical aspects of the work of an IP lawyer, and this too has provided a solid foundation for my work on this book. I would like to thank my colleagues in general and in particular Kenneth Kvistgaard-Aaholm (Partner, Attorney) and Dan Bjerg Geary (Attorney) for taking time to discuss with me some of the legal issues dealt with. Moreover, I would like to thank Lasse Arffmann Søndergaard Christensen (Partner, Attorney) for allowing me the flexibility needed and for ensuring that the tasks that have been relevant to this book have been directed my way.

Last but not least, I would like to thank my wife, Anni, for her patience and moral support.

1. The opinions expressed in this dissertation are my own and do not necessarily reflect those of Gorrissen Federspiel.

Part I Prologue

CHAPTER 1

Introduction

Technical standards have a huge impact on our everyday lives as they allow products from different manufacturers to 'interact' seamlessly and thus establish the very backbone of modern society in which the interoperability of products is essential both for businesses and consumers.[1] Many well-known technologies, such as Blu-ray, USB, WIFI and MP3, originate from standard-setting activities. In fact, the vast majority of technical products, from mobile phones, computers and software to light bulbs and cars, comply with a variety of technical standards. Generally, standardization may take place within the framework of a standard-setting organisation (SSO) or it may result from the efforts of a single, often dominant, company which succeeds in promoting a technical specification so that it becomes the commonly accepted industry standard. Standards set by multiple companies within the framework of an SSO are usually referred to as 'formal standards' while standards set by a dominant company are termed '*de facto* standards', as they arise from consumer choice (market forces) and not from formal standardization efforts.

Despite their commercial and economic importance, technical standards have not traditionally attracted much attention from lawyers and there has been little litigation involving intellectual property rights (IPRs) following the setting of a standard. However, probably fuelled by the increasing number of patents related to information and communications technology (ICT), their inclusion in technical standards, and the complexity of modern technological products, often incorporating several patents and standards, litigation in this field has increased.[2,3] This has resulted

1. Technical standards for instance allow us to use a cell phone to call people regardless of which brand of phone they use, send an e-mail knowing the recipient will be able to read it, access web pages using a single browser, read the documents we receive without installing numerous software programs, and use different peripheral devices, such as Bluetooth headsets, without worrying that said device is incompatible with our existing products.
2. Also see Kühn, Kai-Uwe, Morton, Fiona Scott & Shelanski, *Standard Setting Organisation Can Help Solve the Standard Essential Patent Licensing Problem*, in CPI Antitrust Chronicle, March 2013 (special issue) p. 1, stating that "*...In the ICT sector, rates of patenting have exploded and –*

in what are referred to as the 'patent wars'.[4] These 'wars', in which the focal point has been the assertion of patents that are essential to the implementation of technical standards ('essential patents' or 'SEPs'[5]), have been 'fought' by major corporations such as Microsoft, Nokia, Huawei, Google, Samsung, Motorola and Apple. Thus, the perception of technical standards as mainly involving 'engineerical' challenges has changed dramatically during the last decade in which they have received a tremendous amount of attention, not only from a technical and economic perspective, but also from lawyers, competition authorities and legal scholars.[6]

Not surprisingly, much of this attention has been directed at untangling the competition law issues raised by the assertion of SEPs. Thus, while the competitive benefits of standardization are widely recognized, including by the European Commission, competition authorities strive to ensure that the market power obtained by holding SEPs is not abused to the detriment of effective competition. The power given by SEPs to exclude competitors and the potential for abuse should not be underestimated. In a German court case filed by Motorola against Microsoft, it was revealed that Motorola's own expert characterized SEPs as bullets and noted that "*it only takes one bullet to kill*". This was a reference to the fact that a single SEP is sufficient to block third parties from implementing the standard to which it relates.[7] The market power which is often, but not always, obtained via SEPs is attributable to the fact that there are, by definition, no substitute technologies which enable compliance with the standard in which they are embodied. Simply opting for non-compliance with a well-established standard will often not be a viable option insofar as the market demands compliance. This means that the use of patents that are embodied in standards may become essential, not only to ensure compliance with the standard, but

---

with the convergence among communications technology, device hardware, and software – products have become more complex".

3. As of 29 Aug. 2013, 149,772 patent declarations had been made in respect of the 6,253 standards currently set by the accredited European Telecommunications Standards Institute (ETSI). See ETSI's IPR database available at: http://ipr.etsi.org/. Although the number of patent declarations gives an inflated picture of the actual number of unique and SEPs due to over-declarations and duplications (see Fraunhofer Institute for Communication System and Dialogic, *Study on the Interplay between Standards and Intellectual Property Rights (IPRs)*, OJEU S136 of 18 Jul. 2009, 2011, pp. 19–20) it nonetheless gives an indication of the immense amounts of patents related to technical standards. Also see Biddle, Brad et al., *How Many Standards in a Laptop? (And Other Empirical Questions)*, working paper, 2010 who identify 251 technical interoperability standards implemented in a modern laptop computer of which 44% were developed by consortia, 36% by formal standards development organizations, and 20% by single companies (de facto standards). Available at: http://papers.ssrn.com/sol3/papers.cfm?abstract_id=1619440 (last checked 30 May 2014).
4. See e.g., Hellström, Per & Kramler, Thomas, *Competition, Standards and Patents*, in CPI Antitrust Chronicle, Vol. 2, 2012 p. 2, and Zafar, Osmann, *The junction between competition and IP law*, in Intellectual Property Magazine, April 2012 p. 53.
5. SEP is an abbreviation of 'standard essential patents'.
6. Also see WIPO, *Standards and Patents*, Standing committee on the law of patents, 13th Session, 2009 p. 14.
7. The expert in question was cited in a motion filed by Microsoft with the United States District Court for the Western District of Washington 20 Apr. 2012 (Case C10-1823-JLR). A copy of the motion is available at: www.patentprogress.org/wp-content/uploads/2012/11/Filing-210-Microsoft-Motion-for-Preliminary-Injunction.pdf (last checked 30 May 2014).

to maintain a viable presence in the market. Accordingly, holders of SEPs may effectively be able to act as gatekeepers to the market.

Competition law plays an important role in ensuring that holders of SEPs do not unduly exploit their market power to engage in exploitative or exclusionary conduct once a market has become 'locked-in' to a particular standard, for example by demanding excessive or discriminatory licensing terms or by seeking injunctions against manufacturers of products that comply with a standard. To safeguard against such opportunistic and anti-competitive behaviour, the licensing practices of holders of SEPs are subject to competition law scrutiny as are the IPR polices of SSOs and the conduct of patentees during the standard-setting process. SSOs, patent holders and manufacturers alike all need to be familiar with the restraints imposed by competition law.

Although the exercise of IPRs that are essential to a de facto standard may contravene competition law, special attention should be paid to formal standards since their success, and hence their pro-competitive benefits, does not depend on the efforts of a single company but on cooperation, in good faith, between multiple stakeholders who aim to reach agreement on a common technical specification. To this end, the Commission in its Guidelines on horizontal cooperation agreements (the 'Horizontal Guidelines') states among other things that the IPR policies of SSOs should require participants to provide an irrevocable written commitment to offer to license their essential IPRs to all third parties on fair, reasonable and non-discriminatory terms (FRAND terms) as a prerequisite for having the IPRs included as part of a standard.[8] The purpose of these requirements is to prevent what is commonly known as 'patent hold-up' – that is, the imposition of excessive or discriminatory royalty demands after a standard has been widely adopted in the market and there is no turning back.[9] SSOs whose IPR policies do not comply with this requirement will not be able to benefit from the presumption of legality (the 'safe harbour') established by the Horizontal Guidelines. However, the surge in litigation involving SEPs referred to above and the increase in competition law enquiries is troubling, and some see it as evidence that the FRAND commitments are not effective in ensuring that the pro-competitive effects of formal standardization prevail.[10]

8. See Communication from the Commission, *Guidelines on the applicability of Article 101 of the Treaty on the Functioning of the European Union to horizontal co-operation agreements*, OJ 2011/C 11/1, 14 Jan. 2011, § 285 (in particular). In the USA the term RAND, short for 'reasonable and non-discriminatory', is used in place of FRAND.
9. See for Farrell, Joseph et al., *Standard Setting, Patents, and Hold-Up*, in Antitrust Law Journal, Vol. 74(3), 2007 p. 603 and Bonadio, Enrico, *Standardization Agreements, Intellectual Property Rights and Anti-competitive Concerns*, in Queen Mary Journal of Intellectual Property, 2013 p. 12. Available at: http://ssrn.com/abstract=2237426.
10. See for instance Commission, *Modernising ICT Standardisation in the EU – The Way Forward*, COM(2009) 324 final, White paper, 3 Jul. 2009, point 2.4, where the Commission notes that despite the FRAND principles "*[m]any stakeholders feel that there is room for improvement to reduce complexity and improve predictability of the licensing process*". Also see Bekkers, Rudi et al., *Emerging ways to address the reemerging conflict between patenting and technological standardization*, in Industrial & Corporate Change, Vol. 21(4), 2012 p. 905, and Contreras, Jorge L., *Fixing Frand: A Pseudo-Pool Approach To Standards-Based Patent Licensing*, Forthcoming in Antitrust Law Journal, Fall 2013. Available at SSRN: http://ssrn.com/abstract=2232515.

The aim of this book has been to explore how Articles 101 and 102 of the Treaty on the Functioning of the European Union (TFEU) have been applied, and how it is likely that they will be applied, to prevent, identify and sanction patent-related abuse in the context of technical standards.

Chapter 2

Recent Trends and Developments: An Overview

Much has changed since the Commission published its Communication[1] on IPR and standardization in 1992, but the overall objective of competition law in ensuring the availability of standard-essential IPRs on fair, reasonable and non-discriminatory terms is even more important now than it was then. The economic importance of standards has increased considerably in recent decades, as has the share of standards in which patents are embodied, especially in the field of ICT.[2] A fact-finding study made on behalf of the Commission concluded that the proportion of standards including essential IPRs in the ICT sector had increased by almost 150% from 1999 to 2009.[3] In addition it was found that more than 84% of standards are related to the ICT sector.[4] This trend relates to the increase in litigation seen over the last decade (see below) and has triggered an increased focus on the interplay between standards, patents and competition law. In particular, it has become increasingly evident that competition law is sometimes called for to guide the adoption of pro-competitive standardization agreements and to prevent holders of SEPs from subverting the benefits of standardization by engaging in exploitative or exclusionary conduct.

1. Communication from the Commission, *Intellectual Property Rights and Standardisation*, COM(92) 445 Final, 27 Oct. 1992.
2. Fraunhofer Institute for Communication System and Dialogic, *Study on the Interplay between Standards and Intellectual Property Rights (IPRs)*, OJEU S136 of 18 Jul. 2009, 2011 p. 17. According to the Commission, in 2007 the European ICT industry accounted for a turnover of no less than EUR 670 billion and over 5% of total employment in the EU, but to release the sector's full potential it was acknowledged that "*European ICT needs sound framework conditions to fully contribute to the growth and jobs agenda and in this context standardisation plays an important role*". See Commission, *Modernising ICT Standardisation in the EU – The Way Forward*, COM(2009) 324 final, White paper, 3 Jul. 2009, p. 2.
3. Fraunhofer Institute for Communication System and Dialogic, *Study on the Interplay between Standards and Intellectual Property Rights (IPRs)*, OJEU S136 of 18 Jul. 2009, 2011, pp. 53-55. The study also concluded that 98% of all patent disclosures in SSOs were stated on ICT standards.
4. *Ibid.*, p. 52.

One need merely to look at recent EU case law involving competition law issues including refusals to grant licences, the imposition of non-FRAND licence terms, deception of SSOs and applications for injunctive relief on the basis of SEPs. Thus, within the last decade we have witnessed a number of cases in the EU concerning the interface between standards, competition law and intellectual property law, including the *Microsoft*[5] case decided by the General Court, and the *Qualcomm*,[6] *IPCom*,[7] and *Rambus*[8] cases which were investigated by the Commission. Most recently, the Commission found that Samsung Electronics and Motorola Mobility violated Article 102 TFEU by relying on their SEPs to seek injunctions against competitors.[9] The tension between SEPs and competition law has also played a role in litigation at national level, especially in Germany and the Netherlands. Indeed, the *Spundfass*[10] and *Orange-Book-Standard*[11] cases, and the recent seizure and customs detention (now lifted) of Sony's PlayStation 3 game consoles,[12] all highlight the potential for conflict following the setting of standards, as does the litigation initiated by Samsung and Motorola referred to above. As already noted, these cases have caught the attention of the legal world, stakeholders involved in standardization and policy-makers, including the Commission.

The European Commission (and its US counterpart – the Federal Trade Commission (FTC))[13] is increasingly focusing on the interface between standards, competition and IPRs. For instance, in 2008 the Commission published a communication outlining key initiatives to strengthen the contribution of standardization to innovation and competitiveness in Europe.[14] Among other things the communication stressed that "*due regard needs to be paid to the interrelation between IPRs and standardisation*"[15] and the Commission's fact-finding study, referred to above, was commissioned in 2009 to uncover such interrelation. Moreover, in 2009 the Commission published a white paper focusing specifically on the challenges to standardization in the ICT sector,

5. *Case* T-201/04, *Microsoft Corp. v. Commission*, 17 Sep. 2007.
6. Case COMP/39.247, *Texas Instruments / Qualcomm*, 24 Nov. 2009.
7. Case COMP/39.615, *Nokia/Bosch + IPCom*, 10 Dec. 2009.
8. Case COMP/38.636, *Rambus* and on appeal Case T-148/10 and T-149/10, *Hynix Semiconductor v. Commission*, 5 Jun. 2010 (withdrawn following settlement agreement).
9. COMP/39.939, *Samsung – Enforcement of UMTS standards essential patents* and Case COMP/39.985, *Motorola – Enforcement of GPRS standard essential patents*.
10. KZR 40/02, *Standard Tight-head Drum (Standard-Spundfass)*, Federal Supreme Court of Germany (Bundesgerichtshof), 13 Jul. 2004.
11. Case KZR 39/06, *Philips Electronics N.V. v. SK Kassetten*, German Federal Supreme Court, 6 May 2009, and Case 316533/HA ZA 08-2522 and 316535/HA ZA 08-2524, *Koninklijke Philips Electronics N.V. v. SK Kassetten GmbH & Co. KG*, District Court of The Hague, 17 Mar. 2010.
12. Case 389067/KG ZA 11-269, *Sony Supply Chain solutions (Europe) v. LG Electronics*, District Court of The Hague, 10 Mar. 2011.
13. On the other side of the Atlantic in 2011 the FTC initiated a project to examine the legal and policy issues surrounding the problem of patent 'hold-up' in connection with collaborative standard-setting activities and the role of competition law in preventing such hold-ups. As part of the project, named 'IP Rights in Standard Setting – Tools to Prevent Patent Hold-Up', the FTC conducted a workshop and asked for comments from the public on the issues – see:www.ftc.gov/opp/workshops/standards/index.shtml (last checked 30 May 2014).
14. Communication from the Commission, *Towards an increased contribution from standardisation to innovation in Europe*, COM(2008) 133 final, 11 Mar. 2008.
15. *Ibid.*, point 7.

including those related to competition law and IPRs.[16] In the white paper it was recognized that "*there are certain aspects of ICT standardisation with its focus on functional standards and interoperability, which make the treatment of IPR especially important and delicate in this field*".[17] On the one hand IPRs are important drivers of innovation and hence their exercise should not be unduly restricted, while on the other it is necessary to ensure that the market power obtained by holding IPRs – in particular patents – in the context of technical standards is not abused to restrict effective competition.

There is an overlap between EU competition law and the EU's standardization policy in that promoting compliance with the former is a prerequisite for succeeding with the latter. Thus, if by virtue of their patents certain companies are allowed to 'capture' the benefits of a standard for private gain, public policy objectives will be undermined. Currently the implementation of the EU standardization policy is based on the work undertaken of the officially recognized European Standardisation Organisations (ESOs).[18] However, the Commission has called for greater recognition of standards set by fora and consortia in EU legislation and policies, in so far as they fulfil certain criteria – most of which reflect competition law principles (FRAND licensing, etc.).[19] Thus, the success of such SSOs has not gone unnoticed by the Commission which has pointed out that "*without decisive action the EU risks becoming irrelevant in ICT standard setting which will take place almost entirely outside Europe and without regard to European needs*".[20] This trend towards increased reliance on fora and consortia, alongside the recognized standardization bodies, means that there is a need for clear guidance for the stakeholders involved on how to adopt standardization agreements (including IPR policies) in accordance with competition law, not least because those who control standards endorsed by EU legislation are likely to gain market power.

In an attempt to guide the adoption of pro-competitive standardization agreements, in December 2010 the Commission released new guidelines on horizontal cooperation agreements. Among other things, these contain a revised chapter on

16. See Commission, *Modernising ICT Standardisation in the EU – The Way Forward*, COM(2009) 324 final, White paper, 3 Jul. 2009, point 2.4 (in particular).
17. *Ibid.*
18. See Annex I and II of Directive 98/34/EC of 22 Jun. 1998 laying down a procedure for the provision of information in the field of technical standards and regulations, as amended by Directive 98/48/EC of 20 Jul. 1998, Directive 2006/96/EC of 20 Nov. 2006 and Regulation 1025/2012 of 25 Oct. 2012, provides that ETSI, CEN and CENELEC are the officially recognised ESOs.
19. Commission, *Modernising ICT Standardisation in the EU – The Way Forward*, COM(2009) 324 final, White paper, 3 Jul. 2009, points 2.1, 2.4 and 2.5.
20. *Ibid.*, point 2.5. A number of very successful internet standards (including the HTML standard) have for instance been developed by the independent non-profit World Wide Web Consortium (W3C) based in the USA. For more information see www.w3c.org. In this respect the Commission notes that the market's acceptance of standards for internet protocols established by IETF and web accessibility guidelines produced by W3C is undisputed. Also see Communication from the Commission, *A Digital Agenda for Europe*, COM(2010) 245 final, 19 May 2010, point 2.2.1, where the Commission notes "*...the rise and growing importance of ICT standards developed by certain global fora and consortia*".

standardization with the aim of clarifying how the Commission will assess standardization agreements under Article 101 TFEU.[21] As explained in Chapter 9, these guidelines do not contain a detailed code of conduct, but they do provide an important insight into the Commission's views on technical standards from a competition law perspective.

21. Communication from the Commission, *Guidelines on the applicability of Article 101 of the Treaty on the Functioning of the European Union to horizontal co-operation agreements*, OJ 2011/C 11/1, 14 Jan. 2011.

CHAPTER 3

Relevant Legal Issues

The recent trends and developments highlighted in Chapter 2 shows why it is relevant to examine the role of competition law in dealing with opportunistic behaviour by essential-patent holders – especially with regard to the ICT sector.[1] Among other things, unlocking the economic potential of standardization requires there to be a sound legal framework which is capable of guiding the conduct of patentees and providing an incentive to participate in formal standard-setting activities. The purpose of this book is to provide guidance to stakeholders, policy-makers and courts on how the current competition law regime applies to technical standards and, where gaps exist, to suggest the most likely interpretation of the applicable law. However, despite the increased focus by legal scholars and the Commission's increased vigilance in the field, many questions still remain unanswered.

Many of the legal analyses carried out in this book is of relevance to both de facto standards and formal standards, since the case law relating to the former is used as a basis for determining whether the latter warrants special treatment under the competition rules. However, the primary focus of this book is on formal standards, since the legal framework surrounding such standards is especially in need of clarity. Moreover, they involve collaboration between competitors and therefore warrant special attention from a competition law perspective.

Overall the competition law issues which may arise relate to (1) the conditions governing the standard setting process within SSOs as set out in their standardization agreements (Article 101 TFEU issues), (2) deceit of SSOs by patentees aiming to unduly have their patents embodied in the standards adopted (Article 102 TFEU issue) and (3) the exercise of SEPs after a standard is adopted or the refusal to license them (Article 102 TFEU issues). While the issues stated under point one and two relate to the

1. As noted by the Commission "*... standardisation stakeholders, including public authorities, have been confronted with issues raised by the interplay of IPRs and standards, in particular in the ICT field*". See Communication from the Commission, *Towards an increased contribution from standardisation to innovation in Europe*, COM(2008) 133 final, 11 Mar. 2008,p. 10. As noted in Ch. 2 recent case law underline that these issues are still of relevance.

standard setting process within SSOs (*ex ante* standardization) the third group of issues relate to the unilateral conduct of patentees after a standard has been adopted (*ex post* standardization).[2] In the context of formal standards the *ex ante* and the *ex post* issues are closely interconnected as the very purpose of the Article 101 TFEU requirements which standardization agreements must fulfil is to establish a bulwark against *ex post* abuse. A graphical illustration of the different issues according to the point in time where they arise is provided below alongside references to the sections of this book where they are dealt with.

Figure 3.1 Overview of Potential Issues

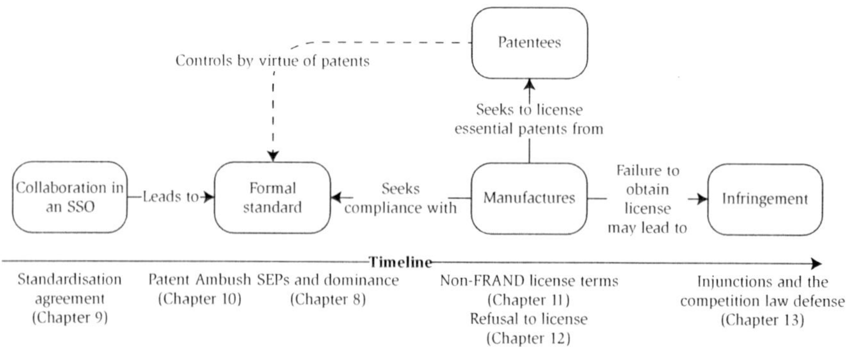

It has been argued that the threat of patent hold-up should not be exaggerated, since *inter alia* relatively few disputes have emerged and intense competition is thriving in the cellular industry to which multiple technical standards and thousands of SEPs relate.[3] This may be true. However, it does not mean that a laissez faire approach is warranted. Fact of the matter is that disputes between SEP holders and prospective licensees continue to emerge and that they pose a risk to effective competition which cannot simply be ignored. What it does mean however is that competition authorities and courts should be cautious not to impose too strict legal standards upon SEP holders based on wrong beliefs about the magnitude of the problem they are dealing with. Unduly restraining the freedom of SEP holders may do more harm than good. It may undermine the incentives of innovative firms to take part in standard setting activities, result in the adoption of inferior standards and, hence, ultimately harm consumer welfare.

2. The different types of standards are described in Ch. 7 s. §7.02 and in s. §7.03 it is explained why the collaborative nature of formal standards poses special competition law challenges.
3. See for instance Brooks, Roger G., *SSO Rules, Standardization, and SEP Licensing: Economic Questions from the Trenches*, Remarks prepared for the Research Roundtable on Innovation and Technology Standards, Searle Center on Law, Regulation, and Economic Growth, Northwestern University School of Law, 2013 pp. 6–7.

§3.01 ISSUES OUTSIDE THE SCOPE OF THIS BOOK

The focus of this book is on the interface between EU competition law, patents and technical standards, and in particular on the IPR-related aspects of standardization agreements and the 'hold-up' issues which may result from the exercise of SEPs. However, some clarification is needed.

It is not possible to deal with all the competition law aspects of standardization within the scope of this book. Accordingly, anti-competitive practices which are of a more general character and which may occur in the context of standardization, but which have no specific relevance to the interface between competition law, patents and technical standards, are not discussed.[4] Practices which are only remotely linked to the interface are also not dealt with. For example, companies may establish patent pools for licensing their SEPs or agree arbitration as means for settling licensing disputes, but such arrangements do not affect the core question of the legality of standardization agreements and the potential 'hold-up' issues raised by the exercise of SEPs. For instance, arbitration may help prevent such a 'hold-up', but it does not have an impact on the competition law assessment to be made if it is unsuccessful, and patent pools may give rise to special competition law issues concerning conditions for access, bundling of rights, etc., but these issues are not specific to standardization.

Non-technical standards can also give rise to conflicts between competition law and intellectual property law, for example when standard terms and conditions are covered by copyright or when a logo which is part of a standard labelling scheme is a protected trade mark. Indeed, in its Horizontal Guidelines the Commission comments specifically on the potential issues associated with standard terms and conditions.[5] However, it is not without reason that the focus in this book (and in general) is on technical standards. As already noted, the economic importance of technical standards has increased in recent decades, as has the risk of disputes between rights holders and implementers of standards, as suggested by recent developments. This means that it is important to uncover how competition law is applied (or is likely to be applied) in this field in order to give guidance to operators in markets where technical standards play a key role, and to increase legal certainty.

It is also important to appreciate that the circumstances surrounding technical standards, including the distinctive characteristics of ICT markets and the reliance on patented technology, give rise to special competition law issues. Patents and technical

4. For instance, SSOs may act as vehicles for collusion between competitors, but this does not concern the interface between competition law and patents. Similarly, a number of anti-competitive clauses – e.g., on market shares, price fixing etc. – might be included in licensing agreements for SEPs, but without having any specific relevance to the interface dealt with in this dissertation.
5. See Communication from the Commission, *Guidelines on the applicability of Article 101 of the Treaty on the Functioning of the European Union to horizontal co-operation agreements*, OJ 2011/C 11/1, 14 Jan. 2011, s. 7.

standards are important drivers of innovation and consumer welfare and it is imperative to ensure that competition law is not applied so as to limit the incentives of undertakings to contribute their patented technologies to SSOs or to hamper innovation. Moreover, technical standards are often adopted on so-called 'network markets' where there is an inherent tendency towards technological unification and consumer 'lock-in'. These special characteristics have an impact on the assessment of market power and hence on the application of Articles 101 and 102 TFEU in the context of technical standards and patents. Thus, although the overall competition law regime does not distinguish between technical and non-technical standards such a distinction does have an influence on the interpretation of the law.

Focus is directed specifically at patents, since these are of greatest importance when discussing the interface between formal technical standards and competition law.[6] This is so because (i) they relate to technical subject matter which is also at the core of technical standards, (ii) are controlled by multiple companies with diverging commercial interests and (iii) may potentially be asserted to prevent companies from manufacturing standard compliant products. Other types of IPRs may also be of relevance to technical standards, but as suggested by case law these are most likely to cause competition law issues in the context of de facto standards where the technical specification underlying the standard itself is controlled by a dominant undertaking. In the *IMS Health* case for instance a copyright protected database was at the core of the dispute whereas in the *Microsoft* case several IPRs, including trade secrets, were relied upon to prevent competitors from implementing certain software interface standards. In these cases the undertakings concerned were able to rely on IPRs other than patents to exclude competitors, because they controlled the technical specification themselves. In the context of formal standards the specification as such is however agreed upon by multiple companies within the framework of an SSO and rules are adopted to ensure third parties access.[7]

Finally, standards mandated by national law must fulfil special legal requirements which do not relate to the conduct of 'undertakings' within the meaning of Articles 101 and 102 TFEU, but which are intended to ensure that Member States do not

6. Also see Lea, Gary & Hall, Peter, *Standards and intellectual property rights: an economic and legal perspective*, in Information Economics and Policy, Vol. 16, 2004 p. 71.
7. In W3C for instance the copyright remains with the original author (which may be the SSO), but rules ensure a right for third parties to distribute and implement the technical specifications underlying the standards adopted (for a good overview see the W3C IPR FAQ available at: http://www.w3.org/Consortium/Legal/IPR-FAQ-20000620.html#libraries). In ETSI the copyright is always vested with the organization as such pursuant to Art. 9 of ETSI's IPR policy dated 19 Mar. 2014 (Annex 6 of the Rules of Procedure) – available at: http://www.etsi.org/about/iprs-in-etsi.

adopt standards that restrict the free movement of goods contrary to Article 34 TFEU. These requirements are not discussed in this book.[8]

8. Any technical standard mandated by law at the national level may present at barrier to trade between Member States for which reason they must fulfil the requirements set out by the so-called *Cassis de Dijon* doctrine created by the CJEU in Case 120/78, *Rewe-Zentral AG v. Bundesmonopolverwaltung für Branntwein*, 20 Feb. 1979. Overall the doctrine entails that the Member States may not in principle prohibit the sale of products lawfully produced and marketed in another Member State even if the product does not satisfy technical or quality requirements imposed on domestic products. Moreover, NSBs must notify with the Commission proposed national technical regulations (at a draft stage) in accordance with Directive 98/34/EC of 22 Jun. 1998 laying down a procedure for the provision of information in the field of technical standards and regulations as amended by Directive 98/48/EC of 20 Jul. 1998, Directive 2006/96/EC of 20 Nov. 2006 and Regulation 1025/2012 of 25 Oct. 2012.

CHAPTER 4
Background

A meaningful legal analysis of how competition law is applied in the field of technical standards relies on contextual and normative frameworks against which the legality of specific commercial practices can be assessed. This is especially true in this case, when the relevant issues have only been sparsely dealt with in EU case law. Articles 101 and 102 TFEU do not directly address the specific questions posed and in the absence of relevant case law these provisions must be infused with meaning by considering the context of the particular issue and the overall objectives of competition law. The importance of these frameworks in supporting the legal dogmatic method is explained in section §4.01 (contextual framework) and section §4.02 (normative framework).

§4.01 CONTEXTUAL FRAMEWORK

The application of competition law, including Articles 101 and 102 TFEU, is a legal discipline based on economic reasoning. Its purpose is to correct inefficiencies caused by the market failures which may result from the anti-competitive exercise of market power.[1] In essence competition law is a hybrid of law and economics.[2] With the exception of 'hardcore'[3] constraints of competition (such as 'price fixing') the application of Articles 101 and 102 TFEU relies on the careful case-by-case assessment of the

1. See, along the same lines, Pacces, Alessio M. & Visscher, Louis T., *Methodology of Law and Economics*, in Klink, Bart van and Taekema, Sanne (Eds.), *Law and Method. Interdisciplinary research into Law*, Series Politika, no. 4, Mohr Siebeck, 2011, pp. 85-107 (p. 91 in particular).
2. Also see Whish, Richard & Bailey, David, *Competition Law*, 7th ed., Oxford University Press, 2012 p. 4, stating that economic performance is of essence to competition law and that "*[to] understand this one must first turn to economic theory*".
3. There is no exhaustive list what constitutes a 'hardcore' restraint of competition, but some such constraints are set out in *inter alia* the Commission's *de minimis* notice – see Commission, *Notice on agreements of minor importance which do not appreciably restrict competition under Article 101(1) of the Treaty on the Functioning of the European Union (De Minimis Notice)*, COM(2014) 4136 final, 25 Jun. 2014, point 13, and the accompanying document Commission, *Guidance on*

actual effects of the commercial practice being scrutinized. This is clear from the Commission's guidelines[4] as well as the case law. In *Delimitis* for instance the court stressed that the legality of an exclusivity clause depended on market barriers and the '*conditions under which competitive forces operate on the relevant market*', whereas in *Irish Sugar*, a case concerning a discriminatory rebate scheme, it was held to be '*necessary to consider all the circumstances*', including whether there was any economic consideration justifying the scheme.[5] Thus, the Court of Justice of the European Union (CJEU) and the Commission acknowledge that per se prohibitions are seldom warranted. It is necessary to distinguish competition on the merits from anti-competitive practices which run counter to the ideal of '*effective competition*'[6] on the basis of empirical data and a sound economic analysis of the market conditions. This also applies in the context of standardization.

The effects-based approach outlined above has implications for the legal methodology applied in this book. As the effects of a commercial practice cannot be determined in a vacuum, it is necessary to set out a contextual framework against which the Treaty provisions, case law and so forth can be interpreted. Only when the specific context of standardization is taken into account it is possible to infuse the broad wording of Articles 101 and 102 TFEU with meaning and distinguish competition on the merits from anti-competitive practices. Accordingly, a contextual framework consisting of a description of the process, meaning and impact of standardization is described in *inter alia* Part II. This description establishes the basis for understanding the pro-competitive benefits of standardization as well as the potential market failures which must be corrected by the application of competition law. The overall framework set out in Part II is elaborated upon in other parts of the book to fit the particular context discussed.

---

restrictions of competition 'by object' for the purpose of defining which agreements may benefit from the De Minimis Notice, SWD(2014) 198 final, 26 Jun. 2014.

4. See e.g., Communication from the Commission, *Guidance on the Commission's enforcement priorities in applying Article 82 of the EC Treaty to abusive exclusionary conduct by dominant undertakings*, OJ 2009/C 45/02, 24 Feb. 2009, point 8, where it is stated that 'the Commission will take into account the specific facts and circumstances of each case'. See also Commission, Guidelines on Vertical Restraints, OJ 2010/C 130/01, 19 May 2010, §§ 9 and 96, and Communication from the Commission, *Guidelines on the applicability of Article 101 of the Treaty on the Functioning of the European Union to horizontal co-operation agreements*, OJ 2011/C 11/1, 14 Jan. 2011, § 29.
5. See Case C-234/89, *Stergios Delimitis v. Henninger Bräu AG*, 28 Feb. 1991, § 22, and Case T-228/97, *Irish Sugar v. Commission*, 7 Oct. 1999, § 114.
6. See e.g., Case 27/76, *United Brands Company and United Brands Continentaal BV v. Commission of the European Communities*, 14 Feb. 1978, § 65, where it is stated that a dominant position within the meaning of Art. 102 TFEU "*relates to a position of economic strength enjoyed by an undertaking which enables it to prevent effective competition being maintained on the relevant market*". See similarly Case T-201/04, *Microsoft Corp. v. Commission*, 17 Sep. 2007, § 332. For an in-depth discussion of the concept of 'effective competition', see Bishop, Simon & Walker, Mike, *The Economics of EC Competition Law: Concepts, Application and Measurement*, Sweet and Maxwell, 2010 p. 15.

§4.02 NORMATIVE FRAMEWORK

A contextual framework provides the basis for assessing the effects of a commercial practice and the effects likely to result from competition law intervention. However, such a framework is not sufficient for a proper interpretation of the relevant legal sources, since it does not provide a standard against which to assess the legality of the market impact in question. In order to determine whether a commercial practice restricts competition within the meaning of Article 101 TFEU or constitutes abuse within the meaning of Article 102 TFEU, it is necessary to consider the overall objective pursued by competition law, i.e., any interpretation of the relevant legal sources must be made within what could be termed a 'normative framework'. A refusal to license SEPs, for instance, would be more likely to be deemed abusive pursuant to Article 102 TFEU if the aim of competition law was solely to optimize consumer welfare by lowering prices and increasing output, whereas it may be justified when (as is the case) innovation is taken into consideration as a factor of effective competition. As noted above, competition law pursues 'effective competition', but there is no clear definition of this concept or of the relevant welfare standard in EU case law.[7] Nonetheless, three overall observations are of particular importance to the analyses in this book.

First, the aim of competition law is to protect effective competition, but this does not necessarily involve protecting competitors. In its Guidance on the enforcement of Article 102 TFEU, the Commission notes that it is *'mindful that what really matters is protecting an effective competitive process and not simply protecting competitors'*.[8] While harm to competitors may be detrimental to effective competition, this need not always be the case. Indeed, the fact that a competitor is excluded from the market may be evidence of fierce competition in the market.[9] That said, there are numerous indications that consumer welfare is considered an important benchmark in assessing the legality of a commercial practice and it follows clearly from case law that harm to competitors, or to the structure of competition, may be deemed to translate (indirectly) into consumer harm and hence be detrimental to effective competition.[10] In *Microsoft*, for instance, the General Court noted that it is settled case law that the scope of Article 102 TFEU extends not only to practices which *'prejudice consumers directly but also those which indirectly prejudice them by impairing an effective competitive structure'*.[11]

7. See *Ibid.* and Whish, Richard & Bailey, David, *Competition Law*, 7th ed., Oxford University Press, 2012 p. 19.
8. Communication from the Commission, *Guidance on the Commission's enforcement priorities in applying Article 82 of the EC Treaty to abusive exclusionary conduct by dominant undertakings*, OJ 2009/C 45/02, 24 Feb. 2009, point 6.
9. See for instance case C-209/10, *Post Danmark A/S v. Konkurrencerådet*, 27 Mar. 2012, § 22. As explained in Ch. 11 s. §11.02 licensing discrimination – while able to distort competition – may potentially signify that some licensees have stronger bargaining positions (countervailing licensee power) or that a competitive pressure is exerted by standards other than those to which the licensors patents relate.
10. See Whish, Richard & Bailey, David, *Competition Law*, 7th ed., Oxford University Press, 2012 p. 19 and Bishop, Simon & Walker, Mike, *The Economics of EC Competition Law: Concepts, Application and Measurement*, Sweet and Maxwell, 2010 p. 29.
11. Case T-201/04, *Microsoft Corp. v. Commission*, 17 Sep. 2007, § 332. Also see point 54 in Commission, *Discussion paper on the application of Article 82 of the Treaty to exclusionary*

The impact on consumer welfare is therefore of primary importance to the application of EU competition law, including the assessment of the legality of standardization agreements and the conduct of SEP holders. Moreover, the objectives of competition law should not be confused with the objectives of fair trade laws since competition law does not rely on an assessment of 'fairness' but on an objective assessment of market impact.[12]

Second, especially in the context of IPRs, effective competition pursuant to Articles 101 and 102 TFEU does not only relate to short-term benefits to consumers (static efficiencies). The importance of long-term benefits (dynamic efficiencies) in the form of innovation is also recognized as an important parameter of effective competition.[13] Thus, focusing solely on short-term benefits to consumer welfare, such as lower prices and higher output, may inhibit companies' investments in R&D out of fear that regulatory intervention will deprive them the possibility of recouping their investment costs. This may lead to a decrease in innovation and product choice, and hence reduce consumer welfare in the long-term. This is why there is no inherent conflict between the exclusivity conferred by patents, the purpose of which is to encourage innovation, and competition law.

Third, competition law is not, and should not be,[14] concerned with economic micro-management. The mere fact that a given commercial practice is not best suited to increase social welfare is not basis for legal intervention. As noted by the CJEU and the Commission on several occasions, the objective of competition law is to ensure that undertakings do not deviate from 'competition on the merits'[15] and to correct the market failures that arise if they do. As explained in Chapter 11 section §11.01, this is part of the reason why the Commission is reluctant to pursue excessive pricing cases and take on the role of price setters. Although the concept is vague, it underlines that competition law intervention should be reserved circumstances where effective competition is at risk because some practice is likely to have appreciable anti-competitive effects.[16]

---

abuses, December 2005, where it stated that the objective of Art. 102 TFEU "*is the protection of competition on the market as a means of enhancing consumer welfare and of ensuring an efficient allocation of resources*".

12. See e.g., Case 85/76, *Hoffmann-La Roche & Co. AG v. Commission*, 13 Feb. 1979, § 91, where abuse is defined as an objective concept. See also Case C-08/08, *T-Mobile Netherlands v. Raad van bestuur van de Nederlandse Mededingingsautoriteit*, 4 Jun. 2009, § 27, where the CJEU held that "*the intention of the parties is not an essential factor in determining whether a concerted practice is restrictive*".
13. See for instance Communication from the Commission, *Guidelines on the applicability of Article 101 of the Treaty on the Functioning of the European Union to horizontal co-operation agreements*, OJ 2011/C 11/1, 14 Jan. 2011, § 269.
14. See Bishop, Simon & Walker, Mike, *The Economics of EC Competition Law: Concepts, Application and Measurement*, Sweet and Maxwell, 2010 p. 32.
15. See e.g., Case C-209/10, *Post Danmark A/S v. Konkurrencerådet*, 27 Mar. 2012, § 25 and Case T-321/05, *AstraZeneca v. Commission*, 1 Jul. 2010, § 354.
16. Even though not explicitly required by the wording of the Arts 101 and 102 TFEU, the CJEU has held that the effect on inter-state trade (and on competition) must be appreciable in order for Arts 101 and 102 TFEU to apply. This was first established in Case 5/69, *Völk v. Vervaecke*, 9 Jul. 1969, § 7, where the Court stated that "*an agreement falls outside the prohibition in Article 85 [now Article 101] when it has only an insignificant effect on the markets, taking into account the*

§4.03 LEGAL METHODOLOGY

Using the commercial and economic aspects of standardization (contextual framework) and the goals of competition law (normative framework) as an analytical framework, the primary objective of this book is to systematize, interpret and describe the applicable law in the field of standards, i.e., overall a legal dogmatic method is applied on the basis of the theory of legal sources. For this, the case law of the CJEU and the decisions of the Commission are of primary relevance for specifying the scope of Articles 101 and 102 TFEU, since the Treaty provisions merely establish a general and non-specific legal framework. However, since it is only recently that attention has been directed at the competition law issues arising in the interface between patents and standards, there is a scarcity of EU case law specifically dealing with these issues. Thus, the CJEU have not given any judgments on this and only a few cases have been dealt with by the Commission. In applying the legal dogmatic method it is necessary to fill out the gaps in the existing case law by drawing on analogous EU cases outside the context of standardization. Any interpretation by analogy must be made in the light of the contextual framework relevant to standardization, since, as mentioned above, the application of Articles 101 and 102 TFEU is based on economic reasoning and hence is context sensitive. In general the nature of the subject matter, including commercial and practical considerations, is of the essence in deducing what is the applicable law in this new and evolving area of competition law, and this underlines the importance of setting out a contextual framework.

The lack of EU judgments that are of specific relevance to the issues studied gives added importance to the Commission's guidelines (soft law) as a basis for deducing applicable law; this applies in particular to the Horizontal Guidelines which deal with standardization agreements. While soft law is not legally binding, its impact should not be underestimated. As the primary enforcer of EU competition law the Commission plays an important role in shaping the competition law regime through its decisions which are likely to reflect the reasoning set out in its guidelines. The authority of the Commission's decisions is seen in the fact that the CJEU will only dismiss a decision on appeal if it finds that there is a manifest error of assessment or abuse of power.[17] From a practical perspective the market is likely to seek to conform to the Commission's guidelines, since legal advisers encourage this. It is therefore only logical to include the Commission's guidelines in the legal analysis in this book.

---

weak position which the persons concerned have on the market of the product in question". See generally Whish, Richard & Bailey, David, *Competition Law*, 7th ed., Oxford University Press, 2012 p. 158.

17. In Case T-201/04, *Microsoft Corp v. Commission*, 17 Sep. 2007, § 87, the General Court for instance observed that "*...the review of complex economic appraisals made by the Commission is necessarily limited to checking whether the relevant rules on procedure and on stating reasons have been complied with, whether the facts have been accurately stated and whether there has been any manifest error of assessment or a misuse of powers*". The grounds of review are specified in Art. 263(2) TFEU. For a more in-depth discussion of the scope of judicial review see Chalmers, Damian et al., *European Union Law: Cases and Materials*, 2nd ed., Cambridge University press, 2010 p. 398.

The relevant case law of the Member States will be included as part of the analysis, both as a source of inspiration and to give a better understanding of the legal issues arising in the context of standardization. National case law may for instance be used as a source of inspiration in determining the extent to which interim injunctions can be sought, threatened or enforced on the basis of FRAND-pledged patents without infringing Article 102 TFEU, since injunctions are granted at the national level and relate to civil proceedings between essential-patent holders and manufacturers of standard compliant products. As for the authority of national law as a source of law, it is noted that the national competition rules of the Members States are largely modelled upon EU competition law, and so many cases will have the same outcome whether investigated under Articles 101 and 102 TFEU or under their national equivalents.[18] Moreover, Article 3(2) of Regulation (EC) No. 1/2003 provides that Articles 101 and 102 shall be applied in parallel with national competition rules in so far as the practice being scrutinized is able to affect trade between Member States. While not necessarily the case, it follows from the foregoing that the judgments of national courts will often reflect the relevant court's interpretation of EU law. That being said, the focus of this book is on EU case law and the purpose is not to engage in an in-depth analysis of the national case law of the Member States.

US sources, including literature, case law and FTC documents, will also be included. Indeed, much of the literature on competition law and standardization is US centric, since case law has developed more rapidly on the other side of the Atlantic. However, it is not the purpose to engage in an actual comparison of US and EU case law. Rather the use of US sources serves to highlight issues which may become of relevance in an EU context and will contribute to the analyses performed to the extent that the economic or legal principles discussed apply universally. Hence, the US sources provide a more solid foundation for analysing applicable EU law in cases where there is a lack of other, more relevant, legal sources and it also gives an idea of how EU competition law might develop in the context of standardization. Having regard to the differences between US law and EU law is of course essential in this respect. For example, section 2 of the US Sherman Act prohibits the wilful acquisition of monopoly power, whereas Article 102 TFEU only prohibits the abuse of a dominant position already achieved and not the mere acquisition of such a position.[19] Such differences need to be filtered out in order to deduce from US sources the commercial and economic reasoning which may be relevant to the interpretation of Articles 101 and 102 TFEU.

---

18. See Whish, Richard & Bailey, David, *Competition Law*, 7th ed., Oxford University Press, 2012 p. 75. However, where EU case-law is lacking or unclear there is a risk that different national courts will apply the competition rules in an inconsistent manner. The German and the Dutch courts have for instance dealt differently with the question as to whether seeking injunctions on basis of SEPs will constitute abuse – see Ch. 13 s. §13.02[D].
19. This difference for instance has profound implications with regard to the Commission's ability to deal with so-called patent ambush scenarios where SSO members subvert the standard setting process by concealing their patents only to subsequently assert them against implementers. In this respect see Ch. 10.

Finally, since the applicable law cannot be established with absolute certainty, due to the lack of EU case law specifically dealing with the interface between patents and standards, there is necessarily a certain normative element to the analyses in this book, i.e., given the nature of the matter, commercial, economic and legal reasoning is used as a basis for substantiating the arguments made and extracting the most likely legal implications of different commercial practices. However, as noted above, the primary objective is nonetheless to deduce how the law is or how it is likely to be (*de lege lata*) and not to comment on how the law ought to be from an ideal perspective (*de lege ferenda*).[20] Perhaps the methodological approach used is best characterized as *de lege sententia ferenda* in so far as the book contains recommendations for how to apply established legal principles and doctrines in the specific context of standardization.[21]

20. Much of the existing literature concerning the interface between patents and standards seems only to give scant attention to settled EU case law in favour of a more 'free' or superficial discussion of legal principles believed to be appropriate.
21. A similar approach was adopted by Haglund, Birgitte, *Erstatningsbetingende medvirkning*, Gyldendal Juridisk, 2012 p. 75 onwards and p. 157.

CHAPTER 5
Structure

This book is divided into six parts, the first part being this prologue.

In the second part, the terminology and process associated with formal standardization efforts is described. The purpose is to provide a contextual framework to support the analyses and conclusions made in the remainder of the book and to establish the terminology used. As already explained, understanding standards and the process of standard-setting is important to the proper application of competition law.

The purpose of the third part is to explore in more detail why market power, often amounting to dominance, is likely to be obtained by proprietors of SEPs and how to properly determine the degree of market power obtained. Thus, Articles 101 and 102 TFEU are only applicable to undertakings which hold market power, since this is a precondition for anti-competitive effects to materialize. However, despite the profound importance of market power to the application of competition law, neither the Commission nor legal scholars have paid much attention to the issue of market power specifically in the context of SEPs. Sometimes there seems to be an idea that the holding of an SEP per se translates into market power, but this is clearly false.

Next, in Part IV, the competition law aspects of the standard-setting processes of SSOs are analysed in the light of the requirements set out by the Commission's Horizontal Guidelines, i.e., there is focus on the pre-standardization phase (*ex ante*). The purpose here is to highlight the role of competition law in preventing patent-related abuse (i.e., Article 102 TFEU issues) arising after a standard is adopted (*ex post*) and to set out the framework under which the legality of standardization agreements must be assessed pursuant to Article 101(1) TFEU. Part IV also contains an analysis of the extent to which concealing patents, contrary to the IPR policies of SSOs, may contravene Article 102 TFEU.

In Part V, an *ex post* perspective is used to shed light on how Article 102 TFEU may be applied to sanction the abusive exercise of SEPs after a standard is adopted. More specifically, the extent to which excessive and discriminatory licensing practices may infringe Article 102 TFEU is analysed, as is the possibility of threatening, seeking or enforcing injunctions on the basis of FRAND-pledged patents.

Finally, Part VI summarizes the main findings of this book and a conclusion on the 'state of the art' – the current legal regime – is provided.

Part II Understanding Technical Standards

CHAPTER 6

What Is a Technical Standard?

As already noted, the benefits of standardization are generally recognized and there has been widespread adoption of standards in all branches of industry; indeed most products today comply with one or more technical standards.[1] However, somewhat ironically there is no commonly agreed definition of a 'technical standard' and, as will be seen in Chapter 7, the terminology used to categorize such standards is quite disparate.[2] Thus, the various definitions adopted by legal commentators as well as in EU directives, public policy documents and by SSOs have been tailored to fit the specific context in which they are used.[3] Likewise, the purpose of this chapter as well as Chapter 7 is not to establish universally applicable definitions, but to describe the nature of technical standards and add to the frame of reference specifically used in this book. From a strictly legal perspective these definitions have no substantive impact, since competition law is not formalistic in nature – what matters is the market impact.

For example, the International Organization for Standardization (ISO) and the International Electrotechnical Commission (IEC) define a standard as a "*document, established by consensus and approved by a recognized body, that provides, for common and repeated use, rules, guidelines or characteristics for activities or their results, aimed at the achievement of the optimum degree of order in a given context*".[4] Similar definitions have been adopted by the World Trade Organization (WTO)[5] as well as the

1. See e.g., WIPO, *Standards and Patents*, Standing committee on the law of patents, 13th Session, 2009 p. 2.
2. See also Lea, Gary & Hall, Peter, *Standards and intellectual property rights: an economic and legal perspective*, in Information Economics and Policy, Vol. 16, 2004 p. 69, Stango, Victor, *The Economics of Standards Wars*, in Review of Network Economics, Vol. 3(1), 2004 p. 4, DLA Piper, Universidade Nova de Lisboa & T.U. Delft, *EU Study on the specific policy needs for ICT standardization, final report*, 2007 p. 4 and WIPO, *Standards and Patents*, Standing committee on the law of patents, 13th Session, 2009 p. 8.
3. DLA Piper, Universidade Nova de Lisboa & T.U. Delft, *EU Study on the specific policy needs for ICT standardization, final report*, 2007 p. 4.
4. ISO/IEC Guide 2:2004, *Standardization and related activities*, definition 3.2.
5. World Trade Organisation Agreement, Agreement on Technical Barriers to Trade (TBT Agreement), Annex 1, § 2, where a standard is defined as a "*[d]ocument approved by a recognized body,*

recognized European Standards Organizations (CEN, CENELEC and ETSI)[6] referenced in Directive 98/34/EC as amended.[7] The tight relationship between these organizations and their common focus on standards adopted by officially recognized SSOs has led to definitions being more or less aligned. However, while the definition quoted above is descriptive of standards set by accredited SSOs, it does not cover the vast number of de facto standards which, as explained in Chapter 7, originate from a purely market driven process, or standards from SSOs which have not been formally recognized and which, as noted in Chapter 2, are playing an increasingly important role. While it is necessary to distinguish between de facto *standards* and formal standards set by SSOs when discussing their competition law implications (see below), there is no need to distinguish between different types of formal standards. It is therefore appropriate to adopt a more general definition for the purpose of this book, since a reference to a 'standard' should not be taken to mean only those standards set by formally recognized SSOs (the terminology for distinguishing different types of standards is provided in the next section). Focusing on its core characteristics, a technical standard can more generally be defined as: any set of technical specifications which sets out requirements with which products, processes, methods or any subset thereof shall or may comply and which are put to common and repeated use.[8] Arguably this definition is sufficiently flexible to encompass all types of technical standards and it suits the purpose of this book well.

A technical standard seldom[9] relates to a product as a whole, but to certain features or characteristics of a product such as a format to be used for data encoding, a protocol to be used for data transmission or the specific design of a connector. While the key purpose of standardization is to promote a common technical specification and accordingly to limit *inter*-technology competition in respect of standardized product

---

that provides, for common and repeated use, rules, guidelines or characteristics for products or related processes and production methods, with which compliance is not mandatory".

6. See www.cenelec.eu/aboutcenelec/whatwedo/whatisastandard/index.html (last checked 30 May 2014).
7. Directive 98/34/EC of 22 Jun. 1998 laying down a procedure for the provision of information in the field of technical standards and regulations, as amended by Directive 98/48/EC of 20 Jul. 1998, Directive 2006/96/EC of 20 Nov. 2006 and Regulation 1025/2012 of 25 Oct. 2012.
8. See, along the same lines, Hovenkamp, Herbert, et al., *Intellectual Property and Antitrust – an Analysis of Antitrust Principles Applied to Intellectual Property Law*, 2002 (suppl. 2006), § 35.1a, where a standard is defined as "*any set of technical specifications which either does, or is intended to, provide a common design for a product or process*". However, this definition ignores the fact that a technical standard seldom relates to a product as a whole. Moreover, use of the term "*is intended to*" results in a too broad definition, covering technical specifications which have not yet been accepted by the market and which are therefore irrelevant from a competition law perspective (see below). Lea, Gary & Hall, Peter, *Standards and intellectual property rights: an economic and legal perspective*, in Information Economics and Policy, Vol. 16, 2004 p. 71, also provide a definition of a technical standard. Also see David, Paul A. & Greenstein, Shane, *The Economics of Compatibility Standards: An Introduction to Recent Research*, in Econ. Innov. New Techno., Vol. 1, 1998 p. 4, who define a standard simply as a specification which is adhered to by producers either tacitly or as a result of a formal agreement.
9. See also Nimmer, Raymond T., *Technical Standards Setting Organizations & Competition: A case for Deference to Markets*, in the University of Houston Public Law and Legal Theory Series, 2009-A-23 p. 4.

features, companies remain free to differentiate their products by means of non-standardized features and characteristics. Thus, standards do not generally aim to minimize competition, but to channel competition into areas where uniform specifications are of less importance to consumers and this process, if carried out properly, will often have considerable welfare enhancing effects – these are discussed in Chapter 9 section §9.01.

Finally, a technical specification first becomes a technical standard in the proper sense of the word when it is adopted by a significant portion of the market to which it relates, i.e., when it is put to common and repeated use.[10] When the participants in an SSO agree on a technical specification, it is in itself nothing more than a document which sets out the characteristics of a standard they would like to see the market adopt. Put, simply SSOs may promote the adoption of standards but, as in the case of de facto standards, it is the market which adopts or rejects them. Thus a *technical standard* must be distinguished from a *standardisation agreement* which governs the process for the adoption of a commonly agreed technical specification by an SSO which may eventually become an industry standard. The Commission defines such agreements as having "*...as their primary objective the definition of technical or quality requirements with which current or future products, production processes or methods may comply*".[11] As noted in Chapter 9, standardization agreements which risk creating market power are subject to evaluation under Article 101 TFEU and must fulfil certain criteria pertaining to openness, transparency and accessibility.

10. See Gifford, Daniel J., *Developing Models for a Coherent Treatment of Standard-setting Issues under Patent, Copyright and Antitrust Laws*, in IDEA: The Journal of Law and Technology, Vol. 43, 2003 p. 333.
11. Cf. Communication from the Commission, *Guidelines on the applicability of Article 101 of the Treaty on the Functioning of the European Union to horizontal co-operation agreements*, OJ 2011/C 11/1, 14 Jan. 2011.

CHAPTER 7

Types of Technical Standards

Technical standards can be categorized in a variety of ways.[1] They may for instance be categorized by reference to their origin, their subject matter, their geographic scope or their legal status.[2] However, as explained below, it is clear that no consistent terminology has been developed. The terms used in this respect often overlap and are contradictory. This section sets out the terminology used in the remainder of this book, taking into account the distinctions that are relevant to competition law.

Given the process by which technical standards originate, a general distinction can be made between de facto standards (section §7.01) and formal standards (section §7.02). As noted below, each of these types of standards is treated differently from a competition law perspective.

§7.01 DE FACTO STANDARDS

While the term '*de facto* standard' is sometimes[3] used to refer to any standard not originating from an officially accredited SSO, the term is most often,[4] and more appropriately, used to refer either to standards arising in the market as a result of the

1. See Nimmer, Raymond T., *Technical Standards Setting Organizations & Competition: A case for Deference to Markets*, in the University of Houston Public Law and Legal Theory Series, 2009-A-23 p. 9, and Park, Jae Hun, *Patents and Industry Standards*, Edward Elgar, 2010 p. 8.
2. For an in-depth analysis of the typology of standardization see Folmer, Erwin & Verhoosel, Jack, *State of the Art on Semantic IS Standardization, Interoperability & Quality*, TNO, Universiteit Twente, NOiV, CTIT, 2011, pp. 16–22 in particular, finding that "*studies have been performed to create some sort of order in the standardization domain, but several authors question definitions given by others, resulting in many different typologies*". The book is available for free download at: www.semanticstandards.org (last checked 30 May 2014).
3. See e.g., UNCTAD, *Addressing the Interface between Patens and Technical Standards International Trade Discussions*, No. 3, 2009 p. 6.
4. See e.g., Nimmer, Raymond T., *Technical Standards Setting Organizations & Competition: A case for Deference to Markets*, in the University of Houston Public Law and Legal Theory Series, 2009-A-23 p. 6, Lea, Gary & Hall, Peter, *Standards and intellectual property rights: an economic and legal perspective*, in Information Economics and Policy, Vol. 16, 2004, pp. 69–70 and Gifford,

unilateral efforts of a single company or to the norms[5] which more indirectly and randomly comes into existence on the basis of consumer choices. Thus, the term '*de facto* standard' distinguishes purely market driven standards from standards resulting from the collaboration and agreement of multiple stakeholders acting within the framework of an SSO (formal standards), whether accredited or not. Obviously, a single company's successful promotion of a technology so that it becomes a de facto standard requires either significant market power and/or technical superiority over competitors. In the absence of market power, the process leading to the adoption of a de facto standard may be lengthy, since it will involve intense competition *for* the market by several companies each trying to convince consumers that their technology is the best. In contrast, technical standards set pursuant to a standardization agreement are often promoted by influential SSOs whose members represent a large proportion of companies active on the relevant market and hence, depending on the competitive pressure exerted by competing SSOs, such standards may be set more effectively.

As with formal standards, de facto standards are most likely to raise competition law issues if their implementation may be obstructed by the existence of IPRs. While de facto standards may be controlled by one or more companies holding proprietary interests, such as patent rights, this will not always be the case. Some de facto standards are 'unsponsored',[6] in the sense that no identified originator holds such proprietary interests. Such standards will seldom lead to restrictions of competition within the meaning of Articles 101 and 102 TFEU. The QWERTY keyboard layout is often highlighted as an example of an unsponsored de facto standard which came into existence due to the success of Remington typewriters.[7] However, de facto standards are often vested with proprietary interests so that their adoption by third parties is at the mercy of one or more rights holders, usually including the company that has been successful in setting the standard.[8] As highlighted in Chapter 2 many formal standards, especially those adopted in the ICT sector, also embody propriety interests in the form of patents.[9]

The default proprietary document format used to handle Microsoft Word documents (.doc and.docx) is another well-known example of a de facto standard as is the

Daniel J., *Competition and Intellectual Property Law and Policy* in the *Knowledge-Based Economy: Standards and Intellectual Property: Licensing Terms: Some Comments*, Federal Trade Commission, 2000 p. 1.

5. See David, Paul A. & Greenstein, Shane, *The Economics of Compatibility Standards: An Introduction to Recent Research*, in Econ. Innov. New Techno., Vol. 1, 1998 p. 4.
6. See *Ibid.* p. 4. However, the term 'unsponsored standards' is not used consistently. While the authors consider unsponsored standards to relate to de facto standards, others use the term to describe all standards that are free of proprietary technology, whether formal or de facto. See e.g.,Stango, Victor, *The Economics of Standards Wars*, in Review of Network Economics, Vol. 3(1), 2004, pp. 3–4.
7. Park, Jae Hun, *Patents and Industry Standards*, Edward Elgar, 2010 p. 12.
8. See Communication from the Commission, *Intellectual Property Rights and Standardisation*, COM(92) 445 Final, 27 Oct. 1992, point 4.2.1, where it is stated that the products or processes which become de facto standards "*will almost certainly embody intellectual property rights*". Also see Lea, Gary & Hall, Peter, *Standards and intellectual property rights – an economic and legal perspective*, in Information Economics and Policy, Vol. 16, 2004 p. 70, and Stango, Victor, *The Economics of Standards Wars*, in Review of Network Economics, Vol. 3(1), 2004, p. 4.
9. Note that the authors referenced in the preceding footnote seem to disagree in this respect.

MP-3 audio compression standard which started its life as a de facto standard, but later became a formally recognized ISO standard. Note however that the term de facto standard is sometimes used in its broadest sense to refer to any product which enjoys widespread diffusion and large market shares. The Microsoft Windows operating system is for instance sometimes referred to as a de facto standard due to the fact that it enjoys a significant market share.[10] However, in a competition law context such use of the term is inappropriate as standard related issues do not arise merely as a result of a products large market share, but because adherence with one or more technical specifications incorporated into a product is demanded by the market.[11] Developers of third party software for the Windows platform needs access, not to the Windows source code as whole, but to the technical specifications describing the interfaces (API's) which allow for software compatibility. Due to the widespread use of the Windows operating system these specifications may accordingly be considered de facto standards specifying how to interact with PC's running said system. In case T-201/04, *Microsoft Corp v. Commission*, the General Court found that *"Microsoft was able to impose the Windows domain architecture as the 'de facto standard for work group computing'"*, and that Microsoft was able to determine independently *"the set of coherent communications rules that will govern the de facto standard for interoperability in work group networks"*, thus clarifying that the technical specification related to said architecture and rules amounted to a de facto standard.[12] A complex product such as Microsoft Windows may contain several such technical standards each of which satisfies different interoperability requirements. In short therefore, a de facto standard, as is the case with other types of standards, refer to the technical specifications underlying products or parts hereof which are put to common and repeated use - not the product itself (see the definition provided in Chapter 6).

§7.02 FORMAL STANDARDS

As opposed to de facto standards which arise as a result of market forces, some standards are established as a result of agreement between two or more stakeholders operating within the framework of which is commonly termed a *standard setting organization (SSO)*.[13] Such organizations may be anything from officially accredited

---

10. See for instance Stango, Victor, *The Economics of Standards Wars*, in Review of Network Economics, Vol. 3(1), 2004 p. 4.
11. Cf. Also Gifford, Daniel J., *Developing Models for a Coherent Treatment of Standard-setting Issues under Patent, Copyright and Antitrust Laws*, in IDEA: The Journal of Law and Technology, Vol. 43, 2003 p. 337.
12. Case T-201/04, *Microsoft Corp v. Commission*, § 392. Also see Commission decision C(2004) 900 final in Case COMP/C-3/37.792, *Microsoft*, 24 Mar. 2004, §§ 24 and 569, where the Commission emphasizes that the refusal in question did not relate to Microsoft's source code, but to the technical specifications of the protocols concerned.
13. Cf. also Rubin, Jonathan L., *Patents, Antitrust, and Rivalry in Standard-Setting*, in Rutgers Law Journal, Vol. 38, 2007 pp. 513–514 and Gifford, Daniel J., *Developing Models for a Coherent Treatment of Standard-setting Issues under Patent, Copyright and Antitrust Laws*, in IDEA: The Journal of Law and Technology, Vol. 43, 2003 p. 336. Sometimes however the term is used to refer solely to officially accredited organizations otherwise referred to as SDO's (see below). See

national, European or international standard setting bodies to trade associations and different types of consortia and fora.[14] Many of these organizations have become hugely influential in deciding which technical product features reach the market and accordingly it is essential for companies active on the market affected to either participate in or closely monitor the activities of SSOs active in their field of business.[15] The telecommunications standards (GSM, 3G, 4G) set by the ETSI are perhaps the ones most well-known.

Note that despite the notion 'organization' a SSO may refer to any affiliation of stakeholders aiming to establish a common standard whether they act within the framework of an incorporated entity, such as a joint venture, or collaborate in a more 'direct' and informal fashion.[16] Moreover, the scope, focus and procedures of SSOs vary greatly.[17] Thus, a SSO may for instance be established on a permanent basis and include a detailed set of by-laws governing its operation (such as is the case with regard to the accredited European SDOs mentioned below or the World Wide Web Consortium (W3C)[18]), or it may be established ad-hoc to fulfil some specific and time-limited purpose (such as is the case with regard to the Full HD 3D Glass Initiative[19] headed by Sony, Panasonic and Samsung) without necessarily relying on such detailed by-laws. In short therefore a SSO, for the purpose of this book, refers to any cooperation between diverse stakeholders, regardless of form, having as its purpose the establishment of a common technical standard. Such use of the term ensures consistency with the majority of texts on the matter and with the Commissions Horizontal Guidelines.[20] However, for the avoidance of doubt note that SSOs do not actually *set* standards – they act as a forum for *selection* of a technical specification after which the market will ultimately decide whether to adopt it as a standard or not. In other words, there is no guarantee that the technical specification adopted by a SSO will necessarily turn into a standard, unless mandated by law, i.e., the term SSO is a bit misleading.

WIPO, *Standards and Patents*, Standing committee on the law of patents, 13th Session, 2009 p. 10, using the notion "consortium" to refers to non-accredited organizations.

14. Communication from the Commission, *Guidelines on the applicability of Article 81 of the EC Treaty to horizontal co-operation agreements*, OJ 2001/C 3/02, 6 Jan. 2001, § 257 (note 95). Also see EICTA, *White Paper on Standardisation and Interoperability*, 2006 p. 6.
15. Cf. also Rubin, Jonathan L., *Patents, Antitrust, and Rivalry in Standard-Setting*, in Rutgers Law Journal, Vol. 38, 2007 pp. 513–514.
16. See along the same lines Rubin, Jonathan L., *Patents, Antitrust, and Rivalry in Standard-Setting*, in Rutgers Law Journal, Vol. 38, 2007 p. 513, stating that the term SSO "*is intended to be agnostic as to the precise nature of the group or association doing the standard-setting and is inclusive of SDOs as well as other forms of SSOs*". As mentioned below the term SDO refers to officially accredited SSOs.
17. Cf. also Nimmer, Raymond T., *Technical Standards Setting Organizations & Competition: A case for Deference to Markets*, in the University of Houston Public Law and Legal Theory Series, 2009-A-23 p. 6.
18. For more information see: www.w3c.org. (Last checked 30 May 2014).
19. For more information see: www.fullhd3dglasses.com. (Last checked 30 May 2014).
20. See Communication from the Commission, *Guidelines on the applicability of Article 81 of the EC Treaty to horizontal co-operation agreements*, OJ 2001/C 3/02, 6 Jan. 2001, s. 7, where the term SSO is used to refer to any organization developing standards pursuant to a standardisation agreement.

As mentioned above some standards are promoted by officially accredited standard development bodies. Indeed over the years a number of very influential standards have been set or subsequently approved by such SSOs – this includes, amongst other things, the 3G and 4G data transmission standards, the PDF document format and the MP3 audio format.[21] To distinguish these accredited bodies from other types of SSOs they are often referred to generally as *Standards Developments Organizations (SDOs)*. Thus, while SSOs are sometimes interchangeably termed SDOs the latter notion is typically reserved a sub-group of SSOs, comprising those which have received official accreditation at the national, regional or international level.[22] From an EU perspective the relevant SDO's are referenced in Directive 98/34 (as amended) and includes both *National Standard Setting Bodies (NSBs)* – one per Member State – as well as the three regional *European Standards Organizations (ESOs)* ETSI, CEN and CENELEC.[23] SDOs exist in other parts of the world as well, such as in the US where the American National Standards Institute (ANSI) is responsible for accrediting SDOs according to specific criteria.[24] The regional SDOs cooperate closely with the international standardization bodies ISO and EIC – most often also embraced under the SDO umbrella – in order to promulgate worldwide standards.[25]

In 1985 the Council adopted the so-called 'new approach' to standardization as a means to facilitate more effective product legislation and contribute to the creation of the single market.[26] The new approach entailed that the ESOs became entrusted with the development of so-called 'harmonised standards' which have as their purpose to ensure that products meet essential requirements, pertaining to for instance health, safety or the environment, set out in EU harmonization legislation. More specifically, the technical specification underlying a harmonized standard set out a path to

21. While the Commission has recently adopted a more positive stance towards standards set by consortia and fora established by private undertakings (see Ch. 2), the official standardisation bodies of the EU will arguably continue to play an important role.
22. See for instance Rubin, Jonathan L. *Patents, Antitrust, and Rivalry in Standard-Setting*, in Rutgers Law Journal, Vol. 38, 2007 p. 513 and EICTA, *White Paper on Standardisation and Interoperability*, 2006 p. 6. While acknowledging that the term SDO is often used to refer to accredited standard setting bodies the EICTA whitepaper itself however used the term SDO solely to refer to well established organizations as opposed to those established on an ad-hoc basis to set a standard with regard to some specific technology.
23. See Annex I and II of Directive 98/34/EC of 22 Jun. 1998 laying down a procedure for the provision of information in the field of technical standards and regulations, as amended by Directive 98/48/EC of 20 Jul. 1998, Directive 2006/96/EC of 20 Nov. 2006 and Regulation 1025/2012 of 25 Oct. 2012.
24. A list of the SDO's currently accredited by ANSI is available at: http://www.standardsportal.org/usa_en/resources/sdo.aspx (Last checked 30 May 2014).
25. As noted by Lea, Gary & Hall, Peter, *Standards and intellectual property rights – an economic and legal perspective*, in Information Economics and Policy, Vol. 16, 2004 p. 69, there is no universal rule to determine what should be recognized as official SDO's (the author uses the term TSO in place of SDO). However, it seems to be commonly agreed that at least the organizations mentioned above to which reference is made in legislation are to be considered as officially accredited SSOs – hence SDO's.
26. See Council Resolution of 7 May 1985 on a new approach to technical harmonization and standards, OJ 1985/C 136/01.

compliance with a new approach directive.[27] Any product manufactured in compliance with such a standard accordingly is presumed to fulfil the essential requirements stated in the directive and may legally be put on the market in the EU. Today a large proportion of the standards adopted by ESOs at the request of the Commission are harmonized standards.[28] However, as noted in Chapter 2 the Commission has recently moved one step closer endorsing non-accredited standards.

Regardless of their status as accredited SSOs any SDO is subject to the same competition law scrutiny as their non-accredited counterparts, i.e., the standardization agreements, including IPR policies, governing their operation will be assessed against the same legal criteria.[29] As all SSOs concern the collaboration between multiple stakeholders, some of which are competitors, the fear of anti-competitive conduct does not vanish merely because the SSO has earned accreditation. Absent effective IPR policies there is an increased risk that some patent owners will take undue advantage of the standard setting process by having its technologies embodied in the standard set, only to subsequently use its patents strategically to foreclose rivals or extract excessive royalties *ex post* when the standard is set. Moreover, the fact that many SDOs are non-profit organizations or that some are partly financed by public funds does not confer upon them immunity from Article 101 TFEU insofar as they are capable of being characterized as undertakings or associations hereof. Overall therefore there is no need to distinguish SDOs from other types of SSOs from the perspective of competition law.

The prohibition contained in Article 101 TFEU applies to '*agreements between undertakings*' and '*decisions by associations of undertakings*'. It follows that standardization agreements are subject to Article 101 TFEU regardless of whether (i) entered into by undertakings directly or (ii) adopted by an SSO which itself is an undertaking or pursuant to a decision insofar as the SSO constitutes an association of undertakings. Since the term 'undertaking' is interpreted broadly as comprising any 'economic activity' consisting of offering goods and services on the market few such agreements will arguably escape the reach of competition law.[30] However, activities connected

27. A list of 'new approach' directives is available at: www.newapproach.org/. (Last checked 30 May 2014).
28. Communication from the Commission, *A strategic vision for European standards: Moving forward to enhance and accelerate the sustainable growth of the European economy by 2020*, COM(2011) 311 final, 1 Jun. 2011, point 1.1.
29. Cf. also Frain, Tim, *Patents in Standards & Interoperability*, paper prepared for the World Intellectual Property Organisation, 2006 p. 2. The application of Art. 101 TFEU to standardisation agreements is discussed in Ch. 9.
30. The entity's legal status and the way in which it is financed is immaterial, cf. for instance Case C-41/90, *Klaus Höfnr and Fritz Elser v. Macrotron GmbH*, 23 Apr. 1991, § 21, Case C-244/94, *Federation française des sociétés d'assurances and Others*, 16 Nov. 1995 § 14, Case C-55/96, *Job Centre*, 11 Dec. 1997 § 21, Case C-35/96, *Commission of the European Communities v. Italian Republic*, 18 Jun. 1998 § 36 and Joined Cases C-180/98 to C-184/98, *Pavel Pavlov and Others v. Stichting Pensioenfonds Medische Specialisten*, 12 Sep. 2000 § 74. Although it may be a relevant factor in determining whether its activities are of an economic nature it is not in itself decisive whether the SSO offers its services for profit. See for instance Case C-49/07, *Motosykletistiki Omospondia Ellados NPID (MOTOE) V Elliniko Dimosio*, 1 Jul. 2009 § 27 and Case C-1/12, *Ordem dos Técnicos Oficiais de Contas*, 28 Feb. 2013, § 57. Indeed, many influential SSOs, such as ETSI (www.etsi.org/about) and W3C (www.w3.org/Consortium/Process/Process-19991111/background.html), are non-profit organizations.

with the exercise of public powers are not economic in nature; hence are not subject to the competition rules.[31] Thus, in *SELEX* the CJEU *inter alia* found the standardization activities of Eurocontrol, an SSO to which the Member States had entrusted the task of defining standards to be used in the sector of air navigation, to be of a legislative rather than a economic nature, since the standards were adopted solely by the Member States for the purpose of establishing a uniform system of air traffic management.[32] In this respect note that although the ESOs pursue the public interest this does not shield them from competition law intervention. As noted by the Commission the ESOs are subject to competition law to the extent that they can be considered undertakings or associations hereof.[33] In *EMC Development* the Commission considered that the question as to whether a standard adopted by CEN (one of the ESOs) could be considered an agreement between undertakings or a decision by an association of undertakings could be left open, because the complaint filed in any event had to be rejected.[34] However, it seems very likely that CEN – as is the case with ETSI – would have been considered an association of undertakings within the meaning of Article 101(1) TFEU. Although CEN being an ESO had to be considered a body entrusted with the general economic interest, the Commission noted that account had to be taken of the fact that the standard in question had been developed by a technical committee whose members were private undertakings.[35]

Standards promoted by SSOs are often collectively referred to as *formal standards*[36] to signify that the process leading to their adoption is more or less

31. See generally for instance Case C-364/92, *SAT Fluggesellschaft*, § 30; Case 107/84, *Commission v. Germany*, §§ 14-15 and Case C-49/07, *MOTOE v. Elliniko Dimosio*, 1 Jul. 2009, § 24.
32. Case C-113/07 P, *SELEX v. Commission*, 26 Mar. 2009, §§ 86-93 (in particular). The fact that SELEX acquired certain prototypes on the market in connection with its activities did not alter this conclusion, since as held by the court at § 102 "*...the fact that technical standardisation is not an economic activity means that the acquisition of prototypes in connection with that standardisation is not an economic activity either*" – as noted above an economic activity consists in offering goods or services – not acquiring them. The Commission in accordance with *SELEX* notes "*...that the preparation and production of technical standards as part of the execution of public powers*" is not covered by the guidelines, cf. Communication from the Commission, *Guidelines on the applicability of Article 101 of the Treaty on the Functioning of the European Union to horizontal co-operation agreements*, OJ 2011/C 11/1, 14 Jan. 2011, § 258.
33. Commission, *Guidelines on the applicability of Article 101 of the Treaty on the Functioning of the European Union to horizontal co-operation agreements*, OJ 2011/C 11/1, 14 Jan. 2011, § 258. By way of example ETSI (ESO responsible for adopting *inter alia* the GSM, 3G and 4G telecommunication standards) explicitly recognizes that "*...all members of ETSI are subject to Article 101 TFEU and thus capable in principle of incurring into anti-competitive behaviour. Furthermore, ETSI itself as an "association of undertakings" is subject to competition law...*", cf. ETSI Guidelines for Antitrust Compliance, 27 Jan. 2011, s. B.2.3. The Commission seems to be of the same opinion, cf. Case IV/35.006, *ETSI interim IPR policy*, 95/C 76/05, 28 Mar. 1995.
34. Commission decision in case COMP/F-2/38.401, *EMC/European Cement Producers*, 28 Sep. 2005, §§ 73-75. The case concerned a complaint that European producers of Portland cement had infringed Art. 101(1) TFEU (then, Art. 81(1) EC) in relation to the development of an industry standard. The rejection of the complaint was upheld on appeal in Case T-432/05, *EMC Development v. Commission*, 12 May 2010.
35. Commission decision in case COMP/F-2/38.401, EMC/*European Cement Producers*, 28 Sep. 2005, § 75.
36. See for Pappalardo, Kylie & Suzor, Nicolas, *Standardisation and patent ambush: Potential liability under Australian competition law*, Competition & Consumer Law Journal, Vol. 18, 2011 p. 269, and Nimmer, Raymond T., *Technical Standards Setting Organizations & Competition: A*

formalized[37] and involve a formal agreement between the stakeholders participating. As noted in Chapter 7 section §7.01 a de facto *standard* to the contrary evolve through a market driven process and therefore does per definition not involve such formal arrangements. As noted in Chapter 7 section §7.03 the difference between the two approaches to standard setting impacts the application of competition law.

Against the above background an overview of the terminology used in this book is shown in the Table 7.1 below.

Table 7.1 Categorization of Standard Setting Organizations and Standards

<table>
<tr><td rowspan="2">Origin:</td><td colspan="2">Standard Setting Organizations (SSOs)</td><td>The Market</td></tr>
<tr><td>Standard Development Organizations (SDOs), including:
• European Standardisation Organisation's (ESBs)
• National Standard Setting Bodies (NSBs)
• International accredited standardization organization's</td><td>Non-accredited SSOs, including:
• Industry organizations
• Consortia
• Fora</td><td>-</td></tr>
<tr><td rowspan="2">Type:</td><td>Accredited standards</td><td>Non-accredited standards</td><td>-</td></tr>
<tr><td colspan="2">Formal standards</td><td>De facto standards</td></tr>
</table>

Some use the term de jure standards specifically to refer to standards set by SDOs while labelling non-accredited standards as for instance consortium standards.[38] The term de jure standard is however misleading as there is normally no legal compulsion for companies to adhere to standards regardless of whether they are set by SDOs or non-accredited SSOs.[39] In fact any standardization agreement mandating compliance

case for Deference to Markets, in the University of Houston Public Law and Legal Theory Series, 2009-A-23 p. 6. Others however use the term solely to refer to standards set by SDOs, cf. for instance Frain, Tim, *Patents in Standards & Interoperability*, paper prepared for the World Intellectual Property Organisation, 2006 p. 2.

37. See however Rubin, Jonathan L., *Patents, Antitrust, and Rivalry in Standard-Setting*, in Rutgers Law Journal, Vol. 38, 2007 p. 514, stating that SSOs also include "*consortia of like-minded companies with few or no formal procedures*" [my emphasis]. In this dissertation such consortia are also referred to as SSOs, since they involve collaboration between multiple companies and, hence, are treated like any other SSO under competition law. Indeed, in order to benefit from the 'safe harbour' established by the Commission's Horizontal Guidelines all SSOs whose standard setting activities risk creating market power must adopt certain formal procedures aimed at safeguarding effective competition – see Ch. 9 s. §9.03.
38. See for instance WIPO, *Standards and Patents*, Standing committee on the law of patents, 13th Session, 2009 p. 10.
39. Gifford, Daniel J., *Developing Models for a Coherent Treatment of Standard-setting Issues under Patent, Copyright and Antitrust Laws*, in IDEA: The Journal of Law and Technology, Vol. 43,

with the standard being developed would fail to comply with the 'safe-harbour' principles set out in the Commission's Horizontal Guidelines as such clause would limit the incentive for members to engage in stand-alone innovation.[40] For this reason the ambiguous term de jure standard will not be used in this book. Instead reference will simply be made to accredited (set by SDOs) and non-accredited (set by non-SDOs) standards where relevant. The term de jure standard should rightly be reserved for technical specifications which are promulgated by government and mandated by law. Such governmental standards typically relates to requirements concerning issues of general public interest such as health, safety or the environment, i.e., areas where there is little incentive for private firms to standardize.[41] In this respect note that products complying with the European Standards adopted by ESOs under the so-called new approach (briefly mentioned above) merely benefit from a presumption that they fulfil the requirements put forward by the relevant new approach directive to which the standard relates, but their use is not strictly required by law. In principle therefore companies are free to deviate from the European Standards and use technologies different from those 'recommended' by the ESOs if these can be documented to fulfil the requirements of the relevant new approach directive.

§7.03 FORMAL STANDARDS ≠ DE FACTO STANDARDS

A distinction between de facto standards and formal standards is not of purely academic interest. Thus, the nature of formal standards triggers special challenges from a competition law perspective since they evolve through agreement rather than a purely market based selection process. Although, as explained in Chapter 9 section §9.02 formal standardization mitigates some of the drawbacks associated with a market based standardization process it also makes topical distinctive risks to effective competition. Thus, since SSOs have as their very purpose to displace the free-markets forces and facilitate technological coordination between competitors vigilance is warranted in order to ensure that consumer interests are not prejudiced. De facto standards on the other hand derive their legitimacy from the market itself and therefore do not give rise to the same competition law issues.

2003 p. 336, and Lea, Gary & Hall, Peter, *Standards and intellectual property rights – an economic and legal perspective*, in Information Economics and Policy, Vol. 16, 2004 p. 69.

40. For more details see Ch. 9 s. §9.03.
41. Cf. also Park, Jae Hun, *Patents and Industry Standards*, Edward Elgar, 2010 p. 12. Note that any technical standard mandated by law at the national level may present a barrier to trade between Member States for which reason they must fulfil the requirements set out by the so-called *Cassis de Dijon* doctrine created by the CJEU in Case 120/78, *Rewe-Zentral AG v. Bundesmonopolverwaltung für Barnntwein*, 20 Feb. 1979. Overall the doctrine entails that the Member States may not in principle prohibit the sale of products lawfully produced and marketed in another Member State even if the product does not satisfy technical or quality requirements imposed on domestic products. Moreover, NSB's must notify with the Commission proposed national technical regulations (at a draft stage) in accordance with Directive 98/34/EC of 22 Jun. 1998 laying down a procedure for the provision of information in the field of technical standards and regulations as amended by Directive 98/48/EC of 20 Jul. 1998, Directive 2006/96/EC of 20 Nov. 2006 and Regulation 1025/2012 of 25 Oct. 2012.

As set out by the Commission's Horizontal Guidelines there is a risk of SSOs being used as a cover for collusion and, as evidenced by case law, a risk that some SSO participants join forces to impose upon the market a proprietary standard to which other market players are subsequently denied access on FRAND terms.[42] To limit the risks to effective competition it is, as explained in Chapter 9, important that the standardization agreements (including IPR policies) governing SSOs include contractual safeguards which (1) promote openness/transparency during the standard setting process and (2) ensure the availability of essential IPR on FRAND terms after the standard is adopted. While the latter aims to ensure that IPRs embodied are not relied upon *ex post* to engage in exploitative or exclusionary conduct the requirements pertaining to openness and transparency have as their purpose to ensure that certain companies are not left in the dark and that innovative technologies are not foreclosed.

As to the exercise of SEPs note that FRAND-pledged patents are subject to special constraints under competition law, since as a main rule refusing to licence such patents (Chapter 12), or enforcing them against licensees willing to take a license (Chapter 13), will violate Article 102 TFEU. Accordingly, engaging in such course of conduct may violate the contractual obligation to license essential IPR to third parties on FRAND terms as well as competition law.[43] Proprietors of patents which have not been FRAND-pledged, including those reading on de facto standards, on the other hand are not subject to the same constraints. Thus, the prerogative to exclude third parties is at the heart of patents and absent a FRAND commitment it has been acknowledged by the CJEU that competition law intervention is only warranted in exceptional circumstances.

To sum up; the fact that formal standards are set 'artificially' pursuant to agreement between different stakeholders (as opposed to de facto standards which arise 'naturally' as a result of market forces) and the legitimate expectations of other market players which arise in light of FRAND commitments, explain why the standard setting process within SSOs as well as the conduct of SSO participants is subject to special scrutiny under Articles 101 and 102 TFEU.

42. Communication from the Commission, *Guidelines on the applicability of Article 101 of the Treaty on the Functioning of the European Union to horizontal co-operation agreements*, OJ 2011/C 11/1, 14 Jan. 2011, §§ 264–266.
43. Cf. also Beurskens, Michael, *An offer you can't refuse*, Comparative IP Academic Workshop Working Paper No. 6, 2009 p. 5. Available for free at http://www.law.washington.edu/Casrip/WWIP/Papers/2009/An offer you cant refuse.pdf. (Last checked 30 May 2014).

PART III Market Power

CHAPTER 8
The Link between Market Power and Standardization

In order for the conduct of undertakings to appreciably impair effective competition within the meaning of Articles 101 and 102 TFEU they must be in possession of market power. Generally, the first step in applying Article 101 or 102 TFEU is therefore to establish a framework for 'measuring' the market power of the undertaking(s) whose actions are the subject of scrutiny – the tool being the definition of one or more relevant markets to which reference can be made in assessing the competitive restraints facing the undertaking(s).[1] Whereas Article 102 TFEU is only applicable to undertakings holding a dominant position the application of Article 101 TFEU does not require a finding of dominance – a lesser degree of market power suffices.

Most of the competition law issues related to standardization revolve around the unilateral conduct of undertakings holding SEPs and the potential for abuse within the meaning of Article 102 TFEU. However, in the context of formal standardization, i.e., standardization taking place within the framework of a SSO, the underlying standardization agreement must fulfil conditions stemming from Article 101 TFEU if there is a risk that it confers upon participant's market power – said conditions, regarding *inter alia* disclosure of patent interests and FRAND commitments, have as their very purpose to prevent abuse in form of 'patent holdup' after the SSO adopts a standard. Accordingly, understanding under what circumstances market power is conferred by SEPs is not only important to the application of Article 102 TFEU, but in determining whether there is a risk that standardization agreements will create market power.

Patents embodied in technical standards will often confer upon their proprietor's appreciable market power. Overall there are two explanations for this – sunk costs and network effects. The former refers to the substantial non-recoverable (sunk) costs which manufactures may have invested participating in the development of a standard

1. See for instance Case 27/76, *United Brands v. Commission*, 14 Feb. 1978, § 10.

and in tailoring their business to the production of standard compliant products.[2] The latter refers to the special characteristics present on markets where standards are set to promote interoperability and compatibility between products from different manufactures. As explained in more detail in the next section consumers on such markets will often be reluctant to opt for products which are not compatible with the standard(s) having achieved the most widespread adoption.

Sunk costs and network effects may act to discourage manufactures from embracing competing standards or non-standardized technologies even if they are met with unreasonable licensing demands from SEP holders.[3] Indeed, the Commission in an open letter to ETSI (an ESO) stated that:

> [o]nce an essential technology is included...in a standard, particularly one that is made mandatory pursuant to Community legislation, the owner of the IPR relating to that technology in most if not all situations occupies a dominant position ... vis-à-vis manufactures requiring licenses.[4]

However, while the statement is arguably true with regard to patents embodied in a de jure standard any perception that holding SEPs automatically translates into dominance is shrouded with error. Although SEP holders are likely to achieve dominance in markets characterized by strong network effects (see below) a careful case-by-case analysis is called for. This has been expressly recognized by the Commission in its most recent Horizontal Guidelines where it is stated that "*...there is no presumption that holding or exercising IPR essential to a standard equates to the possession or exercise of market power. The question of market power can only be assessed on a case by case basis*".[5]

2. Farrell, Joseph et al., *Standard Setting, Patents, and Hold-Up*, in Antitrust Law Journal, Vol. 74(3), 2007 p. 616. Also see Ruikka, Timo, *"FRAND" Undertakings in Standardization – A Business Perspective*, Paper presented at the Fordham IP Conference, New York City, 28 Mar. 2008 p. 6. It has been reported that IBM spent more than USD 500 million on standard setting in 2005 – see Ch. 11, footnote 71.
3. Such network effects may significantly compound the 'lock-in' attributable to the investment costs of manufactures. As noted by Farrell, Joseph et al., *Standard Setting, Patents, and Hold-Up*, in Antitrust Law Journal, Vol. 74(3), 2007 p. 616, "*Hold-up is a particular problem in the context of cooperative standard setting for two reasons. First, when standards are involved, an entire industry may make specific investments that are subject to hold-up. Second, coordination problems can make it especially hard to shift away from an agreed-upon standard in response to excessive royalty demands. If each user's leading alternative to sticking with the standard is unilateral switching, and thus losing compatibility with others, then the patent holder's subsequent advantage . . . includes not only its technology's inherent advantage and the value of the user's own sunk investments, but also the value of compatibility to the user.*"
4. Open letter from the Commission to ETSI and CBEMA, February 1994 *(not published)*. The letter is cited in Dolmans, Maurits, *Standards For Standards*, in Fordham International Law Journal, Vol. 26(1), 2002 p. 187 (footnote 84).
5. Communication from the Commission, *Guidelines on the applicability of Article 101 of the Treaty on the Functioning of the European Union to horizontal co-operation agreements*, OJ 2011/C 11/1, 14 Jan. 2011, § 39.

The Commission's notice on market definition sets out the general principles to be applied when defining the relevant market.[6] The purpose of this section however is not to explain the general principles of market definition and market power in detail, but to apply them specifically in the context of technical standards where legal clarification is called for.[7] While identifying the relevant market(s) and measuring market power can be a daunting task with regard to tangible goods, an extra layer of complexity is added when IPR and standards are part of the equation since, as explained below, the competitive conditions on at least three distinct markets must be taken into consideration – the technology market, the standards market and the product market. Nonetheless, the Commission has not devoted much effort to provide any specific guidance in this respect and the issue of market power often receives only superficial treatment in legal literature addressing the interplay between patents and standards.

As a basis for the discussion of market power it is crucial to understand the market forces at play in the context of standardization – these are analysed in section §8.01. Next, in section §8.02, it is discussed under what circumstances a holder of SEPs can be said to hold a dominant position within the meaning of Article 102 TFEU. Relying on the conclusions made in sections §8.01 and §8.02 it is then discussed in section §8.03 under what circumstances a standardization agreement risks creating market power. This is essential to determine whether contractual safeguards such as those set out by the Commission's Horizontal Guidelines must be put in place in order prevent abuse by IPR holders and bring the agreement outside the scope of Article 101(1) TFEU.

§8.01 RELEVANT MARKET FORCES: A LOOK AT 'NETWORK EFFECTS'

Market power is to be assessed in light of the relevant market conditions – the fact that an undertaking holds a high market share does not necessarily indicate market power.[8] Thus, the market power of those in control of a standard, i.e., the proprietors of SEPs, cannot be properly assessed without understanding the specific market forces at play.

As noted in Chapter 2 many issues concerning the interface between IPRs and standards arise in the ICT field where standards are often adopted to facilitate interoperability. Accordingly, the market mechanisms which act to shape the competitive conditions on so-called 'network markets' are of special importance.[9] Such markets are characterized by network effects which means that the utility of a product

6. Commission notice on the definition of relevant market for the purposes of Community competition law, OJ 1997/C 372/5, 9 Dec. 1997. Note that the Commission's notice has been endorsed by the CJEU – see for instance T-321/05, *AstraZeneca v. Commission*, 1 Jul. 2010, § 86.
7. For a general overview see Whish, Richard, *Competition Law*, 7th ed., Oxford University Press, 2012 pp. 25–48 and 179–189 and Van Bael & Bellis, *Competition Law of the European Community*, 5th ed., Kluwer Law International, 2010 pp. 99–131.
8. See the discussion in Ch. 8 s. §8.02.
9. As noted in Ch. 8 s. §8.03 not all standards are interoperability standards, but such standards are especially likely to confer upon patentees market power due to the effects described below. Moreover, as was noted in Ch. 2, more than 84% of standards related to information and communication technologies.

is directly or indirectly linked to the total number of consumers using compatible/ interoperable products. As explained below, this has several implications with regard to competition and market power. In particular network effects explain why there is a tendency for markets to 'tip' in favour of a single standard and accordingly why significant market power is likely to arise in the context of ICT standardization insofar as select firms are able to control access to the standard by virtue of their patents.[10]

In the following sections it is explained why so-called 'network effects' encourage standardization (Chapter 8 section §8.01[A]) and often result in market power being conferred upon holders of SEPs (Chapter 8 section §8.01[B]). As explained standards are at the heart of network effects as the bundle of technologies facilitating compatibility between products often originate from SSOs or become a de facto standard due to the tendency for network markets to 'tip'.[11]

[A] Network Effects and Standardization

Economists use the term 'network effects' (or network externalities) to describe the forces at play on markets where product compatibility is of significant importance – so-called 'network markets'. A distinction is typically made between two types of network effects – those which are *direct* and those which are *indirect*.[12]

The presence of direct network effects entails that a product's utility, hence its value to the consumer, increases as the total number of consumers using compatible products increases. In other words, products that benefit from network effects derive their value (in part) from the total user base. The value of the cell phone for instance depends largely on the number of users connected to the same network as obviously there is little benefit associated with having a phone if you are only able to call a limited number of other people. Indirect network effects on the other hand refers to the utility value 'indirectly' linked to the number of users in that a large user base encourages companies to offer supplementary products or services which increase the utility of the main product. Again, the cell phone provides an excellent example. As the number of cell phone user's increase so does the potential to earn a profit by offering compatible software products (often referred to as 'Apps') and the resulting increase in product diversity on the downstream software market boosts the utility of the cell phone. Whereas *direct* network effects relate to horizontal compatibility, i.e., interaction between substitute products, *indirect* network effects therefore relate to vertical

10. Also see Farrell, Joseph et al., *Standard Setting, Patents, and Hold-Up*, in Antitrust Law Journal, Vol. 74(3), 2007 p. 632, where it is found that "*[w]hen network effects are important (as a strong role for an SSO suggests), the technology adoption decision is in reality collective. One way or another, the market will tip, and an individual user can hardly decide unilaterally to avoid a technology that is essential to a standard to which it expects others to conform*".
11. Cf. also Hovenkamp, Herbert, *Standards Ownership and Competition Policy*, in Boston College Law Review, Vol. 48(1), 2007 p. 88.
12. See for instance Motta, Massimo, *Competition Policy – Theory and Practice*, Cambridge University Press, 2004 p. 82; Katz, Michael L. & Shapiro, Carl, *Network Externalities, Competition, and Compatibility*, in The American Economic Review, Vol. 75(3), 1985 p. 424, and Whish, Richard, *Competition Law*, 7th ed., Oxford University Press, 2012 p. 11.

compatibility,[13] i.e., the availability of complementary products, services or know-how.[14]

Network effects result in a virtues cycle: as more users adopt a particular technology its utility value increases and this creates an incentive for others to follow the same 'path' of technology adoption. As a result there is seldom room for multiple competing technologies. As a sufficient number of users embrace a given technology in a market characterized by network effects there is a tendency for the market to 'tip' in favour of the technologies having earned most widespread acceptance, leaving competing technologies to fade out and become obsolete on the market(s) concerned.[15] The tendency towards technical standardization is therefore an inherent characteristic in markets on which strong network effects are present. If formal standards are not set by market players within the framework of a SSO de facto standards will often arise as a result of market forces – SSOs merely accelerate the process by means of joint collaboration between companies which would otherwise 'battle' for the market individually.

A recent example can be drawn from the 'battle' between the optical disc formats Blu-ray and HD-DVD each supported by their own consortia consisting of major industry players. Here the latter was eventually abandoned in 2008 as a 'tipping point' was reached when film studios and distributors opted for the Blu-ray standard and left little incentive for consumers to purchase HD-DVD compliant equipment.

It is important to note that network markets do not always 'tip' towards a single technology. Depending on market characteristics, a number of competing technologies may each achieve a sufficiently large user base to render the utility value derived from additional network effects negligible.[16] Hence, while network markets tend to be concentrated competing standards may nonetheless sometimes coexist in effect forming a 'standards market'.[17] From a competition law perspective there is less need to worry when there is competition between standards as this may act to restrain the

13. See Hovenkamp, Herbert, *Standards Ownership and Competition Policy*, in Boston College Law Review, Vol. 48(1), 2007 p. 90.
14. Much of the utility value derived from using Microsoft Windows for instance stems from the ability to interact seamlessly with other windows clients and servers and from the host of compatible devices.
15. Cf. also Besen, Stanley M. & Farrell, Joseph, *Choosing How to Compete – Strategies and Tactics in Standardisation*, in The Journal of Economic Perspectives, Vol. 8(2), 1994 p. 118, Motta, Massimo, *Competition Policy – Theory and Practice*, Cambridge University Press, 2004 p. 84, and Weitzel, Tim, *Economics of Standards in Information Networks*, 2004 p. 24.
16. The size of the relevant product or service market to which the standards relate as well as the extent to which consumers value variety on these markets are decisive factors in this respect See along these lines Motta, Massimo, *Competition Policy – Theory and Practice*, Cambridge University Press, 2004 p. 84.
17. At some point the marginal utility value derived from one additional user or complementary product/service declines, i.e., the impact of network effects becomes less pronounced as more users join the 'network' in question. By way of example consider the smart phone market. Despite strong indirect network effects associated with the amount of software (commonly known as "apps") available several competing platforms (operating systems), including Google Android, Apple IoS and Microsoft Windows Phone, each offering distinct features, exist on the same market. Although there is a great divergence in the number of apps available for each platform there is still sufficient for users not to deselect either platform on basis of network effects.

conduct of SEP holders – see section §8.02. However, if the market becomes 'locked-in' to a single (or a few) standard(s) those conferred control over the standard by virtue of their patents in essence gain the ability to act as gatekeepers to the market as explained in section §8.01[B].

[B] Network Effects and Market Power

While the utility value derived from network effects contributes to increased consumer welfare, and therefore in part explains the pro-competitive benefits of standardization, it also results in the creation of significant market barriers and often confers upon holders of SEPs a dominant position within the meaning of Article 102 TFEU.

The 'tipping' effect described in section §8.01[A] encourages fierce competition between substitute technologies (i.e., *inter*-technology competition) in the pre-standardization phase as companies 'battle' to win the market and harvest the profits associated with having their technologies embodied in the standard that will eventually prevail.[18] However, once the market 'tips' in favour of one or more standards which gain a strong foothold on the market to which they relate the nature of competition will change significantly. Thus, as the utility value of a technology, hence, also the standard to which it relates, increases as it is more widely adopted users are reluctant to opt for technologies which are not compatible with the prevalent standard(s) – in effect the market becomes 'locked-in' by the utility value attributable to network effects and *inter*-technology competition will often cease (or at least be limited) *ex post* standardization. Competition in networks markets is therefore sometimes described as being *for* the market rather than *in* the market since the 'winner(s) take(s) all' once the market 'tips'.[19] As explained in section §8.02 the market outcome of standardization may be more or less persistent depending on the pace of technological development on the market to which the standard(s) relate(s) and the importance of backwards compatibility – in any event however the tendency towards concentration at the technology level (the 'technology market') is likely to confer upon those in control of a standard significant market power on the downstream product market.

Expectations also play a crucial role in this respect. Thus, all things being equal, users[20] decide which technologies to adopt on the basis of their expectations about its diffusion on the market since, as explained above, a larger user base result in larger

18. Cf. also Motta, Massimo, *Competition Policy – Theory and Practice*, Cambridge University Press, 2004 p. 84, Besen, Stanley M. & Farrell, Joseph, *Choosing How to Compete – Strategies and Tactics in Standardisation*, in The Journal of Economic Perspectives, Vol. 8(2), 1994 p. 119, and Paradolesi, Roberto & Renda, Andrea, *The European Commission's Case Against Microsoft – Kill Bill?*, in World Competition, Vol. 27(4), 2004 p. 528.
19. See for instance Spassova, Vesselina, *What kind of competition policy for highly innovative markets with network effects?*, CAE Working Papers 27, Aix-Marseille Université, CERGAM, 2005 p. 7 and Geradin, Damien & Rato, Miguel, *Can Standard-Setting Lead to Exploitative Abuse? A Dissonant View on Patent Hold-Up, Royalty Stacking and the Meaning of FRAND*, in European Competition Journal. Vol. 3, 2007 p. 149.
20. Note that the term 'users' in this respect does not only refer to 'consumers'. Sometimes it may be influential intermediate companies, such as network operators, equipment manufacturers, and distributors, which have the final say in settling a 'standards battle'.

product utility.[21] The technology which eventually becomes a standard therefore need not always be the technology that is best from a technical perspective – the size of the companies supporting the technology and the promotional efforts made, may also be influential in shaping the expectations of users, and hence, the likelihood that a market 'tips'. If enough potential users believe that others will adopt the technology then it will succeed, while it will fail if users expect the user base to be relatively small – the expectations of users in effect becomes a self-fulfilling prophecy. The likelihood that new and emerging technologies succeed therefore to a large extent depends on the prospect of them becoming industry standards since the technologies which lose the battle for the market, as noted above, may become obsolete.[22]

With regard to the competition between the Blu-Ray and HD-DVD format (see above) consumers who purchased equipment and movies conforming with the latter standard for instance had to see their investment wasted when the market 'tipped' due to the decisions made by film studios and distributors. As explained in Chapter 9 section §9.02 companies strive for collaborative standard setting to *inter alia* accelerate the process of technology selection by displacing the free-market forces and to reduce such risks associated with 'going alone'.

The role of expectations in shaping the competitive landscape in effect may result in a reluctance to adopt new technologies due to uncertainty about what other prospective users will do – a phenomenon known to economists' as *excess inertia*: when the private gain for an individual user does not justify it being an early adopter of a new technology the choices made by others are awaited.[23] Any potential entrant will therefore have to convince users not only that its technology is superior from a technical perspective, but that it is able to achieve widespread adoption on the market – a task not easily overcome if established standards have gained a strong foothold.

The effects outlined above explain why network markets are characterized by strong demand side economies of scale,[24] i.e., there is interdependency between the total number users of a specific technology which facilitate compatibility and the value of the products incorporating the technology.[25] This has vital implications with regard

21. Cf. also Besen, Stanley M. & Farrell, Joseph, *Choosing How to Compete – Strategies and Tactics in Standardisation*, in The Journal of Economic Perspectives, Vol. 8(2), 1994 p. 118, Motta, Massimo, *Competition Policy – Theory and Practice*, Cambridge University Press, 2004 p. 82, and Weitzel, Tim, *Economics of Standards in Information Networks*, 2004 p. 24.
22. Cf. also Motta, Massimo, *Competition Policy – Theory and Practice*, Cambridge University Press, 2004 p. 84.
23. See Motta, Massimo, *Competition Policy – Theory and Practice*, Cambridge University Press, 2004 p. 82, and Besen, Stanley M. & Farrell, Joseph, *Choosing How to Compete – Strategies and Tactics in Standardisation, in The Journal of Economic Perspectives*, Vol. 8(2), 1994 p. 119. Also see *Farrell, Joseph & Saloner, Garth, Installed Base and Compatibility – Innovation, Product Preannouncements, and predation*, in The American Economic Review, Vol. 76(5), 1986 p. 943. The authors refer to this as a penguin effect because "*[p]enguins who must enter the water to find food often delay doing so because they fear the presence of predators. Each would prefer some other penguin to test the waters first*".
24. See Farrell, Joseph & Saloner, Garth, *Installed Base and Compatibility – Innovation, Product Preannouncements, and predation*, in The American Economic Review, Vol. 76(5), 1986 p. 940.
25. The value of a given cell phone for instance does not depend on the total number of cell phones in use, but on the number of cell phones the user is able to call as a result of technological compatibility.

to market power, hence the application of Articles 101 and 102 TFEU, since the undertakings which, by virtue of their patents, own the technologies forming part of a standard will be able to control its availability to third parties and in effect prevent them from benefitting from said value – which may be essential for them to remain viable on the market. Network effects therefore may establish almost impenetrable barriers to market access in the aftermath of standard setting activities. Once a market has 'tipped' demand side substitution attributable to competing and well-established standards, as explained in section §8.02, will therefore often be the main source of competitive restraint whereas the prospect of potential competition will seldom act as a restraint. While having profound implications with regard to market power it is however important to note that the tendency towards technological unification is a normal characteristic on network markets and the benefits derived from network effects in terms of utility value is considered pro-competitive. Although said market barriers may force companies to follow a predefined technology-path not deviating from the one already set by the incumbent companies, they do not in themselves pose a problem from a competition law perspective. While *inter*-technology competition is limited the benefits of standardization outlined in Chapter 9 section §9.01 prevail as long as all market players are allowed effective access to the standard(s) – in effect intensifying *intra*-technology competition.

§8.02 ESSENTIAL PATENTS AND DOMINANCE

The first step in applying Article 102 TFEU is to determine whether the undertaking subject to investigation holds a dominant position on the relevant market(s). According to established EU case law dominance follows from the fact that an undertaking enjoys a position of economic strength which enables it to prevent effective competition by "*...affording it the power to behave to an appreciable extent independently of its competitors, its customers and ultimately of the consumers*".[26] In this respect the notion of independence relates to the degree of competitive restraint faced by an undertaking since this indicates whether the undertaking holds the market power necessary to unilaterally influence the parameters of competition to its advantage, e.g., by profitably increasing prices above the competitive level for a significant period of time.[27] In the context of SEPs this means that it must, as a preliminary matter, be assessed to which

26. See for instance Case 85/76, *Hoffmann-La Roche & Co. v. Commission*, 13 Feb. 1979, § 38 and Case 27/76, *United Brands v. Commission*, 14 Feb. 1978, § 65. Also see Communication from the Commission, *Guidance on the Commission's enforcement priorities in applying Article 82 of the EC Treaty to abusive exclusionary conduct by dominant undertakings*, OJ 2009/C 45/02, 24 Feb. 2009, § 10 (including references to additional case law).
27. See Communication from the Commission, *Guidance on the Commission's enforcement priorities in applying Article 82 of the EC Treaty to abusive exclusionary conduct by dominant undertakings*, OJ 2009/C 45/02, 24 Feb. 2009, §§ 10-11. In general the Commission defines market power as the "*ability to profitably maintain prices above competitive levels for a period of time or to profitably maintain output in terms of product quantities, product quality and variety or innovation below competitive levels for a period of time*", Cf. Communication from the Commission, *Guidelines on the applicability of Article 101 of the Treaty on the Functioning of the European Union to horizontal co-operation agreements*, OJ 2011/C 11/1, 14 Jan. 2011, § 39.

extent the patentee enjoys the freedom to profitably set excessive or discriminatory (non-FRAND) royalty rates or other licensing conditions.

Obviously any assessment of market power calls for the delimitation of one or more markets of relevance in identifying the competitive restraints faced by an undertaking.[28] When assessing the market power conferred by SEPs it is necessary to take into consideration three separate, but interconnected market dimensions: the upstream technology market, the standards market to which the SEP(s) relate and the product market to which the standard relates.[29] The purpose of market definition – as is generally[30] the case – is to identify the sources of effective substitution to which licensees will seek recourse in response to a hypothetical small (in the range 5%–10%)[31] but permanent increase in the relative price (royalties) charged by the SEP holder. Thus, market definition establishes a framework for assigning market shares to the various sources of competition and aids in identifying the sources of immediate competitive pressure which may act as restraints.[32]

For illustrative purposes and as a basis for the examples given below, assume that two competing standards (standard$_1$ and standard$_2$) coexists on the market and (to simplify) that three patented technologies have been embodied in standard$_1$ and two in standard$_2$. Also assume that standard$_1$ has achieved a market share of 80% on the product market and standard$_2$ a market share of 10%. The remaining 10% of the product market comprises non-standardized technologies. This scenario is illustrated below:

28. See for instance Case 27/76, *United Brands v. Commission*, 14 Feb. 1978, § 10. Also see Commission notice on the definition of relevant market for the purposes of Community competition law, OJ 1997/C 372/5, 9 Dec. 1997, § 2, where it is stated that "*[t]he main purpose of market definition is to identify in a systematic way the competitive constraints that that the undertakings involved face*".
29. This is supported by the fact that the Commission considers these to be the markets which may be impacted by a standardisation agreement – see Ch. 8 s. §8.03.
30. See Commission notice on the definition of relevant market for the purposes of Community competition law, OJ 1997/C 372/5, 9 Dec. 1997, point 7 and 13 (in particular). Also see Case T-201/04, *Microsoft Corp v. Commission*, 17 Sep. 2007, § 484, where reference is made to point 7 of the notice where it is stated that "*[a] relevant product market comprises all those products and/or services which are regarded as interchangeable or substitutable by the consumer, by reason of the products' characteristics, their prices and their intended use*".
31. The conceptual framework for defining markets is set out in the Commission notice on the definition of relevant market for the purposes of Community competition law, OJ 1997/C 372/5, 9 Dec. 1997, § 17 where the so-called SSNIP-test (short for 'small but significant and non-transitory increase in price test') is adopted for the purpose of defining markets. Also see Commission notice, *Guidelines on the application of Article 101 of the Treaty on the Functioning of the European Union to technology transfer agreements*, OJ 2014/C 89/03, 28 Mar. 2014, § 22 where the SSNIP test is confirmed to apply in the context of licensing.
32. The Commission considers there to be three main sources of competitive constraints: demand substitutability, supply substitutability and potential competition – see Commission notice on the definition of relevant market for the purposes of Community competition law, OJ 1997/C 372/5, 9 Dec. 1997, § 13. However, as stated in § 13 of the notice demand substitutability is of prime importance in defining the relevant market since it constitutes the "*...most immediate and effective disciplinary force*".

Figure 8.1 Relevant Markets and Their Interdependencies

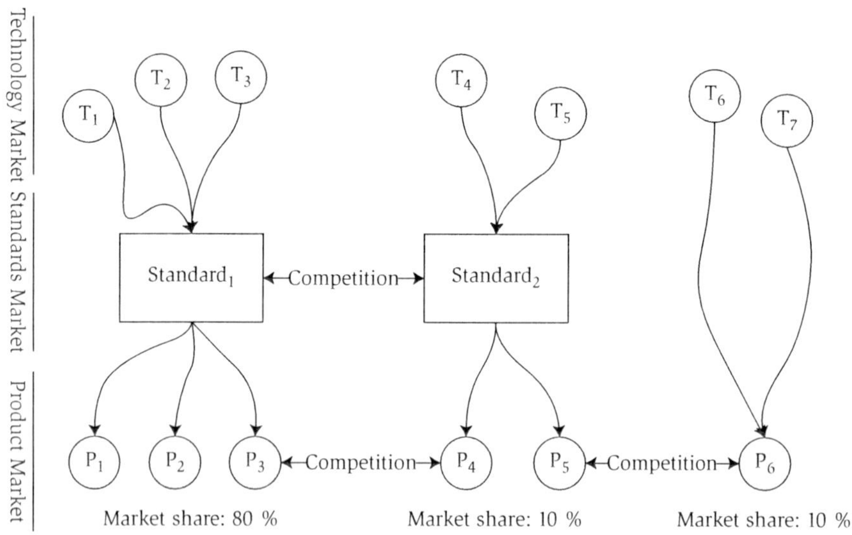

In a licensing context the technology market (also known as the 'licensing market') is of primary relevance. In general technology markets comprise all technologies which are regarded by licensees as interchangeable with or substitutable for the licensed technology by reason of their characteristics, their royalties and their intended use.[33] The CJEU has confirmed that holding a patent (or any other type of IPR) in general does not amount to dominance.[34] This is so because the exclusivity conferred covers only the specific implementation (invention) said out in the patent claims and not alternative implementations able to achieve the same result, i.e., substitute technologies (patented or non-proprietary) may exist and a competitive pressure exert upon the patentee. However, insofar as a patent is essential to comply with a standard there is by definition no substitute technologies available for that purpose, i.e., the bundle of technologies allowing for compliance are complementary rather than substitutable. As to the technology market the Commission in its *Google/Motorola* merger decision accordingly found that "*...each SEP [(Standard Essential Patent)] can be considered as a separate market in itself as it is necessary to comply with a standard and thus cannot be designed around, i.e. there is by definition no alternative or substitute for each such patent*" [addition added].[35] In other words, a distinct upstream technology market is deemed to exist for every patent essential to a standard and as a result the proprietor of such a patent per se holds a market share of 100% on said market – referring to the illustration above (Figure 8.1: Relevant Markets and Their Interdependencies) this

33. Commission notice, *Guidelines on the application of Article 101 of the Treaty on the Functioning of the European Union to technology transfer agreements*, OJ 2014/C 89/03, 28 Mar. 2014, § 22.
34. See for instance Joined Cases C-241/91 P and C-242/91 P, *RTE and ITP v. Commission (Magill)*, 6 Apr. 1995, § 46.
35. Case COMP/M.6381, *Google/Motorola Mobility*, 13 Feb. 2012, § 61.

entails that the proprietor of T_1 to T_7 holds a market share of 100% on the technology market.

As a presumption[36] of dominance is established once it can be grasped that an undertaking holds a market share in excess of 50% this of course is a strong indication that the proprietor of an SEP holds a dominant position. However, as noted by the Commission in its Horizontal Guidelines "*...there is no presumption that holding or exercising IPR essential to a standard equates to the possession or exercise of market power*".[37] It would be wrong to assume that SEPs automatically confer upon their proprietor's market power - let alone dominance - since the presence of competing standards or non-standardized technologies may potentially act to diminish the patentee's market power significantly.[38] In other words, a patent essential to a standard need not be indispensable to licensees in case they are able to switch to competing technologies (whether standardized or not) in response to an increase in royalties or other fees.[39] This is evident when considering that blindly taking into consideration the market share on the technology market would establish a strong presumption of dominance regardless of whether the standard to which the patents relates actually enjoys any success on the downstream product market. Failing to take into account the standards and product market in the example illustrated above (Figure 8.1: Relevant Markets and Their Interdependencies) would for instance support a conclusion that the proprietor of T_4 holds a dominant position despite the fact that 80% of products downstream adhere to a competing standard.

To get a more accurate picture of the market situation and the competitive pressure to which an SEP holders is exposed it is, as stated above, necessary to take into consideration the standards market and products market to which the patents relate in order to identify restraints stemming from substitute standards or non-standardized technologies. The importance of downstream competition in constraining the market power that licensors derive from their position on the upstream technology market has been acknowledged by the Commission. Thus, the Commission in the Technology Transfer Guidelines finds that "*[i]f the downstream product market is competitive, competition at this level may effectively constrain the licensor*" and notes that market shares on the technology market may be calculated by reference to the sales of products

36. Case C-62/86, *AKZO v. Commission*, 3 Jul. 1991, § 60, and Case T-228/97, *Irish Sugar v. Commission*, 7 Oct. 1999, § 70.
37. Communication from the Commission, *Guidelines on the applicability of Article 101 of the Treaty on the Functioning of the European Union to horizontal co-operation agreements*, OJ 2011/C 11/1, 14 Jan. 2011, § 269.
38. Dolmans, Maurits & Ilan, Daniel, *European Antitrust and Patent Acquisitions: Trolls in the Patent Thickets*, in Journal of the Antitrust Committee of the International Bar Association, Vol. 8(2), 2012 p. 8; Geradin, Damien & Rato, Miguel, *Can Standard-Setting Lead to Exploitative Abuse? A Dissonant View on Patent Hold-Up, Royalty Stacking and the Meaning of FRAND*, in European Competition Journal. Vol. 3, 2007 p. 146, and Layne-Farrar, Anne, *Nondiscriminatory Pricing: Is Standard Setting Different?*, in Journal of Competition Law & Economics, Vol. 6(4), 2010 p. 819.
39. While as explained in Ch. 8 s. §8.01[B] there is tendency for standards markets to be concentrated this does not rule out that a limited number of competing standards may coexist - at least for a certain period of time.

incorporating the licensed technology.[40] Indeed, including the product dimension provides a much more valid indication of market power than considering solely the relationship between a specific standard and an SEP.[41] The product market comprises all products which incorporate the licensed technologies or substitute technologies (irrespective of whether they are being licensed[42]) and accordingly it reveals whether SEP holders are constrained by the fact that end users or manufactures may switch to products incorporating alternative technologies in response to a price increase. In the example above (Figure 8.1: Relevant markets and Their Interdependencies) the owner of T_1 would for instance hold a market share of 80% whereas the owner of T_4 and T_6, respectively, would hold a market share of 10%.

It may be necessary to define several distinct product markets. Thus, as is the case with 'traditional' products,[43] a single technology may have several uses. This holds true regardless of the fact that the technology has been embodied in a technical standard. In other words, as a standard may impact several product markets the same applies to any technologies it embodies. The USB standard for instance has been incorporated into a host of different products (such as cell phones, laptops and digital cameras) which each constitute separate product markets. In principle therefore it may be that the patentee - while holding market power in some markets - is not in possession of market power with regard to the specific product market to which the conduct being scrutinized relates because the standard has not gained foothold in this market. In practice however, technical standards are often set with the purpose of facilitating interoperability between a number of different products and therefore seldom achieves success in only one product market.

In addition to defining the downstream products market it is also important to define the standards market as it establishes the basis for concluding whether competition stems solely from non-standardized technologies (which may be especially vulnerable to the 'tipping effect' described in section §8.01, hence risks being abandoned) or whether licensees are able to switch to competing standardized technologies. The Commission in its Horizontal Guidelines recognizes the importance of competing standards finding that:

> in the case of several competing standards or in the case of effective competition between the standardised solution and non-standardised solution a limitation of access may not produce restrictive effects on competition.[44]

40. Commission notice, *Guidelines on the application of Article 101 of the Treaty on the Functioning of the European Union to technology transfer agreements*, OJ 2014/C 89/03, 28 Mar. 2014, § 88.
41. Also see Dolmans, Maurits, *Standards For Standards*, in Fordham International Law Journal, Vol. 26(1), 2002 p. 187.
42. Commission notice, *Guidelines on the application of Article 101 of the Treaty on the Functioning of the European Union to technology transfer agreements*, OJ 2014/C 89/03, 28 Mar. 2014, § 86.
43. In Case 85/76, *Hoffmann-La Roche v. Commission*. 13 Feb. 1979, the Commission for instance found that vitamin C could be used for two different purposes ('bio nutritive' and 'technical') and accordingly defined two distinct markets.
44. Communication from the Commission, *Guidelines on the applicability of Article 101 of the Treaty on the Functioning of the European Union to horizontal co-operation agreements*, OJ 2011/C 11/1, 14 Jan. 2011, § 294. Also see § 277 where the Commission notes that restrictive effects are most unlikely to arise if there is effective competition between a number of voluntary standards.

Similarly, the Commission in its Google/Motorola merger decision highlighted that importance of competing standards to the assessment of market power.[45]

While market definition is an important starting point in assessing dominance it is important to note that it serves primarily to identify the restraints imposed by actual competitors, i.e., it does not give any indication as to the bargaining strength of licensees or other restraints which do not concern the market structure as such.[46] Thus, although a high market share is a strong indicator of dominance it is not by itself to be considered conclusive evidence. According to the Commission market shares must be interpreted "*...in the light of the relevant market conditions, and in particular of the dynamics of the market and of the extent to which products are differentiated*".[47] Indeed, a number of more 'indirect' competitive restraints have been argued to be of relevance in the context of standardization. These are discussed in section §8.02[A]. However, they will most often have little impact in the absence of viable competing standards.

[A] Competitive Restraints Other than Demand Substitutability

In section §8.02 the competitive constraints attributable to demand substitutability were discussed. As was explained the existence of competing standards to which licensees may seek recourse constitutes the most effective competitive restraint on SEP holders. However, other more 'indirect' sources of competitive constraints may as well by of importance to the assessment of dominance. Some such constraints are considered below:

[1] Bargaining Strength of Licensees

One such source of potential competitive constraint is the countervailing power of licensees.[48] The bargaining strength of licensees may be sufficiently strong to effectively deprive the SEP holder the ability to behave to an appreciable extent independently when setting royalty rates or other license conditions. A single company for instance seldom controls all patents essential to the implementation of a standard and the independence, hence market power, of vertically integrated patentees' *vis-à-vis*

45. Case COMP/M.6381 – Google/Motorola Mobility, 13 Feb. 2012, § 53 where it is stated that "*...once a standard has been adopted and widely implemented by the industry* and in the absence of competing standards, *firms that use these technologies may be severely limited in their ability to use another technology*" (emphasis added).
46. See along the same lines Whish, Richard, *Competition Law*, 7th ed., Oxford University Press, 2012 p. 28.
47. See Communication from the Commission, *Guidance on the Commission's enforcement priorities in applying Article 82 of the EC Treaty to abusive exclusionary conduct by dominant undertakings*, OJ 2009/C 45/02, 24 Feb. 2009, § 13.
48. Communication from the Commission, *Guidance on the Commission's enforcement priorities in applying Article 82 of the EC Treaty to abusive exclusionary conduct by dominant undertakings*, OJ 2009/C 45/02, 24 Feb. 2009, § 18. Also see Camesasca, Peter, et al., *Injunctions for Standard-Essential Patents: Justice is not Blind*, in Journal of Competition Law & Economics, Vol. 9(1), 2013 p. 287.

other holders of such patents therefore is likely to be constrained by the fact that their own downstream presence depends on reciprocal licensing. Licensees in possession of non- SEPs or other types of input, e.g., raw materials, may likewise be able to use these inputs as a basis to leverage their bargaining position. Put simply, the prospect of licensees retaliating in case the licensor attempts to impose of non-FRAND license terms may act to keep vertically integrated licensors on the path of virtue. Similarly, preserving the 'goodwill' in the eyes of certain licensees may also be of commercial importance to the licensor insofar as they hold influential positions in SSOs allowing them to exclude the licensor from upcoming revisions of the standard to which the patents in question relate (see immediately below).

Note that the countervailing power of select licensees is obviously not able to shield all licensees from the market power of the SEP holder. In *Irish Sugar* the General Court accepted the Commission's finding that it was necessary to pay attention to weaker buyers.[49] The importance of countervailing licensee power as a competitive restraint is accordingly limited unless the downstream market is concentrated and the conduct being scrutinized is directed at a company actually in possession of bargaining strength.

[2] Dynamic Competition

As explained in section §8.01 there is a tendency for the market to become 'locked-in' to a few (or a single) interoperability standards once they achieve success on a market. Some have however argued that the lock-in is only temporary in the sense that competition *for* the market will be initiated again once it is time to adopt the next generation of a standard and that this factor must be taken into consideration when assessing market power.[50] More specifically, the argument goes that such dynamic competition has a disciplining effect, because SSO members may decide not to include technologies held by patentees who 'misbehave', e.g., by claiming excessive royalties, in future generations of a standard or in unrelated standards. However, in ICT markets where standards are often set to facilitate interoperability the prospect of being excluded from upcoming standards will in many cases not act as an effective competitive restraint. If SSO members were to exclude (vote against) technologies held by a company deemed to have violated its FRAND commitment this may be deemed a collective boycott contrary to Article 102 TFEU – at least if the company in question has not been found guilty of demanding non-FRAND license terms by a court or a competition authority. Moreover, even if SSO members were ready to actually exclude certain technologies this may not be a viable option. In ICT markets there is often a tendency towards path dependency in the sense that the success of next generation technology depends on its ability to achieve backwards compatibility with previous generations. Consumers who have purchased USB 2.0 compliant peripherals (printers,

49. Case T-228/97, *Irish Sugar v. Commission*, 7 Oct. 1999, § 97.
50. Geradin, Damien & Rato, Miguel, *Can Standard-Setting Lead to Exploitative Abuse? A Dissonant View on Patent Hold-Up, Royalty Stacking and the Meaning of FRAND*, in European Competition Journal. Vol. 3, 2007 pp. 148–149.

cameras, etc.) for instance would arguably have been reluctant to buy PCs with USB 3.0 compliant ports if they did not allow for backwards compatibility with USB 2.0. Accordingly, SSOs will often not be in a position to exclude technologies held by patentees who have misbehaved insofar as it prevents the achievement of backwards compatibility. The same applies to a number of other evolutionary technology standards such as WIFI, UMTS and DDR DRAM. Indeed, in the *Rambus* case, which concerned a failure to disclose patents essential to the SDR and DDR DRAM standards adopted by JEDEC (a so-called 'patent ambush'), the Commission held that the "*...the alleged abusive behaviour also extend to subsequent JEDEC standards and not only the SDR and DDR DRAM standards that were adopted during the time in which Rambus was a member of JEDEC*", since Rambus' technologies had become essential to a number of follow-on standards.[51]

[3] Aggregate Royalty Ceiling

A technical standard may consist of several hundreds of essential technologies which for the purpose of standard compliance are complementary rather than substitutes. In this respect it has been argued that holders of SEPs are constrained by the fact that they must take into consideration the royalties charged by third parties in possession of complementary patents when setting their own royalty level since the market, hence also licensees, can only bear a certain aggregate royalty burden.[52] However, while the stakeholders involved in standardization have a common interest in ensuring efficient diffusion of the standard adopted the competitive constraint exerted by the existence of complementary patents is remote and it is unlikely that the Commission will be persuaded by arguments along these lines when evaluating dominance under Article 102 TFEU. Any competitive constraint related to the aggregate royalty level is conditional on transparency with regard to the royalties requested by other patentees, but in many cases such transparency does not exist due to the confidential nature of most licensing agreements. Moreover, it is important to note that once a market becomes 'locked-in'[53] to a specific standard the maximum royalty level bearable by the market to which it relates becomes inflated and licensees (manufactures of standard compliant products) may be able to pass on even excessive royalty claims to consumers whose willingness to pay (price elasticity) - due to the absence of viable alternatives - is high. Although there is likely to be an aggregate royalty ceiling the said ceiling will most often not prevent the SEP owner from acting independently to an appreciable extent as required for a finding of dominance under Article 102 TFEU.

51. Commission decision C(2014) 2891 final in Case COMP/38.636, *Rambus*, 9 Dec. 2009, § 47.
52. See Geradin, Damien & Rato, Miguel, *Can Standard-Setting Lead to Exploitative Abuse? A Dissonant View on Patent Hold-Up, Royalty Stacking and the Meaning of FRAND*, in European Competition Journal. Vol. 3, 2007 p. 146, stating that "*[o]wners of IPR essential to a standard are thus horizontally price-constrained and this absence of price independence will preclude a finding of dominance...*". Also see Layne-Farrar, Anne, *Nondiscriminatory Pricing: Is Standard Setting Different?*, In Journal of Competition Law & Economics, Vol. 6(4), 2010 p. 818.
53. See Ch. 8 s. §8.01 for more details in this respect.

[B] Does 'Super Dominance' Establish a Stricter Norm?

As explained in section §8.02 SEPs, whether reading on a de facto standard or a formal standard, may confer upon their proprietors an unparalleled degree of market power. Thus, due to the networks externalities and switching costs discussed in section §8.01 companies active on the market to which the standard relates may have no choice but to comply with the standard – if left unconstrained SEP holders are accordingly allowed the prerogative of acting as gatekeepers to the market. This raises the question whether the special responsibility[54] of such 'super dominant' undertakings not to distort (the remaining) effective competition on the market extends beyond the obligations imposed on undertakings holding a lesser degree of dominance. If this question is answered in the affirmative it may entail that the notion of fair, reasonable and non-discriminatory (FRAND) implies a norm which is stricter than the one which can be derived from case law dealing with 'ordinary' dominant undertakings outside the context of standardization, i.e., the threshold for finding a royalty excessive (unfair and unreasonable) may for instance be lower.

In *Microsoft*[55] the Commission seemed to imply that the abuse of Microsoft – a refusal to license – was established in light of its super dominant position on the market for client operating systems where the company held a market share of between 90% and 95%. Thus, the Commission in its decision noted that Microsoft "*...can be said to hold an overwhelmingly dominant position*"[56] and referred to the opinion of Advocate General Fennelly in *Cewal* according to which super dominant undertakings have a *"particularly onerous special obligation ... not to impair further the structure of the feeble existing competition"*.[57] Moreover, the notion 'super dominant' was explicitly used in a subsequent press release made by former EU Commissioner Neelie Kroes in which it was stated that the judgment "*...sends a clear signal that super-dominant companies cannot abuse their position to hurt consumers and dampen innovation by excluding competitors ...*".[58] These statements were by some commentators taken to imply that 'super dominance' had been introduced as a new concept in EU competition law.[59] However, although the General Court on appeal[60] confirmed the Commission's

54. As it was established by the CJEU in Case 322/81, *Michelin v. Commission*, 9 Nov. 1983, § 57, that a dominant undertaking has a "*...special responsibility not to allow its conduct to impair genuine undistorted competition on the common market*". See similarly Case C-209/10, *Post Danmark A/S v. Konkurrencerådet*, 27 Mar. 2012, § 23; Case C-280/08 P, *Deutsche Telekom AG v. Commission*, 14 Oct. 2010, § 176 and C-202/07 P, *France Telecom v. Commission*, 2 Apr. 2009, § 105.
55. Commission decision C(2004)900 final in Case COMP/37.792, Microsoft, 24 Mar. 2004.
56. Commission decision C(2004)900 final in Case COMP/37.792, Microsoft, 24 Mar. 2004, § 435. The Commission in § 429 also found that Microsoft held "*...a dominant position which exhibits extraordinary features*".
57. Opinion of Advocate General Fennelly in Joined Cases C-395/96 P & C-396/96 P, *Compagnie Maritime Belge and others v. Commission* (*Cewal*), 29 Oct. 1998, § 137.
58. Neelie Kroes, Former European Commissioner for Competition Policy, *Introductory remarks on CFI ruling on Microsoft's abuse of dominant market position*, SPEECH/07/53, 17 Sep. 2007.
59. See for instance Czapracka, Katarzyna, *Intellectual Property and the Limits of Antitrust: A Comparative Study of US and EU Approaches*, Edward Elgar Publishing, 2009 p. 7.
60. Case T-201/04, *Microsoft Corp v. Commission*, 17 Sep. 2007.

finding that Microsoft held a quasi-monopoly on the relevant market it did not use the notion 'super dominant' nor did the court state that Microsoft was subject to a particularly onerous special obligation as compared to companies with a lesser degree of dominance.

In more recent case law the CJEU has explicitly held that the degree of dominance is not a factor of importance when determining whether conduct is abusive under Article 102 TFEU – hence clarifying that super dominance is not a concept of EU competition law. In the *TeliaSonera*[61] case, which concerned the Swedish network operator TeliaSonera's alleged abuse of a dominant position, the CJEU addressed the question following a reference for a preliminary ruling made by the Stockholm District Court. The abuse of which TeliaSonera was accused regarded so-called margin squeeze, i.e., the adoption of a pricing policy aimed at preventing downstream competitors to which the input sold is essential from earning a profit.

The Stockholm District Court, amongst other things, asked the CJEU whether the degree of dominance is relevant to establish whether the practice in question constituted abuse.[62] The court answered this question in the negative (rightly) stating that Article 102 TFEU "*...does not envisage any variation in form or degree in the concept of a dominant position*".[63] According to the court the degree of market strength is, as a general rule, significant to establish the extent of any anti-competitive effects rather than in relation to the question of whether the abuse as such exists.[64]

Although the court referred to this as a 'general rule' the rather unambiguous interpretation of Article 102 TFEU arguably leaves little room to deviate by establishing exceptions. Contrary to the Commission's decision in *Microsoft* and the opinion of Advocate General Fennelly in *Cewal* (see above) it is therefore clear from the *TeliaSonera*[65] judgment that abuse is an objective concept which does not depend on the degree of dominance. Indeed, this is in line with established case law according to which abuse "*...is an objective concept relating to the behaviour of an undertaking in a dominant position which is such as to influence the structure of a market ...*".[66]

Burying the concept of 'super dominance' was a wise decision.[67] From a policy perspective taking into consideration yet another factor – the degree of dominance – when determining whether there is an abuse would adversely affect the legal certainty of dominant companies and might therefore even discourage pro-competitive conduct. Rather the degree of dominance must be taken into consideration when deciding whether conduct bearing the characteristics of abuse appreciably restricts effective competition. There is therefore no basis for concluding that super dominant patentee's – such as those holding SEPs – are subject to a stricter legal standard than those holding

61. Case C-52/09, *Konkurrensverket v. TeliaSonera*, 17 Feb. 2011.
62. *Ibid.*, § 78.
63. *Ibid.*, § 80.
64. *Ibid.*, § 81.
65. *Ibid.*
66. Case 85/76, *Hoffmann-La Roche v. Commission*, 13 Feb. 1979, § 91.
67. Also see Appeldoorn, Jochen, *He Who Spareth his Rod, Hateth his Son*, in European Competition Law Review, Vol.26(12), 2005, who in the wake of the Commission decision directed a critique at the concept and argued that the degree of dominance was irrelevant to establish abuse under Art. 102 TFEU (then, Art. 82 EC).

a lesser degree of dominance. Accordingly, any argument in favour of holding SEP holders to a distinct legal standard must not be based on their market power, but on the specific circumstances characterizing the process of standard setting. The FRAND commitments given in the context of formal standard setting activities have for instance prompted the Commission to introduce patent enforcement against potential licensees as a new type of abuse in EU competition law – see Chapter 13.

§8.03 STANDARDIZATION AGREEMENTS AND MARKET POWER

As discussed in Chapter 9 section §9.03 the Commission's Horizontal Guidelines sets out certain principles which must be fulfilled by the standardization agreements, including IPR policies, governing SSOs in order for them to benefit from a presumption (the 'safe harbour') that they will not restrict competition within the meaning of Article 101(1) TFEU. The requirements related to IPR disclosures and the procurement of FRAND commitments have as their purpose to ensure that SSOs put in place mechanisms which are suited to prevent the abusive exercise of patents (or other IPRs) *ex post* standardization. The potential for such abusive conduct to materialize in the wake of formal standard setting activities depends on whether the standardization agreement is likely to confer market power upon patentees. Accordingly, the 'safe harbour' principles are only of relevance to standardization agreements which risk creating market power.[68]

There is no presumption that a standardization agreement will create market power. The risk of market power being created by a standardization agreement is inevitably linked to the prospect of patents (or other IPRs) becoming essential to the standard adopted and the proprietors of such patents gaining market power. This aspect was discussed in section §8.02 above and it must be recalled that, in the words of the Commission, "*...there is no presumption that holding or exercising IPR essential to a standard equates to the possession or exercise of market power*".[69]

Bearing in mind the analysis in section §8.02 it seems clear that several factors may be of relevance to the assessment of whether a standardization agreement risks creating market power, such as (i) the market shares of the companies supporting adoption of the standard in question, (ii) the purpose for which the standard is being developed, (iii) the type of standard contemplated adopted, (IV) the characteristics of the market to which the standard relates and (V) the number of competing standards (if any) already established or under development. No single factor is decisive. What matters overall is whether compliance with the standard is likely to become indispensable *and* in the affirmative whether some undertakings may end up in a position as 'gatekeepers' able to control access to the standard.

The market shares of the parties supporting the standard may be used as a proxy for estimating the market share of the standard once it is adopted, since, as noted by the

68. Communication from the Commission, *Guidelines on the applicability of Article 101 of the Treaty on the Functioning of the European Union to horizontal co-operation agreements*, OJ 2011/C 11/1, 14 Jan. 2011, § 278.
69. *Ibid.*, § 269.

Commission, it is fair to assume that those taking part in developing the standard will also implement it.[70] However, the fact that the parties to a standardization agreement holds a high market share on the product market affected (which will often be the case)[71] does not in itself entail a risk that market power will be created. If a standard is supported by influential companies it may be deemed likely to achieve widespread adoption, but this does not necessarily mean that it will become indispensable insofar as there are competing standards able to exert a sufficiently strong competitive pressure. Conversely, compliance with a standard being developed to satisfy regulatory requirements stated in so-called New Approach Directives (see Chapter 7 section §7.02) is likely to become de facto mandatory, hence indispensable. However, if the standard allows for several different implementations market power is unlikely to arise, since then there will be competition between substitute technologies *ex post*, i.e., no rights will be essential. Likewise, standards which relate to 'nice to have' features rather than essential features of products are less likely to create market power.[72] This emphasizes the importance of considering the type of standard contemplated adopted when assessing the likelihood that market power will be created.

While there are a variety of different[73] technical standards, such as interoperability standards, safety standards and performance standards, it is often interoperability standards which attract the attention of competition authorities and legal commentators – and with good reason.[74] Interoperability standards, sometimes also referred to as compatibility or interface standards, enable 'interaction' between substitute or complementary products allowing them for instance to share data through common software protocols or to physically interconnect.[75] To enable such 'interaction' these types of standards are 'low level' in the sense that the technical specifications on which they are based set out specific implementation details and therefore directly impact product design, hence more easily become indispensable. As opposed to for instance safety or performance related standards (which typically set out overall minimum requirements without dictating implementation details) interoperability standards, as a result of their nature, often embody specific technologies needed to achieve compliance – some of

70. *Ibid.*, § 296.
71. Most often the parties to a standardisation agreement will hold a high market share, since strong industry support is a prerequisite for a standard to become widely adopted on the market. As noted by the Commission "*...the effectiveness of standardisation agreements is often proportional to the share of the industry involved in setting and/or applying the standard*" – see *ibid.*, § 296.
72. *Ibid.*, § 293, where it is stated that "*...standards only covering minor aspects or parts of the end-product are less likely to lead to competition concerns than more comprehensive standards*".
73. See e.g., Gifford, Daniel J., *Developing Models for a Coherent Treatment of Standard-setting Issues under Patent, Copyright and Antitrust Laws*, in IDEA: The Journal of Law and Technology, Vol. 43, 2003 p. 334, who distinguishes between safety standards, performance standards, and interoperability standards. There are also other types of standards such as quality standards, information standards and measurement standards. See Swann, Peter, *The Economics of Standardization*, Final Report for Standards and Technical Regulations Directorate Department of Trade and Industry, 2000 p. 14.
74. See also Park, Jae Hun, *Patents and Industry Standards*, Edward Elgar, 2010 p. 12.
75. Rubin, Jonathan L., *Patents, Antitrust, and Rivalry in Standard-Setting*, in Rutgers Law Journal, Vol. 38, 2007 p. 514.

which may be proprietary.[76] Moreover, such standards relate to so-called network markets where there is an inherent tendency for consumers to become 'locked-in' to a single (or a few) standard(s) – see section §8.01. It follows that the risk of market power being created is especially acute with regard to interoperability standards insofar as they specify low level implementation details.

This is not to say that issues may not arise with regard to other types of technical standards, but merely to highlight why interoperability standards are of particular relevance in a competition law context. In the German *standard-spundfass* case the German Federal Supreme Court for instance confirmed the defendant's assertion that it was impossible to comply with an industry standard specifying the size, weight and volume of industrial barrels without infringing a patent related to the manufacture of such barrels.[77] Likewise, the *IMS Health*[78] case (discussed in Chapter 12 section §12.01) did not concern an interoperability standard, but a database structure.

76. For example., consider a performance standard that specifies the minimum efficiency of a light bulb (watt/lumen ratio) and an interoperability standard such as the USB standard which defines the characteristics of cables, connectors and communications protocols. While the goal of the performance standard, i.e., the watt/lumen ratio, may be achieved by a number of substitute technologies, there is no scope for deviating from the technical details of the interoperability standard, as this would result in non-compliance. See Gifford, Daniel J., *Developing Models for a Coherent Treatment of Standard-setting Issues under Patent, Copyright and Antitrust Laws*, in IDEA: The Journal of Law and Technology, Vol. 43, 2003 p. 334, who notes that many safety standards are permissive in the sense that they allow the use different techniques to achieve compliance.
77. Case KZR 40/02, *Standard Tight-head Drum (Standard-Spundfass)*, Federal Supreme Court of Germany (Bundesgerichtshof), 13 Jul. 2004.
78. Case C-418/01 *IMS Health v. NDC Health*, 29 Apr. 2004.

PART IV Adoption of Formal Standards

CHAPTER 9
Standardization Agreements

As stated by economist Adam Smith in the year 1776 the interest of dealers "*...is always in some respects different from, and even opposite to, that of the public. To widen the market and to narrow the competition is always the interest of the dealers*".[1] Although less pronounced this view is still fundamental to modern competition law in the sense that fierce competition is seen as a catalyst able to ensure consumers maximum innovation, product diversity and quality at the lowest possible price while a profound scepticism is directed towards any cooperation between competitors out of fear that such might lead to anti-competitive outcomes. However, at the same time it is acknowledged that a measure of cooperation amongst competitors may sometimes be in the public's interest – formal standard setting is an example hereof. Indeed, the Commission in the Horizontal Guidelines stresses that standardization agreements will frequently give raise to significant efficiency gains.[2] Nonetheless, as stated by Neelie Kroes, former European Commissioner for Competition Policy, "*[a]llowing companies to sit around a table and agree technical developments for their industry is not something that the competition rules would usually allow. So when it is allowed we have to look carefully at how it is done*".[3]

§9.01 BENEFITS OF STANDARDIZATION

Standards give rise to significant pro-competitive benefits. From a practical point of view the benefits derived from technical standards are evident – one need only consider briefly the convenience they allow us to experience in our everyday lives. Just

1. Smith, Adam, *An Inquiry into the Nature and Causes of the Wealth of Nations*, Vol. 1, Book I, first published in 1776, p. 228. Available at: http://www.econlib.org/library/Smith/smWN.html.
2. Communication from the Commission, *Guidelines on the applicability of Article 101 of the Treaty on the Functioning of the European Union to horizontal co-operation agreements*, OJ 2011/C 11/1, 14 Jan. 2011, § 308.
3. Neelie Kroes, Former European Commissioner for Competition Policy, *Being open about standards*, SPEECH/08/317 10 Jun. 2008.

to mention a few examples, compatibility/interoperability between phones (the ability to make and receive calls), in networks (the ability to access files stored at a remote locations, view web content etc.), and between computers and complementary peripherals (printers, mice, displays, cameras, etc.), is possible because competitors adhere to common technical standards.

These conveniences translate into a number of economic and welfare enhancing benefits. As already noted interoperability standards ensure that products from competing manufactures can interact seamlessly and accordingly increase the utility value of products to users. This benefit, which derives from so-called 'network effects', was discussed in more detail in Chapter 8 section §8.01. In addition to enhancing the utility value of products these effects also lower the costs incurred by users when switching between competing products. In effect *intra*-technology competition between companies is intensified and this in turn may lead to lower prices and a more diversified range of products.[4] Moreover, standards fit well with the single market imperative, since the establishment of common technical specifications act to demolish barriers to trade between Member States.[5] Common mobile telephony standards (GSM, 3G, 4G) for instance allows cell phone users to travel in the EU knowing that their phones will be compatible with the network infrastructure in any Member State.

Technical standards are also beneficial to manufactures of standard compliant products and technology developers. Those fortunate enough to have their patent(s) read on a successful technical standard may for instance benefit from the increased licensing revenue bound to flow from the widespread diffusion of the technologies facilitated by the standard. Moreover, to the extent that a standard improves market integration (see above) manufactures of standard compliant products benefit from being able to more effectively serve a broader market without the need to tailor products to each Member State. On high technology markets notoriously known to be characterized by patent minefields (or 'patent thickets') collaborative standardization also enables companies to reduce the risk of being met with infringement claims by securing FRAND licensing commitments from SSO participants. Finally, by aiming for an agreement on a common technical standard rather than wait for the market to eventually select one it may be possible to commercialize new technologies faster and more effectively.

In light of these efficiencies, which are recognized by the Commission,[6] standardization agreements are seen as consistent with the objectives of competition law

4. In his respect note that although standardisation limits *inter*-technology with regard to the standardised product features it allows companies to focus their resources on differentiating non-standardised product features.
5. Note that removing barriers to market integration is one the objectives of competition law. See for instance Joined Cases C-501/06 P, C-513/06P, C-515/06P and C-519/06 P, *GlaxoSmithKline Services and Others v. Commission and Others*, 6 Oct. 2009, where the Court recalled that agreements which "... *frustrate the Treaty's objective of achieving the integration of national markets through the establishment of a single market*" will violate Art. 101(1) TFEU.
6. Communication from the Commission, *Guidelines on the applicability of Article 101 of the Treaty on the Functioning of the European Union to horizontal co-operation agreements*, OJ 2011/C 11/1, 14 Jan. 2011, § 308. Also see Commission, *A strategic vision for European standards: Moving forward to enhance and accelerate the sustainable growth of the European economy by 2020*,

despite having as their purpose to coordinate the market behaviour of competing undertakings. However, to increase the likelihood that the pro-competitive benefits of formal standardization prevail standardization agreements are subject to certain requirements under Article 101 TFEU. These requirements are discussed in section §9.03 by using the Commission's Horizontal Guidelines as a point of departure. Prior to this discussion it is however worth considering why competition law does not simply ban standardization agreements and leave it to market forces to set a de facto standard.

§9.02 WHY NOT WAIT FOR THE MARKET TO SET A DE FACTO STANDARD?

Some commentators have expressed their fear that formal standardization may distort competition, i.e., advantage one competitor over another, and result in standards less preferable than those which would have emerged in the market as a result of consumer choice, i.e., de facto standards.[7] In this respect it is claimed that formal standardization efforts are not based on true and competition neutral consensus, and that SSOs should therefore not promulgate a standard when there is active competition in the market which will be affected by the standard. It is arguably true that the standard setting process in many SSOs resembles an economic power game allowing companies with a significant market presence to have a greater influence on the standard adopted.[8] This is a natural consequence of the fact that the success of standards is measured in terms of their diffusion on the market and that large companies are key players in ensuring such diffusion.

The fears expressed apparently rely on the assumption that social welfare will be higher in cases where the market elects a standard without the intervention of an SSO, simply because the prevailing standards and the competitive structure on the market may be impacted in case of such intervention. However, this view is too simpListic and ignores the benefits that formal standardization may provide if SSOs put in place safeguards able to act as a bulwark against anti-competitive conduct. Resolving competition within the framework of a SSO instead of having recourse to the market may well result in welfare enhancing outcomes. While it cannot be denied that the consensus based process in SSOs is affected[9] by the relative bargaining position of the companies participating, it does not necessarily mean that the process distorts competition to the detriment of consumers or that the resulting standard includes less efficient technologies. Indeed, some companies also prevail over others on the free-market and

COM(2011) 311 final, 1 Jun. 2011 p. 7, where it is stated that "*The benefits of standards for the European industry are tremendous*".

7. See Nimmer, Raymond T., *Technical Standards Setting Organizations & Competition: A case for Deference to Markets*, in the University of Houston Public Law and Legal Theory Series, 2009-A-23 (pp. 1–17 in particular).
8. See Swann, Peter, *The Economics Of Standardization*, Final Report for Standards and Technical Regulations Directorate Department of Trade and Industry, 2000 p. 14.
9. A large and influential would-be implementer may for instance be in possession of de facto veto power due to the fact that the standard will not be able to succeed without its support. Votes may also have been allocated according to firm size.

there is no guarantee that the winners of a market driven 'standards war' will be those objectively in possession of the best technologies. In addition to innovation factors such as financial strength, business relations, marketing efforts and market strength arguably plays an important role in crowning the winner.

As already explained interoperability and compatibility between products from different manufactures are important drivers of consumer welfare. In addition to increased 'interaction' between competing products, interoperability and compatibility may provide at number of indirect positive effects on consumer welfare such as lower prices, reduced search and switching costs and increased product diversity. Waiting for the market to set a de facto standard may prolong the period in which consumers are not able to achieve the optimal degree of interoperability or compatibility. Accordingly, and all things being equal, this therefore results in a suboptimal situation from the perspective of consumer welfare. Furthermore, settling for a standard early on ensures that consumers do no invest in products which will later become obsolete due to the fact that a substitute technology eventually prevails and becomes a standard.[10] Companies offering products incorporating the standard set also benefit as standardization establishes a level playing field allowing them to focus their resources on actual product differentiation rather than offering several similar products based on different interoperability standards or risking that the technology they support become obsolete. These benefits carry on to resellers which are able to offer a larger range of products without risking that some of the products in stock suddenly become obsolete due to the fact that the market tips in favour of a standard different than the one incorporated in the stocked products. While a formal standardization process may lead to the abandonment of technologies which would otherwise have prevailed on the market there is also no basis for concluding that the technologies embodied in the standard set are per se inferior for this reason. Such conclusion presupposes that the market, i.e., consumers, is better equipped to choose the standard providing the largest increase in social welfare. However, the market driven process of technology selection is often influenced by a number of factors not directly associated with technology as such, thus there is no reason to believe that the market outcome would be more beneficial to consumers than the outcome of an SSO.

Against the above background it cannot be denied that consumers and companies alike may be better off with a standard set by an SSO than awaiting market forces to select one. SSOs may accelerate the standardization process by bringing competition within the boundaries of an organization instead of leaving technology selection to the market where the process is often protracted and based on factors others than technological supremacy.

10. The 'standards battle' between the video formats Blu-ray and HD-DVD, which were each promoted by their own consortia, provides a good example in this respect. Following a period of fierce competition between the two formats the market eventually 'tipped' in favour of the Blu-ray format. As movies were no longer published in compliance with the HD-DVD specifications, equipment incorporating the format became obsolete and accordingly consumers were forced to invest in new Blu-ray compatible equipment. Early adoption of a commonly agreed standard would have prevented this scenario.

Taking into consideration the many benefits associated with standardization competition law and policy should not, and does not, attempt to distinguish 'bad' standard setting activities from 'good' standards standard setting activities.[11] Attempts to identify which technological standards are best set by the collaborative efforts of multiple companies within the framework of an SSO is destined to fail. As explained in the next section standardization agreements are as a main rule considered to fall outside the scope of Article 101(1) TFEU, provided that certain contractual safeguards are put in place to increase the likelihood that the pro-competitive benefits of standardization prevail.

§9.03 THE HORIZONTAL GUIDELINES AND THE 'SAFE HARBOUR'

In order to ensure a more efficient process of standardization and mitigate the risk of patent hold-up the most recent version of the Commission's Horizontal Guidelines adopted in 2010 introduced a substantially revised chapter on standardization agreements, i.e., agreements having as "*...their primary objective the definition of technical or quality requirements with which current or future products, production processes, services or methods may comply*".[12] In essence reference is made to agreements which aim at the adoption of formal standards as discussed in Chapter 7 section §7.02. As compared to the previous[13] version of the Horizontal Guidelines from 2001, the current version of the guidelines provide more in-depth guidance to SSOs on how to assess whether their by-laws and polices are in accordance with Article 101 TFEU. Although the guidelines are not legally binding on SSOs their importance should not be underestimated as they clarify how the Commission - which is responsible for enforcing the EU competition rules - intends to assess standardization agreements under Article 101(1) TFEU. Moreover, the General Court, as noted below, seems to have endorsed the principles relied upon by the Commission in this respect.

The Horizontal Guidelines set out a 'safe harbour' in the form of four overall principles which standardization agreement must fulfil in order to benefit from a presumption of legality. More specifically, the 'safe harbour' principles provide that a standardization agreement which risks[14] creating market power will normally not restrict competition within the meaning of Article 101(1) TFEU if:

---

11. Hovenkamp, Herbert, *Standards Ownership and Competition Policy*, in Boston College Law Review, Vol. 48(1), 2007 p. 9. Note that de facto standards and formal standards often coexist and compete on the same market in which case the market is in any event allowed a chance to crown the winner.
12. Communication from the Commission, *Guidelines on the applicability of Article 101 of the Treaty on the Functioning of the European Union to horizontal co-operation agreements*, OJ 2011/C 11/1, 14 Jan. 2011.
13. Communication from the Commission, *Guidelines on the applicability of Article 81 of the EC Treaty to horizontal co-operation agreements*, OJ 2001/C 3/02, 6 Jan. 2001.
14. As explained in Ch. 8 s. §8.03 market power is for instance unlikely to result from a standardisation agreement if the standard contemplated adopted does not have as its purpose to specify implementation details or if viable competing standards or non-standardised technologies can be expected to coexist with the standard adopted.

(1) access to participate in the standard-setting activities is unrestricted;
(2) the procedure for adopting the standard in question is transparent;
(3) there is no obligation to comply with the standard adopted; and
(4) access to the standard, including its underlying specification and any essential IPR (see below), is granted on fair, reasonable and non-discriminatory terms (FRAND terms).[15]

With regard to standards that embody IPR the Commission notes that a:

> clear and balanced IPR policy, adapted to the particular industry and the needs of the standard-setting organisation in question, increases the likelihood that the implementers of the standard will be granted effective access to the standards elaborated by that standard-setting organisation.[16]

To this end the Commission specifies that compliance with the fourth principle, concerning effective access, requires IPR policies to mandate that SSO participants (i) perform good faith disclosures of IPRs potentially essential to the standard under development and (ii) provide an irrevocable commitment in writing to license their essential IPRs on FRAND terms as a precondition for having said IPRs included in the standard adopted.[17]

These 'safe harbour' principles are somewhat special in an Article 101(1) TFEU context in that they mandate the *inclusion* of certain provisions which aim at preventing restrictive effects whereas Article 101(1) TFEU is normally applied to *existing* anti-competitive provisions. Indeed, the 'safe harbour' principles have been devised based on the philosophy that it is better to prevent than to cure.[18] Such approach is important since the adoption of an industry wide standard may affect all companies active on the market to which it relates regardless of whether they take part in the standard setting process or not. Accordingly, measures which ensure that all parties affected are offered a chance to influence and keep themselves informed of the standard setting process are important. Likewise, it is important that all companies are provided access to a standard, including any SEPs, after it is adopted. Absent rules able to promote these objectives there is a risk that standardization agreements will produce anti-competitive effects.

15. Communication from the Commission, *Guidelines on the applicability of Article 101 of the Treaty on the Functioning of the European Union to horizontal co-operation agreements*, OJ 2011/C 11/1, 14 Jan. 2011, §§ 278 and 280–283.
16. *Ibid.*, § 284.
17. *Ibid.*, §§ 284–286. In royalty free licensing are also considered FRAND – see § 285 (footnote 114).
18. The former European Commissioner for Competition Policy, Neelie Kroes, noted that "*...it is a lot better if we can prevent abuses of standard setting processes from occurring in the first place rather than have individual problem cases coming onto our radar screen*". See Neelie Kroes, Former European Commissioner for Competition Policy, *Setting the standards high*, SPEECH/09/475, 15 Oct. 2009.

The General Court seems to have confirmed the validity of the 'safe harbour' principles in *EMC Development*.[19] The court found that the Commission had not erred by examining the applicants claim that a standardization agreement, entered into within the framework of CEN (an SDO), was restrictive of competition in light of the criteria set out in the (former) Horizontal Guidelines "*…in order to assess (i) whether the procedure for adoption of the Standard had not been non-discriminatory, open and transparent, and (ii) whether the Standard was binding*".[20] However, note that being 'safe harbour' principles they are fundamental and guiding rather than mandatory. As noted by the Commission the non-fulfilment of any or all of the principles "*…will not lead to any presumption of a restriction of competition within Article 101(1). However, it will necessitate a self-assessment to establish whether the agreement falls under Article 101(1) and, if so, if the conditions of Article 101(3) are fulfilled*".[21] As explained below, the Commission has for instance accepted that SSOs limit the access to participate in the standard setting activities on the basis of efficiency considerations. That being said, it is unlikely that the Commission will find an IPR policy in accordance with Article 101(1) TFEU if there is a risk of patent hold-up and the policy in question does not contain rules capable of mitigating that risk.

Although contractual mechanisms other than those mentioned in the guidelines may be equally (or more) effective, there can arguably be no objective justification for omitting such rules altogether under such circumstances. In this respect, note that an exemption under Article 101(3) TFEU *inter alia* requires that such omission is necessary to achieve efficiency gains. However, since the obligations relating to disclosures of IPR and FRAND commitments are not very strict it is hard to see how an SSO will be able to successfully argue that omitting them from the IPR policies is necessary to ensure the effectiveness of the standard setting activities. Indeed, the obligations have as their very purpose to safeguard against patent hold-up, hence to ensure effective diffusion of the standard once it is adopted. Thus, SSOs are arguably well advised to construe the 'safe harbour' principles as minimum requirements which may be modified to better suit their particular needs, provided that that they remain effective in preventing patent hold-up.

The chapter on standardization agreements included in the Horizontal Guidelines are directed at the agreements entered into between SSOs and their members – not the licensing practices engaged in by these members (or third parties) after the standard is adopted. While the safe harbour requirements imposed by the Horizontal Guidelines are motivated largely by the desire to prevent SSO members from engaging in unilateral abusive conduct, allegations of such conduct is assessed under Article 102 TFEU – not

19. Case T-432/05, *EMC Development v. Commission*, 12 May 2010, §§ 64–65. The judgment was upheld by the CJEU on appeal – see case C-367/10 P, *EMC Development v. Commission*, 31 Mar. 2011, §§ 91–94. Also see Whish, Richard & Bailey, David, *Competition Law*, 7th ed., Oxford University Press, 2012 p. 609.
20. Case T-432/05, *EMC Development v. Commission*, 12 May 2010, § 65.
21. Communication from the Commission, *Guidelines on the applicability of Article 101 of the Treaty on the Functioning of the European Union to horizontal co-operation agreements*, OJ 2011/C 11/1, 14 Jan. 2011, § 279.

Article 101 TFEU.[22] The potential Article 102 TFEU issues related to the exercise of SEPs *ex post* standardization are discussed in Part V. Below the IPR aspects of the above stated 'safe harbour' requirements are discussed based on the premise that there is a risk that the standardization agreement will confer upon proprietors of SEPs market power.

[A] No Obligation to Comply with the Standard

With regard to the third criterion, that the standardization agreement should not mandate compliance, this is largely self-explanatory and will not be commented on further below. Its purpose is to ensure that *inter*-technology competition is not reduced beyond what already follows from such agreements. Undertakings must be free to opt for alternative - standardized or non-standardized- technologies regardless of their participation in an SSO. Restrictions in this respect are, as noted by the Commission, likely to violate Article 101(1) TFEU, and may even be deemed restrictions of competition by object which entails that it is unnecessary for the purpose of applying Article 101(1) TFEU to demonstrate any actual or likely effects on the market.[23] This was the case in the *Philips/VCR* case where the Commission found that an agreement entered into by Philips and a number of manufacturers of video cassette recorders had as its object to restrict competition, because it obliged the manufactures to exclusively manufacture and distribute products which adhered to the VCR standard promoted by Philips.[24]

[B] Unrestricted Access and Transparency

In order to benefit from the 'safe-harbour' presumption of legality SSO rules must allow for unrestricted access in the standard setting process by all undertakings affected by

22. It is therefore surprising that the Commission has decided to comment on the principles used to determine whether license fees are fair and reasonable, i.e., whether they "*bear a reasonable relationship to the economic value of the patents*", as part of the guidelines. Such guidance should arguably have been included in another document such as for instance the Commission's guidance paper on its enforcement priorities with respect to Art. 102 TFEU. Addressing Art. 102 TFEU issues as part of the Horizontal Guidelines is not logical from a strictly legal point of view. This was also criticized by some when the draft Horizontal Guidelines (SEC(2010) 528/2) were published for public consultation. See for instance European Competition Lawyers Forum (ECLF), *Comments on the Draft Guidelines on the Applicability of Article 101 of the Treaty on the Functioning of the European Union to Horizontal Co-operation Agreements*, 2010 § 52 and § 56. All submissions made to the Commission as part of the public consultation are available at: http://ec.europa.eu/competition/consultations/2010_horizontals/ (last checked 30 May 2014).
23. Communication from the Commission, *Guidelines on the applicability of Article 101 of the Treaty on the Functioning of the European Union to horizontal co-operation agreements*, OJ 2011/C 11/1, 14 Jan. 2011, § 293. For a discussion of the concept 'restriction by object' see for instance Whish, Richard & Bailey, David, *Competition Law*, 7th ed., Oxford University Press, 2012 pp. 117-125.
24. Commission decision 78/156/EEC in Case IV/29.151, *Video cassette recorders*, 20 Dec. 1977, § 23. The Commission decided that the agreement could not be exempted under Art. 101(3) TFEU (then, Art. 85(3) EC), since the restrictions were not indispensable to achieve the claimed benefits arising from establishing of a common standard - see §§ 28-32.

the standard contemplated adopted as well as transparent procedures which "...*allow stakeholders to effectively inform themselves of upcoming, on-going and finalised standardisation work in good time at each stage of the development of the standard*".[25] As to unrestricted participation compliance requires not only that all affected undertakings are allowed a chance to participate, but also necessitates the adoption of (i) objective and non-discriminatory procedures for allocating voting rights between participants as well as (ii) objective criteria (if relevant to the type of standard in question) for selecting the technologies to be included in the standard.[26] Absent such procedures and objective criteria the rules allowing for participation would be rendered illusory. With regard to IPR policies which discriminate against royalty bearing technologies, see section §9.03[B][3] below.

The conditions related to unrestricted participation and transparency work in tandem to limit the risk that companies will be excluded from the market or be placed at a competitive disadvantage as a result of the standard in question being adopted. All companies shall be allowed to take part in the standard setting process, and those who opt not to take part shall have the possibility to keep themselves informed of the standard setting process to avoid being placed at a competitive disadvantage *vis-à-vis* SSO participants once the standard is adopted. If only select companies know the intimate details of the standard being developed they may obtain a significant 'first mover advantage' *ex post* standardization by having had the opportunity to tailor *inter alia* their production machinery, product line-up and marketing campaigns to be in line with the standard in question. This is especially true in rapidly developing technology markets.

[1] The IPR Dimension of Unrestricted Access

Although strictly speaking the conditions outlined above are not IPR related the requirement of unrestricted access nonetheless deserves some attention, because there is an indirect IPR angle to it of relevance. Unrestricted access to participate in the standard setting activities of an SSO ensures that all third parties, including IPR holders, are offered the possibility to impact the technological composition of the standard being developed. Hereby, the risk that innovative technologies are unduly foreclosed from the market decreases. As noted by the Commission "*[t]he risk of elimination of innovation is increased if one or more companies are unjustifiably*

25. Communication from the Commission, *Guidelines on the applicability of Article 101 of the Treaty on the Functioning of the European Union to horizontal co-operation agreements*, OJ 2011/C 11/1, 14 Jan. 2011, §§ 280–282.

26. *Ibid.*, § 281. As explained in Ch. 8 s. §8.01 a technology excluded from a standard may – in particular in markets characterised by strong network effects – be rendered less valuable or even obsolete as the market favours standard compliant products. This explains why the selection of technologies must be based on objective criteria. Absent such criteria there is a risk that influential companies will rely upon the standard setting process to exclude superior technologies held by competitors.

excluded from the standard-setting process".[27] Moreover, a high level of participation is likely to increase the number of technologies which are brought to the table, whether IPR protected or not, and in effect will provide SSO participants with a better opportunity to include the technologies which are most effective and which best meets market demand. Along these lines the Commission in the context of patent pool arrangements state that if "*...participation in a standard and pool creation process is open to all interested parties representing different interests it is more likely that technologies for inclusion into the pool are selected on the basis of price/quality...*".[28] The obligation to disclose potentially essential IPRs in good faith (see section §9.03[C]) also acts to promote the 'quality' of a standard by allowing SSO participants to factor in the cost of licensing when selecting technologies.[29]

The Commission also finds the presence of '*different interests*' to be of importance in ensuring that the license terms and conditions imposed by the members of a technology pool are in accordance with competition law.[30] This reasoning applies by analogy to SSOs. As noted by the Commission upstream-only companies (or NPE's)[31] have as their purpose to maximize royalty revenue whereas to downstream-only companies (manufactures not holding IPR) royalties represent solely a cost which must be minimized to the extent possible.[32] Somewhere in between are vertically integrated firms which operate both at the upstream level and the downstream level and therefore have mixed incentives.[33] These contradictory commercials interests create a system of 'check and balances' which increase the chance that SSO members will reach consensus on a standard which benefit the market as a whole.

Finally, note that IPR policies are by their very nature only binding upon SSO participants. Accordingly, SEPs held by non-participants will evade the IPR related

27. See Communication from the Commission, *Guidelines on the applicability of Article 101 of the Treaty on the Functioning of the European Union to horizontal co-operation agreements*, OJ 2011/C 11/1, 14 Jan. 2011, § 266.
28. Commission notice, *Guidelines on the application of Article 81 of the EC Treaty to technology transfer agreements*, OJ 2004/C 101/02, 27 Apr. 2004, § 231.
29. Having a wide selection of technologies to choose from may increase the technical 'quality' of a standard in terms of performance and effectiveness. However, the ratio between cost and quality must also be taken into consideration in order to ensure its effective commercialization and in this regard IPR disclosures are important, since they allow participants to factor in licensing costs in addition to quality. Participants may for instance be able to ascertain *ex ante* whether IPR holders are willing to provide licenses at a price that the market can bear - and in the negative seek to avoid the technology in question.
30. Commission notice, *Guidelines on the application of Article 81 of the EC Treaty to technology transfer agreements*, OJ 2004/C 101/02, 27 Apr. 2004, § 231.
31. NPE is an abbreviation of 'non practicing entities'. The notion refers to proprietors of patents who do not themselves manufacture products based upon the patented technologies in question. This includes universities, private research laboratories and undertakings which have as their sole purpose to acquire patent portfolios from third parties and to collect licensing fees. The latter type of undertakings has sometimes been labelled with the negative term 'patent trolls'. See for instance Bessen, James E., et al., *The Private and Social Costs of Patent Trolls*, Boston Univ. School of Law, Law and Economics Research Paper No. 11-45, 2011. Available at http://papers.ssrn.com/sol3/papers.cfm?abstract_id=1930272 (last checked 30 May 2014).
32. Communication from the Commission, *Guidelines on the applicability of Article 101 of the Treaty on the Functioning of the European Union to horizontal co-operation agreements*, OJ 2011/C 11/1, 14 Jan. 2011, § 267.
33. *Ibid.*

'safe harbour' conditions (outlined in section §9.03 and discussed in more detail below) which have as their purpose to ensure the availability of essential IPR on FRAND terms after a standard is adopted. In this respect a rule encouraging unrestricted participation reduces the risk that non-participants, having provided no pledge to license on FRAND terms, will obstruct the standard by refusing to license their rights or avail themselves of the opportunity to engage in anti-competitive conduct once the market (eventually) becomes locked-in to the standard adopted. Put simply, SSO policies which encourage participation by all will, all things being equal, reduce the risk of patent hold-up.

[2] Departure from the 'Safe Harbour'

As noted above, SSO policies should, as a main rule, allow all stakeholders in the market to participate in the standard setting process. However, there may be situations where unhindered access may unduly prolong and obstruct the standard setting process, because reaching consensus becomes increasingly difficult as the number of participants increase. This is acknowledged by the Commission which notes that "*...if in the absence of a limitation on the number of participants it would not have been possible to adopt the standard, the agreement would not be likely to lead to any restrictive effect on competition under Article 101(1)*".[34] Even if deemed restrictive of competition pursuant to Article 101(1) TFEU an access restriction may also be able to benefit from an individual exemption pursuant to Article 101(3) TFEU if it is a necessary and proportionate measure to ensure that the pro-competitive benefits of standardization prevail.[35] If access restrictions are put in place the Commission (rightly) considers it to be a mitigating factor if the standard setting process is transparent in the sense that non-participants are kept informed and consulted in a timely manner of the developments taking place.[36] However, for the reasons stated in section §9.03[B][1] this may arguably not be sufficient if the standard is technological complex and its adoption entails a risk that a large number of competing technologies held by non-participants will be foreclosed and become obsolete. Obviously, the likelihood that membership limitations will infringe Article 101 TFEU is directly linked to the importance of SSO participation.[37] If a very influential SSO adopts rules which restricts access the negative impact on competition may be significant. By way of example consider W3C and ETSI which both play a prevalent role in the field of ICT standardization and may possibly be considered dominant in the fields of Internet standards and telecommunications standards, respectively. W3C is responsible for the HTML standard as well as number of other hugely successful internet standards and ETSI standards, such as the 3G and 4G standards, have likewise achieved widespread

34. Communication from the Commission, *Guidelines on the applicability of Article 101 of the Treaty on the Functioning of the European Union to horizontal co-operation agreements*, OJ 2011/C 11/1, 14 Jan. 2011, § 295.
35. *Ibid.* (footnote 2).
36. *Ibid.*
37. Also Dolmans, Maurits, *Standards For Standards*, in Fordham International Law Journal, Vol. 26(1), 2002 p. 172.

success. Accordingly, innovative companies which are excluded from these organizations may incur a significant competitive disadvantage insofar as they are not able to influence the standard setting process and advocate in favour of their technologies.

The Commission has dealt with de jure membership limitations on two occasions - in *X/Open Group*[38] and *Ship classification.*[39] In addition de facto membership limitations caused by mandatory licensing obligations have been scrutinized. In this respect see section §9.03[E][2].

In *X/Open Group*[40] the Commission was asked[41] to assess the legality of a standardization agreement contemplated entered into by a number of software developers who each offered a version of the Unix[42] operating system (or a variety hereof). As the different Unix varieties were incompatible in the sense that software had to be developed specifically for each variation of the operating system, the objective of the agreement was to increase the number of software applications available for each system by establishing a common application environment. However, subject to majority approval, only companies with annual revenue in excess of USD 500 million were able to obtain membership unless they possessed special attributes which would significantly contribute to the objectives of the agreement.[43] Against this background it was initially found that the agreement infringed Article 101(1) TFEU (then, Article 85(1) EC), since there was a risk that it would distort competition to an appreciable extent.[44] However, the agreement was exempted under Article 101(3) TFEU, because (i) the membership limitation was found indispensable to the success of the standard and (ii) "*...the advantages involved in the creation of an open industry standard ... easily outweigh the distortions of competition entailed in the rules governing membership*".[45] The Commission pointed to the fact that unrestricted access to participate in the standard setting activities would "*...create practical and logistical difficulties for the management of the work*", but considered that the X/Open Groups "*...professed aim of making available as widely and quickly as possible the results of the cooperation*" was an essential element in its decision to exempt the agreement under Article 101(1) TFEU (then, Article 85(1) EC).[46]

In *Ship classification*[47] the Commission took the preliminary view that the by-laws of the International Association of Classification Societies and the International Association of Classification Societies Limited (jointly referred to as IACS) infringed *inter alia* Article 101(1) TFEU (then, Article 81 EC), because of restrictive membership

38. Commission decision in Case IV/31.458, *X/Open Group*, 15 Dec. 1986.
39. Commission decision in Case COMP/39416, *Ship Classification*, 14 Oct. 2009.
40. Commission decision in Case IV/31.458, *X/Open Group*, 15 Dec. 1986.
41. The agreement was notified for exemption under Art. 81(3) EEC (now Art. 101(3) TFEU). Note that it is no longer possible to notify agreements to the Commission - instead companies must carry out a self-assessment.
42. The Unix operating system and the different varieties hereof are alternatives to Microsoft Windows.
43. Commission decision in Case IV/31.458, *X/Open Group*, 15 Dec. 1986, § 34.
44. *Ibid.*, § 35.
45. *Ibid.*, § 42.
46. *Ibid.*
47. Commission decision in Case COMP/39416, *Ship Classification*, 14 Oct. 2009.

rules and lack of transparency as to the resolutions (held to be de facto standards) adopted. The case was eventually closed after the Commission made certain commitments made by IACS binding pursuant to pursuant to Article 9(1) of Regulation 1/2003.[48] The Commission did not demand that IACS allowed third party classification societies (CSs) unrestricted access, but accepted certain detailed commitments to (i) adopt objective, transparent, and non-discriminatory membership criteria, (ii) to establish an online subscription based forum allowing non-members to make their voice heard, and (iii) to make available to the public the results of IACS' technical standard setting process.[49] As noted by the Commission the new membership criteria ensured:

> that only technically competent CSs are eligible to become member of IACS, thus preventing that the efficiency and quality of IACS' work is unduly impaired by too lenient requirements for participation in IACS. At the same time, the new criteria will not hinder CSs, who are technically competent and willing to do so, from joining IACS.[50]

[3] Royalty Free IPR Policies

Some SSOs such as Oasis and W3C (see Annex 1) require members to commit to license patents essential to the standards being developed on a royalty free basis to implementers of the standards adopted.[51] Such policies may be pro-competitive if adopted on the basis of objective considerations regarding costs and quality and if they adhere to the principle of proportionality.[52] If the standards set relate to markets characterized by 'patent thickets',[53] i.e., a dense web of overlapping rights, licensing costs may become significant (this problem is often referred to as 'royalty stacking') in the absence of a royalty free IPR policy and may impede efforts to diffuse the standard. Under such circumstances royalty free standards may on balance be best in line with market demands and most beneficial to consumers, provided that less restrictive terms are not able to guarantee the same result.[54] However, while a royalty free IPR policy may be pro-competitive, because it acts to reduce the royalty burden which will eventually be

48. Regulation 1/2003 of 16 December 2002 on the implementation of the rules on competition laid down in Articles 81 and 82 of the Treaty, Art. 9(1).
49. Commission decision in Case COMP/39416, *Ship Classification*, 14 Oct. 2009, Ch. 4.
50. *Ibid.*, § 36.
51. With regard to Oasis this only applies to some technical committees – others mandate licensing on FRAND terms.
52. Also see Dolmans, Maurits, *Standards For Standards*, in Fordham International Law Journal, Vol. 26(1), 2002 p. 181 p. 183.
53. The notion 'patent thicket' is used by for instance Shapiro, Carl, *Navigating the Patent Thicket: Cross Licenses, Patent Pools, and Standard Setting*, in Jaffe, Adam B.; Lerner, Josh & Stern, Scott (eds.), *Innovation Policy and the Economy*, Vol. 1, 2001, and Schöler, Karalona, *Patents and Standards: The Antitrust Objection as a Defence in Patent Infringement Proceedings*, in Wolrad Prinz zu Waldeck et al. (eds.), Patents and Technological Progress in a Globalized World, Springer, 2009 p. 179.
54. One possibility may be for SSOs to require that participants agree not to claim royalty rates which exceed a certain predefined rate (a maximum rate) and to apply said rate to a predefined royalty base.

placed upon standard compliant products, it may also produce anti-competitive effects. When adopted by influential SSOs royalty free IPR policies may be detrimental to innovation, hence, effective competition, to the extent that it discourages participation by R&D intensive companies and prevents them from effectively recouping their R&D costs.[55] In addition royalty free IPR policies may lead to the exclusion of superior technologies which would have been favoured by consumers. Thus, while royalty free IPR policies may act to promote efficient standardization in a static perspective they also entail a risk to dynamic competition by diminishing the incentives to invest in research and development and to contribute to standardization.[56]

In the draft Horizontal Guidelines published for consultation in 2010 it was noted that to comply with the 'safe harbour' principle of unrestricted access "*...the relevant rules should not exclude or discriminate against specific groups of IPR holders. There should be no bias in favour or against royalty free standards, depending on the relative benefits of the latter compared to other alternatives*".[57] This intuitively makes sense since such bias may be considered a de facto membership limitation and contradicts the requirement that technology selection should take place on an objective basis (see section §9.03[B]). Moreover, as noted in section §9.03[E][2], a royalty free IPR policy which does not allow participants to opt-out with regard to specific IPR compounds the potential anti-competitive effects associated with a compulsory licensing policy, because it does not only prevent IPR holders from withholding licences, but also deprives them the possibility of obtaining royalty income. Nonetheless, the phrase cited was removed from the final version of the guidelines following public consultation.[58]

The Horizontal Guidelines in force do not explicitly state that SSOs must abstain from discriminating between specific groups of IPR holders in order to benefit from the 'safe harbour' presumption of legality. This issue is instead discussed under the

55. NPE's for instance rely on royalties as their main source of income and with the exception of 'patent trolls' need such income to finance their R&D activities.
56. Also see Fraunhofer Institute for Communication System and Dialogic, *Study on the Interplay between Standards and Intellectual Property Rights (IPRs)*, OJEU S136 of 18 Jul. 2009, 2011 p. 12, where it is found that "*[t]he broad perception in the market is that while royalty-free regimes may facilitate the standardisation process and the implementation of standards, Fair Reasonable and Non-Discriminatory (FRAND) licensing regimes provide IPR owners with stronger incentives to invest in research and development, to patent, and to contribute to standardisation*".
57. Communication from the Commission, *Draft Guidelines on the applicability of Article 101 of the Treaty on the Functioning of the European Union to horizontal co-operation agreements*, SEC(2010) 528/2, 4 May 2010, § 278. Available at: http://ec.europa.eu/competition/consultations/2010_horizontals/ (last checked 30 May 2014).
58. It is unclear what triggered the removal. However, some of the comments submitted to the Commission expressed concern that depriving royalty free IPR policies the benefit of the 'safe harbour' would discourage SSOs from adopting such policies and accordingly may impede standardization in markets where rapid uptake and low costs are important. It was also claimed that it would disadvantage the open source community which often relies on royalty free licensing. See for instance ECIS, *Comments in reply to the public consultation on the revised rules for the assessment of horizontal cooperation agreements under EU law*, 29 Jun. 2010 p. 3, and CCIA, *Comments of the Computer & Communications Industry Association On the Public Consultation Regarding the Proposed Revised Guidelines for the Assessment of Horizontal Cooperation Agreements under EU Competition Law, 2010* pp. 4-6.

heading 'Effects based assessment for standardisation agreements' which is of relevance to standardization agreements which do not satisfy the safe harbour principles. Hence, in § 297 of the Horizontal Guidelines it is stated that a standardization agreement which "...*clearly discriminates against any of the participating or potential members could lead to a restriction of competition*" and gives as an example that an IPR policy which "...*explicitly excludes upstream only companies (that is to say, companies not active on the downstream production market)*" may restrict competition by leading to the exclusion of potentially better technologies.[59] Following this change it is unclear from the wording of the guidelines whether a royalty free IPR policy is able to benefit from the 'safe harbour' presumption that is not restrictive of competition or whether an individual assessment is called for. It would have been appropriate if the Commission had explicitly made clear (following the change) whether a royalty free IPR policy is deemed to adhere to the principle regarding unrestricted participation. Since the example cited above speaks of rules which *explicitly* exclude upstream only companies it seems likely that the deletion of the original phrase had as its purpose to accede to the concerns during the public consultation phase that excluding royalty free IPR policies from the 'safe harbour' might be detrimental to competition.[60]

From a policy perspective it is open to debate whether allowing royalty free IPR policies to benefit from the presumption of legality established by the 'safe harbour' principles was the right approach. Bearing in mind that the Commission's Horizontal Guidelines stress the importance of unrestricted participation in standard setting activities it seems peculiar that standardization agreements which only allow for the inclusion of royalty free technologies in the standard being developed are able to benefit from an outright *presumption* of legality. It would perhaps have been more appropriate if the legality of royalty free standards policies were to be decided on a case-by-case basis and the 'safe-harbour' presumption of legality conditioned on an IPR-neutral policy. That being said, it must be recalled that adherence with the 'safe harbour' principles only create a presumption of legality and the Commission is not prevented from taking action if the specific circumstances so require. Moreover, there is no guarantee that the CJEU will endorse the Commission's view of such policies.

[C] Disclosure of IPRs and Identification of Essential Patents

As noted above SSO IPR policies must oblige participants to perform good faith disclosures of IPRs potentially essential to the standard under development in order to benefit from the 'safe harbour'.[61] As noted by the Commission the purpose is to enable SSO participants to make informed choices of which technologies to include in the

59. Communication from the Commission, *Guidelines on the applicability of Article 101 of the Treaty on the Functioning of the European Union to horizontal co-operation agreements*, OJ 2011/C 11/1, 14 Jan. 2011, § 297.
60. *Supra* note 59. The Commission also notes that 'FRAND' may cover royalty free licensing. See *ibid.*, § 285 (footnote 114).
61. Communication from the Commission, *Guidelines on the applicability of Article 101 of the Treaty on the Functioning of the European Union to horizontal co-operation agreements*, OJ 2011/C 11/1, 14 Jan. 2011, § 286.

standard adopted.[62] IPR disclosures facilitate technology choice based not only on performance and effectiveness, but also on licensing costs.[63] It allows SSO members to rely on the amount of essential IPR disclosed as a proxy for licensing costs and establishes the basis for engaging in bilateral discussions with the rights holders identified to obtain information (perhaps even commitments) with regard to royalty rates or other licensing conditions. Hence, it may for instance lead to certain patented technologies being deselected, because royalty free alternatives are deemed to provide a cost/benefit ratio better in line with market demand. In addition disclosures establish the basis for procuring FRAND licensing commitments with regard to the IPRs disclosed.

Bearing in mind the importance of patent disclosure and the rather undemanding disclosure standard required to ensure conformity with Article 101(1) TFEU (see below) it seems that IPR policies not containing disclosure obligations will only be able to escape Article 101 TFEU in a limited number of circumstances. As noted by the Commission an IPR policy which (i) does not include a disclosure obligation, but (ii) requires all members to issue a blanket commit to license any essential IPR on FRAND terms, is unlikely to restrict competition within the meaning of Article 101(1) TFEU if (iii) all technologies of potential relevance to the upcoming standard can be expected to be covered by IPR.[64] In such scenario a disclosure obligation plays a less prevalent[65] role in facilitating informed choices between technologies and is not a prerequisite for an SSO to obtain FRAND commitments – the blanket commitment to license (licensing-by-default obligation) covers the latter aspect. In addition the Commission finds that IPR disclosures are irrelevant with regard to SSOs with a royalty free standards policy. However, this reasoning arguably only applies insofar as SSO participants provide a blanket commitment to license their essential IPR on a royalty free basis to all third parties as a precondition for their participation in the SSO.[66] If a royalty free licensing commitment is given as a precondition for participations IPR disclosures are not needed to allow participants to select technologies on basis of their cost/benefit ratio nor to allow SSOs to obtain FRAND commitments.

However, to ensure compliance with Article 101(1) TFEU such licensing-by-default obligations must be combined with a right for SSO participants to exclude specified technologies from the standard setting process if, in the words of the Commission, "*...that exclusion takes place at an early stage in the development of the*

62. *Ibid.*
63. *Ibid.*, at § 327. Also see Schellingerhout, Ruben, *Standard-setting from a competition law perspective*, in Competition Policy Newsletter, no. 1. 2011 p. 7.
64. Communication from the Commission, *Guidelines on the applicability of Article 101 of the Treaty on the Functioning of the European Union to horizontal co-operation agreements*, OJ 2011/C 11/1, 14 Jan. 2011, § 327.
65. The Commission even goes as far as saying that in such scenario "*... any IPR disclosure would not have the positive effect of enabling the members to factor in the amount of IPR when choosing technology since regardless of what technology is chosen, it can be presumed that there is IPR reading on that technology*" – see *ibid*. However, even if all technologies are covered by IPR a disclosure obligation, as noted above, may still have the positive effects of identifying right holders as a basis for bilateral discussions with regard to royalty rates or other licensing conditions.
66. *Ibid.*, at § 286.

standard".[67] The World Wide Web Consortium (W3C), a US based SSO responsible for setting many successful web standards, for instance require that undertakings, as a precondition for participation in the standard setting process, agree to license their SEPs on a royalty free basis, but includes a right to opt-out with regard to specific patent claims if done within certain specified time periods.[68] Such approach arguably fulfils the 'safe harbour' principle regarding disclosure, because it allows patentees to exclude technologies which are of special strategic importance to their business from the generic licensing obligation. The legality of licensing-by-default obligations under Article 101 TFEU is discussed in more detail in section §9.03[E][2].

The disclosure obligation envisaged by the Commission is not a strict one. To ensure compliance with Article 101(1) TFEU it is, according to the Commission, sufficient that SSOs require participants to use their *reasonable endeavours* to identify and disclose in *good faith* any IPRs (and applications for such) which might be essential to the standard under development.[69] In this respect it is clarified that such 'good faith' disclosure obligation does not require participants to identify specific IPR or applications for IPR – generic statements that a participant is likely to hold essential IPRs shall suffice. Moreover, is it stated that "*...the sought after result a good faith disclosure does not need to go as far as to require participants to compare their IPR against the potential standard and issue a statement positively concluding that they have no IPR reading on the potential standard".*[70] While this statement makes clear that SSO participants are not required to make negative declarations that they hold no essential IPR it cannot be inferred from the statement to what extent the 'reasonable endeavours' to identify IPR entails an obligation to actively perform IPR searches. A 2005 investigation (see immediately below) carried out by the Commission however provides a strong indication that IPR policies do not need to mandate IPR searches in order to benefit from the presumption of legality established by the 'safe harbour'.

In 2005, the Commission issued a press release that it had investigated the IPR policies of ETSI – an officially accredited SDO – prompted by concern that the disclosure rules did not sufficiently protect against the risk of 'patent ambush'.[71] The notion 'patent ambush', as explained in Chapter 10, refers to the situation where a company conceals its IPRs during the standard setting process only to subsequently assert them against implementers of the standard adopted. The Commission did not explain exactly what its concern was and how ETSI mitigated that concern. However, the ETSI Guide on IPRs provides some insight in this respect.[72] It is clear that the wording of the Horizontal Guidelines is inspired by the ETSI investigation. The

67. *Ibid.*
68. See ss 3 and 4 of the W3C Patent Policy of 5 Feb. 2005. Available at: http://www.w3.org/Consortium/Patent-Policy-20040205/#def-essential (last checked 30 May 2014).
69. Communication from the Commission, *Guidelines on the applicability of Article 101 of the Treaty on the Functioning of the European Union to horizontal co-operation agreements*, OJ 2011/C 11/1, 14 Jan. 2011, § 286.
70. *Ibid.*, footnote 4.
71. Commission press Release, *Commission welcomes changes in ETSI IPR rules to prevent 'patent ambush'*, IP/05/1565, 12 Dec. 2002.
72. ETSI Guide on IPRs, 19 Sep. 2013, s. § 4.6. Available at: http://www.etsi.org/about/iprs-in-etsi. (last checked 30 May 2014).

Commission was concerned that ETSI's disclosure rules only required members to undertake *"...reasonable endeavours to timely inform ETSI of ESSENTIAL IPRs it becomes aware of"*.[73] In its correspondence with ETSI (cited in ETSI's guidelines) the Commission stated that *"...the deletion of the phrase 'becomes aware of' is important from the Commission's 'patent ambush' perspective..."*, since a member would be expected *"...to have a general awareness of the scope of its IPR rights in that area, and therefore where necessary, 'use its reasonable endeavours' to identify these IPR"*.[74] It is not clear exactly which legal implications the Commission expected to result from the amendment, since as the Commission itself noted its proposed changes did not create a heightened expectation for ETSI members to identify essential IPRs.[75] However, more importantly the Commission, faced with concern about the proposed changes, made clear that it did not expect members of ETSI to conduct searches for patents or other IPR.[76]

While it must be borne in mind that the ETSI decision precedes the adoption of the 2010 Horizontal Guidelines there is no basis for concluding that the assessment will be different today. The rather vague disclosure requirements required for an IPR policy to escape Article 101(1) TFEU are likely attributable to concerns that imposing a stricter norm may discourage SSO participation by rights holders fearing to incur liability by inadvertently failing to identify patents. Indeed, as noted above members of ETSI expressed such concerns when confronted with the Commission's proposed changes to ETSI's IPR Policy. In conclusion, it seems that adherence with the disclosure obligation merely requires SSOs to impose upon their members an obligation to disclose IPR of which they are aware in good faith. As an addition to *ex ante* disclosure obligations it is arguably important that SSOs communicate the patent interests disclosed to the public so as to allow firms interested in producing standard compliant products to make themselves acquainted with the rights to which a license is necessary. Absent such publicly available database the risk of inadvertent infringements and disputes – eventually injunctions – increase. The Commission does not comment on this aspect in the Horizontal Guidelines and there is no case law of relevance to determine to what extent a failure by an SSO to establish such database will violate Article 101(1) TFEU. However, considering the 'safe harbour' principle mandating transparency (see section §9.03[B]) the Commission arguably could attempt to impose such requirement under Article 101(1) TFEU and it may even be held that said principle is not fulfilled absent such disclosure in which case an individual assessment under Article 101(3) TFEU must be performed. It remains to be seen whether, in light of the recent disputes between right holders and implementers at the Member State level, the Commission will focus its attention on this aspect.

73. *Ibid.*, Ch. 4 s. §4.06[B][1].
74. ETSI Guide on IPRs, 19 Sep. 2013, Ch. 4 s. § 4.06[B][1].
75. *Ibid.*
76. *Ibid.*

[D] Disclosure of Licensing Terms

FRAND commitments have as their purpose to reduce the risk that SEPs are used as a means to extract excessive or discriminatory royalties (or other licensing conditions) after a standard is adopted and the market becomes 'locked-in'. However, there is considerable uncertainty as to what fair, reasonable and non-discriminatory means – see Chapter 11 sections §11.01 and §11.02, respectively. Although, as discussed in Chapter 13, competition law limits the ability to use FRAND-pledged patents to obtain injunctions against *willing* licensees it remains that the ambiguity of FRAND commitments deprives them the intended role as a preventive measure to avoid disputes between SEP holders and third parties wishing to adopt the standard.

As an additional measure to ensure efficient diffusion of standards and safeguard the associated pro-competitive effects it has been suggested to allow SSOs to act as repositories and to collect from members *ex ante*, i.e., before the standard is adopted, the most restrictive licensing terms on which they are prepared to grant licenses *ex post*, i.e., after the standard is adopted.[77] Such mechanism concerning disclosure of license terms should not be confused with the obligation, as inherent in most SSO IPR policies, to perform *ex ante* disclosures of IPRs which might be essential to the standard. A mechanism allowing for or mandating *ex ante* disclosures of licensing terms is optional, whereas, as discussed in section §9.03[C], an obligation for SSO members to disclose the existence of essential IPR in good faith is a prerequisite for the standardization agreement to benefit from the safe harbour set out in the Commission's Horizontal Guidelines.

An *ex ante* disclosure mechanism which brings into light the most onerous license terms on which a patentee is prepared to license – at least in principle – will allow for a more transparent process of standard adoption as SSO participants will be better equipped to choose between competing technologies on a cost-benefit basis, i.e., by taking into consideration not only their technical characteristics (as catered for by the *ex ante* disclosure of essential IPR), but also their price – hence improves chances that the standard adopted will be successful in terms of market penetration. Thus, provided that substitute technologies exist, SSO participants will be able to rely on *ex ante* disclosures 1) to circumvent excessively priced patented technologies at an early stage in the technology selection process, and 2) to ensure that the aggregate cost of the technologies selected for inclusion in the standard bears a reasonable relationship to the profits expected to arise from the sale of standard compliant products. The increased transparency may also reduce the risk of *ex post* opportunism by patentees who might otherwise be tempted to rely on their market power to demand excessive or discriminatory royalties (in light of the ambiguity of FRAND commitments). These benefits were acknowledged by former EU Commissioner Neelie Krøes who stated that:

> if we are to include proprietary technology in a standard, then ex ante disclosure may help those involved make a properly informed decision. Competition law

---

77. See for instance Contreras, Jorge L. et al., *An Empirical Study of the Effects of Ex Ante Licensing Disclosure Policies on the Development of Voluntary Technical Standards*, Publication made for the National Institute of Standards and Technology, 2011 pp. 4–5 (with references).

> should not stand in the way. This will almost always entail ex ante disclosure of the existence of essential patents. And it may increasingly entail ex ante disclosure of maximum royalty rates. Both can increase the effectiveness of the standard setting process, lead to more competitive solutions and reduce the risk of later antitrust problems. Standards bodies could very often require disclosure without fear of competition law intervention.[78]

Despite these potential benefits some legal scholars expressed their concern that *ex ante* disclosures of license terms may lead to collusion regarding royalties or conversely allow potential licensees to collectively put pressure on patentees to reduce their royalty rates below the competitive level by threating not to vote for its inclusion in the standard.[79] In addition some find that *ex ante* disclosures are ineffective in facilitating more informed technology choices and prevent problems with excessive pricing, since patentees (it is argued) have an incentive to delay their disclosures until the draft standard becomes 'locked-in' to their technologies.[80] Others have however argued that such criticism is misplaced and that *ex ante* disclosures have proven successful.[81] In the end this remains an empirical question. From a legal perspective fact of the matter is that the Commission looks favourable upon unilateral *ex ante* disclosures of license terms. The Commission in its 2009 white paper on ICT standardization even encourages SSOs to "*...consider a declaration of the most restrictive licensing terms, possibly including the (maximum) royalty rates before adoption of a standard as a potential route to providing more predictability and transparency*".[82] Moreover, the most recent version of the Commission's Horizontal Guidelines explicitly state that standard-settings agreements which provide for unilateral *ex ante* disclosures of the most restrictive license terms will normally not violate Article 101(1) TFEU, because such disclosures allow the parties involved in the standardization process to make informed

78. SPEECH/08/317, *Being open about standards*, 10 Jun. 2008. Also see WIPO, *Standards and Patents*, Standing committee on the law of patents, 13th Session, 2009 p. 41.
79. Contreras, Jorge L. et al., *An Empirical Study of the Effects of Ex Ante Licensing Disclosure Policies on the Development of Voluntary Technical Standards*, Publication made for the National Institute of Standards and Technology, 2011 pp. 5-6 (with references). Also see WIPO, *Standards and Patents*, Standing committee on the law of patents, 13th Session, 2009 p. 41; Fraunhofer Institute for Communication System and Dialogic, *Study on the Interplay between Standards and Intellectual Property Rights (IPRs)*, OJEU S136 of 18 Jul. 2009, 2011, p. 25, and Gilbert, Richard, *Deal Or No Deal? Licensing Negotiations By Standard Setting Organizations*, in *Antitrust Law Journal, Vol.* 77(3), 2011 pp. 856-857.
80. See for instance Dolmans, Maurits, *A Tale of Two Tragedies – A plea for open Standards*, in International Free and Open Source Software Law Review, Vol. 2(2), 2010 p. 124. Although failing to disclose the existence of SEPs in a timely manner may be deemed a 'patent ambush' contrary Art. 102 TFEU this is, as explained in Ch. 10. Patent Ambush, unlikely to happen *inter alia* because the patentee will often not be dominant at the time of the patent ambush.
81. See for instance Contreras, Jorge L. et al., *An Empirical Study of the Effects of Ex Ante Licensing Disclosure Policies on the Development of Voluntary Technical Standards*, Publication made for the National Institute of Standards and Technology, 2011, where the authors, having examined data relating to the US SSOs IEEE and VITA, conclude that the evidence reviewed did not support the criticism directed at *ex ante*disclosure policies.
82. See Commission, *Modernising ICT Standardisation in the EU – The Way Forward*, COM(2009) 324 final, White paper, 3 Jul. 2009, point. 2.4.

decisions "*...not only as to the available technical options and the associated IPR, but also as to the likely cost of that IPR*".[83]

Until now there have been no EU case law dealing with SSO policies allowing for *ex ante* disclosures of the most restrictive license terms. However, the Commission approach seems reasonable. A patent holder's unilateral disclosure of its most restrictive license terms does not involve any coordination between competitors (or other anti-competitive effects) and therefore does not fall within the ambit of Article 101(1) TFEU. If subsequent to a disclosure licensees form a 'buyer cartel' to put pressure on the patentee this may infringe the competition rules, but the issue is distinct from the disclosure itself.

Despite the fact that the Commission takes a favourable view on unilateral *ex ante* disclosures it seems that SSO participants have been reluctant to avail themselves of the option to disclose their license terms.[84] ETSI for instance has allowed such disclosures on a voluntary basis for several years, but until date not a single disclosure has been made.[85] The lack of disclosures may be attributable to fear amongst SSO participants that such disclosures may be deemed a cover to jointly fix prices contrary to competition law. However, bearing in mind the rather clear wording of the Commission's Horizontal Guidelines it seems more likely that patentees abstain from disclosing their terms for commercial reasons.

As opposed to the *ex ante* disclosures of license terms the Commission has not condoned joint license negotiations. Only truly unilateral and independent disclosures are covered by said presumption of legality. The Commission makes clear that an attempt to jointly fix the prices of products or substitute IPR, by relying on the disclosure of the most restrictive licensing terms prior to the adoption of a standard will be deemed a restriction of competition by object in violation of Article 101(1) TFEU.[86] This is in line with established EU case law according to which price fixing agreements constitutes a 'hard-core' restriction of competition. Participants in SSOs accordingly should be wary that engaging in joint discussions regarding license terms with competitors may give rise to liability under the competition rules and SSOs should abstain from any attempt to influence license terms.[87]

83. See Communication from the Commission, *Guidelines on the applicability of Article 81 of the EC Treaty to horizontal co-operation agreements*, OJ 2001/C 3/02, 6 Jan. 2001, § 299.
84. Cf. also Fraunhofer Institute for Communication System and Dialogic, *Study on the Interplay between Standards and Intellectual Property Rights (IPRs)*, OJEU S136 of 18 Jul. 2009, 2011 p. 25, and WIPO, *Standards and Patents*, SCP/13/2, 2009 p. 30.
85. See ETSI Guide on IPRs, 19 Sep. 2013, point. 4.1. See the list of IPR disclosures available at http://www.etsi.org/about/iprs-in-etsi/ex-ante-disclosures (last checked 30 May 2014).
86. See Communication from the Commission, *Guidelines on the applicability of Article 81 of the EC Treaty to horizontal co-operation agreements*, OJ 2001/C 3/02, 6 Jan. 2001, § 274 and § 299 (footnote 124).
87. In accordance herewith ETSI for instance specifically states that "*[n]o detailed licensing terms should be available from ETSI to avoid a misleading impression. ETSI may act as a depository, where IPR owners (licensors) can make available information on how and where to access such disclosed licensing terms, and provide links to URLs of IPR owners*". See ETSI Guide on IPRs, 19 Sep. 2013, point. 4.1. Moreover, none of the SSO IPR policies examined in this dissertation (Annex 1) allows *ex ante* discussions of license terms within the SSO – to the contrary they explicitly state that such discussions must take place on a bilateral basis outside the SSO.

On the other hand bilateral *ex ante* licensing negotiations between SSO members during the standard setting process arguably does not warrant competition law scrutiny for as long as such negotiations does not concern terms and conditions relating to substitute patents (or other IPRs).[88] Indeed, the Commission in its Technology Transfer Guidelines states that undertakings "...*setting up a technology pool ... are normally free to negotiate and fix royalties for the technology package (subject to any commitment given to license on fair, reasonable and non-discriminatory terms, FRAND) and each technology's share of the royalties either before or after the standard is set.*".[89] Although the statement relates to the establishment of technology pools the Commission's reasoning, that it may be more efficient if royalties are agreed *ex ante*, applies with regard to bilateral licensing negotiations as well. Hence, such negotiations may potentially be pro-competitive by allowing manufactures to ascertain whether royalties are commercially reasonable before the standard becomes locked-in to certain technologies and may prevent future disputes.

[E] FRAND Commitments

For a standardization agreement to benefit from the 'safe harbour' presumption that it does not restrict competition within the meaning of Article 101(1) TFEU it must require that SSO participants *prior* to adoption of the standard being developed provide an *irrevocable* commitment in *writing* to offer to license their essential IPR to the *all users of that standard* on *FRAND terms*.[90] A patent is 'essential' if the standard adopted cannot be implemented without infringing the patent.[91] As ETSI (accredited SDO) stated in its IPR policy the term essential:

> as applied to IPR means that it is not possible on technical (but not commercial) grounds, taking into account normal technical practice and the state of the art generally available at the time of standardization, to make, sell, lease, otherwise dispose of, repair, use or operate EQUIPMENT or METHODS which comply with a STANDARD without infringing that IPR.[92]

---

88. Also see WIPO, *Standards and Patents*, Standing committee on the law of patents, 13th Session, 2009 p. 42 (point 156) where it is stated that "...*generally, a patent holder's voluntary and unilateral disclosure of its licensing terms, as well as bilateral ex ante licensing negotiations between an individual SSO member and a patent holder outside the auspices of the SSO, are unlikely to require antitrust scrutiny*".
89. Commission notice, *Guidelines on the application of Article 101 of the Treaty on the Functioning of the European Union to technology transfer agreements*, OJ 2014/C 89/03, 28 Mar. 2014, § 268.
90. Communication from the Commission, *Guidelines on the applicability of Article 101 of the Treaty on the Functioning of the European Union to horizontal co-operation agreements*, OJ 2011/C 11/1, 14 Jan. 2011, §§ 285 and 287.
91. Note that (at least) in the Danish language version of the Horizontal Guidelines the word "essential" has been translated to "væsentlig" which may give the wrong impression that the obligation also applies to 'significant' or 'important' IPRs which are strictly speaking not essential.
92. ETSI IPR Policy (Annex 6 of the Rules of Procedure) of 19 Mar. 2014, p. 41. Available at: http://www.etsi.org/about/iprs-in-etsi (last checked 30 May 2014).

SSOs are not required to actually verify whether participants comply with their FRAND obligations – according to the Commission it is for the participants to self-asses.[93]

Note that FRAND commitments are only required to establish obligations *vis-à-vis* companies seeking a license for the purpose of manufacturing standard compliant products not third parties in general. As noted by the Commission FRAND commitments have as their purpose to ensure that SEPs (or other IPRs) will be made available to implementers of the standard adopted and that they will not be used as a means to extract excessive or discriminatory royalties (or other unreasonable licensing conditions) after a standard is adopted and the market becomes 'locked-in'.[94] The legal implications of FRAND commitments under Article 102 TFEU are analysed in Part V of this book. Two overall findings are made:

- The analyses carried out in Chapter 13 section §11.01 (fair and reasonable) and Chapter 11 section §11.02 (non-discriminatory) reveal that there is considerable uncertainty as to what fair, reasonable and non-discriminatory means when construed in light of Article 102 TFEU.[95] FRAND is not a concept which can be consistently applied as factors specific to the individual licensing transaction must be taken into account. Moreover, there is no basis for concluding that FRAND commitments alters the criteria which according to settled EU case law, and in the absence of such commitments, are decisive in determining whether license fees are unfair, unreasonable (excessive) or discriminatory.
- The analyses carried out in Chapter 12 (Refusals to license) and Chapter 12 (Injunctions) to the contrary indicate that a FRAND commitment – although contractual in nature – has special implications under Article 102 TFEU beyond what follows from settled EU case law. More specifically, it is found that (i) a refusal to license FRAND-pledged patents will infringe Article 102 TFEU as a main rule rather than in 'exceptional circumstances' and that (ii) threating, seeking or enforcing injunctions against 'willing licensees' on basis of FRAND-pledged patents is likely to infringe Article 102 TFEU.

[1] Obligation to Transfer FRAND Commitments

In order to prevent companies acquiring SEPs from evading FRAND commitments previously issued, the Horizontal Guidelines states that the IPR polices of SSOs must oblige members to transfer their FRAND commitments alongside their patents – for

93. Communication from the Commission, *Guidelines on the applicability of Article 101 of the Treaty on the Functioning of the European Union to horizontal co-operation agreements*, OJ 2011/C 11/1, 14 Jan. 2011, § 288.
94. *Ibid.*, § 287.
95. In this respect also see Contreras, Jorge L. et al., *An Emperical Study of the Effects of Ex Ante Licensing Disclosure Policies on the Development of Voluntary Technical Standards*, Publication made for the National Institute of Standards and Technology, 2011 p. 3 (with references). Also WIPO, *Standards and Patents*, Standing committee on the law of patents, 13th Session, 2009 p. 30.

instance by use of a contractual clause between buyer and seller.[96] Absent such clause the standardization agreements does not benefit from the 'safe harbour' presumption that it does not infringe Article 101(1) TFEU.

This requirement is directed at the IPR policies of SSOs. The Horizontal Guidelines does not comment on the extent to which a failure to actually comply with such requirement by the parties to a patent transfer agreement will be deemed a violation of competition law - neither does the Technology Transfer Guidelines. It would have contributed to legal certainty if an opportunity had been seized - for instance when the Horizontal Guidelines were revised in 2010 - to provide some guidance on how the Commission intends to assess the legality of agreements involving the transfer of essential FRAND-pledged patents.[97] There are not cases where the failure to transfer a FRAND commitment has been deemed a violation of competition law. However, the Commission has on several occasions made clear that companies acquiring SEPs are expected to honour existing FRAND commitments covering the patents acquired.

When IPCom (a NPE) in 2007 acquired a portfolio of patents essential to certain telecommunication standards the Commission engaged in discussions with IPCom to ensure that the company was willing to honour a FRAND commitment issued by the transferor, Robert Bosch GmbH, in the course of its participation in the standard setting activities of ETSI (accredited SDO).[98] Following these discussions IPCom declared its willingness to license the patents acquired on FRAND terms pursuant to ETSI's IPR policy and the investigation was ended without any formal decision. The Commission noted that from a competition law perspective, and in order to safeguard the pro-competitive economic effects of standard setting catered for by FRAND declarations, "*...it is important that when patents essential to a standard are transferred from one owner to another, so should any relevant FRAND commitments*".[99] The Commission similarly considered this aspect in its 2012 *Google/Motorola* merger decision where it stated "*...that a purchaser company acquiring a SEP portfolio from a vendor company should be bound by a FRAND commitment previously given by that vendor company*".[100]

The market power conferred by SEPs in the context of formal standards is due to third parties accepting them for inclusion in the standard adopted in reliance on the patentees declared willingness to provide licenses on FRAND terms. In order to prevent patent hold-up the restraints arising from that particular context should - as stated by the Commission - remain in place despite a change of ownership. This is not a

96. Communication from the Commission, *Guidelines on the applicability of Article 101 of the Treaty on the Functioning of the European Union to horizontal co-operation agreements*, OJ 2011/C 11/1, 14 Jan. 2011, § 285.
97. This was also pointed out in connection with the public consultation which preceded adoption of the 2010 Horizontal Guidelines. See Cleary Gottlieb Steen & Hamilton LLP, *European Commission Consultation Draft Guidelines On Horizontal Co-Operation Agreements -Standardization Section*, 25 Jun. 2010, p. 6. Available at: http://ec.europa.eu/competition/consultations/2010_horizontals/. (last checked 30 May 2014).
98. Commission's press release in Case 39615, *Nokia/Bosch + IPCom*, MEMO/09/549 (Commission welcomes IPCom's public FRAND declaration), 10 Dec. 2009.
99. *Ibid.*
100. Case COMP/M.6381, *Google/Motorola Mobility*, 13 Feb. 2012, § 120 (Merger procedure).

controversial requirement as the power obtained by a subsequent acquirer of such patents can be linked directly to the standardization efforts and the FRAND declaration previously issued. Thus, there is no reason why acquirers of FRAND-pledged patents should be allowed to break the boundaries of FRAND and engage in practices which would have been considered a violation of Article 102 TFEU if carried out by the previous owner of the patents.

The statements made by the Commission in the IPCom press release and in the *Google/Motorola* case make clear that the Commission attaches great importance to the transfer of FRAND commitments. Although the Commission has not indicated the legal basis on which it would be prepared to initiate proceedings it seems likely that an agreement involving the transfer of FRAND-pledged patents will be considered restrictive of competition, cf. Article 101(1) TFEU, if it does not ensure that the transferee stays bound by a FRAND commitment issued by the transferor.[101] As a standardization agreement may be deemed restrictive of competition in case it does not oblige SSO participants to transfer their FRAND commitments alongside their patents so may any failure to actually do – obviously this may give rise to the very anti-competitive effects that the transfer obligation aims to prevent in the first place by keeping FRAND commitments intact. There can arguably be no objective justification for not transferring such commitment and if the failure to do so is found to infringe Article 101(1) TFEU an exemption under Article 101(3) TFEU seems unlikely.

The above mentioned stresses the need for undertakings to perform proper due diligence prior to acquiring patents if there is a chance that such patents read on formal industry standards. To aid in this respect is advisable that SSOs keep public available patent databases which allow acquires to become acquainted with existing FRAND commitments. In order to ensure that the patent database is kept up-to-date preferably the SSO polices should also include an obligation on SSO members to inform the SSO in case their patents are transferred to third parties. Such up-to-date database is important to ensure that third parties are able to identify the SEPs to which they need a license in order to avoid infringement and accordingly patent litigation. This is however currently not a requirement included in the Commission's Horizontal Guidelines.

A recent report, which looked into the IPR policies of SSOs, revealed that very few of the polices examined obligated SSO participants to transfer their FRAND commitments.[102] This is unfortunate regardless of the fact that the Commission (as noted above) seems prepared to force transferees of FRAND-pledged patents to respect the

101. In theory Art. 102 TFEU may also be invoked. However, it seems unlikely that this will happen bearing in mind (i) there would be no reason to rely on Art. 102 TFEU – which requires evidence of dominance – when reliance can be placed on Art. 101(1) TFEU which 'merely' requires evidence of market power and (ii) the acquirer of FRAND-pledged patents may not hold a dominant position prior to its acquisition of the SEPs being transferred in which case only the transferee's conduct may be scrutinized under Art. 102 TFEU and it is open to question where failing to impose contractual restraints upon the acquirer constitutes abuse.

102. Fraunhofer Institute for Communication System and Dialogic, *Study on the Interplay between Standards and Intellectual Property Rights (IPRs)*, OJEU S136 of 18 Jul. 2009, 2011 p. 108.

transferors licensing commitment on basis of Article 101 TFEU. Establishing a contractual obligation *vis-à-vis* SSO members in this respect may act to ensure that FRAND commitments are indeed transferred and accordingly that transferees are made aware of their obligation to provide licenses on FRAND terms - hence prevent the need for subsequent competition law enforcement. Competition authorities cannot be expected (and does not possess the resources) to police every single transfer agreement involving SEPs.

[2] Licensing-by-Default

It is important for an SSO to ensure the availability of essential IPR by obtaining FRAND commitments from the companies taking part in the standard setting activities as otherwise implementation of the standards adopted risks being obstructed by patentees who refuse to license their rights on fair, reasonable and non-discriminatory terms - in other words, the absence of FRAND commitments increases the risk of patent hold-up. Timing in this respect is crucial, because the costs associated with altering a standard to avoid technologies which turn out to be unavailable - on FRAND terms or altogether - may increase significantly as the standard setting process progresses and dependency on a specific technology increases.[103] Moreover, any such effort to amend the standard may prove fruitless if no viable substitute technologies exist in which case abandoning the standard or attempting to obtain a compulsory license on the basis of Article 102 TFEU may be the only options left.[104]

The majority of SSOs require that members disclose their SEPs in good faith and confirm their willingness to license the patents disclosed on FRAND terms as a precondition for having them embodied in the standard being developed.[105] This is in accordance with the 'safe harbour' principles set out in the Horizontal Guidelines. However, even if SSO policies mandate timely disclosures of potentially essential IPR in good faith there is still a risk that such IPR is deliberately concealed (a so-called 'patent ambush')[106] or simply overlooked in which case it may not be possible to ascertain the availability of essential IPR at an early stage. In recognition hereof some SSOs have adopted alternative rules. To ensure the availability of licences to essential IPRs *ex post* standardization the DVB Project and W3C (both US based SSOs) for instance require all members to commit themselves to grant licences to IPRs on FRAND or RF[107] terms, respectively, *unless* they explicitly notify the SSO that certain IPRs will not be made available. Such rules seem to be in accordance with Article 101(1) TFEU,

103. This aspect was discussed in Ch. 8 s. §8.01.

104. Compulsory licensing is discussed in Ch. 12.

105. See Eltzroth, Carter, *IPR Policy of the DVB Project: Negative Disclosure, FR&ND Arbitration Unless Pool Rules OK Part 1*, International Journal of IT Standards and Standardization Research, Vol. 6(2), 2008 p. 22, where it is stated that the DVB project's (an SSO) "*...rule on "negative disclosure" turns on its head the duty found in most standards bodies*". This is confirmed by the IPR policies investigated in this dissertation - see Annex 1.

106. See Ch. 10 for a discussion of this issue.

107. W3C require members to grant royalty free licences. A reference to the W3C IPR policy is provided in Annex 1.

since they provide SSO members a chance to opt-out in case they do not wish to license their IPRs.

However, such licensing obligations have been subject scrutiny be the Commission, and it remains somewhat unclear to what extent they will be deemed in accordance with Article 101(1) TFEU. When ETSI, an officially recognized European Standardisation Organisation (ESO), in March 1993 adopted a new interim IPR policy and an IPR undertaking the Commission was reluctant to accept the licensing arrangements envisaged. Overall ETSI foresaw a system where members would agree in advance, i.e., prior to work on a standard commencing, to license any of their IPRs deemed essential to the standard being developed on FRAND terms, provided that they did not issue a negative declaration of unavailability within a six month period.[108] The six month opt-out period was to commence from the time "*...where the scope of the work item relating to the future standard in question is sufficiently clearly defined for the IPR holders to perform a meaningful search*" for essential IPR.[109] The arrangement suggested at the time - referred to as 'licensing-by-default'[110] - overall resembles the one which W3C and the DVB Project have adopted today (see above). However, the Computer and Business Equipment Manufacturers Association ('CBEMA') complained to the Commission that ETSI's IPR arrangements infringed Articles 101 and 102 TFEU (then, Articles 81 and 82 EC).

The CBEMA members, most of which were also members of ETSI, complained *inter alia* that ETSI could not provide the information necessary to facilitate meaningful IPR searches for which reason the interim IPR policy did not offer a genuine possibility to exempt IPRs from the licensing obligation.[111] Thus, CBEMA considered the licensing-by-default undertaking to amount to a compulsory licensing scheme.[112] The Commission was sympathetic to CBEMA's concerns that they risked losing control of their most precious IPR and in a letter to ETSI dated 21 February 1994 took the preliminary view that the 'licensing-by-default' approach, although ensuring the availability of licenses, might be restrictive of competition. The Commission found that a 'licensing-by-default' obligation could be exempted under Article 101(3) TFEU (then, Article 81(3) EC) if it was technically possible (even if financially burdensome) for SSO

108. Commission notice in Case IV/35.006, *ETSI interim IPR policy*, 95/C 76/05, 28 Mar. 1995, point 8.
109. ETSI 1993 IPR undertaking is not published. (unpublished). Cited in Iversen, Eric J., *Standardization and Intellectual Property Rights: ETSI's controversial search for new IPR-procedures*, SIIT'99 Proceedings, IEEE Conference on Standardisation and Innovation, Aachen, Germany, 15–17 Sep. 1999 p. 6.
110. Commission notice in Case IV/35.006, *ETSI interim IPR policy*, 95/C 76/05, 28 Mar. 1995, point 8.
111. See Dolmans, Maurits, *Standards For Standards*, in Fordham International Law Journal, Vol. 26(1), 2002 p. 181; Smith, Graham, *Internet Law and Regulation*, 4th ed., Sweet & Maxwell, 2007 p. 1197, and Iversen, Eric J., *Standardization and Intellectual Property Rights: ETSI's controversial search for new IPR-procedures*, SIIT'99 Proceedings, IEEE Conference on Standardisation and Innovation, Aachen, Germany, 15-17 Sep. 1999 p. 7.
112. Commission notice in Case IV/35.006, *ETSI interim IPR policy*, 95/C 76/05, 28 Mar. 1995, point 9.

members, on basis of the information[113] provided, to perform meaningful IPR searches, but stressed that:

> an undertaking pursuant to which IPR holders are deprived of their freedom to decide whether or not to grant licenses on their existing and future technology is restrictive of competition: it amounts to a mutual renunciation of gaining competitive advantages thanks to technical efforts and thereby deprives the participants of the incentive to develop new technologies.[114]

In addition to CBEMA's compliant ETSI apparently received a number of letters from members who threatened to withdraw their membership of ETSI in case the policy in question was implemented.[115] As a result of the turmoil ETSI eventually decided to abandon the disputed provisions. Accordingly, the complaint filed by CBEMA was withdrawn and never formally decided on by the Commission.[116]

It is clear from the ETSI controversy that, according to the Commission, a compulsory licensing scheme will likely violate Article 101 TFEU as will a 'licence-by-default' scheme which does not provide members the genuine opportunity to exclude select technologies from the FRAND licensing obligation.[117] The Commission in the 2010 Horizontal Guidelines clarifies, that in order to benefit from the 'safe harbour' presumption of legality and escape Article 101(1) TFEU "*...the IPR policy should allow IPR holders to exclude specified technology from the standard-setting process and thereby from the commitment to offer to license, providing that exclusion takes place at an early stage in the development of the standard*".[118] This leaves room for 'licensing-by-default' schemes and indicates that the Commission has adopted a more favourable view of such schemes. Whereas the Commission earlier indicated (see above) that a 'licensing-by-default' scheme would violate Article 101(1) TFEU, but might fulfil the conditions for exemption under Article 101(3) TFEU, it now seems that such schemes will be deemed to fall outside the ambit of Article 101(1) TFEU altogether. This is significant as the burden of proof shifts from the enforcer in Article 101(1) TFEU to the SSO in Article 101(3) TFEU.[119]

---

113. It is unclear exactly how an SSO will be able to guarantee members sufficient information to allow them to perform 'meaningful IPR searches' bearing in mind the often extensive IPR portfolios of multinational companies and the complexity of such search processes.
114. Open letter from the Commission to ETSI and CBEMA dated 21 Feb. 1994 (not published). Referenced by Dolmans, Maurits, *Standards For Standards*, in Fordham International Law Journal, Vol. 26(1), 2002 p. 181.
115. Iversen, Eric J., *Standardization and Intellectual Property Rights: ETSI's controversial search for new IPR-procedures*, SIIT'99 Proceedings, IEEE Conference on Standardisation and Innovation, Aachen, Germany, 15–17 Sep. 1999 p. 6.
116. An amended version of the IPR policy lacking the licensing-by-default obligation was subsequently notified for negative clearance or exemption to the Commission and was accepted as being in accordance with competition law. See Case IV/35.006, *ETSI interim IPR policy*, 28 Mar. 1993.
117. See along the same lines Dolmans, Maurits, *Standards For Standards*, in Fordham International Law Journal, Vol. 26(1), 2002 p. 180.
118. Communication from the Commission, *Guidelines on the applicability of Article 101 of the Treaty on the Functioning of the European Union to horizontal co-operation agreements*, OJ 2011/C 11/1, 14 Jan. 2011, § 285.
119. Council Regulation (EC) No. 1/2003 of 16 Dec. 2002 on the implementation of the rules on competition laid down in Arts 81 and 82 of the Treaty, Art. 2.

The Commission cautious stance towards 'license-by-default' obligations is understandable. A compulsory licensing obligation – whether de jure or de facto – discriminates against companies in possession of large IPR portfolios in favour of those with small portfolios (or none at all) and therefore may be detrimental to innovation as stressed by the Commission.[120] In its 1992 communication on IPR and standards the Commissioned notes that:

> [a]lthough it could be argued that consumers would benefit in the short term if intellectual property rights were compulsively licensed to serve as the basis of standards, in the long-term, investment in research and development in the standardized industrial sectors would dry up within the Community.[121]

Discouraging participation by patentees may also lead to the adoption of inferior standards by limiting the number of substitute technologies available for inclusion.[122] The negative impact of compulsory licensing is compounded if a royalty free standards policy is adopted, since then IPR owners are not only deprived control of their IPR, but also the right to receive remuneration.

That being said, even a compulsory licensing scheme may arguably escape Article 101(1) TFEU or fulfil the conditions for exemption under Article 101(3) TFEU. It must be recalled that ETSI is an influential SSO responsible for adopting many very successful telecommunication standards and this fact most likely acted to shape the Commission's assessment of ETSI's 1992 interim IPR policy. As argued by CBEMA the companies which would be excluded from ETSI, because they refused to sign a licensing-by-default undertaking, would likely suffer a competitive disadvantage.[123] If on the other hand companies can simply avoid the licensing-by-default obligation by joining other SSOs or by 'going alone' there seems to be no basis for finding it restrictive of competition. Moreover, if the members of an SSO constitute a homogenous group whose interests are aligned in the sense that they all possess IPR portfolios of relevance to the standard being developed this may act to mitigate the potential anti-competitive effects and render an exemption under Article 101(3) TFEU more likely.[124]

120. Also see Iversen, Eric J., *Standardization and Intellectual Property Rights: ETSI's controversial search for new IPR-procedures*, SIIT'99 Proceedings, IEEE Conference on Standardisation and Innovation, Aachen, Germany, 15–17 Sep. 1999 p. 4, where it is stated that "*...compulsory licensing has been most strongly advocated by those with the greatest discrepancy between their IPR needs and their IPR portfolios*".
121. Communication from the Commission, *Intellectual Property Rights and Standardisation*, COM(92) 445 Final, 27 Oct. 1992, point 5.1.15.
122. This aspect was discussed in Ch. 9 s. §9.03[A][1].
123. Dolmans, Maurits, *Standards For Standards*, in Fordham International Law Journal, Vol. 26(1), 2002 p. 181.
124. As noted by Iversen, Eric J., *Standardization and Intellectual Property Rights: ETSI's controversial search for new IPR-procedures*, SIIT'99 Proceedings, IEEE Conference on Standardisation and Innovation, Aachen, Germany, 15–17 Sep. 1999 p. 4, ETSI "*...housed a diversity of interest*".

[3] An Overview of Select SSO IPR Policies

A survey of some of the IPR policies adopted by well-known and influential SSOs reveal that (i) members are generally required to submit FRAND commitments as a precondition for having their IPRs included in the standards adopted – either by default (with an option to opt-out) or on a voluntary basis; (ii) members are required to disclose potentially essential IPR in good faith; (iii) members are not required to perform patent searches. For an overview with references to the relevant IPR policies see Annex 1.[125]

All of the SSO policies examined were silent insofar as the meaning of FRAND is concerned and only a single of the SSOs examined has adopted dispute resolution mechanisms, aimed at settling disputes between members arising out of the IPR policy.[126] Accordingly, FRAND commitments as such remain inherently vague and ill-suited to prevent disputes between SEP holders and prospective licensees.[127] However, this is not surprising. The commercial interests of SSO members are often not aligned and it therefore not hard to imagine why an attempt to reach consensus on a definition of FRAND is likely to fail.[128] Moreover, since standard setting activities within an SSO involves collaboration between competitors SSOs generally abstain from interfering with license terms and explicitly state that licensing negotiations are to be undertaken on a bilateral basis outside their reach out of fear that such commercial discussion may give rise to liability under competition law.[129] ETSI in its competition law compliance guidelines for instance states that whenever a unilateral disclosure of license terms is made "*...any discussion and/or negotiation of any licensing terms, including any price term, shall not be conducted in ETSI*".[130] If SSOs specify FRAND in detail and reject technologies for inclusion in a standard on the basis that the owner's licensing terms do not adhere to the definition of FRAND adopted this may be viewed as a collective boycott or be seen as a harmful to innovation in violation of the competition rules. There is also a risk that discussions regarding license terms may be

125. The IPR polices of the following SSOs have been examined: ETSI, CEN, CENELEC, ISO, EIC, ITU, DVB Project, W3C, OASIS, IEEE.
126. Also see WIPO, *Standards and patents*, SCP/13/2, 2009 p. 31 (point 126).
127. This is a common perception. See for instance Contreras, Jorge L., *Rethinking RAND: SDO-Based Approaches to Patent Licensing Commitments*, American University – Washington College of Law, ITU Patent Roundtable, Geneva, 2012 p. 3 and Kühn, Kai-Uwe, Morton, Fiona Scott & Shelanski, Howard, *Standard Setting Organization Can Help Solve the Standard Essential Patents Licensing Problem*, in CPI Antitrust Chronicle, March 2013 (special issue) p. 3.
128. Also see Bekkers, Rudi & West, Joel, *IPR Standardization Policies and Strategic Patenting in UMTS, in Telecommunications Policy*, Vol. 33 (1-2), 2009 pp. 93–96, where it is noted that although several proposals for reform of ETSI's IPR policy have been made by stakeholders the IPR policy remains largely unchanged. According to the authors the "*[t]he difficulty of addressing what is perceived to be a major problem suggests that ETSI has difficulty achieving consensus on more specific IPR policies across the broad range of ETSI member interests*".
129. Also see Eltzroth, Carter, *IPR Policy of the DVB Project: Negative Disclosure, FR&ND Arbitration Unless Pool Rules OK Part 1*, in International Journal of IT Standards and Standardization Research, Vol. 6(2), 2008 p. 25.
130. ETSI, *Guidelines for Antitrust Compliance*, 27 Jan. 2011, Point C.4.2. Available at: http://www.etsi.org/about/iprs-in-etsi.

seen as attempts to fix royalty rates or other terms.[131] The absence of SSO guidelines to aid in the interpretation of FRAND means that competition authorities and courts will play an important role in infusing the notion with meaning.

The fact that many SSO polices contain similar, although not identical, mechanisms to prevent patent-holdup is not surprising. Many of the most influential companies participating in standard setting activities are active worldwide and carry with them prior experiences to new organizations – resulting in a convergence of IPR policies.[132] Moreover, the regulatory landscape, including the Commission's Horizontal Guidelines, likely contributes to this trend by setting out requirements relating to the IPR policies of SSOs. Requiring patentees to issue a FRAND commitment as a precondition for having their patents included in the standard is for instance a way for SSOs to comply with competition law and avoid their organization being viewed as facilitating (illegal) cartel behaviour. In other words, both commercial and regulatory considerations act to shape SSO policies worldwide.

131. As noted in Ch. 9 s. §9.03[D] Disclosure of licensing terms unilateral disclosures of license terms are however permitted under the competition rules and *ex ante* discussions of license terms may potentially be permitted, but subject to a case-by-case assessment.

132. Also see *Brooks, Roger G. & Geradin, Damien, Interpreting and Enforcing the Voluntary FRAND Commitment*, in International Journal of IT Standards and Standardization Research, Vol. 9(1), 2011 pp. 7–8 and Eltzroth, Carter, IPR Policy of the DVB Project: Negative Disclosure, FR&ND Arbitration Unless Pool Rules OK Part 1, International Journal of IT Standards and Standardization Research, Vol. 6(2), 2008 p. 28, where it is stated that DVB's work on its IPR policy was influenced by the parallel activity undertaken within ETSI.

CHAPTER 10
Patent Ambush

As noted in Chapter 9 section §9.03[C] SSOs typically require participants to disclose their potentially SEPs *ex ante*, i.e., before the standard is adopted. Indeed, standardization agreements must require such disclosure in order to benefit from the safe-harbour set out in the Horizontal Guidelines.[1] The purpose of the disclosure obligation is two-fold. Firstly, it serves to promote transparency in the standard setting process so as to ensure that participants are able to make informed decisions on which technologies to include in the standard. Having been informed that a particular technology is subject to patent rights participants may elect to 'circumvent' the patent by altering the draft technical specification underpinning the standard under development or, if the patented technology is deemed the best available option, procure a FRAND commitment from the patentee. Secondly, as patent disclosures establish the basis for procuring FRAND commitments from the patentees identified they also form part of the toolbox aimed at preventing patent holdup, i.e., they aid in ensuring the availability of licenses *ex post* and in preventing patentees from exploiting their market power to demand excessive or discriminatory royalties. Thus, although FRAND commitments, as explained in Chapter 9 section §9.03[E], are of a contractual nature they complement competition law by increasing chances that the pro-competitive benefits of standardization prevail – in particular, they make it possible to sanction the anti-competitive use of injunctions under Article 102 TFEU.[2]

Acknowledging that the disclosure of SEPs or patent applications entails a risk that the SSO initiates evasive manoeuverers to the benefit of non-proprietary technologies SSO participants (who also inhabit the role as patentees) may have an interest in deliberately concealing their patents until work on the standard reaches a point of no return; that is, until the market becomes 'locked-in' to the standard and the patentee

1. See Ch. 9 s. §9.03[B] for more details on the disclosure requirement.
2. See Ch. 13 in this respect, where the possibility of raising a competition law defence against a SEP holder seeking an injunction is discussed.

gains market power.[3] Ignoring SSO disclosure requirements may in effect subvert the standard setting process and unduly increase the market power of patentees by persuading the inclusion of patents which would otherwise have been deselected had other SSO participants been properly informed of their existence.[4] In the words of the Commission a 'patent ambush':

> is a system failure of the standard-setting process. It occurs when a company taking part in the standard-setting process hides the fact that it holds essential Intellectual Property Rights (IPRs) over the standard being developed, and starts asserting such IPRs only after the standard has been agreed and other companies are therefore 'locked in' to using it.[5]

As explained below deceptive conduct which merely allows a non-dominant patentee to obtain market power does not by itself fall within the ambit of Article 102 TFEU, but the subsequent licensing practices engaged in by the patentee once dominant may potentially be deemed abuse in light of earlier conduct – subject to strict preconditions however.[6] Thus, EU competition law does not provide the legal basis for sanctioning such conduct unless it can be shown that (1) it actually lead to the exclusion of technologies which provided a better cost/benefit ratio and (2) in effect the license terms imposed *ex post* are non-FRAND.[7] The evidentiary burden faced by the Commission or any private litigant applying Article 102 TFEU in this context is therefore high. As the analysis of the *Rambus* case below reveals the Commission itself seems to have acknowledged that patent ambush well seldom raise liability under Article 102 TFEU. A representative from the Commission has been cited saying:

> where a non-dominant SSO member intentionally conceals a patent that reads on the ultimate standard, and thereby becomes dominant as a result, [it] is difficult to say liability arises under Article 82...The only apparent area for Article 82 liability might arise if the IP holder applies unfair license terms, engages in excessive pricing or refuses to license in order to monopolize a downstream market.[8]

3. The effects which may lead to such 'lock-in' were discussed in Ch. 8 s. §8.01.
4. Also see Pappalardo, Kylie & Suzor, Nicolas, *Standardisation and patent ambush: Potential liability under Australian competition law*, Competition & Consumer Law Journal, Vol. 18, 2011 p. 271.
5. Commission press release in Case COMP/38.636, *Rambus*, MEMO/09/544 (Commission accepts commitments from Rambus lowering memory chip royalty rates – frequently asked questions), 9 Dec. 2009.
6. See for instance OECD, *Policy Roundtables – Excessive Prices 2011*, DAF/COMP(2011)18, 2012 p. 310 where the Commission notes that Art. 102 TFEU "*...only applies to abusive conduct of firms already having a dominant position. This means that there may be cases where intervention against unilateral exclusionary conduct is legally not possible. In such cases intervention against exploitative conduct may be the only possibility to effectively protect consumers. An example could be action taken against the charging of excessive royalties by a company who has obtained its dominant position as a result of not disclosing its patent when it was involved in discussions on setting a standard for the industry.*"
7. As noted below the first criterion marks a diversion from established case law that there is no need for an anti-competitive practice to succeed in order for Art. 102 TFEU to apply.
8. Hockett, Christopher B. & Lipscomb, Rosanna G., *Best FRANDs forever? Standard-Setting Antitrust Enforcement in the United States and the European Union*, In Antitrust, Vol. 23(3), 2009 p. 23.

In addition it is important to note that the disclosure standard is one of 'good faith' for which reason the lack of disclosure cannot be condemned on an objective basis – there needs to be evidence that the patentee acted contrary to its good faith obligation by either deliberately or negligently concealing its patent interests. As set out by the Commission's Horizontal Guidelines the "*...IPR policy would need to require* good faith disclosure, *by participants, of their IPR that might be essential for the implementation of the standard under development*" and SSO participants are only required to engage in "*reasonable endeavours to identify IPR reading on the potential standard*" [emphasis added].[9] As noted in Chapter 9 section §9.03[C] the Commission does not expect participants to carry out patent searches and few (if any) SSO policies mandate such searches.[10] Thus, while abuse is generally an objective concept which does not rest on proof of anti-competitive intent the Commission seems to recognize that the SSO context requires evidence supporting – if not intent – then at least negligent behaviour.

The Commission's position in this respect seems appropriate and also necessary to safeguard effective competition, hence can be expected to be accepted by the CJEU. It is important to appreciate that standard(s) development within the framework of an SSO is a lengthy process often involving several draft proposals and that SSO participants (often engineers or the like) may not possess the knowledge necessary to identify all their employers patents (or patent applications) of potential relevance.[11] Indeed, as stated in the Common Patent Policy of ISO, IEC, ITU proposals for technical standards "*...are drawn up by technical and not patent experts; thus, they may not necessarily be very familiar with the complex international legal situation of intellectual property rights such as Patents*".[12] Arguably, obliging SSO participants (or SSOs) to identify all relevant IPR by means of patent searches would constitute a disproportionate measure to prevent patent hold-up, since the complexity and costs associated with such searches may delay the standard setting process and/or discourage rights holders from taking part in standard setting activities.

The 'good faith' standard was also relied on by the Commission in the *Rambus* case which provides a good basis for discussing the challenges faced by the Commission in applying Article 102 TFEU in patent ambush scenarios. Indeed, as the CJEU have not yet dealt with patent ambush the Commission's provisional finding in that case represents the only basis for discussing the EU approach with regard to patent ambush.

9. Communication from the Commission, *Guidelines on the applicability of Article 101 of the Treaty on the Functioning of the European Union to horizontal co-operation agreements*, OJ 2011/C 11/1, 14 Jan. 2011, § 286. Note that identifying specific IPR is not required – it is, according to the Commission, sufficient that the SSO participant "*declares that it is likely to have IPR claims over a particular technology (without identifying specific IPR claims or applications for IPR)*".
10. See Ch. 9.
11. Lévêque, François & Ménière, Yann, *Technology standards, patents and antitrust*, in Competition and Regulation in Network Industries, Vol. 9(1), 2008 p. 39.
12. The ISO/IEC/ITU Common patent policy has been adopted by CEN and CENELEC (ESO's). See CEN-CENELEC Guide 8, *Guidelines for Implementation of the Common IPR Policy on Patent (and other statutory intellectual property rights based on inventions)*, 3rd ed., December 2011, Annex 1 (The ISO/IEC/ITU Common patent policy – march 2006).

§10.01 RELEVANT LEGAL TEST

On 30 July 2007, the Commission sent a Statement of Objections (SO) to Rambus in which it expressed its preliminary view that Rambus had violated Article 102 TFEU (then, Article 82 EC) by claiming unreasonable royalties subsequent to a patent ambush.[13] The case was initiated following allegations by DRAM-chip manufacturers Hynix and Infineon that Rambus, during its participation in JEDEC (a US based SSO focusing on developing world wide standards in the field of semi-conductors) had contravened JEDEC's patent policy by failing to disclose patents essential to the SDRAM standard.[14] The Commission's preliminary finding of abuse took place just months after the Federal Trade Commission (FTC) had found Rambus' conduct to constitute illegal monopolization contrary to section 2 of the Sherman Act (as noted below the FTC's decision was later overturned by the U.S. Court of Appeals for the District of Columbia Circuit). However, the Commission on 15 January 2010 decided to shelve the case for lack of community interest having made Rambus' commitments to cap its royalty rates binding pursuant to Article 9(1) of Regulation 1/2003.[15] More specifically, Rambus agreed to claim no royalties with regard to the standards (SDR and DDR DRAM) that were adopted during the time in which Rambus was a member of JEDEC and to cap its royalty rates at 1.5% of the selling price for the subsequent standards which built on top of those first generation standards and likewise included Rambus' technology.

From the perspective of legal certainty the Commission's predilection for relying on Article 9 commitments to settle cases is unfortunate and may send the wrong signal to SSO participants that their 'sins' can be forgiven, hence incentivize abusive conduct due to the absence of risk.[16] However, while the Article 9 decision issued by the

13. Commission press release in Case COMP/38.636, *Rambus*, MEMO/07/330 (Commission confirms sending a Statement of Objections to Rambus), 23 Aug. 2007.
14. The complainants also alleged that the patent ambush had rendered the relevant JEDEC standardization agreement illegal, cf. Art. 101(1) TFEU, since the unintended inclusion of Rambus' patent rights resulted in a anti-competitive closed standard rather than an open standard as envisaged; see Case COMP/C-3/38.636, *Rambus*, 15 Jan. 2010, §§ 7-9 (rejection decision). The Commission however found it unlikely that such infringement could be established – and with good reason. If the standardization agreement itself does not contain provisions likely to result in anti-competitive effects a subsequent unilateral abuse by individual patentees contrary to the spirit of the agreement arguably does not suddenly render the agreement illegal. The legality of standardization agreements is discussed in more detail in Ch. 9 s. §9.03.
15. Commission decision in Case COMP/C-3/38.636, *Rambus*, 15 Jan. 2010. The decision to reject Hynix's complaint (prior to the decision Infineon had withdrawn its complaints) was made pursuant to Art. 7(1) of Regulation 773/2004 of 7 Apr. 2004 relating to the conduct of proceedings by the Commission pursuant to Articles 81 and 82 of the EC Treaty. Hynix appealed the decision to the General Court, but the Case (T-149/10, *Hynix Semiconductor v. Commission*, 5 Jun. 2010) was subsequently withdrawn following settlement agreement between Rambus and Hynix.
16. For a critical view of the Commission's use of Art. 9 decisions see Botteman, Yves & Patsa, Agapi, *Towards a more sustainable use of commitment decisions in Article 102 TFEU cases*, in Journal of Antitrust Enforcement, 2013 (not yet published). Available at: http://antitrust.oxfordjournals.org/content/early/2013/08/13/jaenfo.jnt009.full. On 3 Mar. 2013 Joaquín Almunia, Vice President of the European Commission responsible for Competition Policy, stated that

Commission does not contain an in-depth and fully-reasoned legal assessment it nonetheless provides some indications as to how the Commission intends to deal with patent ambush. As discussed in section §10.01[A] and §10.01[B] below the Commission seemed to apply a two-step test affirming, what was highlighted in Chapter 9; that deception is not by itself actionable conduct under Article 102 TFEU.[17]

[A] Step 1: Establishing Deception *Ex Ante*

The Commission considered that an intellectual property holder would act in bad faith if aware that its IPRs read on a standard under development without drawing the SSOs attention to them.[18] In particular, the Commission held, it would force competitors to accept higher licensing fees than those which could have been negotiated at an earlier stage before adoption of the standard.[19] This of course presupposes that there were substitute technologies competing for inclusion in the standard prior to its adoption as else there is no basis for concluding that *ex ante* negotiations would have led to lower royalty rates, i.e., there would have been no competitive pressure *ex ante* incentivizing the patentee to accept a reduction in royalties. In the absence of competing technologies a patent ambush would also be an unlikely scenario as it is motivated largely by a desire to exclude rival technologies. However, as the deceptive practices of Rambus were found to have resulted in the exclusion of competing non-proprietary technologies the Commission did not comment on these aspects. Nonetheless, for the reasons stated in section §10.01[C] it is safe to conclude that deception does not fall within the ambit of Article 102 TFEU in case it did not result in competing technologies being excluded.

According to the Commission the JEDEC patent policy, and the underlying duty of good faith, stipulated that "*...all members were required, or at the very least expected, to disclose to JEDEC any and all issued or pending patents of which they were aware*" if of relevance to work carried out in JEDEC – the purpose being to allow for the adoption of patent-free standards and, if not a viable solution, to at least obtain FRAND assurances.[20] Despite its provisional conclusion that Rambus may have breached JEDEC's patent policy by concealing its patent interests it was nonetheless stressed that

"*[o]ut of 41 decisions taken by the Commission, we have had 15 prohibitions and 26 commitments*" since Regulation 1/2003 entered into force – see SPEECH/13/210. Hopefully this track record does not extend into the field of standards where market players, as illustrated by this dissertation, are in dire need of better guidance. Although, in addition to the Rambus case, the Commission in 2009 closed formal proceedings into Qualcomm's pricing policy (presumed to be unreasonable) as complaints were withdrawn (MEMO/09/516), the most recent case initiated against Samsung on basis of its exercise of SEPs to seek injunctions seem to indicate a more stringent approach. Thus, despite the fact that Samsung on 12 Dec. 2012 announced its intent to withdraw all injunctions in Europe the Commission found this not to alter its "*preliminary conclusions about the anti-competitive nature of Samsung's conduct*" – see MEMO/12/1021.

17. Cf. also Hockett, Christopher B. & Lipscomb, Rosanna G., *Best FRANDs forever? Standard-Setting Antitrust Enforcement in the United States and the European Union*, in Antitrust, Vol. 23(3), 2009 p. 23.
18. Commission decision in Case COMP/C-3/38.636, *Rambus*, 9 Dec. 2009, § 32.
19. *Ibid.*
20. *Ibid.*, at §§ 36–38.

such breach should generally not be considered a precondition for finding abuse under Article 102 TFEU.[21] Thus, according to the Commission, the duty to act in good faith, and accordingly to disclose potentially SEPs in a timely manner, is inherent in the standard setting process. Establishing a violation of Article 102 TFEU was therefore held merely to require evidence that the conduct in question "*...necessarily distorted the decision making process within a standard-setting body*".[22] In other words, establishing that the deception evidenced has produced exclusionary effects with regard to competing technologies is sufficient (and as mentioned above, seems necessary) to establish abuse.

In this respect the parallel US proceedings provides a contrasting example. Thus, the US court petitioned to review the FTC's decision in *Rambus* cited the Federal Circuit for saying that JEDEC's patent policies suffered from a "*staggering lack of defining details*" and the FTC's own conclusion that the policies "*are not a model of clarity*".[23] Accordingly, the court held that "*...the more vague and muddled a particular expectation of disclosure, the more difficult it should be for the Commission to ascribe competitive harm to its breach*".[24] While clear disclosure rules may aid in supporting a view that the patentee acted in bad faith the Commission arguably will be able to succeed arguing before the CJEU that this aspect is not material to a finding of abuse under Article 102 TFEU. Thus, abuse is an objective concept which does not require a finding of intent.[25] Although patentees (as noted in Chapter 9 section §9.03[C]) are not expected to perform thorough patent searches and delegates participating in SSOs need not have knowledge of all patents possessed by their employer the Commission's finding intuitively makes sense. For the reasons outlined in Chapter 10 it is generally well-known to SSO participants that disclosures are important in the context of collaborative standard setting activities even absent an express provision in this respect. Therefore, a finding of abuse within the meaning of Article 102 TFEU is not conditioned on breach of contract, but of a finding that the conduct in question objectively has as its purpose or effect to harm competition – this leaves room to take into consideration the unwritten expectations of SSO participants. According to the Commission Rambus was well aware of its obligation to disclose patents and patent applications which might be relevant to the standard under development by JEDEC.[26]

[B] Step 2: Establishing Abuse *Ex Post*

As noted above the Commission found that Rambus had deliberately subverted the standard setting process within JEDEC by withholding information regarding patents (and patent applications) later claimed to be essential to the implementation of the standard adopted – the purpose, it was claimed, had been to 'capture' the standard for

21. *Ibid.*, at § 39.
22. *Ibid.*
23. Case No. 07-1086, *Rambus Incorporated v. Federal Trade Commission*, 22 Apr. 2008 p. 22.
24. *Ibid.*
25. See for instance Case 85/76, *Hoffmann-La Roche v. Commission*, 13 Feb. 1979, § 91. The importance of intent is discussed in more detail in Ch. 11 s.§ 11.02[A].
26. Case COMP/C-3/38.636, *Rambus*, 9 Dec. 2009, §§ 40–42.

DRAM interface technology.[27] As part of this strategy Rambus had allegedly tailored its pending patent applications on an on-going basis in order to ensure that the patents, once granted, would cover the standard.[28]

In the Commission's preliminary view Rambus did succeed with its strategy of capturing the standard. Indeed, the Commission considered that a broad range of substitute technologies were at play during the standard setting phase and that absent Rambus' deceit JEDEC members would likely have adopted a standard free of patents since evidence suggested that they favoured low costs over performance.[29] However, although the deceptive tactics engaged in by Rambus were found to have caused the exclusion of substitute non-proprietary technologies from the DRAM standard (hence was anti-competitive) the Commission did not hold the deceptive conduct in itself to constitute abuse. Rather the Commission found that the abuse consisted in claiming royalties at a level which absent the alleged deceptive conduct it had not been possible to charge, i.e., focus was directed at the license terms imposed by Rambus *ex post.*[30]

While at first sight this may seem peculiar there is a good explanation. Indeed, Rambus arguably did not hold a dominant position until after JEDEC adopted the SDRAM standard which embodied its patents and rendered them essential to manufactures of SDRAM chips. As follows from the wording of Article 102 TFEU the provision prohibits the abuse of a dominant position once acquired, but does not sanction the mere acquisition of such position. As Rambus allegedly acquired its dominant position by deceit, but did not hold such position at the time of deceit Article 102 TFEU therefore did not establish the requisite legal basis for sanctioning Rambus' subversion of the standard setting process. Indeed, the objective of SSO participants to postpone patent disclosure is generally to *obtain* market power by persuading SSOs to include patents which otherwise would have been deselected and accordingly this scenario is not unique to the Rambus case, but will be of importance in any case concerning allegations of patent ambush. Arguably the Commission was well aware that Article 102 TFEU did not provide the basis for finding the deceptive practices engaged in by Rambus abusive and accordingly made use of its 'creative' skills to tailor a line of argumentation aimed at circumventing the problem of establishing dominance *ex ante*. As the Commission itself reasoned in *AstraZeneca* "*...it is the date of the implementation of the conduct capable of restricting competition which must be taken as the starting point of the abuse...*" it is clear that considering the deception itself to constitute abuse would have left Rambus of the hook.[31]

The FTC did not face the same challenges as the Commission because Section 2 of the Sherman Act, in contrast to Article 102 TFEU, forbids unlawful monopolization. Accordingly, the FTC did not lack the legal basis for finding the deception itself to be illegal. Thus, it was argued that Rambus had illegally obtained monopoly power, because absent deception its patents would have been excluded from the standard – on

27. *Ibid.*
28. *Ibid.*
29. Case COMP/C-3/38.636, *Rambus*, 9 Dec. 2009, §§ 43–46.
30. *Ibid.*, at § 28.
31. Case T-321/05, *AstraZeneca v. Commission*, 1 Jul. 2010, § 332.

appeal the Court of Appeals for the District of Columbia Circuit however disagreed as there was insufficient evidence to support the accusation.[32]

[C] Standard of Proof

As explained in section §10.01[B] finding a patent ambush abusive under Article 102 TFEU is conditional on a finding that the patentee charges non-FRAND royalties after the standard is adopted. Having found sufficient evidence that the patentee intentionally or negligently deceived during the standard setting process the question therefore is how to determine whether royalties charged *ex post* are indeed non-FRAND. Two approaches comes to mind – either (1) any royalty rate charged following a patent ambush is simply presumed non-FRAND whereas the burden of proof shifts to the patentee *or* (2) it must be established that absent the deceptive conduct the SSO would have chosen alternative solutions or negotiated a lower royalty rate prior to adoption of the standard.

Clearly a finding of deception is not sufficient in itself to consider any royalty charged *ex post* as being non-FRAND. The Commission bears the burden of proof that anti-competitive effects have or are likely to materialize as a result of the patentee's deceit and must substantiate its assessment in this respect.[33] Reversing the burden of proof having merely established deception would in essence relieve the Commission of the burden of proving abuse, because as already explained such must be established by reference to conduct carried out when the patentee held a dominant position – that is, typically after the standard is set. Therefore, there can be little doubt that the Commission (or any other plaintiff in private litigation) is required to establish a connection between the impact of the deceit *ex ante* (when the patentee was not dominant) and the royalty level charged *ex post* (when the patentee acquired a dominant position).[34] In proving this connection it seems that three conditions must be fulfilled:

- *Firstly*, it must be established that technologies which were commercially viable from a cost/benefit perspective competed for inclusion in the standard adopted at the time of deceit.
- *Secondly*, it must be established that the deceit was likely to have caused the exclusion of these technologies – or in other words, that absent the deceit the SSO would likely have considered including them on basis of cost/benefit considerations.
- *Thirdly*, it must be established – by reference to the technologies deemed to have been excluded – that the level of royalties claimed *ex post* would likely have been lower had it not been for the deceit discovered.

32. See Case No. 07-1086, *Rambus Incorporated v. Federal Trade Commission*, 22 Apr. 2008 p. 11.
33. Regulation 1/2003 of 16 December 2002 on the implementation of the rules on competition laid down in Articles 81 and 82 of the Treaty, Art. 2.
34. From the perspective of competition policy one might question this finding and indeed it might on balance be preferable if the burden of proof shifted once a finding of deception had been made. However, under the current legal regime there seems to be no room for such approach.

The first criterion has already been touched upon in section §10.01[A]. Obviously, a patent ambush, being an exclusionary strategy, is unlike to take place if viable competing technologies are not at play at the time of the standard setting activities. Moreover, absent alternatives there is basis for concluding neither that lower royalties could have been obtained through *ex ante* negotiations nor that the technological composition of the standard adopted would have been different, but for the deceit.

The second criterion at a glimpse may seem to conflict with settled case law. Thus, Article 102 TFEU covers behaviour which is aimed at or capable of achieving anti-competitive effects, regardless of its success, and therefore does not require proof that the technological composition of the standard adopted was actually impacted by the patentees deceitful conduct.[35] Even if an attempt to capture a standard by means of deception is obstructed by the SSO, or for other reasons do not lead to the exclusion of competing technologies, this accordingly does not by itself leave out the possibility of applying Article 102 TFEU. However, as already explained deceit is not in itself actionable conduct under Article 102 TFEU insofar as the patentee was not (which will most often be the case) dominant at the time of its conduct. Put simply, as abuse must be established with reference to an impact *ex post* arguably it is necessary to render probable that the deceptive conduct in question lead to the exclusion of alternative (and cheaper) technologies, because absent such finding there is no frame of reference for deciding whether royalties claimed ex post are non-FRAND. From a practical perspective such finding may for be based on records of the discussions which took place within the SSO at the time of deceit or other documents, such as the IPR policy, which are able to substantiate that the objective was to adopt a cost effective (or even royalty free) standard. In *Rambus* for instance the Commission in its preliminary view considered JEDEC had as its objective to adopt an 'open standard' free of proprietary technologies and that cost reductions were favoured over performance improvements.[36]

The third criterion concerns the market impact. As was the case in *Rambus* it must be established that the royalties claimed *ex post* are non-FRAND in light of the patent ambush. Absent a patent ambush the Commission, as discussed in Chapter 11 section §11.01, suggests calculating whether royalties are fair and reasonable by reference to the royalties (or other fees) claimed by the SEP holder prior to adoption of the standard. However, in light of a patent ambush such calculation may take place – not by reference to the patentee's own historical prices – but to the price of the next best alternative which was excluded from the standard due to the patentee's deceptive conduct. In for instance a royalty free or non-proprietary standard have been excluded any royalty claimed may be deemed non-FRAND under such approach.

35. Case T-321/05, *AstraZeneca v. Commission*, 1 Jul. 2010, §§ 356–361 (in particular).
36. Commission decision in Case COMP/C-3/38.636, *Rambus*, 9 Dec. 2009, § 38.

[D] Relevant Remedies

It follows from Regulation 1/2003 that the Commission has the power to impose "*…any behavioural or structural remedies which are proportionate to the infringement committed and necessary to bring the infringement effectively to an end*".[37] However, it is not evident how to remedy a patent ambush. Thus, once a patentee through deceptive tactics succeeds in having its patents embodied in a standard there is no going back – whatis done cannot be undone. Therefore, any remedy must necessarily relate to the licensing practices of the patentee *ex post* the aim being to reflect the outcome which would have resulted from competition between substitute technologies *ex ante*, but for the patentee's deceit.

Bearing in mind that a patent ambush has the effect of deriving the market the comfort of the FRAND commitments which would have been obtained in case of disclosure the licensing practices of an undertaking found guilty hereof at the very least must be treated under Article 102 TFEU as if such commitment had been issued. Most notably, this has the effect of severely limiting the possibility of seeking injunctions on basis of the patents concealed during the standard setting process (in this respect see Chapter 13). In addition only two remedial options are on the table. Either the patents in question are held unenforceable against manufactures of standard compliant products *or* the threshold for finding a royalty rate excessive in light of a patent ambush is lowered so as to somehow compensate manufactures.[38]

The former option can quickly be dismissed. Thus, it would be disproportionate if per se a patent ambush had the effect of rendering the patents concealed unenforceable – in essence it would entail considering any royalty claimed subsequent to a patent ambush as being non-FRAND. There are no indications that the Commission intends to impose such remedy in case of patent ambush and it seems unlikely that the CJEU would find it to adhere to the principle of proportionality as set out in Regulation 1/2003. Rather the Commission in *Rambus* argued along the lines of the second option and considered the market impact brought about by Rambus' deceptive tactics. Thus, having found that the patent ambush might have resulted in the exclusion of non-proprietary technologies *ex ante* the Commission found it proportionate that Rambus would abstain from claiming any royalties covering the SD and DDR standards developed at the time of deceit.[39] However, the Commission found the effects of the alleged abusive behaviour to have impacted the follow-on DDR standards – DDR2 and DDR3 – as well. With regard to these standards the Commission accepted a royalty cap of 1.5% of the selling price as being proportionate likely because the effects the patent ambush had on these standards was more uncertain. However, to the extent that a subsequent revision of a standard is likely to follow the technology-path established by

37. Regulation 1/2003 of 16 December 2002 on the implementation of the rules on competition laid down in Articles 81 and 82 of the Treaty, Art. 7(1).
38. The meaning of the notion fair and reasonable in general is discussed in Ch. 11.
39. See Case COMP/C-3/ 38 636, *Rambus*, 9 Dec. 2009, §§ 49–50 (commitments decision). Also see Commission's press release in Case COMP/38.636, *Rambus*, MEMO/09/544 (Commission accepts commitments from Rambus lowering memory chip royalty rates – frequently asked questions), 9 Dec. 2009.

standard established in the shadows of deceit (in order to ensure backwards compatibility) it may however be possible to establish that such follow-on standard has been impacted to the same extent as the original revision of the standard, i.e., in such case there is no reason why the royalty implications should not extent to subsequent versions as well.

§10.02 SUMMARY

Competition law only requires SSO members to perform good faith disclosures of SEPs and not to actually search their patent portfolios for such patents and issue a negative declaration that they have none. This means that the Commission faces a high burden of proof in patent ambush cases, since it must be established that the SSO member being scrutinized acted in bad faith.

Even if it can be proved that the patentee acted in bad faith by deliberately concealing its patent interests this will not be sufficient for the conduct to have implications under Article 102 TFEU. Article 102 TFEU only prohibits the abuse of an *existing* dominant position and not the *acquisition* of such position by deceit or otherwise. Unless it can be showed that the patentee held a dominant position at the time of its deceit the deceptive conduct itself therefore does not fall within the ambit of Article 102 TFEU. If evidence of a patent ambush can be procured Article 102 TFEU may however play a (limited) role in restraining the licensing practices of the patentee in question after the standard is adopted.

First, proof of deceptive conduct *ex ante* arguably will establish a licensing obligation *ex post* under Article 102 TFEU similar to that arising from a FRAND commitment. In this respect note that mere participation in an SSO does not establish a licensing obligation pursuant to competition law.

Second, if a patentee fails to disclose its patent rights and said failure is found (i) to be a breach SSO disclosure rules, and (ii) to have impacted the technological composition of the standard adopted, then (in light of earlier conduct) in principle Article 102 TFEU can be applied to ensure that the license fees charged does not exceed those which would have prevailed, but for the deceit. However, in this respect the evidentiary burden faced by the Commission is especially hard to overcome, since it must be showed, not only that the patentee contravened disclosure rules, but also that competing technologies were excluded from the standard and that the proprietors of these technologies would have licensed them for a lower fee.

In conclusion; Article 102 TFEU is ill-suited to deal with patent ambush issues. SSOs accordingly should not lean back and expect competition law to provide remedies if a patentee carries out a patent ambush, but introduce contractual safeguards in their IPR policies. These safeguards may for instance take the form of stricter disclosure obligations than those required under Article 101(1) TFEU and/or so-called 'licensing-by-default' obligations according to which participants must license all rights which have not disclosed and individually exempted from the licensing obligation.

PART V Exercise of Essential Patents

CHAPTER 11
Non-FRAND License Terms

As explained in the previous chapters, the IPR policies of SSOs typically require members to issue FRAND commitments as a precondition for having their patents embodied in the standards adopted – not least because this allows them to benefit from a rebuttable presumption of legality according to the Horizontal Guidelines (see Chapter 9 section §9.03). The purpose of the Commitment is to ensure that IPR holders do not exploit the market power gained once a standard is adopted and the market becomes 'locked-in' to impose upon licensees unreasonable or discriminatory license terms to the detriment of the success of the standard concerned and effective competition. However, while there can be little doubt that refusing to license FRAND-pledged patents will satisfy the criteria for finding abuse as set out in the *Microsoft* test discussed in Chapter 12 it is more unclear whether licenses actually granted pursuant to such pledge must satisfy a stricter legal test under Article 102 TFEU than is the case with regard to patents which the patentee has not pledged[1] to license on FRAND terms. Does FRAND have any autonomous meaning in this respect or is it merely a reminder of the principles forming part of established EU case law?

Although the acronym FRAND has evolved in the context of standardization it covers a well-known concept of competition law which has been enshrined in Article 102(a) and (c) TFEU in which unfair and discriminatory trading practices, respectively, are mentioned as examples of prohibited abuse. The FRAND concept (although not the acronym) was introduced in EU case law as early as 1978 when the CJEU passed its judgment in the *United Brands*[2] case where it *inter alia* found the charging of unfair

1. If such agreement was not reached due to the patentees deceit of the SSO there is basis for concluding that the patentees licensing practices *ex post* will be assessed as if an agreement had been entered into. In this respect see Ch. 10 where the ability of Art. 102 TFEU to deal so-called 'patent ambush' was discussed.
2. Case 27/79, *United Brands v. Commission*, 14 Feb. 1978. Also see Case 26-75, *General Motors v. Commission*, 13 Nov. 1975.

(excessive) and discriminatory prices to violate Article 102 TFEU (then, Article 86 EC).[3] Although the specifics of standardization must be taken into consideration it is clear that the FRAND concept is to be construed in light of established case law pertaining to other areas of commerce.[4] Indeed, as noted in section §11.01 below, the Commission in its Horizontal Guidelines relies on the reasoning applied by the CJEU in *United Brands*[5] when stating that "*...the assessment of whether fees charged for access to IPR in the standard-setting context are unfair or unreasonable should be based on whether the fees bear a reasonable relationship to the economic value of the IPR*".[6]

The purpose of this Chapter 11 is to explore in more detail the likely licensing implications of a FRAND commitment under applicable EU case law bearing in mind the legal framework applicable in general and the specific context of formal standardization. The prohibition against unfair and unreasonable license terms is analysed in section §11.01, whereas the prohibition against discriminatory licensing is analysed in section §11.02. As explained there seems to be a basis for concluding that the overall legal regime applicable outside the FRAND context applies within that context as well, i.e., novel legal criteria are not called for. On the other hand the factual circumstances underpinning formal standard setting activities are likely to have special implications when 'reasonableness' and 'fairness' is to be assessed under the existing legal regime.

§11.01 [FR]AND: FAIR AND REASONABLE LICENSE TERMS

Although a central part of the FRAND regime it is unclear exactly which implications the 'fair and reasonable' component of FRAND has under Article 102 TFEU. The reluctance to attempt any precise definition of 'fair and reasonable' is however not surprising. Competition law is packed with imprecise legal terms (such as 'abuse', 'distortion of competition' and 'exceptional circumstances') which are infused with meaning on a case-by-case basis depending on the economic context in which they are applied. This most often leads to the development of overall legal frameworks rather than precise rules.[7]

3. Cf. also Meibom, von Wolfgang & Nack, Ralph, *Patents without injunctions? – Trolls, Hold-ups, Ambushes, and Other Patent Warfare*, in Wolrad Prinz zu Waldeck et al. (eds.), Patents and Technological Progress in a Globalized World, Springer, 2009 p. 507.
4. The Commission in its Horizontal Guidelines states that "*...high royalty fee can only be qualified as excessive if the conditions for an abuse of a dominant position as set out in Article 102 of the Treaty and the case-law of the Court of Justice of the European Union are fulfilled*". See Communication from the Commission, *Guidelines on the applicability of Article 101 of the Treaty on the Functioning of the European Union to horizontal co-operation agreements*, OJ 2011/C 11/1, 14 Jan. 2011, § 269.
5. In Case 27/79, *United Brands v. Commission*, 14 Feb. 1978, § 250, the CJEU similarly stated that "*...charging a price which is excessive because it has no reasonable relation to the economic value of the product supplied...*" amounts to abuse. Also see case 26-75, *General Motors v. Commission*, 13 Nov. 1975, § 12.
6. Communication from the Commission, *Guidelines on the applicability of Article 101 of the Treaty on the Functioning of the European Union to horizontal co-operation agreements*, OJ 2011/C 11/1, 14 Jan. 2011, § 289.
7. The General Court in Case T-167/08, *Microsoft Corp v. Commission*, 27 Jun. 2012, § 84, stated that "*...the use of imprecise legal concepts in making rules, breach of which entails the civil,*

As explained below the CJEU and the Commission have suggested various methods which may be of relevance to determine whether the price charged by a dominant undertaking is unfair and unreasonable (excessive), but legal certainty remains an issue. However, establishing very clear and strict criteria (while improving legal certainty) may unduly restrict the freedom of companies to operate their business and/or the possibility of the Commission to cope with anti-competitive conduct. Indeed, in the context of formal standards the Commission has noted that:

> [it] is not feasible or appropriate to be more specific as to what constitutes 'fairness' or 'reasonableness' since these are subjective factors determined by the circumstances surrounding the negotiation. If the rightholder is to be satisfied that his investment in research and development can be adequately recovered, he would expect the royalty rate to relate in some way to the normal freely negotiated commercial rate, allowing for the greatly increased market for his technology which standardization will bring.[8]

The latter part of the citation indicates that the royalty should somehow reflect a 'freely negotiated commercial rate' and not be so excessive as to prohibit diffusion of the standard concerned.When assessing whether license terms are fair and reasonable (as well as non-discriminatory - see section §11.02) a number of factors must be taken into consideration, including the specific license terms agreed, the risks incurred by the licensor and the value of the technology being licensed. Indeed, the licensor will have multiple reasonable royalty rates to choose from within the boundaries of 'fair and reasonable' and those boundaries will change depending on the context at hand. This has been recognized by the General Court.[9]

Often participants in SSOs will find little interpretative guidance as to the meaning of FRAND by turning to SSO policies.[10] As noted in Chapter 9 section §9.03[E][3] SSOs have generally abstained from adopting any rules or guidelines as to the understanding of FRAND – most often explicitly stating that license terms must be negotiated on a bilateral basis outside the framework of the SSO.[11] Absent any

administrative or even criminal liability of the person who contravenes them, does not mean that it is impossible to impose the remedial measures provided for by law, provided that the individual concerned is in a position, on the basis of the wording of the relevant provision and, if need be, with the help of the interpretation of it given by the courts, to know which acts or omissions will make him liable" (also see § 91). It is open to question whether indeed the legal frameworks developed allows the individual concerned to know which acts or omissions will make him liable – not least, as set out below, in the context of the FRAND requirement.

8. Communication from the Commission, *Intellectual Property Rights and Standardisation*, COM(92) 445 Final, 27 Oct. 1992, point 4.3.3.
9. See *supra* note 8 at § 95, where the Court states that "*Microsoft is, on the other hand, right to maintain that several rates may be covered by the notion of 'reasonable remuneration rates'*". At § 120 the Court also notes that subject to the prohibition against discrimination "*...the 2004 decision remains neutral as regards the possibility for each of Microsoft's potential licensees to enter into an agreement with Microsoft adapted to its business model*".
10. Indeed, on basis of interviews with a number of stakeholders in SSOs a report in 2009 revealed that there was no agreement as to how [F]RAND should be interpreted. See Fraunhofer Institute for Communication System and Dialogic, *Study on the Interplay between Standards and Intellectual Property Rights (IPRs)*, OJEU S136 of 18 Jul. 2009, 2011 p. 78.
11. While not all SSO polices have been investigated as part of this dissertation it is expected that this approach has been adopted by most (if not all) SSOs. Thus, as mentioned in Ch. 9 s. §9.03[E][3]

interpretative guidance the notion 'fair and reasonable' remains imprecise and without any substantial meaning. This of course increases the risk of disputes between SEP holders and those seeking a license for the purpose of achieving compliance with a standard as to what exactly constitute fair and reasonable license terms. Such disputes eventually may end up on the table of competition authorities or courts insofar as licensees (if the terms are accepted) or would-be licensees (if the terms are rejected) claim the license terms imposed to violate Article 102 TFEU. As explained in Chapter 13, there is also a tendency that infringers of SEPs seek to rely on competition law as a defence in injunction proceedings claiming that they had been willing to take a license on FRAND terms, but that the SEP holder insisted on non-FRAND terms.

That being said, it is in any event necessary to distinguish the contractual implications of a FRAND commitment from those arising under Article 102 TFEU. Although SSO policies may act to minimize the risk of anti-competitive effects and disputes *ex post* standardization they are not by themselves able to ensure that Article 102 TFEU issues will not arise. As noted by the Commission when opening formal proceedings against Qualcomm "*...a finding of exploitative practices by Qualcomm in the WCDMA licensing market contrary to Article 82 of the EC Treaty may depend on whether the licensing terms imposed by Qualcomm are in breach of its FRAND commitment*".[12] However, as indicated by the Commission's language - in particular the phrase "*may depend on*" - contractual compliance with FRAND commitments will not automatically guarantee competition law compliance. Indeed, even if SSO policies were to contain elaborate definitions of FRAND such definition, as agreed between SSO members, would not necessarily be FRAND *vis-àis* non-members. In this respect it must be recalled that the interests of SSO members cannot be presumed always to be aligned with those of the public, let alone in harmony with effective competition.[13] Moreover, note that excessive pricing accusations in the context of SEPs - as evidenced by the *Microsoft*[14] case which concerned IPR essential to a de facto standard - are not conditional on the patentee having issued a FRAND commitment to an SSO. Disputes may also arise with regard to patents which have not been FRAND-pledged in which case there will be no contractual obligations upon the patentee.[15] As mentioned by way of introduction (section §11.01) the FRAND concept is no alien outside the context of formal standardization.

SSOs generally abstain from defining FRAND or interfering in licensing negotiations out of fear that they may otherwise be accused of cartel like behaviour in violation of competition law.

12. Commission press release in Case COMP/39.247, *Texas Instruments / Qualcomm*, MEMO/07/389 (Commission initiates formal proceedings against Qualcomm), 1 Oct. 2007. The case was eventually closed following withdrawals of the complaints lodged with the Commission - see Commission's press release in Case COMP/39.247, *Texas Instruments / Qualcomm*, MEMO/09/516 (Commission closes formal proceedings against Qualcomm), 24 Nov. 2009.
13. See along the same lines Farrell, Joseph et al., *Standard Setting, Patents, and Hold-Up*, in Antitrust Law Journal, Vol 74(3), 2007 p. 658.
14. Case T-167/08, *Microsoft Corp v. Commission*, 27 Jun. 2012.
15. Note however, that if the patentee participates in the SSO in question and it can be proven that the absence of a FRAND-commitment is attributable to a 'patent ambush', i.e., a deliberate concealment of patents during the standard setting process, it may arguably be possible to impose a FRAND-commitment as a remedy under Art. 102 TFEU - see the discussion in Ch. 10.

The analysis carried out below seeks to reveal which criteria the Commission and the CJEU rely upon to determine whether a royalty is unfair and unreasonable within the meaning of Article 102(a) TFEU and whether the threshold for finding abuse is lower in light of a FRAND commitment. The question as to what constitutes a fair and reasonable royalty is best answered in the negative, i.e., by seeking to extract from case law the legal framework used to determine whether royalties (or other license terms) are unfair and unreasonable.

[A] The Prohibition against Excessive Pricing

The CJEU has consistently held that restraining the exercise of IPRs is only warranted in 'exceptional circumstances' since the right to exclude constitutes the very subject matter of an exclusive right.[16] This is not to say that IPRs, including patents, are immune to intervention under Article 102(a) TFEU. As noted by the Court in Case 238/87, *AB Volvo v. Erik Veng*, which concerned a refusal to license certain design rights related to spare parts, "*...the exercise of an exclusive right...may be prohibited by Article 86 if it involves, on the part of an undertaking holding a dominant position, certain abusive conduct such as ... the fixing of prices for spare parts at an unfair level*".[17] With regard to Motorola's potential abuse of FRAND-pledged patents to seek injunctions EU competition commissioner Joaquin Almunia in a press release also stressed that "*[t]he protection of intellectual property is a cornerstone of innovation and growth. But so is competition*".[18] This was a clear signal that the freedom to exercise IPRs is not unlimited.

According to the wording of Article 102(a) TFEU, a dominant firm that imposes "*unfair purchase or selling prices or other unfair trading conditions*" may be subject to liability. Relying on the market power conferred by SEPs to impose unfair or unreasonable royalties (excessive royalties) may therefore constitute abuse regardless of whether the SEP holder has issued a FRAND commitment – in effect the prohibition contained in Article 102(a) TFEU applies in the context of both de facto standards and formal standards. However, although there is clearly a legal basis for intervening against excessive royalties there have until date been no CJEU judgments or Commission decisions where a royalty rate charged by a patentee has been condemned as excessive. Indeed, relatively few excessive pricing cases have in general been dealt with under Article 102 TFEU. This is likely attributable to the practical difficulties

16. See Case 238/87, *AB Volvo v. Erik Veng*, 5 Oct. 1988, §§ 8–9, Joined cases C-241/91 P and C-242/91 P, *Radio Telefis Eireann (RTE) and Independent Television Publications Ltd (ITP) v. Commission* (Magill), 6 Apr. 1996, § 50, Case T-198/98, *Micro Leader Business v. Commission*, 16 Dec. 1999 § 56, Case C-418/01, *IMS Health v. NDC Health*, 29 Apr. 2004 §35 and Case T-201/04, *Microsoft Corp v. Commission*, 17 Sep. 2007, § 691.
17. Case 238/87, *AB Volvo v. Erik Veng*, 5 Oct. 1988, § 9.
18. Commission press release in Case COMP/39.985, *Motorola – Enforcement of GPRS standard essential patents*, MEMO/13/403 (Commission sends Statement of Objections to Motorola Mobility on potential misuse of mobile phone standard-essential patents- Questions and Answers), 6 May 2013. The case is discussed in Ch. 13 s. §13.02[C][2].

facing the Commission in proving a price excessive as well as considerations that capping prices may reduce the incentives of undertakings to innovate.

As to the practical difficulties these are plenty. It is in general very difficult to determine, in a non-arbitrary manner, what constitutes an excessive price.[19] Doing so requires an appropriate benchmark against which the price being scrutinized can be compared and an idea of how much the price may legally deviate from the benchmark for it to be considered excessive. This is no different in the context of SEPs. If for instance the pricing of comparable technologies is used as a benchmark it is necessary (1) to determine to what extent the value of said technologies differs from the licensed technology being scrutinized, (2) whether the comparable technologies in question are being licensed in a different commercial setting and in the affirmative the resulting impact on royalties, and (3) having established a 'level playing field' (if possible at all) to decide whether the difference between the benchmark and the price being investigated is substantial enough to support a case under Article 102(a) TFEU bearing in mind that bilateral license negations may yield different outcomes. The difficulties highlight why the application of Article 102(a) TFEU to excessive prices is prone to error and may risk doing more harm than good – as explained below restraining the ability of dominant undertakings to recoup costs may be detrimental to innovation.

Speaking of innovation, one of the common objections against applying Article 102 TFEU to regulate prices is that it may be detrimental to innovation, hence also to consumer interests, because it creates uncertainty as to whether investments in R&D can be effectively recouped. In the words of the US Supreme Court:

> [t]he mere possession of monopoly power, and the concomitant charging of monopoly prices, is not only not unlawful; it is an important element of the free-market system. The opportunity to charge monopoly prices – at least for a short period – is what attracts 'business acumen' in the first place; it induces risk taking that produces innovation and economic growth.[20]

Such reasoning also echoes in the EU. The Commission has for instance acknowledged that "*...high profits may often be the result of superior innovation and risk taking, which should not be penalized as this would work as a disincentive to innovate and invest*".[21] This holds true in the context of standardization as well.[22] Indeed, SEP holders may have invested substantial resources in developing the patented technologies due to the prospect of having them included in a formal standard. Fear of upsetting the delicate balance between investment and reward may explain in part why there has been no cases concerning the abusive pricing of patents – after all patents have as their primary purpose to encourage such investments.

19. Also see Whish, Richard & Bailey, David, *Competition Law*, 7th ed., Oxford University Press, 2012 p. 719, and Mariniello, Mario, *European Antitrust Control and Standard Setting*, Bruegel Working Paper, 2013 p. 13.
20. *Verizon Communications Inc. v. Law Offices of Curtis V. Trinko*, LLP, 540 U.S. 398, 407 (2004).
21. OECD, *Policy Roundtables – Excessive Prices 2011*, DAF/COMP(2011)18, 2012 p. 311.
22. Cf. also Mariniello, Mario, *European Antitrust Control and Standard Setting*, Bruegel Working Paper, 2013 p. 13.

Another source which may cause competition authorities to exercise restraint is the perception that the 'market failure' evidenced by the presence of excessive royalties will 'self-correct' and therefore does not warrant competition law intervention. Economic theory predicts that, depending on market barriers, the prospect of earning high profits will attract market entry and the resulting increase in competition will put a downwards pressure on prices.[23] However, in this respect it must be noted that once a standard is established and has become widely diffused – especially if network effects are at play (see Chapter 8 section §8.01[B]) – there may be impenetrable barriers to the market. Accordingly, the likelihood that the market will correct itself in due course should not be exaggerated.

In any event it is important to appreciate that the issues outlined above relate to competition policy and that from a strictly legal point of view such reasoning does not shield dominant patentees from intervention. In the *Microsoft* case (see Chapter 12) it was for instance unsuccessfully argued in Microsoft's defence that the Commission's finding of abuse and the imposition of a periodic penalty was "*...a source of risk and uncertainty which will discourage innovation to the detriment of the consumer*".[24] Indeed, the risk of distorting incentives exists in all cases where Article 102 TFEU is applied to constrain the exercise of IPR (and market power in general), but this has not kept the Commission at bay.[25] Nonetheless, it seems fair to expect that excessive pricing cases will remain relatively scarce.[26]

Excessive pricing may be purely exploitative in nature, i.e., aimed at increasing royalty revenue, or may have as its purpose (often in combination with a discriminatory licensing scheme)[27] to exclude certain licensees from the downstream product market on which the licensor has a presence itself. In either case consumer welfare is

23. Whish, Richard & Bailey, David, *Competition Law*, 7th ed., Oxford University Press, 2012 p. 718. Also see OECD, *Policy Roundtables – Excessive Prices 2011*, DAF/COMP(2011)18, 2012 p. 313, where the Commission notes that capping profits by use of Art. 102 TFEU may undermine the markets own mechanism to restore competition.
24. Case T-167/08, *Microsoft Corp v. Commission*, 27 Jun. 2012, § 77.
25. Also see the Commission's statement in OECD, *Policy Roundtables – Excessive Prices 2011*, DAF/COMP(2011)18, 2012 p. 311. In Case T-201/04, *Microsoft Corp v. Commission*, the argument that a compulsory license would harm Microsoft's incentives to innovate was for instance rejected by General Court which recalled that there is basis for applying Art. 102 TFEU to issue compulsory license in exceptional circumstances and that the presence of IPR does not in itself constitute an objective justification for refusing to license insofar as such exceptional circumstances exist. See Case T-201/04, *Microsoft Corp v. Commission*, 17 Sep. 2007, §§ 688–712.
26. Also see Taffet, Richard, *Further Reflections on the Impact of the EC Horizontal Cooperation Guidelines on Intellectual Property Rights and Innovation*, in CPI Antitrust Chronicle, Vol. 2, 2011 p. 6, who in the context of SEPs and excessive pricing notes that *"a fair reading of the Guidelines in connection with issues of "hold up" and "excessive pricing" suggests that the circumstances giving rise to a violation of Article 102 should be quite limited and, before any conclusion of a violation can be made, a full assessment of competitive effects will be necessary."*
27. Although not always the case (for instance if combined with a 'margin squeeze') a licensor seeking to exclude competitors by demanding excessive royalties will most often have an interest in licensing its own downstream operation at 'arms length', i.e., at a non-excessive price, so as distort competition and put competitors at a relative disadvantage. In such case the licensing scheme is not only unreasonable, but also discriminatory, and in effect two distinct types of abuses are committed – with regard to discriminatory licensing reference is made to s. §11.02.

at stake. In the former case consumers are prejudiced by having to pay a premium for standard compliant products (assuming that licensees are able to pass on their licensing costs) whereas in the latter *indirect* harm will come from the fact that the intensity of downstream competition decreases alongside innovation and product diversity. However, in the words of the Commission, the "*...balance in the EU over the last 50 years has been tilted towards addressing exclusionary conduct, to prevent that exclusionary conduct leads to market conditions which allow exploitation of consumers, rather than intervening directly against exploitative conduct*".[28] Although Article 102 TFEU can be applied to sanction conduct which is directly exploitative of consumers this statement underlines that excessive pricing is most likely to catch the attention of the Commission if it forms part of an exclusionary strategy.[29] It is also clear from case law and policy documents that the Commission's primary focus is not on exploitative abuses, such as excessive pricing, but on exclusionary abuses aimed at foreclosing market access or eliminating competitors.[30]

[B] Legal Test

Overall the purpose of any legal test applied within the ambit of Article 102(a) TFEU is to ascertain whether the dominant undertaking makes use of its market power to reap benefits which it would not have been possible to achieve had there been, in the words of the Court, "*normal and sufficiently effective competition*".[31] Thus, the overall benchmark is the hypothetic royalty rate which would have been offered had it not been for the SEP holder's dominant position. This supports the Commission's reasoning that the reasonableness of a royalty rate imposed *ex post* (after a standard is adopted) may be decided by comparing it to the royalty rate imposed *ex ante* (before the standard was adopted) where competition between substitute technologies was still intact - presupposing of course the patentee licensed its patents prior to adoption of the standard concerned. This test, which is arguably the one most reliable to substantiate a finding of abuse, is discussed in Chapter 11 section §11.01[E].

The legal test generally relied upon as a basis to determine whether a price is excessive was established in the 1978 *United Brands* case, but as noted below the test has since been elaborated upon and modified to better fit the IPR context. In *United*

28. OECD, *Policy Roundtables – Excessive Prices 2011*, DAF/COMP(2011)18, 2012 p. 312.
29. See for instance Case 6/72, *Continental Can v. Commission*, 21 Feb. 1973, § 26, where it is stated that Art. 102 TFEU (then, Art. 86 EC) "*...is not only aimed at practices which may cause damage to consumers directly, but also at those which are detrimental to them through their impact on an effective competition structure*". Also see Whish, Richard & Bailey, David, *Competition Law*, 7th ed., Oxford University Press, 2012 p. 321.
30. Cf. also Geradin, Damien, *Abusive pricing in an IP licensing context: An EC competition law analysis*, paper prepared for the 12th EU Competition Law and Policy Workshop: A Reformed Approach to Article 82 EC, European University Institute, 2007 p. 9. In this respect note that the Commission's guidance on enforcement priorities published 3 Dec. 2008 concerns only exclusionary conduct - see Communication from the Commission, *Guidance on the Commission's enforcement priorities in applying Article 82 of the EC Treaty to abusive exclusionary conduct by dominant undertakings*, OJ 2009/C 45/02, 24 Feb. 2009.
31. Case 27/76, *United Brands v. Commission*, 14 Feb. 1978, § 250. Also see Case 26/75, *General Motors v. Commission*, 13 Nov. 1975, § 249.

Brands the Court held that "...*charging a price which is excessive because it has no reasonable relation to the economic value of the product supplied*..." will constitute abuse.[32] This reasoning has also been applied in cases dealing with the pricing of IPRs[33] and (as already noted) is relied upon by the Commission in the Horizontal Guidelines in relation to SEPs.[34] The question of course is how to assess objectively the 'economic' value of an asset (such as a patent) and how to determine whether the price (royalties etc.) charged 'bears a reasonable relationship' to said value. In *United Brands* the Court considered that one way of doing so would be to determine:

(1) whether the difference between the price charged and the costs of supply is excessive; and
(2) in the affirmative whether the price charged is unfair in itself or when compared to competing products.[35]

The test devised by the Court in *United Brands* makes clear that a price cannot be considered excessive merely because there is a high profit margin – as provided by the second criteria it must somehow also be unfair.[36] Indeed, in some subsequent cases (see below) profits have not been taken into consideration at all. This is not to be seen as contrary to the *United Brands* case, since the court stressed that other ways of determining whether a price bears a reasonable relationship to the economic value of an asset may also be applied if relevant.[37]

As to the first criteria the Court accepted that there may be "...*considerable and at times very great difficulties in working out production costs which may sometimes include a discretionary apportionment of indirect costs and general expenditure*...".[38] This acknowledgement is not without relevance, since patents (and other IPRs) are often associated with high upfront costs stemming from investments in R&D, but low marginal costs of supply (licensing costs). As allocating fixed R&D costs, including the costs of failed projects, with any precision is close to impossible, cost based measures are unfit for deciding whether the royalties requested by SEP holders are excessive. This has been acknowledged by the Commission which in its Horizontal Guidelines

32. Case 27/76, *United Brands v. Commission*, 14 Feb. 1978, § 250. Also see Case 26/75, *General Motors v. Commission*, 13 Nov. 1975, § 12, Case 226/84, *British Leyland v. Commission*, § 27, and Case T-198/98, *Micro Leader Business v. Commission*, 11 Dec. 2008, § 54.
33. See Case C-52/07, *Kanal 5 v. STIM*, 11 Dec. 2008, § 29. In Case T-167/08, *Microsoft Corp v. Commission*, 27 Jun. 2012, this guiding principle was applied to mean that a price will only be reasonable if it bears a reasonable relationship to the innovative character of the technology being licensed. The case is analysed in s. §11.01[C].
34. Communication from the Commission, *Guidelines on the applicability of Article 101 of the Treaty on the Functioning of the European Union to horizontal co-operation agreements*, OJ 2011/C 11/1, 14 Jan. 2011, § 289.
35. Case 27/76, *United Brands v. Commission*, 14 Feb. 1978, § 252.
36. Also see Case COMP/A.36.568/D3, *Scandlines Sverige AB v. Port of Helsingborg*, 23 Jul. 2004 where the Commission, referring to the United Brands case stated that "...*even if it were to be assumed that the profit margin of HHAB is high (or even 'excessive'), this would not be sufficient to conclude that the price charged bears no reasonable relation to the economic value of the services provided.*"
37. Case 27/76, *United Brands v. Commission*, 14 Feb. 1978, § 253.
38. *Ibid.*, § 254.

state that "*[i]n principle, cost-based methods are not well adapted to this context because of the difficulty in assessing the costs attributable to the development of a particular patent or groups of patents*".[39] Leaving profits aside which factors may be of relevance in determining whether a royalty is excessive?

As to the second criteria of the *United Brands* test the Court did not elaborate on the notion 'unfair', but indicated that the price of competing products may be a factor of relevance. In the context of IPR this means that the price of comparable technologies - whether patented or not - may be considered a benchmark able to substantiate a finding that a royalty scheme is abusive. However, although recent case law supports the relevance of such criteria (as explained in section §11.01[C]) it is important to note that the price charged by an IPR holder according to the *Parke, Davis* judgment is not to be deemed abusive merely because providers of comparable non-patented technologies charge lower prices.[40] As explained by Advocate General Mischo "*[t]his appears to mean that 'the inventor' is entitled to recover not only his production costs in the strict sense and a reasonable profit margin but also his research and development expenditure*".[41] This statement was made in light of the *Parke, Davis* judgment which stressed that a comparison between the price of a patented and a non-patented product does not suffice to prove abuse, but arguably the reasoning extends to comparisons between different patented products (or technologies) as well. The costs associated with developing patented technologies are not uniform and therefore cost divergences may explain why one patented technology is being licensed at a lower rate than another. Accordingly, relying on comparisons with other technologies as a basis for finding a royalty rate (or other licensing conditions) excessive is not sufficient to establish a violation of Article 102(a) TFEU. Moreover, any such comparison must take into consideration to what extent the business models of the licensors are equivalent – comparing the remuneration charged by a vertically integrated patentee with the one charged by a pure upstream company for instance would be like comparing apples to oranges. While the former earns an income on both the technology and the product market the latter must recoup all R&D costs through licensing, i.e., on the technology market.

Perhaps acknowledging that using comparable technologies as a benchmark is often inappropriate the Commission in its Horizontal Guidelines instead highlights that the royalty rates charged for the *same IPR* in other comparable standards may provide

39. Communication from the Commission, *Guidelines on the applicability of Article 101 of the Treaty on the Functioning of the European Union to horizontal co-operation agreements*, OJ 2011/C 11/1, 14 Jan. 2011, § 289. Also see Case T-167/08, *Microsoft Corp v. Commission*, 27 Jun. 2012, § 144, where the General Court finds that "... *fixed development costs are not ... a correct basis for valuing intellectual property*".
40. Case 27/79, *Parke, Davis v. Probel*, 29 Feb. 1968 p. 72, where it is stated that "...*a higher price for the patented product as compared with the unpatented product does not necessarily constitute an abuse*".
41. Opinion of Advocate General Mischo delivered 21 Jun. 1988 in Case 238/87, *AB Volvo v. Erik Veng*, 5 Oct. 1988.

an indication as to whether the rate being scrutinized is FRAND compliant.[42] Performing a comparison with prices charged in relation to other standards may seem a sensible approach, since it avoids the issue of diverging R&D costs outlined above. Assuming that the patent in question is actually embodied in several standards such comparison may be of particular relevance if one of the standards is subject to competitive pressure (from other standards or non-standardized technologies) while the other is not, since then the royalty rate divergence identified, all things being equal, may be taken to reflect solely the patentees market power. Thus, a SEP holder cannot objectively justify charging a higher royalty rate with regard to a standard (A) by reference to the fact that another standard (B), in relation to which the patent in question is also being licensed, is subject to more intense competition from other standards or licensors. Such argument will to the contrary substantiate that the royalty rate relating to standard A is excessive, because it reflects the market power of the licensor – in this respect see section §11.01[C] where the distinction between 'intrinsic value' and 'strategic value' is discussed.

Making comparisons for the purpose of establishing whether a royalty is excessive is however not without difficulties. Thus, transactions cannot be considered equivalent merely because they revolve around the same patent – licensing transactions are context sensitive. When performing comparisons between different licensing transactions it is therefore necessary to eliminate from the equation the price impact attributable to for instance diverging risks, cross-licensing arrangements and covenants provided by the licensor before drawing any conclusions. A valid comparison, as hinted by the Commission, also requires the standards to be 'comparable'. The Commission does not provide any guidance in this respect, but it seems reasonable to conclude that for standards to be deemed 'comparable' they (1) must relate to the same or at least similar product markets and (2) concern the same or similar product features, since otherwise economic or commercial conditions may differ to such extent that the basis for a consistent and valid comparison vanishes. If for instance the standards compared relate to different products markets it cannot be ruled out that the patentee has set his remuneration rates to reflect the fact that profit margins differ. This is not necessarily to be considered a reflection of market power, but may simply signify an attempt to recoup investment costs effectively without placing too high costs on manufactures present on 'low profit markets', i.e., the purpose of the high rate may be to compensate for the low rates on other markets, since the latter rates do not allow the patentee to recoup investment costs. Moreover, it may be that a patent, although

42. Communication from the Commission, *Guidelines on the applicability of Article 101 of the Treaty on the Functioning of the European Union to horizontal co-operation agreements*, OJ 2011/C 11/1, 14 Jan. 2011, § 289. It may also be possible to make comparisons with royalty rates charged to other licensees to determine whether these are lower and in the affirmative seek to identify whether there is an objective justification able to explain the difference identified. If no such objective justification exists it may be taken as an indication that the licensor seeks to extract excessive rents from some licensees. Obviously, this issue relates to discrimination which is being discussed in s. §11.02, but since discrimination requires a showing that competition is distorted whereas excessive pricing does not, it may be of interest to licensees to supplement a complaint that a royalty is discriminatory with a claim that it is excessive.

essential to several standards, does not contribute equal value to them all and this as well may explain why different rates of remuneration are charged.

While the cases mentioned above provide some guidance as to the factors which may be of importance in evaluating whether a royalty is excessive they only establish a somewhat vaporous legal framework. More recently the General Court has however rubber-stamped a legal test based on valuation principles devised specifically with standard-essential IPRs in mind – the overall principle being that a royalty is excessive if it reflects the strategic value of a technology as opposed to its intrinsic value. This test is discussed in the next section.

[C] Intrinsic versus Strategic Value

The General Court's judgment in case T-167/08, *Microsoft Corp v. Commission*, added some clarification, although as explained below it remains difficult to assess whether a royalty is unfair and unreasonable.[43] The judgment traces back to a decision[44] passed by the Commission in 2004 in which Microsoft was found to have abused its dominant position by refusing to grant competitors access to certain interoperability information (on protocols) deemed to be a de facto standard on the market for work group server operating systems. The Commission's finding of abuse was upheld by the General Court on appeal.[45] In accordance with the Commission's 2004 decision Microsoft was accordingly ordered to provide its competitors on said market access to the information in question and to authorize its use on reasonable and non-discriminatory conditions for the purpose of developing interoperable work group server operating system products.[46] In response Microsoft began licensing interoperability information as well as patents allegedly reading on the technology underlying the protocols concerned. Focusing on what Microsoft had been able to charge prior to its acquisition of a dominant position – the Commission stressed that the remuneration rate charged by Microsoft should "*... not reflect the strategic value stemming from Microsoft's market power in the client PC operating system market or in the work group server operating system market*".[47] However, the Commission subsequently found that Microsoft had failed to license said information on FRAND terms and therefore imposed a periodic penalty payment on Microsoft – the aggregate value of the penalty was set out in a decision adopted by the Commission in 2008 and amounted to EUR 899 million.[48] Although the decision concerned solely the interoperability information being licensed,

43. Case T-167/08, *Microsoft Corp v. Commission*, 27 Jun. 2012.
44. Commission decision C(2004)900 final in Case COMP/C-3/37.792, *Microsoft*, 24 Mar. 2004.
45. Case T-201/04, *Microsoft Corp v. Commission*, 17 Sep. 2007.
46. Commission decision C(2004)900 final in Case COMP/C-3/37.792, *Microsoft*, 24 Mar. 2004, Art. 5(a).
47. *Ibid.*, § 1008(ii). As noted above the same line of reasoning has found its way to the Horizontal Guidelines where the royalties charged prior to the acquisition of market power is held to be a good indicator of whether the royalties subsequently charged are excessive.
48. Commission decision C(2008) 764 final (fixing the definitive amount of the periodic penalty payment imposed on Microsoft Corp. by Decision C(2005) 4420 final) in Case COMP/C-3/37.792 – *Microsoft*, 27 Feb. 2008. The General Court subsequently lowered the fine to EUR 860 million on appeal in Case T-167/08, *Microsoft Corp v. Commission*, 27 Jun. 2012.

and not the patents which allowed for its implementation, the legal test applied (and endorsed by the General Court – see immediately below) was meant to apply universally. Accordingly, it also signals to SEP holders which criteria the Commission may apply to determine whether their license agreements are fair and reasonable.

As a basis for arriving at its finding that the remuneration rates requested were unreasonable the Commission applied a three-step test.[49] Thus, in order to determine whether the remuneration rates reflected "*...value conferred upon a licensee to the exclusion of the strategic value stemming from Microsoft's market power...*" it was assessed:

(1) whether the protocols concerned were Microsoft's own creations or an implementation of a publicly available standard;
(2) whether they were innovative; and
(3) whether comparable technologies were offered at a lower rate, excluding the strategic value that stems from the dominance of any such technologies.[50]

Having established the overall (cumulative) criteria the Commission set the outer boundaries of 'reasonable' by explaining in the negative under what circumstances any remuneration would be deemed unreasonable.

With regard to the *first criterion* the Commission made clear that Microsoft should not be allowed to charge anything for information concerning protocols which were taken from the public domain, e.g., because they were described in a publicly available standard.[51] As noted above the 2008 decision concerned only the remuneration rates relating to the interoperability information licensed and not Microsoft's patents which were also being licensed. The first criterion will obviously be of no relevance in the context of patents, including those reading on a standard, since these are per definition not part of the public domain.

Moving on to the *second criterion* the Commission explained that Microsoft was only entitled to claim remuneration if its protocol technology was innovative in the sense that it was novel (did not form part of the state of the art) and non-obvious to a person skilled in the art.[52] Those acquainted with patent law will recognize these

49. The test was based on pricing principles drawn up following discussions between the Commission and Microsoft – *ibid.*, at §§ 39 and 111. In addition to the three-step test the pricing principles made clear that Microsoft's remuneration would only be fair insofar as it "*enables implementation of the protocols by a licensee in a commercially practicable manner*". The Commission did not comment further on this aspect in its decision. Bearing in mind that the purpose of competition law as set out in Ch. 4 s. §4.02 is to protect consumers, and not competitors as such, it seems appropriate to construe the principle as meaning that a price should not be so high as to obstruct the business of an *efficient* competitor, i.e., if an inefficient competitor is not enabled to compete this may not be attributable to the prices being unreasonable.
50. *Ibid.*, §§ 116–117.
51. *Ibid.*, § 129 read together with § 117. Also see Case T-167/08, *Microsoft Corp v. Commission*, 27 Jun. 2012, § 34.
52. The Commission concluded that the majority (166 out of 173) of the non-patented technology being licensed by Microsoft pursuant to the 2004 decision were not innovative and therefore did not warrant any remuneration at all. See Commission decision C(2008) 764 final (fixing the

criteria as being decisive to the grant of patents. Indeed, as recognized by the General Court, the Commission assessed the innovative character of the protocols on basis of criteria which corresponds to those set out in Articles 54 (novelty) and 56 (inventive step) of the European Patent Convention.[53] Again, it must be recalled that the Commission applied the criteria when assessing the innovative character of Microsoft's *non-patented* protocol technology as disclosed with the licensed technical documentation. This begs the question whether the Commission, for the purpose of applying Article 102(a) TFEU in the context of SEPs, intends to apply these criteria as well and substitute the assessment of novelty and non-obviousness made by the patent office which granted the patents with its own?

In this respect the Commission made clear that it will presume provisionally "*...that the fact that a patent has been granted and has not been found invalid creates a presumption that the ... technology covered by this patent is innovative*".[54] SEP holders therefore need not fear that the Commission begins to second guess the assessment which lead to the grant of their patent as a basis for questioning the whether the royalty rate (or other license terms) imposed by the patentee is appropriate – doing so would not only run counter to the Commission's own statement, but also be contrary to settled EU case law which provides that it is not for the Commission to question the existence (as opposed to the exercise) of an established right.[55] As noted by the Commission itself its position is in line with that of the General Court which has held that:

> it is inherent in the fact that the undertaking concerned holds an intellectual property right that the subject-matter of that right is innovative or original. There can be no patent without an invention and no copyright without an original work.[56]

The first two criteria set out by the Commission were arguably meant to replace the first criteria of the *United Brands*-test (discussed in section §11.01[B]) according to which it had to be determined whether the difference between the price charged and the costs of supply is excessive. Recognizing that supply costs are a poor proxy in relation to IPRs the Commission focused on the value of the technology in terms of innovation instead – if the remuneration charged exceeds the value of the technology in terms of

definitive amount of the periodic penalty payment imposed on Microsoft Corp. by Decision C(2005) 4420 final) in Case COMP/C-3/37.792 – *Microsoft*, 27 Feb. 2008, §§ 175 and 219.

53. Case T-167/08, *Microsoft Corp v. Commission*, 27 Jun. 2012, § 149. The Convention on the Grant of European Patents of 5 Oct. 1973, as amended (European Patent Convention) is available at: http://www.epo.org/law-practice/legal-texts/html/epc/2010/e/ma1.html (last checked 30 May 2014).
54. Commission decision C(2008) 764 final (fixing the definitive amount of the periodic penalty payment imposed on Microsoft Corp. by Decision C(2005) 4420 final) in Case COMP/C-3/37.792 – *Microsoft*, 27 Feb. 2008, § 132.
55. See for instance Joined Cases C-241/91 P and C-242/91 P, *RTE and ITP v. Commission*, 6 Apr. 1995 ('Magill'), § 276, where the Court stressed that "*...determination of the conditions and procedures for granting protection of an intellectual property right is a matter for national rules*". For a more in-depth discussion of the distinction between existence and exercise see Anderman, Steven & Ezrachi, Ariel, Intellectual Property and Competition Law, 2nd ed., Oxford University Press, 2011 p. 129.
56. Case T-201/04, *Microsoft Corp v. Commission*, 17 Sep. 2007, § 695.

innovation it is excessive. Since as noted above the criteria set out in *United Brands* were not meant to be exhaustive there is no conflict between the criteria relied upon by the by the Commission and prior case law. Indeed, as noted below the criteria were endorsed by the General Court on appeal.

As to the *third criterion*, concerning the comparison with other technologies, this is a reflection of the second criterion of the *United Brands*-test according to which a price must be unfair either by itself or in comparison with competing products. As the Commission noted the purpose was to determine whether Microsoft's remuneration rates were *reasonable* in that they were in "*...line with a market valuation of technologies deemed comparable to the protocol technology described in the Technical Documentation*".[57]

Interestingly, the Commission prior to its 2008 decision dismissed a request from Microsoft to specify the exact remuneration rates which would be considered reasonable and non-discriminatory pursuant to the 2004 decision, stating that its role was not to prescribe the precise rates, but to ensure that those set by Microsoft were FRAND.[58] Feeling left in the dark Microsoft decided to appeal the Commission's 2008 decision.

On appeal the General Court had to determine whether the Commission could lawfully impose a periodic penalty without having specified the 'reasonable remuneration rates' which Microsoft was forced to accept pursuant to the 2004 decision and whether the Commission was correct in finding that Microsoft's rates were unreasonable pursuant to the above criteria. With regard to the former the court sided with the Commission stating that there may be multiple[59] reasonable rates of remuneration, depending *inter alia* on the business models employed by the licensees, and it was not for the Commission to choose and impose one specific rate upon Microsoft – it was for Microsoft to self-assess whether its rates of remuneration were reasonable.[60] Thus, the Commission was entitled to impose the penalty in question relying on the above mentioned pricing principles, since according to the General Court they provided "*...cumulative, sufficiently precise criteria that enable Microsoft to assess whether a given technology has an intrinsic value distinct from its strategic value*".[61] The Court's endorsement[62] of the criteria sets an important precedent and provides much needed guidance to SEP holders although as explained below determining whether a royalty is reasonable is still a highly complex task prone to error. Although it remains to be seen whether the Commission will apply the test in future cases this seems a likely scenario bearing in mind that it has been blue stamped by the General Court.

Turning to the question of reasonableness the General Court stressed the need to distinguish between intrinsic value and strategic value as a basis for determining

57. Commission decision C(2008) 764 final (fixing the definitive amount of the periodic penalty payment imposed on Microsoft Corp. by Decision C(2005) 4420 final) in Case COMP/C-3/37.792 – *Microsoft*, 27 Feb. 2008, § 139.
58. *Ibid.*, § 75.
59. The statement highlights that determining whether a royalty rate is reasonable is not an exact science.
60. Case T-167/08, *Microsoft Corp v. European Commission*, 27 Jun. 2012, § 95 (in particular).
61. *Ibid.*, § 87.
62. Also see *Ibid.*, §§ 133–146.

whether the remuneration requested by Microsoft was excessive.[63] In essence the court hereby made clear the IPR specific meaning of the overall principle set out in *United Brands* that a price should bear a reasonable relationship to the economic value of the product sold. A reasonable remuneration reflects solely the intrinsic value stemming from a technology's innovative character whilst the strategic value attributable to for instance network effects (see Chapter 8 section §8.01) or the fact that a technology constitutes a trade secret, according to the General Court, cannot be relied upon to substantiate a claim that a royalty is reasonable.[64] The court did not use the term network effects, but to the same effect stated that Microsoft should not be allowed to charge remuneration rates which reflected the strategic value stemming from "*...the mere ability to interoperate with Microsoft's operating systems*".[65] SEP holders which seek to exploit the success of a standard by increasing their royalty rates after the standard is adopted and the market becomes 'locked-in' therefore cannot evade Article 102(a) TFEU arguing that they increased their royalties merely to reflect the fact that licensees were willing to pay a higher price insofar as said willingness stems from network effects (strategic value) rather the innovative character (intrinsic value) of the licensed technology. The distinction between intrinsic and strategic value guides the application of Article 102 TFEU in excessive pricing cases and underlines that holders of FRAND-pledged patents will not be subject of a special legal standard. It seems reasonable to conclude that the intrinsic value of a patented technology does not diminish merely because it is embodied in a formal standard and there is therefore nothing to suggest that the threshold for finding a royalty rate excessive in light of a FRAND commitment is lower.

So where are SEP holders left in the wake of the Microsoft judgment? Since patented technologies, as noted above, are not publicly available and presumed to be innovative the first and second criteria of the Microsoft-test are of little relevance in this context of SEPs. Thus, faced with task of determining whether royalties charged with such patents are excessive the Commission will have to adopt other methods capable of clarifying whether the royalty scheme, comprising the royalty rate and the royalty base, is excessive in comparison with the innovative character of the licensed technology.[66] It goes without saying that determining the value of a patent is a very challenging task. In this respect note that proof that comparable technologies are offered at a lower rate (the third criterion) is not sufficient to substantiate a finding of abuse on its own – see section §11.01[B].

[D] Expert Assessments

The Commission in the Horizontal Guidelines suggests that another method may be to obtain an assessment from an independent expert regarding the objective centrality

63. *Ibid.*, § 138.
64. *Ibid.*, §§ 143–144.
65. *Ibid.*, § 142.
66. The issues regarding choice of royalty base are discussed in s. §11.01[F].

and essentiality of the relevant IPRs to the standard at issue.[67] However, if indeed the patent is essential such approach in itself cannot substantiate a finding of abuse. Even if the patented technology is found to make only a minor contribution to the standard it will still be necessary to determine how much remuneration that contribution is worth – is there a reasonable relationship between its intrinsic value to the standard and the remuneration demanded by the patentee? Moreover, an expert assessment of the 'centrality and essentiality' may aid in determining whether the remuneration charged is *excessive*, but not whether it is *unfair* in itself or in comparison with other technologies as required by the test set out in the *United Brands* case discussed in section §11.01[B]. As clarified in the *Microsoft* case it must be determined whether the remuneration reflects strategic value attributable to market power. The CJEU's judgments in Microsoft and United brands indicated that it might be possible to determine whether the remuneration is also unfair on the basis of a comparison with the remuneration charged by other patentees who have contributed more significant innovations to the standard in question. However, in order for such comparisons to provide any such indication it is necessary to take into consideration the business model of the patentees to which reference is made. Vertically integrated patentees (those manufacturing standards compliant products), may be inclined to demand lower royalty rates than pure upstream companies (those which do not exploit SEPs themselves), because licensing revenue is not the only source of income on which they can rely to recoup R&D costs.

The strongest case for intervention against excessive remuneration charged by SEP holders is arguably when the patentee increases its royalties *ex post* standardization without any objective justification. This scenario is discussed in the next section.

[E] Comparing *Ex Ante* and *Ex Post* Royalty Rates

As a basis for determining whether the royalty rate charged bear a reasonable relationship to the economic value of the patent licensed, or whether in the words of the General Court in *Microsoft* (see section §11.01[C]) the royalty rate exceeds its 'intrinsic value', the Commission has suggested that it may be possible to compare *ex ante* royalty rates with *ex post* royalty rates.[68] Such method to assessing whether royalty rates are fair and reasonable has also been suggested by some legal scholars.[69] It presupposes that the patent in question was licensed prior to adoption of the standard on the market to which the standard relates and for the purpose of allowing

67. Communication from the Commission, *Guidelines on the applicability of Article 101 of the Treaty on the Functioning of the European Union to horizontal co-operation agreements*, OJ 2011/C 11/1, 14 Jan. 2011, § 290.

68. Communication from the Commission, *Guidelines on the applicability of Article 101 of the Treaty on the Functioning of the European Union to horizontal co-operation agreements*, OJ 2011/C 11/1, 14 Jan. 2011, § 289.

69. See for instance Shaprio, Carl & Varian, Hal, *Information Rules: A strategic guide to the network economy*, Harvard Business School Press, 1999 p. 241, where the author along the same lines finds that "*[r]easonable should mean the royalties that the patent holder could obtain in open, up-front competition with other technologies, not the royalties that the patent holder can extract once other participants are effectively locked in to use technology covered by the patent*".

the licensee to implement features similar to those covered by the standard – otherwise the basis for a valid comparison vanishes. However, if these conditions are fulfilled such comparison arguably establishes a strong basis for determining whether a royalty rate is excessive.

If the patent subject to scrutiny was licensed *ex ante* at a certain rate the licensor must have determined that rate to be sufficient to allow for the costs associated with developing the patented technology to be recouped and to compensate for the risks undertaken in this respect. In other words, there will be a strong presumption[70] that anything in excess of that rate will reflect 'strategic value' attributable to the fact that the market has become 'locked-in'. Some legal scholars have nonetheless questioned the appropriateness of such test arguing that presupposing an increase in royalty rate *ex post* to be supra-competitive and evidence of exploitative behaviour fails to appreciate that given the investments in time, effort and money made by firms participating in formal standard setting activities such increase is to be expected.[71] However, the need to recoup such investment costs by increasing royalty rates should probably not be exaggerated. It must be borne in mind that a patentee which succeeds in having its technology embodied in a standard will greatly (unless already a de facto standard) increase the market share of said technology and the resulting increase in licensing profit will arguably most often be more than adequate to offset the costs incurred participating in the standard setting process within an SSO.

Another argument which puts the validity of the Commission's proposed method in to question has been advanced as well. Thus, as outlined above the method suggested by the Commission rests on the premise that the market power of a patentee is increased when his technology is embodied in a standard and that accordingly any increase in royalties after a standard is adopted (*ex post*) will be indicative of *ex post* opportunism, i.e., an attempt to extract rents in excess of a the technology's intrinsic value. In this respect it has been argued that in the absence of substitute technologies prior to adoption of a standard the inclusion of a patented technology in a standard does not confer upon the patentee additional market power since under such circumstances "*...market power pre-exists the standard and is due to the uniqueness of the technology in question*".[72] If a valid argument it would deprive the method outlined

70. Although difficult to explain such increase in royalty rate it may nonetheless be possible. It may for instance be that the technology was only licensed for a short period prior to adoption of the standard and that the increase *ex post* merely signifies that the licensor did not manage to align prices properly with market evaluation *ex ante*. It is also necessary to take account of the fact that the licensor may have adopted an aggressive pricing strategy *ex ante* in which case an increase to a 'normal level' *ex post* does not indicate abuse of a dominant position.

71. See Layne-Farrar, Anne & Padilla, Jorge, *Assessing the link between standard setting and market power*, 2010 p. 12. Available at: http://dx.doi.org/10.2139/ssrn.1567026 (last checked 30 May 2014). These costs may sometimes be significant. It has been reported that IBM spent more than USD 500 million on standard setting in 2005 – see Blind, Knut et al., *Standard essential patents to boost financial returns*, Paper at the 6th Annual Conference of the EPIP Association, 8–9 September 2011 p. 1 (footnote 4). Available at: http://www.epip.eu/conferences/epip06/.

72. Geradin, Damien, *Abusive pricing in an IP licensing context: An EC competition law analysis*, paper prepared for the 12th EU Competition Law and Policy Workshop: A Reformed Approach to Article 82 EC, European University Institute, 2007 p. 19. See similarly, Richard T. & Stiroh, Lauren J., *Standard Setting and Market Power*, Comments provided for Joint Hearing of the

above its validity in cases where the SEP being scrutinized covers a technology determined to have been unique *ex ante*, since then the link between market power and standardization would be severed. Indeed, if the patentee held market power *ex ante* royalty rates may have been excessive already at that time.

It is arguably true that the proprietor of a unique technology may have held a strong market position (even amounting to dominance) prior to it being part of a standard, but this need not be the case. The fact that a technology is unique, in the sense that it is the only one able to achieve a particular technical result, does not per se confer upon its proprietor market power. Market power does not stem from the fact that a technology is unique, but from the fact that it is subject to inelastic demand. In other words, if the market does not demand compliance with that particular technology uniqueness alone does not allow the patentee to act to an appreciable extent independent of licensees and impose upon them non-FRAND license terms. However, the inclusion of a patented technology – whether unique or not – in a standard will increase the market power of the patentee insofar as the market demands compliance with the standard (and accordingly the technology), since then demand becomes inelastic. It follows that the uniqueness of a technology *ex ante* does not necessarily deprive the method suggested by the Commission its validity – it needs to be determined not if the technology was unique, but if the patentee held market power *ex ante* and whether said market power has increased as a result of the technology becoming embodying in a standard. Such increase in market power does not always result from having a patent embodied in a standard – it may for instance be that the technology formed part of a dominant de facto standard *ex ante* in which case its inclusion in a formal standard may have merely increased its *value* by broadening the market and not its market power.[73]

In conclusion; the *ex ante* – *ex post* method is arguably the one best suited to establish whether royalties are excessive bearing in mind what was concluded in section §11.01[C], namely that 'strategic value' not attributable to the innovative character of a technology must be excluded for the purpose of determining whether royalties are unfair and unreasonable. Arguably a SEP holder will face difficulties explaining why royalty rates were suddenly increased once confirmed that the patent in question read on a technical specification underlying a widely adopted standard.

[F] Royalty Base

As opposed to tangible products which are sold for a fixed price IPRs are most often licensed in return for payment of a royalty rate (typically a percentage) calculated on basis of revenue, turnover or some other royalty base – this fact adds an extra level of complexity. Thus, it entails that the legality of a royalty rate cannot be assessed in

United States Department of Justice and the Federal Trade Commission, Competition and Intellectual Property Law and Policy in the Knowledge-Based Economy, 18 Apr. 2002 p. 13.

73. See along the same lines Layne-Farrar, Anne & Padilla, Jorge, *Assessing the link between standard setting and market power*, 2010 p. 12. Available at: http://dx.doi.org/10.2139/ssrn.1567026 (last checked 30 May 2014).

isolation.[74] A seemingly law rate may very well lead to excessive royalty payments, hence violate Article 102 TFEU, if calculated on basis of a factor which does not adequately reflect the value contributed by the licensed technology – in the words of the Commission and the CJEU the royalty rate would then not bear a "*reasonable relationship to the economic value of the IPR*" licensed.[75]

In *Kanal 5*, a preliminary ruling concerning royalty rates imposed by television broadcast companies, the CJEU held that imposing royalty rates calculated on basis of revenue was in principle reasonable in relation to the economic value of the service provided, since revenue reflected the value of the licensed rights in trade.[76] However, the court added that the proportion of revenue extracted should reflect the actual or likely use of the licensed rights (in that case musical works protected by copyright) as precisely as possible.[77] Accordingly, it was found that "*...in certain circumstances, the application of such a remuneration model may amount to an abuse, in particular when another method exists which enables the use of those works and the audience to be identified and quantified more precisely*", provided that this method does not lead to a disproportional increase in the licensors management costs.[78] The court did not condemn any particular royalty base as illegal, but made a point that the method of royalty calculation should reflect as precisely as possible – to the extent viable – the actual value in trade of the licensed rights. Transposed to the context of SEPs it is therefore clear that the royalty base and the methods of calculation applied must be linked to the value provided by the SEPs licensed.

In the *Microsoft* case it was revealed that Microsoft (which pursuant to a 2004 Commission decision had to license certain rights related to software protocols)[79] calculated its royalties *inter alia* on basis of the licensee's net revenue derived from the sale of products implementing the software protocols.[80] In this respect the General Court, along the lines of *Kanal 5*, noted that the 2004 Decision did not preclude Microsoft from charging remuneration rates which are a proportion of the revenue of the licensees, but added that "*...such rates may be sought only if they represent value other than the strategic value of the technologies in question*".[81] In essence the court

---

74. It may also be difficult to rely on comparisons with other technologies to determine whether a royalty rate is excessive if the rates do not apply to a similar base. If for instance one royalty rate is calculated on basis of sale price per unit and another on basis of revenue it is not possible to directly compare those rates.
75. See s. §11.01[B] above.
76. Case C-52/07, *Kanal 5 and TV 4 v. STIM*, 11 Dec. 2008, §§ 36–37.
77. *Ibid.*, § 41. The amount of royalties collected by the Television broadcast companies varied in accordance not only with the revenue of the television broadcasting companies but also with the amount of music broadcast.
78. *Ibid.*, § 40. Also see Case 395/87, *Ministère public v. Jean-Louis Tournier*, 13 Jul. 1989, § 45, where the court found that "*[t]he fact that a flat-rate royalty is charged can only be criticized by reference to the prohibition contained in Article 86 if other methods might be capable of attaining the same legitimate aim, namely the protection of the interests of authors, composers and publishers of music, without thereby increasing the costs of managing contracts and monitoring the use of protected musical works*".
79. Commission decision in Case COMP/C-3/37.792, *Microsoft*, 24 Mar. 2004.
80. Case T-167/08, *Microsoft Corp v. Commission*, 27 Jun. 2012, § 45.
81. *Ibid.*, § 120.

stressed that the payments made under the royalty scheme should be a reflection of the intrinsic value of the licensed technologies in trade.

The above judgments suggest that there is no such thing as a 'blacklisted' royalty base the use of which will per se violate Article 102 TFEU. A royalty scheme will arguably escape Article 102 TFEU if the royalty rate and the base against which that rate is *applied* ensure a reasonable relationship between the royalties paid and value of the licensed technology in trade.[82] However, some legal uncertainty remains. If for instance a SEP relates only to one particular feature (e.g., WIFI) of a product (e.g., a phone) which, as is often the case, contains multiple features, should the royalty base be set to reflect the value of the specific component (e.g., a chip) facilitating the feature in question or the whole product? To what extent does it make a difference to the application of Article 102 TFEU?

[1] Calculating Royalties on Basis of the 'Smallest Saleable Patent Practicing Unit'

With regard to these questions some interesting submissions were made to the US International Trade Commission (ITC) in connection with a 2012 patent roundtable having as its purpose to allow industry players to share their views on standards SEPs and FRAND licensing.[83] While not related to Article 102 TFEU these submissions (made by major players in the standards arena such as Apple, Nokia, Samsung etc.) nonetheless indicate which issues the Commission and the CJEU may be forced to deal with under that provision in the future. Obviously the views submitted reflect each company's commercial interest in SEPs and it is not unlikely that eventually Article 102 TFEU will be invoked in an attempt to defend those interests.

With regard to the royalty base it is clear from the submissions made to the ITC that some companies interpret FRAND as meaning that royalties must be calculated at the component level while others find such approach unjust and argues in favour of calculating royalties on basis of the average selling price (ASP) of the product. Apple for instance argued, referring to US case law, that royalties should be calculated on basis of the component that practices all or substantially all of the standardized technology ('smallest saleable patent practicing unit') to prevent the patentee from collecting "*...value unassociated with its contribution to the standard...*". According to Apple using the ASP of the end product "*...as the royalty base has the effect of distorting the value of essential patents and discriminating against companies with high value products, like Apple*".[84] The statement of the CJEU in *Kanal 5* (see above), indicating that the royalty base should allow for the use of the licensed technology to be identified and quantified as precisely as possible, seems to support Apple's reasoning in an Article 102 TFEU context. However, while in theory calculating royalties at the

82. As noted by the CJEU in Case C-52/07, *Kanal 5 and TV 4 v. STIM*, 11 Dec. 2008, § 36 "*...royalties must be analysed with respect to the value of that use in trade*".
83. The submissions made to the ITC can be seen at: http://www.itu.int/oth/T065B000034 (last checked 30 May 2014).
84. Apple's submission to the ITC dated 12 Oct. 2012 p. 2.

'component level' will provide the most accurate reflection of the value of the licensed technology there is reason to believe that the use of such royalty base does not necessarily render a royalty scheme less arbitrary - explanation provided below.

As the court stated in *Kanal 5 "...royalties must be analysed with respect to the value of that use in trade"*.[85] This entails that the licensee cannot demand that the relevant component's cost is used as the royalty base.[86] In effect the value contributed by the component in question must be established by reference to its proportional contribution to revenue, selling price or some other measure reflecting the value of the product as a whole. A simplified example will serve to clarify the difficulties associated with such approach:

> A product which sells for EUR 1,000 contains five components. One of these components practices, in the words of Apple, all or substantially all of a standardised technology. There are 5 SEPs reading on the component in question and it can be determined that without the component the product would only sell for EUR 900, i.e. the value of the component in trade is EUR 100.

In the example above it may be argued that the royalty base (if established by reference to selling price) should be EUR 20 per product sold (EUR 100/5 patents), since this reflects the value of the component incorporating the standard. However, such approach is very simplistic and would likely fail to achieve an appropriate balance between the interests of right owners and those of licensees.[87] *First*, this method presupposes that the five SEPs contributes equally in terms of innovation to the features practiced by the component in question, but that may not be the case.[88] *Second*, the method rests on the premise that the EUR 100 reflects the 'intrinsic' - as opposed to the 'strategic' - value of the component to end users. However, it may be very difficult to determine the intrinsic value of a component practicing a standard. Consumers will for instance be reluctant to pay anything for a cell phone not compliant with the 3G (and soon 4G), since the market has become 'locked-in'[89] to this standard. Obviously this does not mean that a FRAND compliant royalty base in such case will be

85. Case C-52/07, *Kanal 5 and TV 4 v. STIM*, 11 Dec. 2008, § 36.
86. This is fortunate since the production cost is a poor proxy of the components value to the product as whole. As (rightly) noted by Nokia in its contribution to the ITC dated 10 October (p. 4) "*...the value of intellectual property cannot always be defined as a fraction of the cost of some physical building blocks required for its implementation, as this would be analogous to forcing prices of software on a disk to be set as a percentage of the cost of the blank media carrying such software*".
87. In this respect note that the court in Case C-52/07, *Kanal 5 and TV 4 v. STIM*, 11 Dec. 2008, § 31, stressed the need to obtain such balance by stating that "*...is appropriate to seek an appropriate balance between the interest of composers of music protected by copyright to receive remuneration for the television broadcast of those works and those of the television broadcasting companies to be able to broadcast those workers under reasonable conditions*".
88. Also see Geradin, Damien & Rato, Miguel, *Can Standard-Setting Lead to Exploitative Abuse? A Dissonant View on Patent Hold-Up, Royalty Stacking and the Meaning of FRAND*, in European Competition Journal. Vol. 3, 2007 p. 140 who note that " *Not all IPR are of equal value. While some cover "earth shattering" inventions, others concern minor evolutions of existing technologies*". See similarly Layne-Farrar, Anne, *Antitrust And Intellectual Property Rights: Assessing The Link Between Standards And Market Power*, in Antitrust, Vol. 21(3), 2007 p. 49.
89. Reference is made to Ch. 8 s. §8.01 for more information on the market characteristics - so-called 'network effects' - which may lead to such consumer 'lock-in'.

the total selling price of the phone,[90] but how to determine the value contributed by the component practicing such standard? This requires seeking recourse to some sort of hypothetical (and error prone) assumption about the value of the licensed technology prior to it becoming part of a standard.

Even if it is possible to establish the value of the component in trade with any certainty this arguably does not entail that using some other royalty base, such as net revenue, will necessarily violate Article 102 TFEU. As noted by way of introduction neither the royalty rate nor the royalty base can be assessed in isolation. As Nokia stated in its submission to the ITC "*...as 1% of a base of 100 leads to the same result as 10% of a base of 10, which royalty structure is actually used has no economic relevance, as long as the result reflects the appropriate value for a license*".[91] This reasoning does not contradict the CJEU's overall reasoning in *Kanal 5* and *Microsoft* that the royalties paid should bear a reasonable relationship to economic value of the licensed rights. Indeed, it may be that a SEP holder who claims royalties based on the perceived value of a component will charge a higher royalty rate than one opting for revenue assuming that both patentees need to recoup the same amount of R&D related sunk costs. This effect has been explicitly acknowledged by the CJEU in *Windsurfing International* where the court was faced with the task of determining the legality of a royalty scheme related to sailboards; defined as an "*apparatus composed of a 'board' (a hull made of synthetic materials equipped with a centre-board) and a 'rig' (an assemblage consisting essentially of a mast, a joint for the mast, a sail and spars)*".[92] The focal point in this respect (other issues were dealt with as well) was whether a provision stating that royalties had to be calculated on the basis of the price of a the complete sailboard regardless of whether licensees sold only a component (the 'rig') constituted a violation of Article 101(1) TFEU (then, Article 85 EC). The CJEU found that not to be the case since "*...licensees acknowledged that it would be equitable to accept a higher rate of royalty once the licensor's remuneration was to be calculated on the price of the rig alone*", i.e., it was shown (in line with Nokia's reasoning) that shifting the royalty base from the sale board as a whole to the component did not result in payment of less royalties since the royalty rate was adjusted accordingly.[93]

[2] Conclusion

Against the above background it seems fair to conclude that neither the royalty rate nor the royalty base can be assessed in isolation – the two are interconnected. In determining whether a remuneration scheme violates Article 102(b) TFEU what matters is whether the royalty rate *and* the royalty base taken together results in the licensee paying remuneration which bears a reasonable relationship to the economic

90. As set out in the *Microsoft* case as analysed in s. §11.01[C] extracting royalties in excess of a technology's intrinsic value (innovative character) will violate Art. 102 TFEU.
91. Nokia's submission to the ITC dated 10 Oct. 2012 p. 4.
92. Case 193/83, *Windsurfing International Inc. v. Commission*, 25 Feb. 1986. § 2.
93. *Ibid.*, §§ 65–66.

value of the licensed technology in trade. This applies regardless of whether the patentee has pledged to license its patent(s) on FRAND terms.

[G] The Aggregate Royalty Level

As noted in Chapter 9 section §9.03[D] competition law does not preclude SSOs from adopting policies which mandate or allow for a unilateral disclosure of licensing terms at an early stage before the standard is adopted. However, SSO policies seldom make use of this option and even if policies allow for *ex ante* disclosure of licensing terms members abstain from actually doing so. Accordingly, there is typically no mechanism in place to ensure that the aggregate royalty burden does not impede the commercialization of standard compliant products.

While under 'normal' circumstances a company is able to control the amount of royalties' payable, by deselecting certain patented features for inclusion in their products, this is not a viable option when a given set of technologies becomes standardized. To the extent that companies present on the downstream market to which a standard relates are forced to comply with the standard due to consumer demand they must obviously license all third-party patents reading on it. Without a cap on aggregate royalties the cost of obtaining licensees for all SEPs may in principle exceed total product turnover (exceed 100%) – hence, prevent commercialization of the standard by companies not fortunate enough to hold SEPs usable as 'bargaining chips' to obtain royalty free cross-licenses.[94] Some have accordingly argued that FRAND should be construed as a commitment to set royalty rates in a way which ensures that the cumulative royalty burden does not exceed a certain (low) percentage of a products sale price.[95] It has for instance been argued that:

> the result of five, or ten, or twenty separately-negotiated 'reasonable' royalties can easily be a single aggregate royalty that is unreasonably high. It is thus critical that, in the context of technical standards, any assessment of the 'reasonableness' of an individual patent holder's royalty rate take into account the overall number of SEPs applicable to a standard and the aggregate royalty burden on the standard.[96]

Others have argued that royalty stacking is not a threat to standardization.[97] However, these discussions have not been rooted in competition law.

---

94. See Lemley, Mark A. & Shapiro, Carl, *Patent Holdup and Royalty Stacking*, in Texas Law Review, Vol. 85, 2007 pp. 2001–2011 and 2025 and Lemley, Mark A. & Shapiro, Carl, *Ten Things to do about Patent Holdups of Standards (and one not to)*, in Boston College Law Review, Vol. 48 p. 150.
95. *Ibid*. Also Miselbach, Roger & Nicholson, Ron, *Determination of Fair and Reasonable Royalty Rates, N&M Consultancy Limited*, 2000, Ch. 6 s. §6.01.
96. Contreras, Jorge L., *Rethinking RAND: SDO-Based Approaches to Patent Licensing Commitments*, American University – Washington College of Law, ITU Patent Roundtable, Geneva, 2012 pp. 14–15. Available at SSRN: http://ssrn.com/abstract=2159749 (last checked 30 May 2014).
97. Fraunhofer Institute for Communication System and Dialogic, *Study on the Interplay between Standards and Intellectual Property Rights (IPRs)*, OJEU S136 of 18 Jul. 2009, 2011 p. 24 (with references). Also see Geradin, Damien, *What's Wrong with Royalties in High Technology Industries?*, TILEC Discussion Paper Series No. 2009-043, 2009, who conclude that the problem of royalty stacking has been exaggerated by focusing solely on the "*…highest cumulative royalty*

From a competition law perspective the question is whether a royalty rate which assessed in isolation is fair and reasonable may be considered abusive, cf. Article 102 TFEU, if the cumulative royalty burden is considered too high to be commercially viable. Neither the CJEU nor the Commission has taken a stance in this respect. However, the question which must be asked in determining if a royalty rate is fair and reasonable from a competition law perspective is not whether the licensor asks for remuneration which prevents the success of the standard or attempts to extract a large share of the cumulative 'royalty-pie', but whether the royalty requested, in the words of the Commission and the CJEU, bears "*... a reasonable relationship to the economic value of the IPR*".[98] The role of competition law is not (and should not be) to dictate the commercial terms which – in the view of policy-makers and courts – ensures efficient commercialization of products, but to prevent conduct which does fall within competition on the merits.Commercial autonomy and the freedom to conduct business as protected by the Charter of Fundamental Rights of the European Union[99] should be maintained as should the prerogative of IPR owners to exercise their rights to claim royalties which in isolation are reasonable. Only such legal standard is able to ensure a proper balance between competition and the incentives to innovate as catered for by intellectual property laws and competition law alike – while in a static perspective capping royalties on basis of the cumulative royalty burden may lower prices of standardized products, the method is not able to guarantee patent proprietors a reasonable return on their investment in R&D, hence may be detrimental to innovation as well as standardization in a dynamic perspective.[100] As noted in Chapter 4 section §4.02 the purpose of competition law is not to promote the ideal of *perfect* competition by focusing only on prices and supply, but to ensure that *effective* competition is prevalent by also safeguarding innovation.

In addition it must be noted that imposing a cap on aggregate royalties on the basis of Article 102 TFEU would deal a serious blow to the legal certainty of SEP holders. Hence, they would be faced with the impossible task of taking into consideration the confidential royalty rates requested by third parties when settings their own license terms (unless the SSO sets an aggregate royalty ceiling) and would also need to assess whether indeed the patents declared essential are essential as a matter of fact.[101]

---

rates (e.g., 30%) paid only by a limited number of industry players". Available at SSRN: http://ssrn.com/abstract=1104315 or http://dx.doi.org/10.2139/ssrn.1104315.

98. See s. §11.01[B].
99. Article 16 of the Charter of Fundamental Rights of the European Union.
100. Also see Dolmans, Maurits, *Standards For Standards*, in Fordham International Law Journal, Vol. 26(1), 2002 pp. 138–140 who argues that seeking to impose a cap on royalties would "*...crush pure innovators for which royalties represent the main or unique source of revenue*".
101. See Layne-Farrar, Anne, *Be My FRAND: Standard Setting and Fair, Reasonable and Non-discriminatory Terms*, 2010 p. 5 noting that " *[t]he numeric proportionality formula is not, however, as simple, as fair, or as reasonable as it might at first seem*", and that "*[r]ather than revolving around the worth of any given patent and the royalties it can command, the uncertainty instead would revolve around whether any given patent was in fact "essential" for the standard at hand*". Available at: http://www.aipla.org/learningcenter/library/papers/SM/2010-Spring-Meeting-Speaker-Materials/Documents/ED_2010_SM_Layne-Farrar_PPR.pdf.

Any attempt to cap aggregate royalties will also give rise to a number of practical difficulties in general. One such difficulty would be determining in a non-arbitrary manner what the royalty ceiling should be.[102] Another would be to allocate royalties between patentees. As already noted not all IPRs are necessarily equally valuable to the standard and not all firms are equally dependent on royalty income. Simply distributing royalties between licensors in proportion to the number of SEPs they contribute to the standard at issue would therefore be detrimental to innovation.[103] The number of SEPs may also change over time and this entails that royalties must be redistributed on an on-going basis.[104]

It is also important to appreciate that the problem of royalty stacking (as opposed to the problem of patent hold-up) cannot be characterized as originating from the exercise of market power – hence is not a problem to be dealt with under Article 102 TFEU. Indeed, royalty stacking may be an issue even if all SEP holders claim the same royalty rate *ex post* as they did in the competitive environment existing before the standard was adopted. Royalty stacking is a problem well-known in the ICT industry (even outside the context of standardization) and stems from 'imperfections' in patent law which allows for the creation of what has been termed the 'patent thicket', i.e., a dense web of overlapping rights which must be hacked (licensed) trough in order to ensure the legitimate commercialization of products.[105] The problem of royalty stacking (if such exists) therefore should be addressed within the boundaries of patent law (or possibly in SSO IPR policies)[106] and not by competition law.

[H] Patent Ambush and Refusals to License

This legal framework set out above is not the only one of potential relevance in excessive pricing cases. To the extent that patents have become essential to a formal standard as result of deceit during the standard setting process – a so-called 'patent ambush' – the reasonableness of the royalties requested by the patentee *ex post*, according to the Commission, may be established taking into consideration the royalty

102. See Layne-Farrar, Anne, *Be My FRAND: Standard Setting and Fair, Reasonable and Non-discriminatory Terms*, 2010 p. 9.
103. *Ibid.* See to the contrary Contreras, Jorge L., Fixing Frand*: A Pseudo-Pool Approach To Standards-Based Patent Licensing*, Forthcoming in Antitrust Law Journal, Fall 2013 p. 31, who argues that " *[i]n the case of SEPs, allocation on the basis of numeric proportionality is reasonable, as every SEP, by definition, should be essential to the standard, and the lack of a license to any one SEP should prevent a compliant product from being sold. It is thus plausible that every patent be given the same value*". However, this reasoning is flawed. The fact that a number of patents are necessarily infringed by those implementing the standard does not mean that the value of the underlying technologies is identical.
104. Not all companies take part in the standard setting process and new patent claims may accordingly surface over time.
105. See for instance Shapiro, Carl, *Navigating the Patent Thicket: Cross Licenses, Patent Pools, and Standard Setting*, in Jaffe, Adam B.; Lerner, Josh & Stern, Scott (eds.), *Innovation Policy and the Economy*, Vol. 1, 2001, and Schöler, Karolina, *Patents and Standards: The Antitrust Objection as a Defence in Patent Infringement Proceedings*, in Wolrad Prinz zu Waldeck et al. (eds.), Patents and Technological Progress in a Globalized World, Springer, 2009 p. 179.
106. The difficulties outlined above will however most likely present an obstacle in this respect.

rate which would have prevailed absent deceit. Thus, in *Rambus* the Commission considered that the Royalties charged by chipset manufacturer Rambus may be excessive in light of earlier conduct.[107] In effect the legal test normally applied to determine the reasonableness of a royalty rate (as set out above) is supplemented by a distinct test in light of a patent ambush. This test is discussed in Chapter 10. However, as also explained in that section Article 102 TFEU is not well suited to deal with patent ambush scenarios, since the wording of the provision merely prohibits abuse of a dominant position and not the acquisition of such position whether by deceit or otherwise. Accordingly, it can be expected that the Commission will only invest resources in pursuing patent ambush strategies under Article 102 TFEU in a limited number of cases. This issue is not discussed further below.

Also note that imposing exorbitantly high royalty rates or other clearly unreasonable license terms may be deemed a constructive refusal to license. In order to avoid the practical difficulties associated with excessive pricing cases the Commission when facing such circumstances may try instead to build their case on basis of the refusal to license regime discussed in Chapter 12 claiming that royalties are in fact so exorbitant that they signify an abusive refusal to license. In case a FRAND-pledged has been issued such case is definitely more clear cut, since as noted, there can be little doubt that refusing to license in light of a FRAND commitment will be deemed abusive.

[I] Cash-Only Licensing Option and Reciprocity

In addition to the requirement that a FRAND license must be non-excessive it follows from the Commission's decisional practice that the 'fair and reasonable' concept requires patentees to offer a cash-only licensing option – a license cannot be made conditional on the cross-licensing of patents which are *not* essential to the standard in question. Thus, in the context of a merger decision regarding Google's acquisition of Motorola Mobility the Commission held that a refusal to offer a cash-only option would potentially violate Google's FRAND commitment and Article 102 TFEU.[108] The Commission however noted that a license may generally be made conditional on reciprocity with regard to the licensee's SEPs insofar as they read on the same standard as the licensed patents.[109] Allowing for reciprocity is important in order to minimize the risk

107. Case COMP/38.636 – RAMBUS is discussed in Ch. 10.

108. Case COMP/M.6381 – Google/Motorola Mobility, 13 Feb. 2012, § 147 (Merger procedure).

109. *Ibid.*, § 107, footnote 57 (Merger procedure). Also see Commission notice in Case IV/33.667, *Philips//Matsushita-D2B*, 23 Aug. 1991. The case concerned a standardisation agreement (in the form of a joint venture agreement) which was notified to the Commission for negative clearance or exemption pursuant to Art. 101(3) TFEU (then, Art. 85(3) EC). The agreement *inter alia* provided that the parties would license their IPRs to all third parties interested in applying the standard (an extended D2B-standard) being developed and that the license agreements would contain a mutual worldwide non-assertion clause covering all existing and future patents pertinent to the standard. Such mutual non-assertion covenant has the same effect as a reciprocal licensing agreement. Although the Commission considered that the agreement could possibly contain some restrictions of competition it did not mention the non-assertion arrangement and in any event concluded that the agreement would merit exemption.

of patent hold-up and promote effective adoption of the standard. The ETSI IPR policy for instance provides that the FRAND commitment *"may be made subject to the condition that those who seek licensees agreed to reciprocate"*.[110]

The Commission's reasoning intuitively makes sense. While it cannot be considered abusive for a holder of SEPs to ensure its freedom to operate by demanding reciprocal licensing of complementary SEPs extending the reciprocity requirement to non-SEPs may limit technical development to the prejudice of consumers. Forcing third parties into licensing their non- SEPs deprives them their innovative edge and the ability to compete on basis of their patented technology by means of product differentiation – hence, stifles *inter*-technology competition. Moreover, preventing third parties from enjoying the fruits of their innovative efforts by refusing to license might diminish their incentive to invest in research and development. If proprietors of FRAND-pledged patents were allowed to cripple their competitors by forcibly extracting cross-licensees for non-standardized technologies this would accordingly be harmful to effective competition (including innovation). It would also run counter to the 'spirit' of the FRAND commitment which acts to constrain the market power leveraged as a result of the standardization process.

Cash-only licensing has also been discussed in a policy context. Thus, from the perspective of competition policy it has been suggested by some authors that SSOs could mitigate the hold-up problem associated with the exercise of SEPs by putting in place internal dispute resolution mechanisms or arbitration provisions.[111] In this respect it has been stated that that requiring the licensor to specify a cash price for its SEPs will aid the third party responsible for resolving the dispute in determining whether the license offer is FRAND compliant in that *"determining if a complex package of crosslicenses satisfies F/RAND is difficult for a third party"*.[112] The authors do not make clear whether they intend to impose such obligation on basis of Article 101(1) TFEU or leave the decision to SSOs on a voluntary basis. However, as highlighted above there seems to be basis for concluding that the cash-only licensing obligation is already inherent in Article 102 TFEU and extending it to SSO polices on basis of Article 101(1) TFEU to create clarity at the standard adoption stage is therefore only to be seen as a natural step. As explained in Chapter 7 section §7.03, the market power held by proprietors of FRAND-pledged patents is not obtained solely by their own innovative effort, but in reliance on SSO participants who voted for inclusion of their technology in the standard concerned. Therefore, they are under a special responsibility not to abuse the market power so obtained.

110. ETSI IPR Policy (Annex 6 of the Rules of Procedure) of 19 Mar. 2014. Available at: http://www.etsi.org/about/iprs-in-etsi (last checked 30 May 2014) p. 36.
111. See for instance Kühn, Kai-Uwe, Morton, Fiona Scott & Shelanski, Howard, *Standard Setting Organization Can Help Solve the Standard Essential Patents Licensing Problem*, in CPI Antitrust Chronicle, March 2013 (special issue), and Lemley, A. Mark & Shapiro, Carl, *A Simple Approach To Setting Reasonable Royalties For Standard-Essential Patents*, Stanford Public Law Working Paper, No. 2243026, 2013. Available at: http://dx.doi.org/10.2139/ssrn.2243026 (last checked 30 May 2014).
112. Lemley, A. Mark & Shapiro, Carl, *A Simple Approach To Setting Reasonable Royalties For Standard-Essential Patents*, Stanford Public Law Working Paper, No. 2243026, 2013 p. 4.

Finally, note that a clause prohibiting the licensee from enforcing rights against the licensor, or allowing the licensor to terminate the license agreement in such case, will most likely run counter to Article 101(1) TFEU. Companies in need of a license to SEPs cannot simply shift to alternative sources of supply and therefore such clauses effectively amounts to de facto cross-licensing obligations. In essence they confer upon the licensor a permit to infringe the licensee's rights and may deprive the licensee its competitive edge in the same way as a cross-licensing obligation related to non-SEPs.[113] The legality of non-challenge and termination clauses is discussed in the next section.

[J] Non-challenge and Termination Clauses

Non-challenge clauses generally impose upon the licensee an obligation - either directly or indirectly - not to challenge the validity of the licensed patents. If the patents licensed have been declared essential to a formal standard the licensor may in addition want such clause to prevent challenges to their essentiality.

Although a patent has been declared essential to the implementation of a standard pursuant to SSO policies this does not necessarily mean that it is essential as a matter of fact, i.e., it might not read on the technical specification underlying the standard. Indeed, criticism has been directed at what appears to be an over-declaration of potentially SEPs by SSO members.[114] As noted in Chapter 10, SSOs typically do not require their members to ascertain whether the patents they disclose are actually essential neither do SSOs assess for themselves. Instead, the disclosure obligation inherent in most SSOs mandate that any IPR which may *potentially* read on the standard under development be brought to the attention of the SSO. This compromise is understandable as requiring SSO participants to verify on an on-going basis whether any of their patents or patent applications read on the technical specification being developed would considerable increase the costs[115] and risk associated with formal standard setting activities, hence discourage participation. Several factors may encourage SSO members to over-declare patents as being essential:

- Profit.
- Pure innovators in particular may have incentives to declare a large number of patents essential in order to maximize their royalty revenues, relying on the

113. See to the contrary Lemley, Mark. A., *Intellectual Property and Standard Setting, in California Law Review*, Vol. 90, 2002 p. 1965 (footnote 325), stating that "*...IP owners might reasonably want to reserve the right to refuse to license those who later sue them for infringement on a different IP right*".
114. See for instance Ruikka, Timo, *"FRAND" Undertakings in Standardization – A Business Perspective*, Paper presented at the Fordham IP Conference, New York City, 28 Mar. 2008 p. 4, Fraunhofer Institute for Communication System and Dialogic, *Study on the Interplay between Standards and Intellectual Property Rights (IPRs)*, OJEU S136 of 18 Jul. 2009, 2011 p. 20, and Lemley, Mark A., *Intellectual Property and Standard Setting*, in California Law Review, Vol. 90, 2002 p. 1965 (footnote 323).
115. Cf. also Ruikka, Timo, *"FRAND" Undertakings in Standardization – A Business Perspective*, Paper presented at the Fordham IP Conference, New York City, 28 Mar. 2008 p. 5, stating that "*[t]he cost of having definitive technical assessments of whether all patents declared essential are really essential would be very great and would in any event have to be subject to court review*".

perception that implementers will seldom commit resources to ascertain whether each patent declared essential actually reads on the standard adopted.[116]

- Bargaining power.
- As is generally the case with regard to patents numbers do matter when undertakings engage in licensing negotiations.[117] Thus, a significant portfolio of SEPs increases the ability of a licensor to obtain royalty free cross-licenses from other SEP holders – hence improves the potential for profit on the product market to which the standard relates. Moreover, such a portfolio sends a warning signal to other SEPs holders present on the downstream product market that the patentee has the capability to retaliate in case they initiate patent litigation.[118]
- Competition law.
- As competition law encourages early stage disclosure of patents which may potentially be essential to the implementation of the standard under development, SSO participants, in order to avoid allegations of anti-competitive patent ambush, may have incentives to err on the safe side by declaring too many patents as being potentially essential.[119]

As non-challenge clauses may compound the problem of over-declaration and increase licensing costs, hence the price of standard compliant products, it is appropriate to consider to what extent such clauses are in accordance with EU competition law. In this respect note that non-challenge clauses may be found to violate not only Article 102 TFEU, but also Article 101(1) TFEU the application of which is not conditioned on a finding of dominance. Although there is currently no EU case law dealing specifically with clauses forbidding essentiality challenges, the stance taken by the CJEU and the Commission with regard to clauses prohibiting (or discouraging) invalidity challenges provide a strong indication of things to come. Thus, the effect of such clauses are highly similar – non-challenge clauses relating to invalidity may result in licensees paying for invalid patents whereas those relating to essentiality may result in licensees paying for patents the scope of which do not cover the standard being implemented. As explained below there is good reason to believe that not only clauses which outright prohibit such challenges, but also those entitling the licensor to terminate the agreement in case of such challenges, may be illegal. One may of course argue that the issues could have been evaded by licences had they examined the patent claims prior to procuring a license. However, acknowledging the time and effort associated with such *ex ante* analysis companies may be inclined to 'take a license and worry later' in order to

116. Depending on the type of standard hundreds or even thousands of patents may be declared essential. See *supra* note 5.
117. Cf. also Cook, William, *FRAND or foe*, in Managing Intellectual Property, June 2006 p. 1.
118. However, that the ability to rely on SEPs to seek or threaten injunctions is severely limited in some jurisdictions and may violate Art. 102 TFEU. In this respect see Ch. 13 s. §13.02[C].
119. Cf. also Camesasca, Peter, et al., *Injunctions for Standard-Essential Patents: Justice is not Blind*, in Journal of Competition Law & Economics, Vol. 9(1), 2013 p. 287.

ensure that their products can legally be put on the market quickly.[120] Moreover, knowledge of the licensed technology provides a better basis for succeeding with such challenges as acknowledged by the Commission (see below).

First a look at case law relating to validity challenges. Non-challenge clauses which impose upon licenses an obligation not to challenge the validity of the licensed rights may be considered restrictive of competition within the meaning of Article 101(1) TFEU and are excluded from the safe harbour of the Technology Transfer Block Exemption Regulation (TTBER).[121] Validity challenges are an important tool in promoting effective competition, because invalid IPR confer upon their proprietor's market power to which they are not entitled, hence unduly distorts competition on the market. As noted by the Commission in its Technology Transfer Guidelines "*[i]nvalid intellectual property stifles innovation rather than promoting it*" and licensees are generally those best equipped to challenge the validity of a patent, since they have been utilizing the licensed technology.[122] Invalid IPRs therefore should be eliminated.[123] A similar reasoning was expressed by the CJEU in *Windsurfing International.* Here the Court found a non-challenge clause to constitute an unlawful restriction of competition within the meaning of Article 101(1) TFEU (then, Article 85 EEC) "*...in view of the fact that it is in the public interest to eliminate any obstacle to economic activity which may arise where a patent was granted in error*" and because "*..such a clause clearly does not fall within the specific subject-matter of the patent...*".[124]

The Courts assessment in *Windsurfing International* was rather cursory and gave the impression that any non-challenge clause would be considered contrary to Article 101(1) TFEU. However, in *Bayer v. Süllhöfer*, the CJEU held that a non-challenge clause *may*, depending on the legal and economic context, restrict competition within the meaning of Article 85(1) EEC (now, Article 101(1) TFEU).[125] The Court in this respect found that a non-challenge clause does not restrict competition if the license provided is royalty free[126] or if the right being licensed relates to a technically outdated

120. In a dispute between the companies Nokia and InterDigital, Nokia for instance initiated a case before the UK Patents Court to have a number of InterDigital's patents declared non-essential to the 3G UMTS standard. See *Nokia Corporation v. Interdigital Technology Corporation* [2007] EWHC 3077. For more information see Helmers, Christian & McDonagh, Luke, *Trolls at the High Court?*, LSE Law, Society and Economy Working Papers, No. 13, 2012 pp. 12–13. Available at: http://papers.ssrn.com/sol3/papers.cfm?abstract_id=2154958.

121. Commission Regulation (EC) No. 316/2014 of 21 Mar. 2014 on the application of Art. 101(3) of the Treaty on the Functioning of the European Union to categories of technology transfer agreements, Art. 5(1)(b).

122. See Commission notice, *Guidelines on the application of Article 101 of the Treaty on the Functioning of the European Union to technology transfer agreements*, OJ 2014/C 89/03, 28 Mar. 2014, § 134.

123. *Ibid.*

124. Case 193/83, *Windsurfing International v. Commission*, 25 Feb. 1985, §§ 92–93.

125. Case 65/86, *Bayer v. Süllhöfer*, 27 Sep. 1988, § 16.

126. The court focused exclusively on whether the license was royalty-free. However, as many royalty-free license agreements involves cross-licensing the fact that a license is royalty-free does not necessarily entail that it is free of charge – rather monetary payment are in such cases substituted by a payment in kind. In case a royalty-free cross-licensing agreement contains a non-challenge clause the party (or parties) prohibited from initiating validity challenges may arguable be placed at a competitive disadvantage as absent such clause it would have been possible to invalidate the licensed subject matter and obtain a royalty income on basis of its

process not used by the licensee, since then the licensee would not suffer a competitive disadvantage by having its freedom of action constrained.[127] In addition the court stressed that even if confirmed that the licensee's freedom of action was constrained it would have to be determined, taking into consideration the positions of the parties to the agreement on the market for the products in question, whether competition is restricted to an appreciable extent.[128] It is not clear under which circumstances the Court considered that such appreciable restriction would manifest. The Commission in its Technology Transfer Guidelines interprets the judgment as meaning that Article 101(1) TFEU is likely to apply (and the exemption in Article 101(3) TFEU unlikely to apply) "*...where the licensed technology is valuable and therefore creates a competitive disadvantage for undertakings that are prevented from using it or are only able to use it against payment of royalties*", hence (rightly) seems to presuppose that under such circumstances a non-challenge clause will likely give rise to an appreciably restriction of competition.[129] A licensed technology is 'valuable' when it – such as is the case with an SEP – creates a barrier to market entry because it cannot be invented around, i.e., the commercial importance of the right is at the core of the analysis.[130] Arguably this reasoning applies by analogy with regard to clauses prohibiting essentiality challenges. As noted above licensees may not have had the resources or the time to assess in advance whether all patents (potentially hundreds or even thousands) declared essential to an SSO are essential in fact and depriving them the possibility of doing so *ex post* will act to maintain artificially high licensing costs, hence create an obstacle to economic activity.

Contrary to non-challenge clauses which outright prohibit validity challenges it has been common for license agreements to include a clause allowing the licensor to terminate the agreement in case the licensee challenges the validity of the patent(s) licensed. As opposed to clauses prohibiting validity challenges such clauses 'merely'

own rights. It remains to be seen whether the CJEU, if provided the opportunity to rule in this context, will insist on a narrow interpretation of its former judgment in Case 65/86, *Bayer v. Süllhöfer*, 27 Sep. 1988.

127. *Ibid.*, §§ 17–18 and 21.

128. *Ibid.*, § 19.

129. Also see Commission notice, *Guidelines on the application of Article 101 of the Treaty on the Functioning of the European Union to technology transfer agreements*, OJ 2014/C 89/03, 28 Mar. 2014, § 134. However, the use of the notion 'competitive disadvantage' (also found in the Court judgment) is a bit confusing, since it usually refers to the harm inflicted upon companies subject to anti-competitive discrimination. Arguably this is not to be interpreted as meaning that the licensee has to be put at a competitive disadvantage *vis-à-vis* other licensees by having to pay royalties for such clause to violate Art. 101(1) TFEU. Even absent such distortion of competition it is clear that consumers (hence effective competition) will be harmed by having to pay artificially inflated prices for products incorporating the licensed technology insofar as invalid rights are being maintained. This is supported by Case IV/32.736, *Moosehead/Whitbread*, 23 Mar. 1990, § 4 (cited *infra* footnote 131).

130. See by analogy Case IV/32.736, *Moosehead/Whitbread*, 23 Mar. 1990, § 4 where the Commission in the context of a trademark licensing agreements notes that "*...Only where the use of a well-known trademark would be an important advantage to any company entering or competing in any given market and the absence of which therefore constitutes a significant barrier to entry, would this clause which impedes the licensee to challenge the validity of the trademark, constitute an appreciable restriction of competition within the meaning of Article 85 (1).*"

allowing for termination have traditionally not been considered restrictive of competition. Although a right to terminate will arguably discourage some licensees from initiating validity challenges Article 5(1)(c) of the former TTBER explicitly stated that clauses "*...providing for termination of the technology transfer agreement in the event that the licensee challenges the validity of one or more of the licensed intellectual property rights*" are not excluded from exemption.[131] The Commission clarified that the purpose of the exemption was to ensure that a "*licensor is not forced to continue dealing with a licensee that challenges the very subject matter of the licence agreement...*".[132] Indeed, if licensors were to tolerate validity challenges by licensees without having the opportunity to terminate the license agreement they would probably think twice before providing a license in the first place – knowing that licensees, having learned the specifics of the licensed subject matter, are those most likely to succeed with such a challenge.[133] As license agreements are generally seen as pro-competitive, because they ensure diffusion of technology which would otherwise have been reserved exclusively for the rights holder, this would be unfortunate. However, as explained below the situation is different in the context of SEPs and the Commission has since acknowledged that such termination clauses may violate Article 101(1) TFEU.

Recently the Commission has changed its opinion in this respect and has suggested a more strict approach towards any type of non-challenge clause. According to the 2014 TTBER a clause in a non-exclusive license agreement which allows the licensor to terminate the agreement in case of a validity challenge no longer benefits from the safe harbour of the block exemption, since it is expressly stated that "*...any direct or indirect obligation on a party not to challenge the validity of intellectual property rights which the other party holds in the Union...*" is excluded from its scope.[134] In the associated Technology Transfer Guidelines the Commission, referring to *Windsurfing International* (see above), explains that a balance between the interests of the licensor in terminating the agreement and the "*...public interest to eliminate any obstacle to economic activity...*" must be reached.[135] The Commission in this respect acknowledges that a termination right can have the same effect as an outright non-challenge clause if the licensee has become 'locked-in' to the licensed rights and accordingly cannot afford the risks and costs associated with a termination of the licensee agreement. This acknowledgement is particularly important with regard to SEPs having earned widespread adoption since a termination of a license agreement

131. Commission Regulation (EC) No. 772/2004 of 27 Apr. 2004 on the application of Art. 81(3) of the Treaty to categories of technology transfer agreements, Art. 5(1)(c).
132. Commission notice, *Guidelines on the application of Article 81 of the EC Treaty to technology transfer agreements*, OJ 2004/C 101/02, 27 Apr. 2004, § 113.
133. See for instance Anderman, Steven & Schmidt, Hedvig, *EU Competition Law and Intellectual Property Rights – The Regulation of Innovation*, 2nd ed., Oxford University Press, 2011 p. 289, and Ivo Van Bael & Bellis, Jean-Francois, *Competition Law of the European Community*, 5th ed., Kluwer Law International, 2010 p. 638.
134. Commission Regulation (EC) No. 316/2014 of 21 Mar. 2014 on the application of Art. 101(3) of the Treaty on the Functioning of the European Union to categories of technology transfer agreements, Art. 5(1)(b).
135. Commission notice, *Guidelines on the application of Article 101 of the Treaty on the Functioning of the European Union to technology transfer agreements*, OJ 2014/C 89/03, 28 Mar. 2014, § 138.

relating to such patents may potentially expel the licensee concerned from the market. Thus, with regard to such patents a non-challenge clause allowing the licensor to terminate the agreement may, as envisaged by the Commission, de facto amount to an obligation not to challenge the validity of patents, thereby give rise to the same anti-competitive effects as an outright non-challenge prohibition. As mentioned above there is reason to extend the reasoning related to validity challenges to essentiality challenges - regardless which type of challenge is prohibited the potential adverse effects on competition are highly similar.

As follows from the above it is likely that a non-challenge or termination clause - whether related to the invalidity or essentiality of SEPs - will violate Article 101(1) TFEU and/or Article 102 TFEU.

[K] Is the Initial License Offer Special?

As there is and can be no universal formula suited for determining a FRAND royalty rate it is important to appreciate that the parties negotiating a license should be left considerable 'room' to do so without risking competition law intervention. Imposing upon licensors to strict requirements may handicap them in licensing negotiations and reduce their ability to effectively recoup investments costs. Put simply, the negotiation process might become frustrated if holders of SEPs have to fear that the potential license suddenly breaks of negotiations and files a competition law complaint that the royalties requested are excessive.

A US court order concerning a dispute between Microsoft and Motorola raises an interesting question in this respect. Motorola had made an offer to license Microsoft its SEPs relating to the WIFI (802.11) and MPEG4 video encoding (H.264) standards at a royalty rate of 2.25% of the price of the end product, but Microsoft claimed that rate to be in breach of Motorola's RAND commitment. In this respect the court held that initial offers do not have to be on RAND terms so long as a RAND license eventually issues.[136] However, the court stressed that this did not mean that Motorola could "*...make blatantly unreasonable offers to implementers*", since "*[s]uch behaviour would frustrate the purpose behind the agreements by allowing the standard essential patent owner to abuse its power as a standard essential patent holder and extract higher than reasonable royalty rates*".[137] The court found that the freedom to negotiate should not be unduly constrained, but at the same time held that the licensor had to oblige by the duty of good faith inherent in any contract.[138] Although the court's order was based on contract law the issue may as well turn up in a competition law context - does every offer have to be FRAND compliant?

The overall reasoning of the US court is in line with the view (stated in the beginning of this section) that competition law should not be applied so strictly that it deprives the parties the freedom to negotiate in place licenses on a bilateral basis.

136. Case C10-1823JLR, *Microsoft Corp v. Motorola*, United States District Court Western District of Washington at Seattle, Document no. 335, 6 Jun. 2012, p. 25.
137. *Ibid.*
138. *Ibid.*

However, the purpose of licence negotiations is not to "*negotiate towards a RAND licence*" as claimed by Motorola (and accepted by the US court), but to negotiate within the boundaries of what is fair and reasonable taking into consideration the overall guidelines specified above. The boundaries of the FRAND concept itself should (and arguably does) provide sufficient room for the patentee to manoeuvre in licensing negotiations – as established by the General Court in *Microsoft* there may be multiple fair and reasonable royalty rates the patentee merely has to choose one of them (see Chapter 11 section §11.01[C]). While the exact license terms are first established when eventually a license is concluded each and every license proposal arguably must be FRAND compliant.[139] If the patentee is obliged to license under Article 102 TFEU (pursuant to a FRAND commitment or otherwise) there can be no objective justification for attempting to impose unfair and unreasonable royalties, regardless of whether this takes place as part of an initial license offer. Conferring upon SEP holder's immunity from competition law with regard to offers made during the course of license negotiations may result in supra-competitive royalty rates or other unreasonable terms being imposed. Indeed, in *Microsoft* the General Court recalled that pursuant to the Commission's decision, obliging Microsoft to license certain interoperability information, the company was under an obligation "*...to* propose *reasonable remuneration rates to its potential licensees*" [emphasis added].[140]

If a non-FRAND license offer is actually accepted by what then becomes the licensee the above issue is of course of little relevance since then the terms agreed will be those subject to scrutiny. However, as noted in Chapter 13, the Commission has clearly indicated that good faith license negotiations requires the patentee not to stray from the path of FRAND and that doing so will render the seeking of injunctions abusive. Thus, if a would-be licensee rejects a license proposal finding it non-FRAND and subsequently starts infringing the patent in question, a successful competition law defence on basis of Article 102 TFEU against an action for an injunction will likely be conditional on proof that the license offers as a matter of fact were non-FRAND.[141]

[L] Summary

While overall it is clear that an excessive price is one which does not bear a reasonable relationship to the economic value of a patented technology being licensed it is equally clear that no consistent legal framework has yet developed as to the application of Article 102(a) TFEU to the pricing of SEPs.

The test applied in the Microsoft case clearly highlights the difficulties in determining in a non-arbitrary manner whether royalty rates or other license conditions are unreasonable. The Commission in accordance with case law presumed patented technologies to be innovative in character and therefore did not question the remuneration scheme applied by Microsoft with regard to its patented technologies.

139. As noted above this requires the whole 'package' of license terms to be taken into consideration as the royalty rate cannot be assessed in isolation.
140. Case T-167/08, *Microsoft Corp v. Commission*, 27 Jun. 2012, § 219.
141. See Ch. 13 for a detailed discussion of the competition law defence under Art. 102 TFEU.

Having (rightly) done so the Commission needs to seek other benchmarks against which patents can be compared if it is to succeed in an excessive pricing case against a company holding patents essential to a standard. In this respect looking at the prices charged for other comparable - patented or non-patented technologies - may give useful indications. However, since R&D costs, licence conditions and market conditions may differ establishing a valid and consistent basis for such comparison is likely to be very difficult. Recognizing that R&D costs differ across technologies case law suggests that a comparison with other non-patented technologies, and likely also patented technologies, is not by itself able to substantiate a finding of abuse under Article 102(a) TFEU - stronger evidence is needed.

The Commission therefore must look elsewhere for evidence. One place to look may be comparable standards. If the same IPR is priced differently depending on the standard in which the technology is incorporated this might suggest that the highest prices charged is excessive - what else could explain the difference? Unfortunately, difficulties as to establishing consistent and valid comparisons are also bound to arise in this respect. If the standards relate to different product markets or concern different product features this might explain a price divergence and hence the impact of such differences needs to be eliminated for the comparison to be valid. It goes without saying that this is not an easy task.

As outlined above proving license condition non-[FR]AND is very difficult. However, this is not to say that it is impossible and as evidenced by case law the Commission may go great lengths to obtain evidence and also does not fear engaging in complex economic assessments. Perhaps the strongest case for intervention is if it can be established that the price charged for a patent license *ex post* (after a standard is adopted) exceeds the one charged *ex ante* (before the standard was adopted), provided that the licenses relate to the same products and features. It is likely that if presented with such evidence the CJEU will conclude that it is for the patentee to objectively justify the price increase.

§11.02 FRA[ND]: NON-DISCRIMINATORY LICENSE TERMS

Legal scholars have focused a great deal of attention on determining the meaning of the notion 'fair and reasonable', i.e., the [FR] part of FRAND. Although not possible to precisely define the notion a number of guiding principles able to aid courts, competition authorities and stakeholders involved in standard setting activities have resulted from these efforts - see Chapter 11 section §11.01. To the contrary the [ND] part of FRAND which dictates that license terms should be 'non-discriminatory' has received little attention.[142] This is surprising as the risk that SEP holders engage in anticompetitive discrimination is arguable no less than the risk that they demand excessive

142. Cf. also Farrar-Layne, Anne, *Nondiscriminatory pricing - is standard setting different*, in Journal of Competition Law & Economics, Vol. 6(4), 2010 p. 812, Chaffer, Chris, *Prohibiting discriminatory cross-licensing*, in Information & Communications Technology Law, Vol. 21(2), 2012 p. 91, and Crane, Daniel A., *Patent Pools, RAND Commitments, and the Problematics of Price Discrimination*, Cardozo Legal Studies, Working Paper No. 232, 2008 p. 26.

royalties (or other unreasonable license terms) in violation of competition law - the objectives are merely distinct.[143] Thus, whereas licensors may have incentives to increase their royalty income by means of excessive pricing (exploitative abuse) they may also - provided that they are vertically integrated - be tempted to engage in discriminatory licensing in order to disadvantage competing manufactures of standard compliant products (exclusionary abuse). Moreover, the Commission, as noted in Chapter 11, seems to prioritize taking action against exclusionary abuses, such as discriminatory licensing, whereas resources are seldom committed to deal with exploitative abuses.

The limited focus on discriminatory licensing in the context of standard setting may be attributable to the fact that despite the Commission's declared enforcement priorities no cases at the EU level have concerned the latter half of the FRAND commitment. Thus, while in the context of standards the Commission has performed a number of investigations with regard to excessive royalty claims, deceptive conduct and enforcement of SEPs, none have concerned the issue of discrimination. The lack of case law should not necessarily be taken to mean that discriminatory licensing issues are purely hypothetical. Indeed cases at the Member State level[144] as well as in the United States[145] underline that allegations in this regard may arise. Most likely the relatively few cases are instead attributable to the difficulties facing competition authorities and licensees in identifying and proving the existence of discriminatory licensing practices. Thus, as discrimination is a relative concept a finding of abuse requires insight into the, often confidential, license agreements entered into by the patentee - what licensees do not know will not hurt them. Although there are also major challenges involved in determining whether a royalty is unfair and unreasonable the assessment required in this respect can to the contrary be made in isolation with reference to factors such as the intrinsic value of the technology being licensed.

The divergence in focus may also be caused by the perception that the term 'discriminatory' is to a large extent self-explanatory. Thus, the terms unfair and unreasonable are in themselves nothing more than 'placeholders' which need to be supplied with actual substance by courts and competition authorities and therefore there is room for different interpretations. On the contrary the term discriminatory is, from a linguistic perspective, more unambiguous and may be perceived as providing a clearer indication of the behaviour which runs contrary to Articles 101 and 102 TFEU. Notwithstanding the linguistic clarity the commercial realities facing patentees and licensees however means that *illegal* discrimination is not easily distinguished from

143. Depending on the magnitude of the royalty rate imposed on the disfavoured licensee it may not only be deemed discriminatory, but also unfair and unreasonable (excessive) in violation of Art. 102 (a) TFEU, but this need not be the case. A discriminatory royalty rate may very well place the licensee at a competitive disadvantage without being excessive, since what matters is not the royalty level, but whether other licensees received more favourable terms. To the contrary the 'fairness' of the royalty rate under Art. 102(a) TFEU is assessed without regard to the rates offered to other licensees - see s. §11.01.

144. Case KZR 40/02, Standard Tight-head Drum (Standard-Spundfass), 13 Jul. 2004 as decided by the German Federal Supreme Court which, amongst other things, concerned allegations of discriminatory licensing.

145. Case 501 F.3d 297 (3d Cir. 2007), *Broadcom Corp. v. Qualcomm Inc.*

legal discrimination. Patentees enter into diverse license agreements for a number of completely legitimate reasons. Royalty rates and other licensing conditions agreed between patentees and licensees most often reflect a prior bargaining process just as is the case with other types of agreements.[146] There may therefore be a number of objective justifications able to bring the conduct outside the scope of Articles 101 and 102 TFEU. Indeed, as explained in more detail in section §11.02[C][3], economic theory supports that discriminatory licensing may in fact increase economic welfare and accordingly there is no room for a per se prohibition under Article 101 or 102 TFEU.[147] This does not change merely because a FRAND commitment has been issued by the licensor. Dealing with discriminatory licensing under Articles 101 and 102 TFEU is therefore not a simple and straightforward process. A careful analysis of the actual or potential effects caused by discriminatory licensing of SEPs needs to be performed in order to establish whether the conduct in question risks harming competition.[148]

Against this background the purpose of this section is to uncover (1) under what circumstances a differentiated licensing scheme may violate competition law and (2) whether there is basis for concluding that the presence of a FRAND commitment has any substantive impact on the competition law assessment to be carried out in this respect. Before turning to the legal framework in section §11.02[B] some thoughts on the intentions of licensors with respect to licensing discrimination are presented in section §11.02[A].

[A] Motives for Discrimination

The [ND] portion of FRAND has as its purpose, in accordance with Article 102(c) TFEU, to ensure that the licensing practices of SEP holders do not distort competition between licensees wishing to manufacture standard compliant products. However, whereas it is intuitively clear what licensors may gain from imposing excessive (unfair and unreasonable) royalties contrary to the [FR] portion of FRAND the incentives to discriminate are more ambiguous.

Considering the motives of patentees to discriminate is useful as a basis for discussing the associated legal implications and in unearthing when in particular there is reason to be concerned that anti-competitive effects may materialize. That being said, note that price discrimination, regardless of the underlying motivations, may

146. Cf. also Farrar-Layne, Anne, *Nondiscriminatory pricing – is standard setting different*, in Journal of Competition Law & Economics, Vol. 6(4), 2010 p. 813.
147. Cf. also *Whish, Richard & Bailey, David, Competition Law*, 7th *ed.*, Oxford University Press, 2012 p. 760.
148. Farrar-Layne, Anne, *Nondiscriminatory pricing – is standard setting different*, in Journal of Competition Law & Economics, Vol. 6(4), 2010 p. 814 concludes that "*...only those practices which have actually harmed or stand a good chance to actually harm consumer welfare should be prohibited*". The fact that risk of an adverse impact on effective competition, comprising consumer welfare, needs to be proved however already follows from established EU case law. In case C-95/04 P, *British Airways plc v. Commission*, § 145, the Court notes that discrimination may be regarded as abusive when "*the behaviour of the undertaking in a dominant position tends, having regard to the whole of the circumstances of the case, to lead to a distortion of competition*".

violate Article 102(c) TFEU as a matter of law.[149] According to settled case law abuse is an objective concept[150] and hence, in the context of discrimination, it must be established by considering the potential competitive disadvantage inflicted upon licensees and the resulting distortion of effective competition – intent is of secondary importance. In other words, the application of Article 102(c) TFEU is not conditional on a finding that the licensor deliberately aimed to harm competition by discriminating between licensees. Even though it may be tempting for a licensor simply to 'go with the flow' of licensing negotiations and attempt to extract the largest royalties possible caution is therefore warranted. This is however not to say that proof of anti-competitive intent does not play a role to the application of Article 102 TFEU. Proof of anti-competitive intent may substantiate a finding of abuse and constitute an aggravating factor with regard to the level of fines imposed. In *AstraZeneca* for instance the General Court stressed that "*...although proof of the deliberate nature of conduct ... is not necessary for the purposes of identifying an abuse of a dominant position, intention none the less also constitutes a relevant factor...*".[151] Even if not a prerequisite, evidence of subjective intent may tip the scale in favour of intervention in cases where it is unclear to what extent the discriminatory practice actually is detrimental to competition.[152]

Overall a SEP holder may have an interest in engaging in licensing discrimination either (1) to increase royalty revenue by setting royalties to reflect the individual licensee's perceived willingness or ability to pay or (2) to increase sales revenue on the downstream product market to which the license relates by inflicting upon certain (likely the strongest) rival companies a competitive disadvantage.

As to the *first objective* (to increase royalty revenue) it may be exploitative of licensees, to the extent that those which have become 'locked-in' to the standard in question are deliberately charged higher royalty rates, but it may also signify a more genuine strategy; the adoption of a royalty scheme which is consistent with the business model of the individual licensee. There is no denying that competition may be distorted in both scenarios, but as discussed in section §11.02[C][3] adopting royalties to fit the characteristics of the individual licensee need not always yield anti-competitive effects on balance if it allows a more effective way of recouping investment costs.

149. Some authors give a different impression. See for instance Farrar-Layne, Anne, *Nondiscriminatory pricing – is standard setting different*, in Journal of Competition Law & Economics, Vol. 6(4), 2010 p. 813, who state that in the presence of market power "*the second step in any investigation would generally need to center on the patent holder's motivations*".

150. See for instance Case 85/76, *Hoffmann-La Roche & Co. AG v. Commission*, 13 Feb. 1979, § 91.

151. Case T-321/05, *AstraZeneca v. Commission*, 1 Jul. 2010, § 359. Also see Case C-08/08, *T-Mobile Netherlands v. Raad van bestuur van de Nederlandse Mededingingsautoriteit*, 4 Jun. 2009, § 27, where the CJEU held that "*...while the intention of the parties is not an essential factor in determining whether a concerted practice is restrictive, there is nothing to prevent the Commission of the European Communities or the competent Community judicature from taking it into account*".

152. See generally Anderman, Steven & Ezrachi, *Intellectual Property and Competition Law*, Oxford University Press, 2011 p. 130, who note that subjective intent plays a role in 'grey areas'.

In any event it seems that a rational licensor seeking to optimize royalty income in the long-run will have an incentive not to distort competition between licensees appreciably. A uniform increase in license fees is arguably more likely to yield the desired result. Thus, if *all* licensees are imposed upon high (even excessive royalties) each licensee will, all things being equal, be able to pass on the costs involved to consumers without incurring a competitive disadvantage *vis-àis* other licensees since these incur the same costs. In effect it may be possible to sustain increased royalty flows in the long-run provided that the price of the end products supplied as a result does not increase beyond what the market can bear. To the contrary discriminatory licensing – unless objectively justified by diverging economic or competitive conditions – will distort competition between licensees insofar as passing on costs will render the disfavoured licensees' products unattractive to consumers relative to those of the favoured licensees'. In comparison with a uniform licensing scheme discriminatory licensing is therefore ill-suited as a method to increase the aggregate royalty revenue, because the disfavoured licensees will experiences a drop in sales which might offset any increase in royalty revenue stemming from sale of products by favoured licensees. This highlights why typically discriminatory licensing, if devised as part of an anti-competitive plan, will constitute *exclusionary* rather than *exploitative* abuse.[153]

As to the *second* objective outlined above (to exclude rivals), the question is under what circumstances discrimination can effectively be put to use as a strategy aimed at placing the licensor's downstream competitors (secondary line injury) or competing licensors (primary line injury) at a competitive disadvantage.[154] In unmasking the incentives of licensors in this respect it is necessary to distinguish between two groups of patentees – those vertically integrated and those not.

A non-vertically integrated patentee (i.e., a 'pure innovator' with no presence on the downstream product market to which its patent(s) relate) arguably has little to gain from engaging in discrimination with the aim inflicting upon licensees, with whom it does not compete, a competitive disadvantage (secondary line injury).[155] The fact that the licensed patent(s) read on a technical standard does not give rise to a different conclusion. Indeed, manufactures of standard compliant products act as 'ambassadors'

153. In any event charging higher prices from 'locked-in' licensees quickly becomes a question of excessive pricing contrary to the [FR] portion of FRAND (in essence an Art. 102(a) TFEU issue) since it signifies an attempt to increase the price to a level which does not reflect the intrinsic value of the licensed technology, but rather the strategic value of the licensors patents.

154. The terms primary- and secondary line injury refers to the level of trade where the anti-competitive harm materializes. As to the distinction between primary- and secondary line injury see for instance Geradin, Damien & Petit, Nicolas, *Price Discrimination Under EC Competition Law: Another Antitrust Doctrine In Search Of Limiting Principles?*, in Journal of Competition Law and Economics, Vol. 2(3), 2006 p. 487, and Jones, Alison & Sufrin, Brenda, *EC Competition Law- Text*, Cases and Materials, 3rd ed., Oxford University Press, 2008 p. 442.

155. Legal scholars generally seem to agree. See for instance Geradin, Damien & Petit, Nicolas, *Price Discrimination Under EC Competition Law: Another Antitrust Doctrine In Search Of Limiting Principles?*, in Journal of Competition Law and Economics, Vol. 2(3), 2006 p. 502 and p. 517, Farrar-Layne, Anne, *Nondiscriminatory pricing – is standard setting different*, in Journal of Competition Law & Economics, Vol. 6(4), 2010 p. 813, and Hovenkamp, Herbert, et al., *Unilateral Refusals to License*, in Journal of Competition Law and Economics, Vol. 2(1), 2006 p. 5.

for the standard in question and disadvantaging certain of them will entail a risk to the success of the standard, hence to royalty income. This is especially true in the midst of a 'standards war', since weakening the 'ambassadors' of a standard may limit its diffusion and accordingly risk 'tipping' the market in favour of competing standards.[156] Moreover, disadvantaging certain licensees relative to other may produce exclusionary effects and lead to consolidation on the downstream market.[157] This in effect will increase the bargaining power of the remaining licensees which in turn may be able to suppress royalty rates going forward.[158] It follows that SEP holders may in fact gain financially from effective downstream competition and accordingly has little incentive to discriminate with a view to disadvantaging select licensees.

While apparently non-vertically integrated licensors do not gain *directly* from discriminating between licensees, one might argue that they could gain *indirectly* from such action as part of a strategy to harm other licensors (primary line injury). Thus, there are numerous cases concerning tangible products and services where non-vertically integrated suppliers have been found to abuse their dominant position by discriminating between their trading partners downstream (by use of fidelity rebates, tying/bundling practices or selective price cuts) as a means to shield their dominant position upstream from the perils of competition.[159] While obviously a proprietor of SEPs has no incentive to harm licensor's of complementary patents, i.e., patents relating to the standard in which the licensors technology is embodied, benefit may potentially be derived by giving preferential treatment (for instance by means of a royalty reduction) to licensees who abstain from producing products incorporating a competing standard - such exclusionary strategy in effect harms other licensors. However, from a commercial perspective such strategy seems unlikely to be employed since it entails a risk that the disfavoured licensee's will retaliate by abandoning the standard in which the licensors patents are embodied. In order to lure licensees away from competing standards it therefore seems much more likely that the licensor would resort to general, rather than selective, price cuts so as keep all licensees satisfied during the crucial stage where competing standards battle to win the market.

On the other hand vertically integrated patentees, i.e., those utilizing their patents downstream to produce standard compliant products, may have strong incentives[160] to price discriminate in favour of their own subsidiaries or to refuse their

156. This 'tipping' effect was discussed in Ch. 8 s. §8.01 (network effects).

157. See Geradin, Damien & Petit, Nicolas, *Price Discrimination Under EC Competition Law: Another Antitrust Doctrine In Search Of Limiting Principles?*, in Journal of Competition Law and Economics, Vol. 2(3), 2006 p. 518, for a similar view.

158. Whether licensees will be able to exert such competitive pressure upon the licensor in the short run will, amongst other things, depend on whether they are in a position to 'abandon' the licensor and opt for competing standards or non-standardised technologies. Even if licensees are not able to do so in the short run an increase in bargaining power may potentially materialize when an upcoming version of the standard is negotiated.

159. For an overview of the cases involving secondary line injury and primary line injury, respectively, see Geradin, Damien & Petit, Nicolas: "*Price Discrimination Under Ec Competition Law: Another Antitrust Doctrine In Search Of Limiting Principles?*", in Journal of Competition Law and Economics, Vol. 2(3), 2006 p. 491.

160. See for instance Geradin, Damien & Petit, Nicolas: "*Price Discrimination Under Ec Competition Law: Another Antitrust Doctrine In Search Of Limiting Principles?*", in Journal of Competition

strongest rivals a license altogether as a means to leverage their dominant position from the technology market to the relevant downstream market (secondary line injury).[161] Several EU cases[162] have dealt with discrimination by vertically integrated firms aiming to disadvantage select competitors on the downstream market. As illustrated in the *Broadcom v. Qualcomm* case decided by the U.S. Court of Appeals for the Third Circuit such allegations of primary-line discrimination may potentially also arise in the context of SEPs.[163] In that case the plaintiff, Broadcom, alleged that the defendant, Qualcomm, had violated competition law (§ 2 of the Sherman Act) *inter alia* by discriminating against licensees despite having issued a FRAND commitment to ETSI and other SDO's which induced them to include the licensed technology (WCDMA) in the so-called UMTS standard. In particular, it was claimed that once Qualcomm's patents were accepted for inclusion in the UMTS standard, the company engaged in a course of discriminatory behaviour which involved charging double royalty rates to licensees who made use of chipsets manufactured by rival companies and by granting discounts and other unlawful payments to manufactures who agreed to exclusively use standard compliant chipsets manufactured by Qualcomm. Qualcomm's conduct was therefore not motivated by a desire to harm other licensors, but to protect its downstream chipset business against competition. As stated in the plaintiff's complaint the discriminatory licensing policy was "*...part of Qualcomm's effort to obtain a monopoly in the UMTS chipset market because it views competition in that market as a longterm threat to its existing monopolies in CDMA technology*",[164] i.e., in essence it was claimed that Qualcomm aimed to exclude rival chipset manufactured by use of a leveraging strategy.

The incentives outlined above highlight that vertically integrated patentees may potentially gain from discriminatory licensing and accordingly that resources, as a matter of competition policy, should spent scrutinizing the conduct of such patentees. Below the legal framework under which such scrutiny must take place is analysed.

[B] The Prohibition against Discriminatory Conduct

While in principle Article 101(1) TFEU may be applied to sanction discriminatory conduct most cases are decided with reference to Article 102 TFEU. This is a reminder that for discrimination to have an appreciable effect on competition (cause a 'competitive disadvantage') the market must be sufficiently concentrated to deprive the contracting partner the possibility of shifting to alternative sources of supply in response to an undertakings discriminatory conduct. Moreover, as noted in Chapter 8,

Law and Economics, Vol. 2(3), 2006 p. 512 and 519 (in particular), Farrar-Layne, Anne, *Nondiscriminatory pricing – is standard setting different*, in Journal of Competition Law & Economics, Vol. 6(4), 2010 p. 813, and Hovenkamp, Herbert, et al., *Unilateral Refusals to License*, in Journal of Competition Law and Economics, Vol. 2(1), 2006 p. 5.

161. As explained in s. §11.02[E] an outright refusal to license is the ultimate type of discrimination.
162. See for instance Case T-301/04, *Clearstream v. Commission*, 9 Sep. 2009; Case T-111/96, *ITT Promedia v. Commission*, 17 Jul. 1998, and Case T-229/94, *Deutsche Bahn AG v. Commission*, 21 Oct. 1997.
163. Case 06-4292, *Broadcom Corp. v. Qualcomm Inc.*, 501 F.3d 297 (3d Cir. 2007). 28 Jun. 2007.
164. *Ibid.*

SEPs often confer upon the patentee a dominant position for which reason the need to rely on Article 101 TFEU to sanction anti-competitive discrimination is in any event limited. In the remainder of this section focus will therefore be on Article 102 TFEU.

It follows explicitly from Article 102(c) TFEU that "*applying dissimilar conditions to equivalent transactions with other trading parties, thereby placing them at a competitive disadvantage*" is prohibited. Moreover, the Commission and the CJEU have made clear that applying equivalent conditions to transactions characterized by different factual circumstances may infringe Article 102(c) TFEU – a type of 'reverse discrimination'.[165] There is no doubt therefore that discriminatory licensing may violate EU competition law. As the Commission has put it the imposition of license terms according to a "*friend/enemy*" scheme may fall within the scope of Article 102 TFEU.[166] This statement is a reminder of what was said in Chapter 11 section §11.02[A]; that anti-competitive discrimination will often have as its purpose to exclude certain 'enemies' from the market by placing them at a competitive disadvantage *vis-à-vis* other trading partners – likely the licensor himself.

It must be recalled however that there is no per se prohibition against licensing discrimination. It may be that only positive effects result or that such effects on the balance outweigh any negative effects – both scenarios will bring the conduct outside the scope of Article 102(c) TFEU.[167] As explained in Chapter 11 section §11.02[C][3] the application of Article 102(c) TFEU, bearing in mind that innovation forms part of 'effective competition', should be reserved those cases where the risk to downstream competition overshadows the licensors legitimate interest in effectively recouping R&D costs.The provision (and the extended interpretation hereof given by the CJEU) does not in itself provide a foundation for distinguishing illegal discrimination from legal discrimination. In particular, it is necessary to unearth under what circumstances transactions should be considered 'equivalent' within the meaning of Article 102(c) TFEU as this, as explained below, is by no means self-evident. It is for instance unclear to what extent non-cost related commercial factors, such as the individual licensee's willingness to pay or perceived risks, may impact the equivalence of transactions, hence the legality of a discriminatory licensing scheme under applicable law. Clarity in

165. See Case C-209/10, *Post Danmark A/S v. Konkurrencerådet*, 27 Mar. 2012, § 30 (cited below) and COMP/A.36.568/D3, *Scanlines Sverige v. Port of Helsingborg*, 23 Jul. 2004, § 276. Also see case 13-63, *Italian Republic v. Commission*, where the Court stated that "*...discrimination could also be caused if different situations were treated in the same manner.*" (the case concerned discrimination in the context of the ECSC Treaty).

166. See the Commission's press release in Case COMP/37.792, *Microsoft*, IP/01/1232 (Commission initiates additional proceedings against Microsoft), 30 Aug. 2001. The Commission dropped the allegations concerning discrimination in its final decision in Case COMP/37.792, *Microsoft*, 24 Mar. 2004, for which reason the General Court did not consider the issue on appeal in Case T-201/04, *Microsoft Corp. v. Commission*, 17 Sep. 2007.

167. See for instance Case C-95/04 P, *British Airways v. Commission*, 15 Mar. 2007, §§ 69 and 86. Also see Communication from the Commission, *Guidance on the Commission's enforcement priorities in applying Article 82 of the EC Treaty to abusive exclusionary conduct by dominant undertakings*, OJ 2009/C 45/02, 24 Feb. 2009, point 28 (with references to additional case law). As stated by the Commission in the aforementioned enforcement guidelines a dominant undertaking may justify its conduct "*...so either by demonstrating that its conduct is objectively necessary or by demonstrating that its conduct produces substantial efficiencies which outweigh any anti-competitive effects on consumers.*".

this respect is essential to patentees in ensuring compliance with competition law since such factors will often be the only ones they can rely upon to justify a discriminatory licensing scheme.

While the Horizontal Guidelines contain some guidance as that which license terms can be considered fair and reasonable[168] they do not address the issue of discriminatory licensing in any detail – neither does the Commission's Technology Transfer Guidelines.[169] Thus, despite the fact that the draft Horizontal Guidelines published for consultation on 4 May 2010 were subject to critique[170] for not elaborating on the notion 'non-discriminatory' the Commission's final guidelines remains silent in this respect. However, the lack of specific guidance is not surprising. After all the Horizontal Guidelines concerns the application of Article 101 TFEU to standardization agreements and not the licensing practices engaged in by SSO members after the standard concerned has been adopted – these will usually be scrutinized under Article 102 TFEU. That being said, it is noteworthy that the Commission felt the need to provide guidance on assessing whether at royalty is fair and reasonable while completely ignoring the 'non-discriminatory' part of FRAND. The Commission silence with regard to discriminatory licensing is arguably a strong indication that a FRAND commitment does not entail a special obligation to ensure equal treatment of licensees different from the one to which dominant licensors of patents in general must comply with. Thus, while as explained below, there is reason to assess the legality of licensing discrimination according to criteria distinct from those used with regard to tangible goods and services there is nothing to suggest that the 'non-discriminatory' component of FRAND imposes a stricter licensing norm. Indeed, it seems that the only way of imposing a stricter norm would be to interpret the [ND] portion of FRAND as being the equivalent of a most-favoured-licensee clause, but doing so would be contrary to Article 102(c) TFEU which as noted above have been construed as prohibiting 'reverse' discrimination, i.e., equal treatment of non-equivalent transactions.

Rewinding a bit; according to the wording of Article 102(c) TFEU, there are two overall steps associated with evaluating the legality of discrimination. It must be determined (1) whether the license agreements being compared relate to equivalent transactions and in the affirmative (2) whether a competitive disadvantage is inflicted on a licensee or a would-be licensee which is not objectively justified.As the most common argument put forward to substantiate an objective justification is that there is no discrimination, because transactions are not equivalent, there is clearly an overlap between the first and second criteria.[171] Indeed, if dissimilar conditions are applied to equivalent transactions (or *vice versa*) arguably there is little room to argue that the

---

168. Communication from the Commission, *Guidelines on the applicability of Article 101 of the Treaty on the Functioning of the European Union to horizontal co-operation agreements*, OJ 2011/C 11/1, 14 Jan. 2011, §§ 289-291.
169. Commission notice, *Guidelines on the application of Article 101 of the Treaty on the Functioning of the European Union to technology transfer agreements*, OJ 2014/C 89/03, 28 Mar. 2014.
170. The contributions filed with the Commission are available at: http://ec.europa.eu/competition/consultations/2010_horizontals/ (last checked 30 May 2014).
171. With regard to objective justifications Ivo Van Bael & Bellis, Jean-Francois, *Competition Law of the European Community*, 5th ed., Kluwer Law International, 2010 p. 816, notes that "*[t]he most common justification raised against an allegation of discriminatory pricing is that the*

conduct was objectively justified owing to the nature of the equivalence-test which, as highlighted below, involves taking into consideration circumstances (cost considerations etc.) which are also of relevance to substantiate an objective justification.[172] Accordingly, the question of 'equivalence' and that of 'objective justification' are discussed collectively in section §11.02[C], whereas the criterion relating to 'competitive disadvantage' is discussed in section §11.02[D].

[C] Equivalence of Transactions

Assessing whether a license agreement is discriminatory may seem as simple as comparing it to other agreements concerning the same patent(s) to determine if royalty rates or other license conditions differ.[173] However, it quickly becomes obvious that transactions cannot be considered 'equivalent' within the meaning of Article 102(c) TFEU merely because they concern the same patent(s). Such an approach would completely ignore that diverging license terms may in fact reflect dissimilarities as to the circumstances underpinning the transactions being compared. What at first sight appears to be discrimination may upon closer scrutiny turn out merely to signify a genuine attempt to offset dissimilar economic or competitive conditions. In the words of the CJEU an "*[a]pperance of discrimination in form may correspond in fact to an absence of discrimination in substance*".[174] Thus, it is clear that competition law does not require licensors, including those holding SEPs, to treat all licensees the same insofar as they are able to justify not doing so. The application of Article 102(c) TFEU requires a careful case-by-case analysis taking into consideration all the factual circumstances at hand.[175] In this respect note that discrimination is the norm rather than the exception, even in markets characterized by intense competition, and that for discrimination to be a commercially viable strategy the licensor does not need to hold market power.[176] This is an important reminder that diverging license terms do not necessarily signify an abuse of market power.

pricing is not discriminatory because the costs of the goods or services, or the customers to which a price is charged, are not identical".

172. See for instance Case T-301/04, *Clearstream v. Commission*, 9 Sep. 2009, § 181. Here the applicants claimed that the price difference in question was justified by cost considerations which, as explained below, also play a role in establishing whether transactions are equivalent in the first place.
173. Comparing royalty rates may itself be a complex task if the royalty base is different. If for instance a rate of 2.5% is calculated on basis of net revenue whereas another rate of 1.5% is calculated on basis of sale price it is not immediately clear which one is the most favourable to the licensee.
174. Case 13-63, *Italian Republic v. Commission*, 17 Jul. 1963 (the case concerned discrimination in the context of the ECSC Treaty).
175. This has been acknowledged by the CJEU. See for instance Case 322/81, *Michelin v. Commission*, 9 Nov. 1983, § 73, and Case T-228/97, *Irish Sugar v. Commission*, 7 Oct. 1999, § 114.
176. Cf. also Farrar-Layne, Anne, *Nondiscriminatory pricing – is standard setting different*, in Journal of Competition Law & Economics, Vol. 6(4), 2010 p. 813, Whish, Richard & Bailey, David, *Competition Law*, 7th ed., Oxford University Press, 2012 p. 760, and Bishop, Simon & Walker, Mike, *The Economics of EC Competition Law: Concepts, Application and Measurement*, Sweet and Maxwell, 2010 p. 250. See to the contrary Geradin, Damien & Petit, Nicolas, *Price*

As stated by the German Federal Supreme Court, the anti-discrimination provision in section 20(1) of the Act Against Restraints of Competition (the German equivalent of Article 102(c) TFEU) *"does not contain any blanket most-favoured-status clause intended to force the dominant undertaking ... to provide the same favourable conditions, especially prices, to all"*[177] – this reasoning applies in the context of Article 102(c) TFEU as well and extends to FRAND-pledged patents.Thus, there is nothing to support that the 'non-discriminatory' component of a FRAND commitment should be considered the equivalent of a 'most favoured licensee' clause which confers upon the patentee an obligation to extend the benefits offered to one licensee to all licensees. It is important to appreciate that too strict an application of Article 102(c) TFEU entails a risk of 'reverse discrimination' which as noted above is also prohibited, i.e., failing to take account of the fact that transactions are different may also be deemed to constitute abuse.[178]

Having confirmed that Article 102(c) TFEU does constitute an implicit most-favoured-licensee clause the question is which economic and competitive conditions may justify differential treatment of licensees. With regard to tangible products and services supply costs have typically played an important role in this respect, since transactions have been held non-equivalent if characterized by different costs of supply. However, as explained in the next section costs are a poor proxy for 'equivalence' in a licensing context. Accordingly, alternative proxies of potential relevance are considered in section §11.02[C][2] (focusing on the license terms) and §11.02[C][3] (focusing on the licensee's willingness or ability to pay).

[1] Supply Costs as a Proxy for 'Equivalence'

In the field of economics price discrimination is often defined as selling a specific good or service to different customers at different prices which do not reflect different supply costs.[179] The application of uniform pricing where supply costs do differ is also

---

Discrimination Under EC Competition Law: Another Antitrust Doctrine In Search Of Limiting Principles?, in Journal of Competition Law and Economics, Vol. 2(3), 2006 p. 482, stating that "*[a] firm must have some market power (i.e. the ability to set supracompetitive prices) to be able to price discriminate*".

177. Case KZR 40/02, Standard Tight-head Drum (Standard-Spundfass), Federal Supreme Court of Germany (Bundesgerichtshof), 13 Jul. 2004. See translation in International Review of Intellectual Property and Competition law (IIC), Vol. 36(6), 2005 pp. 741–752 (p. 746 in particular). The German Act Against Restraints of Competition is accessible at: http://www.gesetze-im-internet.de/englisch_gwb/ (last checked 30 May 2014).

178. According to Brooks, Roger G. & Geradin, Damien, *Interpreting and Enforcing the Voluntary FRAND Commitments*, in International Journal of IT Standards and Standardization Research, Vol. 9(1), 2011 p. 16, this interpretation seems to holds true from the perspective of contract law as well. Thus, based on an analysis of the history underpinning the ETSI IPR policy (and presuming no substantial difference amongst SSOs) the author concludes that there is no basis for interpreting the FRAND commitment as a Most Favoured Licensee clause.

179. See for instance Bishop, Simon & Walker, Mike, *The Economics of EC Competition Law: Concepts, Application and Measurement*, Sweet and Maxwell 3rd ed., 2010 p. 251, *Whish, Richard & Bailey, David, Competition Law*, 7th *ed., Oxford University Press, 2012* p. 759, Farrar-Layne, Anne, Nondiscriminatory pricing – is standard setting different, in Journal of Competition Law & Economics, Vol. 6(4), 2010 p. 814.

considered price discrimination.[180] Thus, according to these definitions the equivalence of transactions is to be assessed with reference to the underlying supply costs which accordingly become a focal point in determining whether the terms and conditions in question are discriminatory. Clearly inspired by such definition the CJEU in *Post Danmark* described price discrimination as "*...charging different customers or different classes of customers different prices for goods or services whose costs are the same or, conversely, charging a single price to customers for whom supply costs differ*".[181]

This definition has clearly been devised with tangible products and services in mind and is in need of slight modification to be applicable in a licensing context. Thus, whereas the supply of goods or services has a number of direct cost implications attributable to for instance diverging transport costs, taxes, handling costs or regulatory requirements, such costs are often negligible (or non-existing) in the context of IPR licensing.[182] While developing the technology to become patented may have incurred upon the licensor high upfront-costs, licensing it once developed only has limited cost implications. Transaction costs may of course differ depending on the time it takes to reach a license agreement as may monitoring/policing costs associated with ensuring that the licensee pays the correct amount of royalties, but it is unlikely that this will have a significant impact on the amount of royalties claimed under the agreement.

The weak link between supply costs and royalty rates entails that the former are not well suited as a benchmark for determining whether license transactions are equivalent under Article 102(c) TFEU. Thus, focusing merely on supply costs would fail to take into consideration the often significant non-monetary 'value transfers' ancillary to the patent itself.[183] Due to the insignificance of supply costs in this context it would also in effect impose upon the patentee an obligation equivalent to the one arising from a most-favoured-licensee clause – as explained above doing so would be contrary to the extended interpretation of Article 102(c) TFEU made by the Commission and the CJEU. The above definition therefore must be expanded to cover indirect costs stemming from the risks undertaken by the licensor and the value transferred between the parties to the license agreement.[184]

180. See Bishop, Simon & Walker, Mike, *The Economics of EC Competition Law: Concepts, Application and Measurement*, Sweet and Maxwell, 2010 p. 251 (footnote 108), where it is stated that in "*in theory, selling a product to different consumers at the same price when the costs of supply are different is also price discrimination*". Also see Whish, Richard & Bailey, David, Competition Law, 7th ed., Oxford University Press, 2012 p. 759, and Farrar-Layne, Anne, *Nondiscriminatory pricing – is standard setting different*, in Journal of Competition Law & Economics, Vol. 6(4), 2010 p. 814.

181. Case C-209/10, *Post Danmark A/S v. Konkurrencerådet*, 27 Mar. 2012, § 30.

182. Also see Farrar-Layne, Anne, *Nondiscriminatory pricing – is standard setting different*, in Journal of Competition Law & Economics, Vol. 6(4), 2010 p. 815.

183. If not taken into consideration under the first step of the discrimination-test (equivalence) such 'value transfers' would in any event have to be taken into consideration under step two which requires proof that the licensee is placed at a competitive disadvantage. Step two is discussed in s. §11.02[D].

184. Although this severely complicates establishing discrimination it is necessary in order to avoid type I-errors (false positives), i.e., the incorrect finding of abuse when in reality there is none.

While the CJEU in *Post Danmark* (cited in section §11.02[C][1]) adopted a narrow definition focusing solely on supply costs it was must likely adopted to fit the particular pricing practice dealt with and should be not understood as preventing other factors of relevance from being taken into consideration. Indeed, in *United Brands for* instance the Court acknowledged *inter alia* that the conditions of marketing, the density of competition, the interplay between supply and demand as well as the wages of the labour force may factors of relevance.[185] Moreover, in addition to arguments concerning supply costs the applicant in *Clearstream* argued that the price difference in question was justified by the fact that it had provided the alleged disfavoured trading party with insurance against civil liability. While the Court rejected the argument on basis of insufficient evidence regarding the existence of an insurance agreement it did not dismiss the potential validity of risk related arguments as such.[186] While these cases did not specifically concern patent licensing they at least underline that supply costs – in the narrow sense of the word – is not the only parameter of relevance in assessing the equivalence of transactions under Article 102(c) TFEU. Indeed, as already noted the licensor not only has the right, but also the obligation to ensure that the remuneration charged reflects any dissimilarity as to the terms and conditions agreed in order to avoid applying similar conditions to non-equivalent transactions.

[2] License Terms as a Proxy for 'Equivalence'

In determining whether transactions are equivalent in a licensing context it is more appropriate to think of differences in terms of licensee 'traits'.[187] It then becomes clear that a number of factors not related directly to costs may render license transactions non-equivalent, hence provide an objective justification under Article 102(c) TFEU.[188] License agreements are seldom confined to a 'pure' one-way license at a fixed royalty rate, but contain a number of additional components such as for instance grants-backs, field of use or territorial restrictions, indemnity undertakings, transfer of know-how and/or lump sum payments. Such components relating to the scope of the license, the risks of the licensor and the 'value' transferred between the parties, will often have a significant impact on the monetary payment made under the agreement.[189] Indeed, while not strictly related to supply costs, the terms and conditions impact both the value of the patent licensed as well as the risks – hereby the potential costs – of the parties to the agreement. Accordingly, differences as to the terms agreed will therefore most often translate into diverging royalty payments or other fees. All things being

185. Case 27/76, *United Brands v. Commission*, 14 Feb. 1978, §§ 228–229.
186. Case T-301/04, *Clearstream v. Commission*, 9 Sep. 2009, § 181 and § 187.
187. See Farrar-Layne, Anne, *Nondiscriminatory pricing – is standard setting different*, in Journal of Competition Law & Economics, Vol. 6(4), 2010 p. 815, who (rightly) argues that discrimination in an IP context is "*thought of in terms of licensee traits rather than cost justifications*".
188. As noted in s. §11.02[C][3] even factors completely unrelated to costs might establish the basis for a non-discrimination counter-claim.
189. Cf. also Mariniello, Mario, Fair, Reasonable And Non-Discriminatory (Frand) Terms: A Challenge For Competition Authorities, in Journal of Competition Law & Economics, Vol. 7(3), 2011 p. 536.

equal a licensee provided with an indemnity undertaking can for instance be expected to pay more than those who are not since additional remuneration may be required to offset the potential risks associated with such undertaking. This is not different than when a bank sets its interest rate to reflect the perceived risk associated with the individual loan transaction. Thus, while the costs of supply are strictly speaking low other costs incurred by the licensor may vary between licensees and as the royalty rate set needs to cover such costs in addition to the costs of upfront R&D they may likewise render transactions non-equivalent.

In the context of standard setting vertically integrated patentees offering standard compliant products themselves may also make their patent license (and their FRAND commitment) conditional on reciprocity, thus securing their own freedom to operate on the downstream market to which the standard relates by obtaining a license to complementary essential technologies in return.[190] In such cases payment under the agreement may be very small (even non-existing) as the value of the licensed rights are offset against each other, i.e., reciprocal licensing in essence constitutes a payment in kind. Obviously this entails that some licensees – being in possession of patents (or other rights) to offer in return – will be able to secure lower royalty rates than those not in possession of such rights. However, this does not in itself signify discrimination within the meaning of Article 102(c) TFEU since, as noted above, the value of the license granted in return would have to be neutralized from the equation prior to any comparison of license agreements.

There is nothing sinister about cross-licensing agreements. On their face cross-licensing agreements are important means to clear 'blocking positions' and allow standard compliant products to effectively reach the market. Arguably they also reduce transaction costs and uncertainty associated with negotiating multiple distinct agreements to obtain the rights needed. As rightly noted by Carl Shapiro:

> If two patent holders are the only companies realistically capable of manufacturing products that utilize their intellectual property rights, a royalty-free cross license is ideal from the point of view of ex post competition. But any cross license is superior to a world in which the patents holders fail to cooperate, since neither could proceed with actual production and sale in that world without infringing on the other's patents[191]

As follows from the above evaluating 'equivalence' under Article 102(c) TFEU involves establishing a level 'playing field' as basis for the comparison of license agreements by extracting the effective price paid by the individual licensee, i.e., the price paid taking into consideration the economic value of all terms and transfers made under the

---

190. Making the FRAND commitment conditional on reciprocity is considered justified by the Commission. See case No. COMP/M.6381, *GOOGLE/ MOTOROLA MOBILITY*, footnote 57 in which the Commission notes "*...that a SEP holder is generally considered as entitled to condition a cross-licence from the counter-party to that counter-party's SEPs reading on the same standard*" (SEP refers to "Standard Essential Patent").

191. See Shapiro, Carl, *Navigating the Patent Thicket: Cross Licenses, Patent Pools, and Standard Setting*, in Jaffe, Adam B.; Lerner, Josh & Stern, Scott (eds.), *Innovation Policy and the Economy*, Vol. 1, 2001 p. 123.

agreement. Obviously, this is a very challenging[192] task as it requires valuating each component forming part of the license agreements being compared. If, as argued in the next section, the willingness and ability of licensees to pay is also a factor or relevance things are bound to get even more complicated. In effect licensors will arguably have considerable freedom to argue non-equivalence on basis of factors such as those mentioned above albeit within the boundaries of reasonableness. However, while evaluating the value transferred between a licensor and a licensee under a cross-license agreement or monetizing the risks associated with an indemnity clause is difficult it is not impossible to do with some discrepancy and such complexity will not by itself safeguard licensors from intervention - nor should it.[193] Put simply, even if license agreements are different this does not grant the licensor a blanket permission to discriminate. A royalty difference (or any other difference) must reflect dissimilarities as to economic conditions characterizing the transactions. If for instance an indemnity undertaking is given only to select licensees which as a result pay a higher royalty rate than other licensees then the magnitude of the royalty difference identified should (with a margin of discretion) reflect the risks incurred by the licensor in this respect in order to support an objective justification and render the pricing scheme non-arbitrary.

Taking into consideration the uncertainties highlighted above it is unfortunate that neither the Commission nor the CJEU have provided more clear guidance as to the criteria used to determine whether transactions are equivalent in cases where dissimilar conditions cannot be explained on basis of cost considerations. Indeed, there is a tendency for the CJEU and the Commission to perform a rather cursory assessment in discrimination cases.[194] In the context of licensing the resulting legal uncertainty may cause dominant companies to abstain from perfectively legitimate licensing practices out of fear that they might infringe competition law and as already noted there is a risk that innovation hence effective competition, will suffer as a result.

Taking the above analysis one step further, one might ask if discrimination will always violate Article 102(c) TFEU if it cannot be explained on basis of licensee terms, but is claimed merely to result from the outcome of bilateral negotiations and being aimed at effectively compensating the licensor for the costs and risks incurred *ex ante* during the research and development phase leading to the patent grant. In the next section it is considered to what extent EU case law leaves room for such argument and whether indeed it should. While the definition of discrimination provided by Article 102(c) TFEU provides a broad framework allowing courts and competition authorities to take into consideration factors other than costs and risks they have, as

192. See along the same lines Farrell, Joseph et. al., *Standard Setting, Patents, And Hold-Up*, In Antitrust Law Journal, Vol. 74(3), 2007 p. 638.

193. In Case T-167/08, *Microsoft Corp v. Commission*, 27 Jun. 2012, the Commission had compiled a complex body of evidence in support of its argument that the protocols licensed by Microsoft were non-innovative and therefor did not justify the remuneration requested by Microsoft. Although the case concerned excessive pricing and not discrimination it highlights that the Commission does not refrain from carrying out complex economic assessments if the competition law violation at issue is of sufficient importance.

194. See along the same lines Van Bael & Bellis, Jean-Francois, *Competition Law of the European Community*, 5th ed., Kluwer Law International, 2010 pp. 811–812.

explained below, been reluctant to provide any clear statements in this respect – perhaps fearing to open the floodgates to abuse.

[3] Willingness and Ability to Pay as a Proxy for 'Equivalence'

In the preceding sections it was discussed to what extent the costs incurred and the license terms agreed may render transactions non-equivalent under Article 102(c) TFEU. However, price differentiation may also take place on basis of commercial considerations not related to such factors, but to the characteristics of individual licensee's signalling their willingness or ability to pay (the 'licensee situation') – as explained in section §11.02[A] shady motives need not be the driving force. Indeed, positive welfare effects may result from such strategy, but there is also a risk that it will distort competition amongst licensees and accordingly limit their ability to compete. This inevitably raises the question as to what extent Article 102(c) TFEU leaves room for a SEP holder to tailor his licensing scheme on basis of considerations pertaining to the characteristics of the individual licensee if competition as a result is distorted.[195] The insight granted by economics is an important starting point in this respect – after all competition law pursues an objective of effective competition the obtainment of which relies on economic reasoning. Although the welfare effects of discrimination are ambiguous it is generally accepted that licensing discrimination may be beneficial – not only to the licensor – but also to consumers.[196] This finding applies in the context of standardization as well and regardless of whether FRAND commitments have been issued.

First, discrimination as noted above allows the licensor to license firms which otherwise would not have had the financial capabilities or the willingness to take a license. This can be welfare enhancing since establishing lower prices for price sensitive licensees (those with high price elasticity) and higher prices for less sensitive licensees (those with low price elasticity) will increase 'licensing output' and in effect the intensity of downstream competition.[197] If forced to license under a uniform scheme the licensor might realize that setting the royalty rate to fit the most price sensitive companies (those with high price elasticity) will result in a decrease of profits,

195. If competition is not distorted Art. 102(c) TFEU does not apply, since the provision requires that a 'competitive disadvantage' is inflicted upon certain companies relative to others. In this respect see s. §11.02[D].

196. See for instance Bishop, Simon & Walker, Mike, *The Economics of EC Competition Law: Concepts, Application and Measurement*, Sweet and Maxwell, 2010 p. 253, Rapp, Richard T. & Stiroh, Lauren J., Standard Setting and Market Power, Comments provided for Joint Hearing of the United States Department of Justice and the Federal Trade Commission, Competition and Intellectual Property Law and Policy in the Knowledge-Based Economy, 18 Apr. 2002 p. 13, Hausman, Jerry A., Price Discrimination and Patent Policy, in RAND Journal of Economics, Vol. 19(2), 1988 p. 264, and Kao, Kuo-Feng & Hwang, Hong, *Input Price Discrimination and Social Welfare in the Presence of Technology Licensing*, working paper, 2013 p. 17. Available at: http://www.apeaweb.org/confer/osaka13/papers/Hwang_Hong.pdf (last checked 30 May 2014).

197. See Rapp, Richard T. & Stiroh, Lauren J., Standard Setting and Market Power, Comments provided for Joint Hearing of the United States Department of Justice and the Federal Trade Commission, Competition and Intellectual Property Law and Policy in the Knowledge-Based

and accordingly may set a royalty rate which reflects the willingness/ability of less price sensitive companies – this will force some companies to exit the market and may prevent new entry.

Second, discrimination may increase effective competition in a dynamic perspective by encouraging innovation. Such pro-competitive effect is particularly likely to arise in markets characterized by high sunk costs and low marginal costs insofar as adopting prices to fit the individual customer's (or in this case, licensee's) willingness to pay allows upfront investment costs to be more effectively recouped.[198] Since proprietors of SEPs may have incurred high sunk costs (stemming from investments in R&D, including failed projects) it follows that a too strict prohibition against licensing discrimination which denies them the possibility of effectively recovering said costs and secure a reasonable rate of return may produce adverse welfare effects. Moreover, the potential increase in competition between licensees (mentioned above) may also enhance innovation at the product level.

To ensure that the welfare effects outlined above are allowed a chance to prevail it is necessary to construe Article 102(c) TFEU, as allowing licensors to adopt their remuneration scheme to fit the characteristics of the individual licensee – even if the resulting differences in treatment cannot be explained on basis of diverging costs or license terms. In other words, treating different situated licensees differently should not be deemed anti-competitive.[199] In order to maintain the autonomy of the market place competition law should only intervene in cases where a divergence as to the license terms agreed is unlikely to have resulted merely from the legitimate outcome of licensing negotiations and has no basis in objective factors related to the situation of licensees. Similar reasoning reflects in case law at the national level. In the German *Standard Spundfass* case, which concerned alleged discrimination on basis of patents essential to a de facto standard for industrial barrels, the Federal Supreme Court rightly emphasized that an abuse of a dominant position cannot simply be inferred by the fact that the pursuit of the most favourable business conditions by the dominant undertakings trading partners has not resulted in the same ratio between expenditure and

Economy, 18 Apr. 2002 p. 13. Also see Kao, Kuo-Feng & Hwang, Hong, *Input Price Discrimination and Social Welfare in the Presence of Technology Licensing*, working paper, 2013 p. 17. Available at: http://www.apeaweb.org/confer/osaka13/papers/Hwang_Hong.pdf (last checked 30 May 2014).

198. Bishop, Simon & Walker, Mike, *The Economics of EC Competition Law: Concepts, Application and Measurement*, Sweet and Maxwell, 2010 pp. 255–256, Jones, Alison & Sufrin, Brenda, *EC Competition Law- Text, Cases and Materials*, 3rd ed., Oxford University Press, 2008 p. 441, and Hausman, Jerry A., *Price Discrimination and Patent Policy*, in RAND Journal of Economics, Vol. 19(2), 1988 pp. 263–264.

199. Farrar-Layne, Anne, *Nondiscriminatory pricing – is standard setting different*, in Journal of Competition Law & Economics, Vol. 6(4), 2010 p. 815, similarly finds that "*...offering different licensing terms to "similarly situated" licensees is generally viewed as discriminatory, as is offering the same licensing terms to "differently situated" licensees*". Also see Rapp, Richard T. & Stiroh, Lauren J., Standard Setting and Market Power, Comments provided for Joint Hearing of the United States Department of Justice and the Federal Trade Commission, Competition and Intellectual Property Law and Policy in the Knowledge-Based Economy, 18 Apr. 2002 p. 13, who in a US context suggests only prohibiting licensor from offering "*the same royalty to "similarly situated licensees"*.

reward.[200] The court hereby made clear that the autonomy of the parties to negotiate in place terms and conditions without fearing subsequent competition law intervention should be safeguarded – regardless of the fact that some trading partners may be put at a competitive disadvantage. Although the case was decided on basis of German competition law there is no reason to believe that Article 102 TFEU operates by a different overall norm.[201]

This should not be taken to mean however that licensors will be able to justify their licensing scheme merely be reference to the fact that the terms were negotiated in place on a bilateral basis.It would be wrong to assume that the outcome of such negotiations always reflects a genuine compromise between the parties since as between dominant licensors and licensees the bargaining power will often be asymmetric. The CJEU and the Commission, as highlighted by the case law mentioned below, can therefore be expected only to accept discrimination claimed to result from bilateral negotiations if supported by evidence that the licensee's business models are somehow different. To support an argument that differential license terms are attributable to divergent outcomes of the bargaining process, licensors holding market power will therefore be well advised to secure documentation able to prove that the terms in question have not been imposed unilaterally, but results from genuine bilateral licensing negotiations and reflects objective factors relating to the licensee. After all, potential licensees will often have no knowledge of the license agreements already entered into by the patentee and therefore will not be in a position to safeguard their business against anti-competitive discrimination. In this respect it must be recalled that dominant undertakings have a special[202] responsibility not to impair genuine undistorted competition in the market. SEP holders therefore clearly do not have unfettered freedom to discriminate – the question is which objective criteria (if any) relating to the licensee situation may legitimately be taken into consideration?

Arguably differentiating between licensees on basis of factors such as the use to which the licensed technology is put and expected revenues will not violate Article 102(c) TFEU, since doing so is not a reflection of market power, but an acknowledgement that each licensee has a different willingness or ability to pay. The type of product in which the licensee intends to incorporate the licensed technology may have a significant impact on the licensee's valuation hereof.[203] A licensee utilizing a SEP to sell high-end products with a considerable profit margin may for instance be willing (and able) to pay a higher royalty rate than a competitor with a smaller profit margin. Bilateral negotiations may also lead to different outcomes in terms of license terms simply as a reflection of the bargaining position of the parties and in this respect the

200. Case KZR 40/02, *Standard Tight-head Drum (Standard-Spundfass)*, Federal Supreme Court of Germany (Bundesgerichtshof), 13 Jul. 2004. See translation in International Review of Intellectual Property and Competition law (IIC), Vol. 36(6), 2005 pp. 741–752 (p. 746 in particular).

201. Although the German courts are known to be patentee friendly the reasoning referred seems consistent with the fact that positive welfare effects may arise from discriminatory patent licensing for which reason caution should be displayed when applying Art. 102(c) TFEU as a tool to mingle with market outcomes in this respect.

202. See for instance T-321/05, *AstraZeneca v. Commission*, § 671 (with references).

203. Cf. also Farrar-Layne, Anne, *Nondiscriminatory pricing – is standard setting different*, in Journal of Competition Law & Economics, Vol. 6(4), 2010 p. 820.

goliath is not always the licensor.[204] By way of example consider a licensee holding an input important to the business of a vertically integrated licensee; say a patent which is not standard-essential, but which nonetheless adds consumer valued functionality to the products made by the licensor. In such scenario the licensor may very well accept lower royalties than offered to other licensees in order to obtain a cross-license, knowing that the licensee is not obliged to license its rights in return.[205] Another scenario may arise for instance if some would-be licensees currently manufacture products which adhere to a competing standard (hence, standards incorporating the technologies of competing licensors). In this case the licensor may be inclined to offer these firms better license conditions to persuade them that it makes sense to adopt the standard to which its patents relate (or in a more hostile jargon; to lure them away from competitors), whereas companies 'locked-in'[206] to the standard are offered less preferential treatment – this may however be deemed both exploitative of locked-in licensees and exclusionary with regard to competing licensors.

Unfortunately there are no clear[207] answers to be extracted from EU case law, but there are indications that the 'licence situation' is potentially a factor which may render transactions non-equivalent and therefore help a discriminatory licensing scheme escape Article 102(c) TFEU.The notorious *Rambus* case, which concerned an alleged 'patent ambush'[208] by a holder of FRAND-pledged patents, for instance provides an indication that the 'licensee situation', according to the Commission, is of relevance to the assessment of discrimination. Thus, Rambus had originally submitted a licensing commitment (pursuant to Article 9 of Regulation 1/2003) which included a most-favoured-licensee clause, but having aired the commitment (pursuant to Article 27 of Regulation 1/2003) the Commission received a number of responses that the clause should be removed "*...as Rambus would likely refuse to agree to any royalty rate below*

204. As explained in Ch. 8 s. §8.02[B] this bargaining position of licensees is also a factor of relevance to the assessment of market power.
205. As noted in s. §11.01[I] a holder of FRAND-pledged patents can only demand reciprocity with regard to patents essential to the same standard as the patents being licensed – absent such connection a cash-only license has to be offered. Therefore in this scenario the licensor would have to accept licensing its FRAND-pledged rights without being sure to get a license in return – this, as argued, increases the bargaining strength of the licensee and may prompt the acceptance of lower royalty rates.
206. Such 'lock-in' may for instance be attributable to the fact that their production machinery during the standard setting phase was tailored to be able to meet the demands relating to the specific standard in question or because the licensee has become 'path-dependant' since backwards compatibility is valued by consumers and the licensees products adhere to prior versions of the standard.
207. In Geradin, Damien & Petit, Nicolas, *Price Discrimination under EC Competition Law: The Need for a caseby-case Approach*, GCLC Working Paper 07/05, 2005 p. 17, the authors find that "*[t]he Commission and the Community courts have not, however, resolved the issue of whether customers with different price elasticity could be considered as being in a different situation, thereby rendering Article 82(c) inapplicable*".
208. See Ch. 10 for more details on this phenomenon. A 'Patent ambush' occurs when SSO participants conceal their Intellectual Property Rights (IPRs) essential to the standard being developed, and starts asserting them after the standard has been agreed and the other participants 'locked in' to using it. See Commission's press release in Case COMP/38.636, *Rambus*, MEMO/09/544 (Commission accepts commitments from Rambus lowering memory chip royalty rates – frequently asked questions), 9 Dec. 2009.

those specified [in the commitment made] because it arguably would have to offer those rates to every other licensee, thereby preventing licensees from obtaining better rates through negotiations" [addition added].[209] In essence this reasoning points to the fact that royalty rates, as noted above, may increase if discrimination is prohibited. Rambus subsequently agreed to remove the clause from its template license agreements and the Commission's endorsement indicates a willingness to accept (at least to some extent) that bilateral license negotiations should be allowed to yield different results. It is more unclear to what extent the CJEU are prepared to accept the outcome of bilateral negotiations if distortion of competition results.

In Case T-167/08, *Microsoft Corp v. Commission*, which concerned a fine imposed on Microsoft for breach its duty to license on FRAND terms in accordance with a decision adopted by the Commission in 2004, the General Court stated that "*...subject to the obligation to provide interoperability information on non-discriminatory terms – the 2004 decision remains neutral as regards the possibility for each of Microsoft's potential licensees to enter into an agreement with Microsoft adapted to its business model*". The statement is somewhat ambiguous. While on the one hand making clear that license negotiations – in accordance with *Rambus* – are allowed to yield different results depending on the potential licensee's business model, it is stressed that the prohibition against discrimination must nonetheless be respected. The General Court did not provide any guidance to aid in distinguishing between legal and illegal discrimination in this respect. Arguably the General Court's statement is to be taken as a reminder that although there is some scope to negotiate in place terms and conditions on basis of objective criteria relating to the 'license situation' it is for the dominant undertaking to ensure that competition is not unduly distorted.

In *United Brands*[210] and *Irish Sugar,*[211] which concerned tangible products, it was similarly held that the willingness or ability of customers – the interplay between supply and demand as it was put – may be taken into consideration when a dominant undertaking sets its prices. However, the reasoning put forward by the CJEU in these cases does not add clarification. Quite to the contrary the cases seem to have blurred the line between illegal and legal clarification by introducing a rather artificial distinction between supply and demand at different stages of the supply chain.

In *United Brands*[212] an undertaking (UBC) importing and distributing brand name (Chiquita) bananas in the EU was, amongst other things, found guilty of price discrimination contrary to Article 102 TFEU (then, Article 86 ECC). UBC had charged customers different prices according to the Member State for which the bananas supplied were destined to be sold. Having concluded that the transactions were equivalent in that supply costs were not able to explain the price difference identified it was found that "*[t]his being so all those customers going to Rotterdam and Bremerhaven to obtain their supplies might be expected to find that UBC offers them all*

209. Case COMP/C-3/ 38 636, *Rambus*, 15 Jan. 2010, §§ 56–59 and 82 (rejection decision).
210. Case 27/76, *United Brands v. Commission*, 14 Feb. 1978.
211. Case T-228/97, *Irish Sugar v. Commission*, 7 Oct. 1999.
212. Case 27/76, *United Brands v. Commission*, 14 Feb. 1978, § 225.

the same selling price for 'Chiquita' bananas".[213] The Court rejected UBC's argument that the prices charged were not discriminatory because they had merely been adapted to what each market could bear and reflected the fact that retail prices varied between Member States.[214] The Commission had argued that charging "*...each Member State the highest price which the market of that State could bear is not a reason justifying the application of different prices*". Signalling a limited scope to take into consideration the law of supply and demand the Court added that "*...the interplay of supply and demand should, owing to its nature, only be applied to each stage where it is really manifest*".[215] According to the Court the applicant was therefore not justified in taking into account the "*...law of supply and demand as between the vendor and the ultimate consumer and not as between the vendor (UBC) and the purchaser (ripener/distributors)*" – it was primarily for UBC's trading partners (and not UBC) to take into consideration the factors which could result in different retail selling prices in different Member States (such as the density of competition, wages, etc.).[216]

In *Irish Sugar*, the General Court similarly found market mechanisms to have been distorted because prices had been set "*...not by reference to supply and demand on the industrial market in Ireland, but by reference to current and potential buyers from its customers according to their location*".[217] In accordance with the reasoning of *United Brands* the Court therefore found the pricing scheme in question to constitute abuse because it was not adapted to reflect supply and demand as between the supplier and its customer, but concerned an unrelated stage in the supply chain.

As noted above the judgments rendered in *United Brands* and *Irish Sugar* supports that it may be justified to price discriminate by reference to factors relating to the 'licensee situation'. However, insofar as the dominant undertaking does not deal directly with end users the conditions on the downstream product market are not of relevance in this respect, since according to the Court the interplay between supply and demand should only be considered at the stage where it is really manifest – being between the seller and the buyer. While the courts' reasoning was based on the premise that adjusting prices on a state-by-state basis is detrimental to the goal of market integration in the EU (the single market imperative) it does arguably not make much sense upon closer scrutiny. Thus, inevitably the downstream market conditions (which cannot be taken into consideration) will also impact the trading partner's willingness to pay insofar as the trading partner offers products on said market. Nonetheless, it remains that a licensor seeking compliance with competition law cannot adopt its prices to match conditions (such as the end users price elasticity) of the product market on which the licensed technology will be put to use. Instead reference must be made to factors related exclusively to the licensee such as for instance its profitability or use of the licensed technology.

213. Case 27/76, *United Brands v. Commission*, 14 Feb. 1978, § 207.
214. *Ibid.*, §§ 215–218.
215. *Ibid.*, § 229.
216. *Ibid.*, §§ 227–230.
217. Case T-228/97, *Irish Sugar v. Commission*, 7 Oct. 1999, § 141.

In conclusion case law supports that objective factors related to the licensees commercial situation may render transactions non-equivalent within the meaning of Article 102(c) TFEU, hence substantiate a finding of non-discrimination. However, clarity is still called for since it is unclear which factors may be relied upon in this respect and how the CJEU intends to decide whether the positive benefits outlined above outweigh the negative impact on competition in cases where subjective intent (see section §11.02) does not support a finding of abuse.

[D] Competitive Disadvantage

As highlighted by the wording of Article 102(c) TFEU competition law is concerned only with discrimination capable of placing select trading partners at a 'competitive disadvantage' relative to others. Thus, as noted by the CJEU in *British Airways* Article 102(c) TFEU (then, Article 82(c) EC) "*...forms part of the system for ensuring, in accordance with Article 3(1)(g) EC, that competition is not distorted in the internal market*".[218] A finding that dissimilar conditions have been applied to equivalent transactions is accordingly not by itself sufficient for Article 102 TFEU to apply: in the words of the CJEU, referring to the competitive relationship between travel agents, "*...there must be a finding not only that the behaviour of an undertaking in a dominant market position is discriminatory, but also that it tends to distort that competitive relationship...*".[219] This requirement is based on the reasoning that a distortion of competition may indirectly harm consumers because crippling the ability of certain companies to compete may lead to market concentration and accordingly higher prices.[220] In this respect note that it is sufficient for competition law to apply that the licensing scheme on its face *could* result in discrimination – there is no need to show that the effect has actually materialized itself in that competition has been distorted.[221]

It is clear therefore, that a differential licensing scheme can only be detrimental to competition if as a result the licensees' receiving the least favourable terms and conditions risks being placed at a competitive disadvantage – otherwise there is no distortion of competition. As noted above a precondition for such competitive disadvantage to materialize is that the licensors patented technologies are sufficiently important (translates into market power) to discourage mistreated licensees to simply

218. Case C-95/04 P, *British Airways v. Commission*, 15 Mar. 2007, § 143. When the Lisbon Treaty was signed on 13 Dec. 2007 the rule in Art. 3(1)(g) EC, to which the court referred, was moved to Protocol No. 27 on the internal market and competition. The protocol states "*that the internal market as set out in Article 3 of the Treaty on European Union includes a system ensuring that competition is not distorted*".

219. Case C-95/04 P, *British Airways v. Commission*, 15 Mar. 2007, § 144.

220. In Case C-209/10, *Post Danmark A/S v. Konkurrencerådet*. 27 Mar. 2012, § 44 it was for instance held "*...necessary to consider whether that pricing policy, without objective justification, produces an actual or likely exclusionary effect, to the detriment of competition and, thereby, of consumers' interests*".

221. See for instance case T-219/99, *British Airways v. Commission* (§ 235 in particular), where the General Court held it to be sufficient that a performance reward scheme *could* result in anti-competitive discrimination.

opt for alternatives – in the context of SEPs this requirement is typically fulfilled because per definition there are no substitute technologies.

[1] Non-competitors: Different Product Markets

Market definition is an important starting point in determining whether the use of differential license terms distorts competition, hence inflicts a competitive disadvantage. Clearly a violation of Article 102 TFEU is conditional on a finding that the 'trading partners' (licensees) subject to differential treatment are active on the same product market as otherwise the divergence identified – while perhaps not objectively justified according to the criteria discussed in section §11.02[C] – does not distort competition. In other words, if a differentiated royalty scheme reflects merely the product market to which the licensed technology is put to use there can be no discrimination within the meaning of Article 102 TFEU. Indeed, with respect to licensing in the context of technology pools the Commission in its guidelines on technology transfer agreements states that *"[i]t is in general not considered restrictive of competition to apply different royalty rates to different product markets, whereas there should be no discrimination within product markets"*.[222] As a technical standard may relate to several distinct product markets this is important to bear in mind. Thus, if for instance the proprietor of a patent essential to the USB standard decides to impose a royalty of 2% on licensees producing USB sticks and a royalty of 2.5% on licensees incorporating the licensed technology into laptop computers this does not constitute a violation of Article 102 TFEU simply because there is no discrimination *within* products markets, i.e., USB sticks and laptop computers are not substitute products, hence each comprise a distinct market.

[2] Non-competitors: Different Geographic Markets

The above logic may on its face substantiate a conclusion that differential treatment of licensees' active on the same product market, but on different geographical markets, likewise does not inflict a competitive disadvantage within the meaning of Article 102 TFEU. However, in this respect potential competition is likely to be a factor of decisive relevance. Thus, standards often promote interoperability between competing products at the regional or global level, hence facilitates cross-border competition, but geographic price discrimination may discourage select licensees from entering new markets by placing them at a (potential) competitive disadvantage *vis-à-vis* other licensees already present on said markets and accordingly present a barrier to potential competition. Moreover, even if there is no actual or potential competition between licensees, discriminating between licensees according to the market on which they are active may still distort competition due to arbitrage, i.e., because the cheaper products

222. Commission notice, *Guidelines on the application of Article 101 of the Treaty on the Functioning of the European Union to technology transfer agreements*, OJ 2014/C 89/03, 28 Mar. 2014, § 269.

offered by the favoured licensee(s) are likely to end up on the market in the Member State(s) where the licensees receiving less preferential treatment are present.

[3] Competitors

In case there is competition between licensees it must be determined on a case-by-case basis whether the nature of the divergence identified is such as to place the disfavoured licensee(s) at a competitive disadvantage. However, despite the express requirement that a 'competitive disadvantage' must be inflicted the CJEU have traditionally only paid scant attention – if any at all – to this aspect.[223] In *Suiker Unie* for instance, a case concerning discrimination in the context of loyalty rebates, the court merely affirmed that there was competition between the buyers of the dominant undertaking and hinted that the scheme would therefore necessarily lead to a distortion of competition.[224] It was not before the judgment in *British Airways* that the CJEU provided some express guidance with regard to the Court's position in this respect.

In *British Airways* the Court, as noted above, stressed that Article 102 TFEU is only applicable to discriminatory practices able to distort competition, but at the same time it set a very low threshold for establishing the likelihood of such distortion. The CJEU took the position that if the discriminatory conduct in question impacts factors of importance to competition in the relevant market then there is no need to prove an "*actual quantifiable deterioration in the competitive position of the business partners taken individually*" – it is sufficient to show that the discriminatory practice at hand "*tends, having regard to the whole of the circumstances of the case, to lead to a distortion of competition*".[225] Thus, in light of the fact that the ability of travel agents to compete was determined by their ability to provide seats on flights at a reasonable cost as well as by their individual financial resources the CJEU held that the General Court had not erred by not verifying, or in verifying only briefly, whether competition had been distorted, i.e., the court found that the likelihood of such distortion was evident from the circumstances of the case. As operating costs are of importance to competition in most industries the reasoning of the court seems to entail that price discrimination, if applied to equivalent transactions, is per se capable of inflicting a competitive disadvantage, hence may distort competition. Arguably however a certain *de minimis* threshold applies – not least in light of the fact that Article 102 TFEU is only applicable to practices capable of restricting competition to an 'appreciable' extent. If the disfavoured licensee is able to pass the increase in royalty costs on to its customers without incurring a competitive disadvantage there is arguably no basis for applying Article 102(c) TFEU.

---

223. Cf. also Whish, Richard & Bailey, David, Competition Law, 7th ed., Oxford University Press, 2012 p. 762 and *Van Bael & Bellis*: Competition Law of the European Community, Aspen Publishers, 2010 p. 813.
224. Joined Cases 40 TO 48, 50, 54 TO 56, 111, 113 and 114/73, *Suiker Unie and Others v. Commission*, 16 Dec. 1975, § 525.
225. C-95/04 P, *British Airways v. Commission*, 15 Mar. 2007, §§ 144–149.

[E] Refusals to License: The Clash of Inconsistent Legal Tests

Until now focus has been on the situation where the IPR owner grants a license to *all* interested parties on a given market, but where some licensees receive preferential treatment relative to others present on said market. In this section focus is directed at a slightly different scenario. Thus, if the IPR owner does not 'merely' grant some companies terms and conditions which are unfavourable relative to others, but refuses to license certain companies altogether, this may similarly be considered a violation of Article 102(c) TFEU – especially if, as explained below, the refusal concerns a patent which is essential on a downstream market. In essence, a refusal to license only select companies is the ultimate type of discrimination.[226]

The CJEU have however developed a distinct legal doctrine used to assess whether a refusal to license constitutes abuse within the meaning of Article 102(b) TFEU. Said doctrine has evolved through a series of cases, the latest being the *Microsoft*[227] case in which the General Court passed its judgment in 2007. Referring to the framework established by prior case law the Court held that an undertaking can only be forced to grant a compulsory license in 'exceptional circumstances' such as those where:

(1) the refusal relates to a product or service indispensable to the exercise of a particular activity on a neighbouring market;
(2) the refusal is of such a kind as to exclude all effective competition on that neighbouring market; and
(3) the refusal prevents the appearance of a new product for which there is potential consumer demand or limits technical development to the prejudice of consumers.[228]

It is evident that the legal test outlined above relies on criteria which are different from, and inconsistent with, the criteria relevant to determine whether the imposition of a differentiated licensing scheme amounts to discrimination, cf. Article 102(c) TFEU. In particular, a finding of abuse in this respect requires that the refusal is likely to eliminate *all* effective competition whereas for the purpose of finding discrimination it is sufficient that competition is distorted, i.e., that a competitive disadvantage is inflicted upon the would-be licensee relative to those having obtained a license. As a result determining the point of collision between the two legal tests it not merely of

226. See generally Whish, Richard, *Competition Law*, 7th ed., Oxford University Press, 2012 p. 760 and Buttigieg, Eugène, *Competition Law: Safeguarding the Consumer Interest: a Comparative Analysis of US Antitrust Law and EC Competition Law*, Wolters Kluwer (International competition law series, 40), 2009 p. 195.

227. Case T-201/04, *Microsoft Corp v. Commission*, 17 Sep. 2007. Prior cases dealing with refusals to license include Joined Cases C-241/91 P and C-242/91 P, *RTE and ITP v. Commission*, 6 Apr. 1995 ('Magill'), and Case C-418/01, *IMS Health*, 29 Apr. 2004.

228. T-201/04, *Microsoft Corp v. Commission*, 17 Sep. 2007, §§ 332, 564 and 647 (in particular). Note that prior case law focused exclusively on whether the refusal at hand prevented the appearance of a new product, whereas the General Court in *Microsoft* held that a refusal which limits technical development to the prejudice of consumers may also be abusive.

theoretical importance, but will in many cases be crucial in deciding whether a refusal to license constitutes abuse.

> Example: Company A owns a patent essential to a dominant de facto standard and grants a license to a number of companies, but decides not to license company B. Said refusal does not eliminate all effective competition, but merely limits it, as some companies have obtained a license. A is therefore not obliged to grant a license pursuant to the legal test applicable to refusal to license situations. However, competition is nonetheless distorted as B is placed at a competitive disadvantage relative to its competitors (which may include A itself). This raises the question as to whether B can raise a non-discrimination claim in order to obtain a license or whether the refusal to license-test rules out such action because it takes precedence.

In the context of SEPs resolving the conflict described above is primarily of practical relevance with regard to patents not covered by a FRAND commitment, i.e., patents reading on a de facto standard or patents which read on a formal standard, but which have not been FRAND-pledged.[229] Thus, clearly a patentee cannot legally[230] refuse to license SEPs insofar as a FRAND commitment has been issued.

If the legality of a discriminatory refusal to license is always to be determined against the criteria inherent in Article 102(c) TFEU, patentees might want to think twice before granting licenses in the first place. Thus, once a patent essential to a dominant standard has been licensed to a single company a subsequent refusal to license competitors of said company will almost certainly be deemed abusive under the legal test applicable to discriminatory licensing. More specifically, the question of equivalence becomes irrelevant in this scenario because cost and risk related factors are not able to justify a refusal to license – neither is the interplay between supply and demand. Moreover, there can be little doubt that a selective refusal to license is capable of distorting competition insofar as the right in question is essential to operations on a downstream market. Indeed, if the refusal concerns a patent essential to comply with a dominant technical standard any company denied a license may very well be expelled from the market because end users, as explained in Chapter 8 section §8.01, often demand compliance – especially if so-called network effects are at play.[231]

229. Note that if the patentee has participated in standard setting activities within the framework of an SSO and the lack of FRAND-commitment is attributable to a failure to disclose patents in accordance with SSO policies this may be deemed a 'patent ambush' contrary to Art. 102 TFEU (see Ch. 10).
230. In this respect see Ch. 12 where FRAND commitments are discussed in light of the case law regarding refusals to license.
231. In short, network effects arise because end users value interoperability between products – the cell phone being a good example. Users would gain little from buying a phone if they had no one to call, but as the number of phone users increase so does the utility value derived by the individual user owning one, provided of course that the phones in question form part of the same 'network' in that they are able to interact. In this respect standards (such as GSM, 3G/4G etc.) are of essence because they facilitate interaction, referred to in technical terms as 'interoperability'. Accordingly, as a standard increases its market share so does the utility value attributable to it by end users and in effect compliance with the standard in question at some point becomes de facto mandatory for companies present on the market to which the standard relates.

On the outset one might argue that a refusal does not involve applying "*dissimilar conditions to equivalent transactions*" (as no transaction is carried out) for which reason the test applicable to discrimination is of no relevance. In this respect it is however important to note that Article 102(c) TFEU forms part of a *non-exhaustive* list of potential anti-competitive practices, i.e., competition authorities and courts are not bound to apply the provision in a strictly formalistic way. As competition law is not concerned with formalism, but actual or potential market impact, clearly the test applicable to determine whether discrimination constitutes abuse may, depending on the circumstances, also be of relevance in case of an arbitrary refusal to license select companies. Thus, to the extent that a refusal to license gives rise to a distortion of competition patentees cannot shield themselves from competition law intervention relying on formalistic arguments that they did not carry out a transaction with the would-be licensee and therefore did not discriminate, cf. Article 102(c) TFEU.[232]

This was highlighted in *Clearstream*[233] where it was found that Clearstream International SA had abused its dominant position by *inter alia* (1) refusing to supply certain clearing and settlement services to Euroclear Bank SA for more than two years despite having provided competitors (including its own sister company) with undelayed access and (2) by discriminating against Euroclear Bank SA as a result hereof. Thus, the Commission noted that a refusal[234] to deal by a dominant undertaking may violate Article 102 TFEU when the refusal either limits production, markets or technical development, cf. Article 102(b) TFEU, or results in discrimination, cf. Article 102(c) TFEU.[235] On appeal the General Court accepted the Commission's reasoning that the (de facto) refusal to deal and the resulting discrimination were "*...not two separate offences but rather two manifestations of the same course of conduct*".[236] Clearly therefore a refusal to deal may in effect also amount to discrimination, cf. Article 102(c) TFEU. Thus, although in *Clearstream* the conduct condemned was found capable of both eliminating all effective competition and of distorting it, the case nonetheless highlights that a refusal to deal may be scrutinized under Article 102(c) TFEU regardless of the fact that such conduct is normally subject to a distinct (and more

232. While legal scholars seem to agree that a refusal to supply select undertaking may amount to discrimination there has been few (if any) commenting on the interface with the refusal to license test.
233. Case T-301/04, *Clearstream v. Commission*, 9 Sep. 2009.
234. Note that the term 'refusal' is not confined to outright refusals, but according to case law also includes constructive (de facto) refusals to deal caused by for instance the imposition of unfair terms or terms which the supplier/licensor knows to be unacceptable. See for instance COMP/38.096 – Clearstream (Clearing and Settlement), § 223, as the case was upheld on appeal. Also see Van Bael & Bellis, Competition Law of the European Community, 5th ed., Kluwer Law International, 2010 p. 837. In effect this means that an exploitative abuse caused by requesting a royalty rate which is unfair and unreasonable (see s.§11.01 above with regard to the [FR] component of FRAND) may also amount to a de facto refusal as may tactics employed to delay the licensing negotiation process.
235. See COMP/38.096 – Clearstream (Clearing and Settlement), 2 Jun. 2004, § 222.
236. Case T-301/04, *Clearstream v. Commission*, 9 Sep. 2009, paras 150–151.

strict) legal test.[237] Similarly in *United Brands* the CJEU held that the refusal of United Brands, an importer of Chiquita brand bananas, to supply a distributor in Denmark was inconsistent with Article 102(b) and (c) TFEU (then, Article 86 EEC) "...*since the refusal to sell would limit markets to the prejudice of consumers and would amount to discrimination which might in the end eliminate a trading party from the relevant market*".[238]

So does the reasoning set out in the above cases apply by analogy with regard to refusal to license situations or does these warrant different treatment bearing in mind the specifics of IPR?

There is no clear answer to this question to be found in EU case law. It is of course important to appreciate that the very purpose of an intellectual property right is to grant the proprietor the right to exclude others from practicing the claimed invention and to freely set the terms and conditions under which third parties may obtain a license. One might therefore argue that IPR owners should be entitled to refuse certain companies a license so as to preserve their autonomy to benefit from their rights as they see best. Economics may perhaps support such view. If the mere fact that a license to essential IPR has been granted to some companies on a given market entails an obligation to license all companies on said market this may deprive IPR owners the incentive to license their IPR altogether – even though licensing might in fact intensify competition, i.e., some licenses are better than none.

Considering the refusal to license-test as *lex specialis,* hereby allowing it to overrule the test inherent in Article 102(c) TFEU, would however give rise to a peculiar situation. Thus, it would entail that a discriminatory refusal to license select undertakings, must be assessed in light of the *Microsoft*-test, which requires proof that *all* effective competition is likely to be eliminated, whereas a differential licensing scheme – which in comparison have less detrimental effects on competition – is subject to the less licensor friendly test in Article 102(c) TFEU which 'merely' requires proof that competition is distorted. In this respect it must also be borne in mind that the licensee friendly refusal to license-test relies on the reasoning that the IPR owner should, as a main rule, not be forced to grant a license as this would run contrary to the very substance of its exclusive right and the objective underlying the patent system. However, once the patentee decides to provide certain undertakings with a license this reasoning arguably does not bear must weight insofar as the refusal to license distorts competition.

While there is no EU case law dealing with discriminatory refusals to license the German Federal Supreme (BGH) Court in *Standard-Spundfass*[239] decided along the lines of *Clearstream* making some useful observations in this respect. The case concerned a patent related to the manufacture of industrial drums which was essential

237. The legal test of relevance in determining whether a refusal to deal amounts to abuse is largely similar to the one set out in the *Microsoft* judgment (see Ch. 12), with the one exception that a finding of abuse is not conditional on the refusal preventing the emergence of a new product or limiting technical development.

238. Case 27/76, *United Brands v. Commission*, 14 Feb. 1978, § 183.

239. Case KZR 40/02, Standard Tight-head Drum (Standard-Spundfass), Federal Supreme Court of Germany (Bundesgerichtshof), 13 Jul. 2004.

in order to comply with certain guidelines and related technical specifications set up by the Association of the Chemical Industry (Verband der Chemischen Industrie e.V. (VCI)) deemed to constitute a de facto standard. Relying on its patent the plaintiff had, prior to the action before the court, succeeded in having the Düsseldorf District Court impose a preliminary injunction against the defendant – an unlicensed German subsidiary of an Italian drum manufacturer.[240] In the case before the BGH the defendant did not dispute that the patent had been infringed, but claimed that the plaintiff's refusal to grant it a royalty free license violated the anti-discrimination provision in § 20(1) of the German Act against Restraints of Competition, relying on the fact that such licenses had been granted to three German competitors which participated in the VCI working group (in addition a number of paid-for licenses had been granted to companies based in other EU Member States). The BGH agreed that the referring court had erred in not properly considering this aspect. Thus, according to the BGH:

> The fact that the plaintiff, as the patent proprietor, is free to decide whether to grant licences for the disputed patent at all and, if so, to whom does not release the plaintiff from the obligation to observe the anti-discrimination provision and accordingly does not shelve the assessment of the question of whether there was an objectively justifiable reason for refusing the defendant a licence.[241]

While there is no guarantee that German case law is aligned with EU law this substantiates the above reasoning: if a single course of conduct, in this case a refusal to license, impacts competition in several ways in that it has exclusionary as well as discriminatory effects, then a finding of abuse may be based on a reference to either effect, i.e., the less strict legal test prevails. Thus, if the dominant undertaking is allowed to refuse a license according to the criteria set out in *Microsoft*, but nonetheless decides to license certain companies this triggers the special responsibility of a dominant undertaking*"not to allow its behaviour to impair genuine, undistorted competition on the internal market"*[242] and accordingly the obligation to observe the anti-discrimination provision inherent in Article 102(c) TFEU.

[F] Summary

For royalty rates (or other types of remuneration) to be non-discriminatory they must be non-arbitrary, i.e., they must be set according to objective criteria relating to each license transaction. However, since there have been no cases before the CJEU concerning discriminatory licensing it cannot be established with certainty which

240. Case No. 4 O 395/98, Düsseldorf District Court, 9 Feb. 1999.
241. Case KZR 40/02, Standard Tight-head Drum (Standard-Spundfass), Federal Supreme Court of Germany (Bundesgerichtshof), 13 Jul. 2004. Citation based on unofficial translation in International Review of Intellectual Property and Competition law (IIC), Vol. 36(6), 2005 pp. 741–752.
242. See for instance case C-209/10, *Post Danmark A/S v. Konkurrencerådet*, § 23, Case C-280/08 P, *Deutsche Telekom AG v. Commission*, § 176, C-202/07 P, *France Telecom v. Commission*, § 105, and 322/81, *Michelin v. Commission*, § 57.

objective criteria are able to justify a differential licensing scheme under Article 102(c) TFEU. Some guiding principles can however be extracted from case law.

In general discriminatory pricing practices have been condemned under Article 102(c) TFEU where the price difference identified could not be explained on basis of diverging transaction costs. Transaction costs - if construed narrowly - are however ill-suited as a benchmark in a licensing context. When assessing whether differential licensing constitutes abuse within the meaning of Article 102(c) TFEU focus must instead by directed at the license agreements being compared. There can be little doubt that licensors of SEPs - whether FRAND-pledged or not - are allowed to adapt licensing fees to reflect the specific license terms agreed. This of course may result in royalty differentiation, but will not constitute discrimination, cf. Article 102(c) TFEU, insofar as there is a link between the royalty rates charged and the monetary impact of the terms agreed. In determining whether license agreements are 'equivalent' for the purpose of applying Article 102(c) TFEU it must accordingly be assessed whether diverging license terms are able to explain the different remuneration rates identified. An indemnity undertaking for instance represents a risk to the licensor and a value to the licensee, which all things being equal, will increase the fee charged under the agreement. Conversely, licensees which cross-license IPR of their own will, all things being equal, pay less than those who do not. In sum, Article 102(c) TFEU does not oblige SEP holders to apply a uniform royalty scheme nor does it translate FRAND commitments into implicit most-favoured-licensee clauses. Indeed, failing to adopt remuneration rates to reflect differences as to the terms agreed may be deemed to constitute 'reverse' discrimination contrary to Article 102 TFEU. In addition, licensees may be situated differently insofar as they for instance offer different types of products and this as well may potentially render transactions non-equivalent.

Some authors have cautiously suggested that the problem of discrimination could be coped with by SSO IPR policies. If these were to require members to disclose publicly their license agreements this would, it is argued, make it possible to ascertain whether the licenses offered are non-discriminatory.[243] However, as already mentioned above the anti-discrimination portion of FRAND does not in itself require licensors to act as if subject to a 'Most Favoured Nation'-clause. Indeed, the flexibility of bilateral licensing negotiations should be preserved. Thus, while terms and conditions may differ across license agreements this is not necessarily indicative of anti-competitive discrimination - rather such differentiation, as noted above, may reflect completely legitimate business considerations. Making available all agreements for public scrutiny would deprive licensors of their business secrets and most likely subject them to a number of unwarranted accusations and claims - in effect an IPR policy requiring such disclosure is therefore likely to discourage SSO participation by innovators and may even be considered restrictive of competition, cf. Article 101(1) TFEU. Thus, when imposing requirements aimed at preventing anti-competitive conduct by patentees it is important to appreciate that competition law is concerned with safeguarding effective competition as a whole and not merely the interests' of implementers. As noted in

243. See Lemley, Mark. A, *Intellectual Property and Standard Setting*, in California Law Review, Vol. 90, 2002 p. 1965.

Chapter 9 section §9.03[E][2] the Commission has for instance expressed its unwillingness to accept provisions which require SSO members to issue a blanket licensing commitment as a precondition for participation, so-called 'license-by-default' clauses, on grounds that these may discourage SSO participation and harm the incentives to innovate. Confining the freedom of patentees to differentiate between licensees may similarly yield unwarranted results.

CHAPTER 12
Refusals to License

In the preceding sections there is a discussion of the Article 102 TFEU prohibition of unfair, unreasonable and discriminatory licensing and the implications of FRAND commitments in this respect. In this section, the focus is on the circumstances in which an outright refusal to license standard- SEPs may infringe Article 102(b) TFEU. This issue is closely related to the one discussed in Chapter 13 which concerns the extent to which seeking injunctions on basis of SEPs is in conformity with Article 102 TFEU - hence, a prerequisite for an action for an injunction to constitute abuse of a dominant position is that the patentee initiating the action is obliged to grant a license under Article 102 TFEU.

There has until date been no cases dealing with outright refusals to license FRAND-pledged patents. However, in the context of de facto standards there have been several cases. The purpose of this section is not to make a detailed analysis of the case law regarding de facto standards, since this has already been dealt with extensively in the legal literature.[1] Rather, the aim is to outline the legal test of relevance as a basis for substantiating the conclusion that refusing to license FRAND-pledged patents is likely to be deemed an infringement of Article 102(b) TFEU.

In section §12.01 the general legal framework applied in refusal to license cases is outlined whereas in section §12.02 the applicability of said framework in light of a FRAND commitment is discussed.

§12.01 ESSENTIAL PATENTS

In principle a patentee is entitled to refuse to license third parties to use its patents. Indeed, the right to exclude third parties from exploiting the patented invention is at the

1. See for instance Steven Anderman & Hedvig Schmidt, *EU Competition Law and Intellectual Property Rights – The Regulation of Innovation*, 2nd ed., Oxford University Press, 2011, pp. 93-125, and Lévêque, François, *Innovation, Leveraging and Essential Facilities: Interoperability Licensing in the EU Microsoft Case*, in World Competition, Vol. 28(1), 2005 pp. 71-91.

core of patent law. However, according to settled EU case law a dominant undertaking's refusal to license may in 'exceptional circumstances' constitute abuse within the meaning of Article 102(b) TFEU which prohibits conduct *"limiting production, markets or technical development to the prejudice of consumers"*. These 'exceptional circumstances' have evolved through a series of cases discussed briefly below.

The first case concerning the potentially abusive exercise of IPR was *Volvo v. Veng.*[2] In this case, which concerned a reference for a preliminary ruling, the CJEU was asked whether Volvo was obliged to license certain design rights to third-party manufactures in order to allow them to produce spare parts for Volvo's vehicles. The Court held that the right to prevent third parties from exploiting an intellectual property right constitutes the very essence of such a right and that a mere refusal to license does not in itself constitute an abuse of a dominant position.[3] However, the Court found that Volvo's exercise of an exclusive right may violate Article 102 TFEU (then, Article 86 EC) if such exercise involves "*...certain abusive conduct such as the arbitrary refusal to supply spare parts to independent repairers, the fixing of prices for spare parts at an unfair level or a decision no longer to produce spare parts for a particular model even though many cars of that model are still in circulation*".[4] Although these scenarios do not strictly concern refusals to license, the overall reasoning has been relied upon in subsequent cases concerning IPR and hence this case marked the first cautious step towards the compulsory licensing regime which has subsequently been developed under Article 102(b) TFEU.[5] In order to establish the legal framework that applies in this context it is sufficient to refer to the *IMS Health*[6] and *Microsoft*[7] cases. These cases are of special interest as they are the latest cases on refusals to license and set out the 'exceptional circumstances' in which a refusal to license will constitute abuse of a dominant position.

The 'exceptional circumstances' test set out in *IMS health* was consistent with the one adopted in *Magill.*[8] In this case a refusal to license copyright protected TV programme listings was found to constitute a violation of Article 102(b) TFEU, because the refusal was not objectively justified, concerned an indispensable input (TV programme listings) which prevented the appearance of a new product on a secondary market (a comprehensive weekly TV guide) for which there was a potential consumer demand. The Court in *IMS Health*, however, used the opportunity to clarify a few issues.

In *IMS Health*, a case referred to the CJEU for a preliminary ruling pursuant to Article 267 TFEU, the focal point was a copyright protected format (the so-called '1860

2. Case 238/87 *AB Volvo v. Erik Veng* 5 Oct. 1988.
3. *Ibid.*, § 8.
4. *Ibid.*, § 9.
5. These include Joined Cases C-241/91 P and 242/91 P *RTE and ITP v. Commission* (Magill), 6 Apr. 1995, Case T-504/93 *Tiercé Ladbroke SA v. Commission*, 1997, Case C-418/01 *IMS Health v. NDC Health*, 29 Apr. 2004 and Case T-201/04 *Microsoft Corp v. Commission*, 17 Sep. 2007.
6. Case C-418/01 *IMS Health v. NDC Health* [2004] ECR I-5039.
7. Case T-201/04 *Microsoft Corp v. Commission* [2007] ECR II-3601.
8. Joined Cases C-241/91 P and 242/91 P *RTE and ITP v. Commission* (Magill), 6 Apr. 1995.

brick structure') which had become a de facto industry standard held to be indispensable to the presentation of regional sales data on pharmaceutical products. The 1860 brick structure had been relied upon by IMS Health to seek an injunction against a competitor (NDC Health) in Germany and the German court handling the injunction case sought clarity as to the circumstances under which IMS Health's refusal to license a competitor, NDC Health, contravened Article 102 TFEU (then, Article 82 EC). The Court reiterated its reasoning in *Volvo v. Veng* and *Magill* that the exercise of an exclusive right may constitute abuse in 'exceptional circumstances'.[9] Based on the premise that the 1860 brick structure was indeed an indispensable input the CJEU held that for a refusal to constitute abuse it is 'sufficient' that three cumulative conditions are satisfied:

(1) The refusal prevents the emergence of a new product or service for which there is a potential consumer demand.
(2) The refusal is not objectively justified.
(3) The refusal is such as to eliminate all competition on the secondary market to which the refusal relates.[10]

As to the indispensability requirement the Court stressed that it would only be fulfilled in case there are no viable "...*alternative solutions, even if they are less advantageous...*" and if "...*obstacles capable of making it impossible or at least unreasonably difficult...*" to create such alternative solutions were present.[11] The Court in this respect added that it was necessary to determine whether users of the 1,860 brick structure had become 'locked-in' unable to switch to alternative data format.[12] In the context of SEPs there is per definition no substitute technologies allowing for compliance with the standard to which they relate, but still a license may not be indispensable if it is possible for the would-be licensee to operate on the market by employing competing standards or non-standardized technologies. Whether this is possible will depend largely on the state of the market. If, due to 'network effects' (discussed in Chapter 8 section §8.01) the market has 'tipped', or is about to 'tip', in favour of the standard incorporating the technology to which a license is refused there may be no viable alternative solutions. At the end of the 'standards battle' between the optical disc formats, Blu-ray and HD-DVD, it would for instance have made little sense for manufactures who were refused a license to embrace the HD-DVD format which was about to be expelled from the market.

With regard to the third criteria the Court also recalled that according to the *Bronner*[13] Judgment, an earlier case which concerned a refusal to grant access to an essential facility in form of a nationwide newspaper home-delivery scheme, it was

9. Case C-418/01 *IMS Health v. NDC Health*, 29 Apr. 2004 § 35.
10. *Ibid.*, § 38 and §52. Note that the third criterion does not require a finding that all competition has in fact been eliminated – as follows from the *Microsoft* case (see below) it is sufficient that there is a *risk* of all effective competition being eliminated.
11. Case C-418/01 *IMS Health v. NDC Health*, 29 Apr. 2004§ 28.
12. *Ibid.*, § 29.
13. Case C-7/97, *Bronner v. Mediaprint*, 26 Nov. 1998.

necessary to distinguish an upstream market and a (secondary) downstream market on which a refusal would eliminate all competition. It was held to be sufficient that a potential or even a hypothetical secondary market could be identified.[14] Applied to the fact of the IMS Health case it meant that it was a matter for the national court to determine whether the 1,860 brick structure in dispute constituted "*...upstream, an indispensable factor in the downstream supply of German regional sales data for pharmaceutical products*".[15]

Having stated that it was 'sufficient' that the three cumulative conditions outlined above were satisfied for a refusal to license to be abusive the Court in *IMS Health* left behind some uncertainty as to which other exceptional circumstances (if any) could substantiate a finding of abuse under Article 102(b) TFEU. In this respect some clarity was added in the *Microsoft* case decided by the General Court. The case concerned a refusal by Microsoft to license certain interoperability information related to its Windows operating system (primary market) to competitors on the market for server operating systems (secondary market). The General Court confirmed that a refusal to license will only constitute abuse in exceptional circumstances, but at the same time clarified that those circumstances had not been exhaustively set out in *Magill* and *IMS Health*.[16] More specifically, the court stated that:

> the circumstance relating to the appearance of a new product, as envisaged in Magill and IMS Health ... cannot be the only parameter which determines whether a refusal to license an intellectual property right is capable of causing prejudice to consumers.[17]

As noted by the court Article 102(b) TFEU after all refers more generally to limitations "*...not only of production or markets, but also of technical development*".[18] This finding was decisive in the Microsoft case since the undertaking which was refused a license was already present on the secondary market for server operating systems where it offered a product in competition with Microsoft, i.e., the refusal did not, strictly speaking, prevent the emergence of a 'new product'. Rather, the refusal prevented said product from attaining a sufficient degree of interoperability with Microsoft's dominant client operating system on the primary market. In this respect the General Court accepted the Commission's reasoning that the refusal to licence would 'lock-in' consumers to Microsoft's products, since the ability to achieve interoperability was valued to such extent that products on the secondary market unable to achieve it would be deselected even if superior to Microsoft's product offer (in essence an argument relating to strong network effects – see Chapter 8 section §8.01).[19] There was no doubt

14. Case C-418/01, *IMS Health v. NDC Health*, 29 Apr. 2004, § 44.
15. *Ibid.*, §§ 40–46.
16. Case T-201/04, *Microsoft Corp v. Commission*, 17 Sep. 2007, § 331 and § 647.
17. *Ibid.*, § 647.
18. *Ibid.*
19. *Ibid.*, §§ 422 and 650–651. At § 422 the General Court stated that the refusal would reinforce "*Microsoft's competitive position on the work group server operating systems market, particularly because it induces consumers to use its work group server operating system in preference to its competitors', although its competitors' operating systems offer features to which consumers attach great importance*".

therefore that the interoperability constituted an indispensable input on the secondary market. Against this background the General Court accepted the Commission's finding that the 'artificial advantage' retained by Microsoft as a result of its refusal (i) discouraged technical development on the secondary market, (ii) channelled consumer demand towards Microsoft's products and (iii) entailed a risk that all effective competition on the secondary market would be eliminated.[20]

The Commission has also pointed to the fact that Microsoft's refusal to license involved a disruption of "*previous levels of supply*" because the interface information had previously been disclosed to third party developers.[21] In early EU case law concerning refusals to supply goods and services this has been held to be a circumstance of importance. In *United Brands* for instance the CJEU held that "*an undertaking in a dominant position for the purpose of marketing a product ... cannot stop supplying a long-standing customer who abides by regular commercial practice, if the orders placed by that customer are in no way out of the ordinary*".[22] However, in the *Microsoft* case the General Court did not seem to attach great importance to this issue. Nonetheless, it is likely to be seen as an aggravating circumstance if an IPR owner relied on a business relationship to 'build' a secondary market and suddenly seeks to reserve said market for itself by refusing to license.[23]

In the wake of the *Microsoft* case the current state of the 'exceptional circumstances' test can be summarized as follows; for a refusal to license to constitute abuse within the meaning of Article 102 TFEU it is sufficient that the refusal (i) concerns an IPR indispensable to a certain economic activity on a secondary market, (ii) prevents the emergence of a new product for which there is potential consumer demand or otherwise limits technical development to the prejudice of consumers, (iii) is objectively unjustified, and (iv) entails a risk that all effective competition is eliminated on said secondary market.[24]

It is important to appreciate that the need to distinguish a secondary market stems from the reasoning that an IPR owner (or any other owner of an asset) should not be forced to subsidize competitors, but at the same time should not be allowed to leverage a monopoly position on one market to an aftermarket and hereby limit

20. *Ibid.*, §§ 618, 650 and 653 (in particular).
21. Commission decision in case COMP/C-3/37.792, *Microsoft*, 24 Mar. 2004, § 578 et seq.
22. Case 27/76, *United Brands v. Commission*, 14 Feb. 1978, § 182.
23. See Anderman, Steven & Schmid, Hedvig, EU Competition Law and Intellectual Property Rights – The Regulation of Innovation, 2nd ed., Oxford University Press, 2011 p. 118.
24. As noted by the General Court in the *Microsoft* case "*...it is for the dominant undertaking concerned, and not for the Commission, before the end of the administrative procedure, to raise any plea of objective justification and to support it with arguments and evidence. It then falls to the Commission, where it proposes to make a finding of an abuse of a dominant position, to show that the arguments and evidence relied on by the undertaking cannot prevail and, accordingly, that the justification put forward cannot be accepted*". See Case T-201/04, *Microsoft Corp v. Commission*, 17 Sep. 2007, § 668. So far no objective justification has been able to bring a refusal outside the scope of Art. 102(b) TFEU when the other exceptional circumstances (criteria 1,2 and 4) have been fulfilled. According to the CJEU the mere possession of an IPR does not constitute an objective justification under such circumstances and in the *Microsoft* case arguments that a compulsory license would diminish the incentives of Microsoft to innovate were dismissed – see *ibid.*, §§ 688–711.

technical development to the prejudice of consumers. However, since, as explained in Chapter 8 section §8.02, the technology market, comprising SEPs, is a market separate from the product market to which the patented technology is put to use this condition will per se be fulfilled in the context of IPR, i.e., it will always be possible to distinguish two markets – a technology market and a product market.

The 'exceptional circumstances' test is not only of relevance to patents essential to a de facto standard, but also to those reading on formal standards insofar as the patentee has not issued a FRAND commitment. Absent such commitments, which as explained in the next section provide better opportunities to extract compulsory licences, SSOs cannot properly safeguard the standard adopted from 'outside' patent-holdup engaged in by companies not taking part in the standard setting process within the SSO. This is why it is important for SSOs to convince as many companies as possible to take part in the standard setting activities and to secure from them FRAND commitments.

§12.02 ARE FRAND-PLEDGED ESSENTIAL PATENTS DIFFERENT?

There is no special obligation upon patentees to make their patents available for the purpose of aiding in the development of a formal industry standard within the framework of an SSO. An alternative strategy may be for the patentee to 'go alone' and seek to establish a proprietary de facto standard with the aim of 'capturing' the profits associated and avoid the restraints imposed by FRAND commitments.[25] If a non-FRAND-pledged patent turns out to read on a formal standard manufactures of products complying with said standard are left with no other option than to ask for a license and if the request is denied, demand a compulsory license under Article 102 TFEU arguing that the 'exceptional circumstances' outlined in section §12.01 are present. However, if a patentee takes part in formal standard setting activities to avoid the risks of 'going alone' and pledges to license its SEPs on FRAND terms the situation changes.[26]

Provided that a patentee has issued a commitment to an SSO affirming its willingness to license its patents on FRAND terms it is obvious that a subsequent refusal to do so may constitute a violation of that promise pursuant to contract law. In this respect the would-be licensee will need to convince the relevant court that the FRAND commitment issued to the SSO must be construed as a third party beneficiary clause. That being said, discussing the contractual implications of FRAND commitments falls outside the scope of this book. Here the relevant question is whether, bearing in mind the aforementioned case law relating to de facto standards, a FRAND

25. On the strategic considerations a company faces when deciding whether to pursue standard development alone, see *Lea, Gary & Hall, Peter, Standards and intellectual property rights: an economic and legal perspective*, in Information Economics and Policy, Vol. 16, 2004 p. 75.
26. This only applies to the extent that the refusal relates to undertakings seeking a license for the purpose of manufacturing standard compliant products, since these are the beneficiaries of FRAND commitments. Accordingly, a refusal to license third parties wishing to utilize the patented technologies for other purposes must be assessed under Art. 102 TFEU according to the 'traditional' legal test set out in Ch. 12 s. §12.01.

commitment will impact the assessment to be made under Article 102 TFEU if the patentee decides to renege on its promise and refuses to grant a license. As noted below there is much too suggest that this question must be answered in the affirmative.

In principle there can be no objective justification for refusing to license FRAND-pledged patents to companies seeking a license for the purpose of manufacturing standard compliant products. It may be that the specific terms of an existing license agreement allows the licensor to terminate the agreement, but an outright refusal to bring into existence such agreement in the first place contradicts the very purpose of a FRAND commitment. As already explained FRAND commitments have been designed to ensure the availability of SEPs after a formal standard is adopted. It is clear therefore that a refusal to license can only be objectively justified in very limited circumstances.

A refusal to license may for instance be objectively justified if the prospective licensee refuses to cross-license its own essential patents reading on the same standard, since as noted in section §11.01[I] a FRAND commitment may be made conditional on reciprocity.[27] Moreover, a refusal may arguably be justified if the patentee, on basis of objective data, has reason to anticipate a material breach of contract in case a license agreement is entered into. It may for instance be that financial records substantiates that that the prospective licensee will be unable to honour its obligation to pay royalties or that the undertaking concerned has repeatedly breached contractual obligations *vis-à-vis* the patentee in the past.

Nonetheless, the fact that the patentee has no objective justification for refusing to license is not sufficient to succeed with a claim for a compulsory license under Article 102 TFEU pursuant to the 'exceptional circumstances' test set out in *Microsoft* (and preceding case law). If for instance the SEP holder refuses to license only one rival on a market characterized by fierce competition between multiple companies it may not be possible to prove that the refusal entails a risk that all effective competition will be eliminated.[28] A strict application of the 'exceptional circumstances' test is therefore not able to guarantee the effectiveness of FRAND commitments, since it entails a risk that patentees may evade liability under Article 102 TFEU despite having no objective justification for refusing to license their FRAND-pledged patents.[29] However, this scenario is unlikely for several reasons.

While FRAND commitments are contractual in nature they are also creatures of competition law. Hence, as noted in Chapter 9 section §9.03[E], in order to benefit from a presumption that they fall outside the ambit of Article 101(1) TFEU the IPR policies of SSOs must obligate members to issue a FRAND commitment as a precondition for having their patents embodied in the standard developed. Bearing this in mind, it is

27. Cf. also Dolmans, Maurits & Ilan, Daniel, *European Antitrust and Patent Acquisitions: Trolls in the Patent Thickets*, in Journal of the Antitrust Committee of the International Bar Association, Vol. 8(2), 2012 p. 9.
28. Likewise, the test may fail if there are viable competing standards, since then the SEP in question cannot be considered indispensable for remaining in or entering the downstream product market to which the standard in question relates.
29. If such refusal distorts competition the SEP holder may incur liability under Art. 102(c) TFEU which prohibits discriminatory licensing – see Ch. 11 s. §11.02[E] where the interface between the exceptional circumstances test and the discrimination test is discussed.

very likely that Article 102 TFEU will be invoked to ensure the effectiveness of FRAND commitments even if this requires a departure from the 'exceptional circumstances' test. Refusing to license FRAND-pledged patents is arguably an 'exceptional circumstance' in its own right in the absence of an objective justification. Moreover, it must be recalled that the General Court explicitly held the list of exceptional circumstances set out in *Magill* and *IMS Health* to be non-exhaustive – what matters is whether the refusal is likely to be *"limiting production, markets or technical development to the prejudice of consumers"* within the meaning of Article 102(b) TFEU. In effect the court left itself considerable room to manoeuvre in future cases and it requires little effort to place a refusal to license a FRAND-pledged patent within this overall framework. A distinct, but nonetheless related, issue also supports that refusing to license FRAND-pledged patents will be considered a per se like violation of Article 102 TFEU. Hence, the analyses performed in Chapter 13 reveal that holders of FRAND-pledged patents are most likely obliged under Article 102 TFEU to engage in good faith licensing negations with prospective licensees prior to seeking recourse to injunctions. All the less, an outright refusal to license will violate Article 102 TFEU.

§12.03 SUMMARY

In the absence of a FRAND commitment there is, in principle, no obligation under Article 102 TFEU to license third parties. The right to exclude third parties from exploiting a patented invention constitutes the very essence of a patent. Thus, according to the *Microsoft* case (and preceding cases) Article 102 TFEU only provides a basis for issuing compulsory licenses in exceptional circumstances.

In contrast, there is in principle no objective justification for refusing to license FRAND-pledged patents and there is little doubt that doing so will constitute an abuse within the meaning of Article 102 TFEU. Thus, while contractual in nature, FRAND commitments ensure that Article 102 TFEU can be relied upon to ensure the availability of SEPs once a formal standard is adopted. Although no case so far have dealt with a refusal to license FRAND-pledged patents there is basis for arguing that any such refusal would constitute an 'exceptional circumstance' in itself and in essence a per se like abuse, distinct from the exceptional circumstances set out in the *Microsoft* case. This highlights why it is important that SSOs obtain FRAND commitments from their members in accordance with the 'safe harbour' principles set out in the Commission's Horizontal Guidelines.[30]

Given that they are aware that a refusal to license will most likely result in liability under Article 102 TFEU (as well as contract law) patentees probably think twice before doing so. Instead, holders of FRAND-pledged patents with nefarious intentions of excluding their rivals will probably use discriminatory licensing tactics and excessive pricing, as these are much more difficult to deal with under Article 102 TFEU. These

30. These principles were discussed in Ch. 9 s. §9.03.

issues were discussed in Chapter 11. In the next section it is discussed to what extent enforcing SEPs against infringers will violate Article 102 TFEU if the infringer in question is entitled to a compulsory license under the very same provision, cf. above, but disagreements arises as to the meaning of FRAND.

CHAPTER 13
Essential Patents and Injunctive Relief

Patent rights are exclusive rights allowing their proprietors to prohibit third parties from utilizing the patented subject matter without prior authorization. The fundamental characteristics of the patent system is the prerogative of patentees' to freely set their licensing terms, decide to whom a license should be granted and to enforce their patents before the courts against any unlicensed third party. However, as already discussed, competition law may under certain circumstances limit these prerogatives. Thus, in the event of a patent-holdup, competition law may intervene to prevent a dominant right holder from abusing his market power within the meaning of Article 102 TFEU, by requiring a (compulsory) license to be granted on FRAND terms. This provision has fundamental importance in the context of technical standards as undertakings in possession of patents declared essential to a standard will often hold a dominant position on the relevant technology market due to the fact that no substitute patents allowing for compliance with the standard exist.[1]

Against this background there has been a growing tendency in recent years for alleged infringers of SEPs to rely on competition law as a means to quash the patent owners request for an injunction or action for damages – a so-called competition law defence.[2] Such defence is based on the reasoning that the patentee, if he had acted in accordance with competition law, would have no basis for asserting the patents in question, and therefore should accordingly be deprived his right to do so by the court handling the infringement claim. Thus, competition law, at least in some jurisdictions, may provide the defendant with an extra line of defence should the 'traditional' non-infringement and/or invalidity counter-claims fail. More specifically, the alleged infringer, depending on the merits of the case, may counter-claim that the plaintiff's

1. Reference is made to Ch. 8 s. §8.02 where the assessment of market power with regard to technical standards is discussed.
2. Sometimes also referred to as a 'FRAND defence'. See for instance Camesasca, Peter, et al., *Injunctions for Standard-Essential Patents: Justice is not Blind*, in Journal of Competition Law & Economics, Vol. 9(1), 2013, p. 295.

request for injunctive relief violates Article 102 TFEU, hence should be dismissed, in light of the fact that the plaintiff:

- has refused to license the disputed patents;
- has requested non-FRAND license terms;
- has carried out a patent ambush; and/or
- has failed to negotiate a license in good faith although obliged to do so pursuant to a FRAND commitment.

From the defendants point of view this can be crucial, because the link established between the technical specification agreed upon in an SSO and the patents claimed to be essential to the implementation hereof, makes it easier for the patentee to prove that infringement of the patents concerned has taken place. If the defendant offers products in compliance with a formal standard, the patentee merely has to prove that its patents read on the standard in question, i.e., the underlying technical specification set by the SSO, in order to prove infringement – in effect the cumbersome task of performing a technical analysis of the defendant's product is often superfluous.[3] In other words, if the defendant claims its products to adhere to a standard, the question is often not whether the disputed patents read on the products, but whether they are essential in the sense that they read on the standard itself.[4] This may prompt defendants, in cases involving infringement of SEPs, not to focus their effort on disputing that infringement has taken place, but instead seek to rely on counter-claims based on contract law or competition law. A prerequisite for such defence to succeed is that the would-be licensee has a claim to a compulsory license under Article 102 TFEU. This aspect was discussed in Chapter 12 where it was concluded that (i) absent a FRAND commitment the SEP holder is only obliged to license in exceptional circumstances, whereas (ii) in light of a FRAND commitment the opposite applies – a refusal to license can only escape Article 102 TFEU in exceptional circumstances. The analyses carried out below presuppose that the would-be licensee is entitled to license on FRAND terms pursuant to Article 102 TFEU and that a FRAND commitment has been given.

Before turning to the competition law issues in section a brief note on the contractual implications of FRAND commitments are made in Chapter 3 section §3.01. While it falls outside the scope of this book to deal with all aspects of contract law a short notice shall be made in this respect in order to highlight the possible implications of a FRAND undertaking under contract law and clarify their interplay with those arising under competition law. To the extent that a FRAND undertaking as construed under contract law is able to prevent the use of injunctions in ways which are detrimental to effective competition the role of competition law becomes less pronounced.

3. Such analysis may be necessary however if the standard in question is drafted broadly so as to allow for implementation by a number of substitute technologies.
4. It may turn out that the patents are not essential despite the fact that they have been declared by the patentee to be so. As noted in Ch. 11 s. §11.01[J] several factors may lead patentees to over-declare patents as potentially essential.

§13.01 CONTRACT LAW

Although the possibility of succeeding with a competition law defence (as explained below) is closely linked to the existence of a FRAND undertaking, such undertaking is in essence a contractual commitment and may potentially be relied upon as such by a defendant in an injunction case. Thus, although FRAND undertakings are creatures of competition law – in that they originate[5] from Article 101 TFEU – they impose on the patentee contractual obligations *vis-à-vis* the SSO and may in some jurisdictions be construed as third party beneficiary clauses enforceable by any potential licensee wishing to implement the standard in question. Depending of the specific wording of a FRAND undertaking and the SSOs IPR policy, defendants in patent litigation may therefore be able to successfully rely on contract law to prevent the patentee from obtaining an injunction or, as was the case in *LG Electronics v. Sony,*[6] a border seizure (this case is commented on below).

Sometimes legal commentators do not draw a sharp line between contract law and competition law, but in the context of injunctions discuss both under the heading 'FRAND defence'. This may give the (wrong) impression that the implications of FRAND undertakings under contract law and competition law, respectively, are identical. There is however no basis for concluding that such contractual promise given by the patentee would (or should) be construed in accordance with the economic and legal principles underlying competition law. The outcome of a case may deviate significantly depending on the legal basis against which a FRAND obligation is construed – a license offer may very well be FRAND compliant if construed in the context of contract law, while being non-FRAND in the light of competition law and *vice versa*. Although a FRAND commitment, in accordance with the objectives of competition law, is relied upon by SSOs as a preventive contractual measure to minimize the likelihood of patent hold-up and ensure efficient commercialization of the standard once adopted, there is no guarantee that contract law provides sufficient safeguards in this respect. It is for instance a common tradition in both civil law and common law jurisdictions to take into account the intent of the parties to an agreement.[7] To the contrary competition law is aimed at enhancing consumer welfare on the market as such to the benefit of consumers and in this respect intent is, as was discussed in Chapter 11 section §11.02[A], of secondary importance. Moreover, competition law is only concerned with damage sustained by individual companies to the extent that it harms effective competition, whereas proof of such damage may be sufficient under contract law. Also note that the application of competition law is conditioned on a finding that the patentee has market power, whereas this is irrelevant under contract law. Finally, it must be recalled that if an SSO adopted a definition of FRAND such definition need not be in accordance with public interest – it may for

5. In this respect see Ch. 9.
6. Case 389067/KG ZA 11-269, *Sony Supply Chain solutions (Europe) v. LG Electronics*, District Court of The Hague, 10 Mar. 2011.
7. Cf. also Brooks, Roger G. & Geradin, Damien, *Interpreting and Enforcing the Voluntary FRAND Commitment*, in International Journal of IT Standards and Standardization Research, Vol. 9(1), 2011 p. 4.

instance be discriminatory against non-members, hence lead to distortions of competition.

Keeping in mind that the very purpose of requiring a patent owner to issue a FRAND commitment is to ensure efficient diffusion of the standard by allowing any interested third party to implement its underlying technical specifications, it seems obvious that a patent owner, having issued such commitment with regard to SEPs, cannot subsequently deny to license these patents on FRAND terms. From the perspective of contract law such undertaking clearly indicates a willingness to licence.[8] By way of example ETSI (an accredited SDO) for instance requires members and their affiliates, who wish to have their patented technologies included in a standard, to declare that they are *"prepared to grant irrevocable licenses"* for such patents on fair, reasonable and non-discriminatory terms.[9] However, as highlighted below the fact that the plaintiff has indicated its willingness to license does not necessarily provide sufficient basis for a defence under contract law. The likelihood of success largely depends on the jurisdiction handling the case; whereas national courts applying EU competition law (under the powers conferred by Regulation 1/2003[10]) must do so in accordance with EU case law the rules and principles governing interpretation of contracts have not been harmonized.

Firstly, the defendant must show the existence of an agreement to which the patentee is party and which confers upon the defendant rights. Even if the defendant is a member in the SSO which has adopted the standard in question it must be recalled that FRAND undertakings are directed at the SSO as such and not its members, i.e., there is typically no direct contractual relationship between the defendant and the plaintiff regardless of whether they are both members of the same SSO. In order to succeed with a counter-claim on basis of contract law it is therefore necessary for the defendant to establish that the FRAND undertaking in question constitutes a third-party beneficiary clause which the defendant may rely on. This is obviously not a requirement for finding abuse under Article 102 TFEU.

Secondly, it must be shown that any rights conferred upon the defendant – on basis of the wording of the agreement and/or the intent of the parties to it – precludes the plaintiff from seeking injunctive relief or results in an implied license to the patents allegedly infringed. In this respect the two Dutch cases outlined below serves well to exemplify:

> *Samsung v. Apple*
>
> In *Samsung v. Apple*[11] the District Court of The Hague was faced with the task of deciding whether Samsung could successfully obtain an injunction against Apple

8. This holds true from the perspective of competition law as well. In this respect see Ch. 12 regarding the assessment of refusals to license under Art. 102 TFEU.
9. ETSI IPR Policy (Annex 6 of the Rules of Procedure) of 19 Mar. 2014. Available at: http://www.etsi.org/about/iprs-in-etsi (last checked 30 May 2013) p. 41.
10. Council Regulation (EC) No. 1/2003 of 16 Dec. 2002 on the implementation of the rules on competition laid down in Arts 81 and 82 of the Treaty.
11. See combined cases 400367/HA ZA 11-2212, 400376/HA ZA 11-2213 and 400385/HA ZA 11-2215, District Court of The Hague, 14 Mar. 2012. For a case summary see Kuipers, Gertjan; Groenevelt, Douwe and Lamme, Oscar, *A further perspective on Apple v. Samsung: How to*

which allegedly had infringed certain of Samsung's FRAND-pledged patents essential to the UMTS standard. Apple raised a FRAND defence on basis of both competition law and contract law. With regard to the latter Apple argued *inter alia* for dismissal of the action on grounds that it had in fact obtained an (implied) license to the disputed patents by applying the standard in question – in other words, it was claimed that Samsung's FRAND undertaking should be construed as an unconditional license offer capable of acceptance by implementation. This argument was (as one might expect) rejected by the court. Since Samsung had merely declared that it was generally *"prepared to grant licenses to its essential IPRs on a fair, reasonable, and non-discriminatory basis"* in accordance with SSO policies, the court found that the undertaking lacked the very essence of a readily acceptable license offer, namely the license terms. Rather than a license offer the FRAND undertaking, according to the court, was to be considered an irrevocable commitment to enter into good faith license negotiations with any company wishing to take a license for the purpose of implementing the standard in question. Moreover, the court held that the mere application of a standard cannot in any event constitute 'acceptance' of a license offer as it does not imply a willingness to actually enter into a license agreement. Accordingly, there was found no basis for reaching the conclusion that Apple had obtained an (implied) license to Samsung's FRAND-pledged patents.

To the contrary Apple was able to convince the court that the request for an injunction should be dismissed because it constituted an abuse of rights and was contrary to pre-contractual good faith. In this respect, see Chapter 13 section §13.02[D].

LG Electronics v. Sony

In *LG Electronics v. Sony*[12] the existence of an arbitration clause proved to be decisive. The case concerned an allegation by LG Electronics that Sony's PlayStation 3 gaming console infringed certain of its patents essential to the Blu-ray standard adopted by the Blu-ray Disc Association – an SSO where both LG and Sony were members. LG Electronics had issued a commitment that it was willing to license the disputed patents on FRAND terms, but as license negotiations stranded the company applied for an injunction and instructed the Dutch customs authorities to perform a border seizure of PlayStation 3 consoles – in effect approximately 300,000 consoles were detained.

Sony substantiated its defence by reference to the fact that the relevant SSO by-laws obliged members to settle any dispute regarding license terms by use of arbitration and that it has never refused to take a licence. These arguments were found persuasive. According to the preliminary relief judge, the arbitration mechanism meant that the parties would 'inevitable' enter into a license agreement on FRAND terms and therefore LG's action was considered incompatible

successfully enforce Standard Essential Patents in the Netherlands, in berichten industriële eigendom, August 2012 pp. 222–228.

12. Case 389067/KG ZA 11-269, *Sony Supply Chain solutions (Europe) v. LG Electronics*, District Court of The Hague, 10 Mar. 2011. For a case summary see Kuipers, Gertjan; Groenevelt, Douwe and Lamme, Oscar, *A further perspective on Apple v. Samsung: How to successfully enforce Standard Essential Patents in the Netherlands*, in berichten industriële eigendom, August 2012 p. 225, and Blaseby, Matthew, *Fighting Counterfeits on the European Frontline*, in Intellectual Property Counsellor, No. 176, 2011 p. 3.

with SSO by-laws, which had as their purpose to ensure efficient commercialization of the Blu-ray standard to the benefit of all members. Accordingly, Sony was successful in having the border seizure lifted and the injunction dismissed.

The case law discussed above highlights that FRAND commitments may potentially provide an effective defence against injunctions depending on the specific circumstances at hand. However, as already mentioned, there is no guarantee that they will provide sufficient protection against vexatious litigation contrary to Article 102 TFEU. While the rights derived from a FRAND commitment under contract law may provide an effective bulwark against injunctions and have a precautionary effect in preventing competition law disputes there is no guarantee that they will sufficiently safeguard effective competition let alone because the focal point under contract law is the rights of the defendant (as construed in light of divergent national laws) and not community interest as safeguarded by competition law. Moreover, notwithstanding the existence of an agreement to which the defendant is part seeking or merely threatening an injunction may amount to abuse under Article 102 TFEU provided that the action aims to impose onerous license terms upon or exclude a company willing to take a license on FRAND terms. In the words of the Commission "*...a FRAND commitment cannot be considered a guarantee that a SEP holder will not abuse its market power. Although a FRAND commitment may influence a company's incentives to significantly impede effective competition, it remains true that the company would still have the ability to do so*".[13] It follows therefore that competition law forms an important instrument in infusing FRAND commitments with the ability to act as a bulwark against anti-competitive conduct. Since there is not necessarily an overlap between competition law and contract law it is important that patentees and implementers alike are aware not only of the restraints imposed by the latter.

§13.02 COMPETITION LAW

The question as to the availability of the competition law defence and how to ensure a proper balance between right holders and public interest has spurred a heated debate amongst legal scholars, industry and competition authorities. While there is no doubt that an undertaking wishing to implement a technical standard is able to initiate legal action against the patentee before a national court or file a complaint with the Commission (or a national competition authority) in order to obtain a FRAND license, it is more uncertain to what extent a claim to such license can be raised as a defence in infringement proceedings to avoid an injunction. This section sets out to explore the admissibility of such a competition law defence and the extent to which assertion of SEPs may violate Article 102 TFEU.

EU Commissioner Joaquin Almunia, in the context of an investigation into Samsung's assertion of SEPs, noted that:

13. Case COMP/M.6381, *Google/Motorola Mobility*, 13 Feb. 2012 (Merger procedure), § 113.

> [w]hen companies have contributed their patents to an industry standard and have made a commitment to license the patents in return for fair remuneration, then the use of injunctions against willing licensees can be anti-competitive.[14]

As explained below the overall concern is that by threatening to use injunctions (or by actually doing so), holders of SEPs may succeed with making anti-competitive demands which would not have been accepted under normal circumstances, i.e., before the standard concerned was adopted, or exclude rivals actually willing to take a license on FRAND terms.

[A] The Views of the Industry

Major cooperation's have stated their concerns regarding the enforcement of SEPs against unlicensed implementers. For instance, in a joint response sent to the Federal Trade Commission by Cisco, HP, IBM and RIM these companies state that *"giving a RAND commitment should mean that a patentee gives up the right to enjoin or exclude the use, manufacture, sale, or importation of products that implement the standard for which the patentee claims to own essential patents"*.[15] Statements to a similar effect were issued by Ericsson,[16] Verizon[17] and Broadcom.[18] Microsoft and Apple have likewise declared that they will not seek injunctive relief based on SEPs - Apple, in a letter to ETSI (SDO), has stated that *"A party who made a FRAND commitment to license its cellular standards essential patents or otherwise acquired assets/rights from a party who made the FRAND commitment must not seek injunctive relief on such patents"*.[19]

14. See Commission's press release in Case COMP/39.939, *Samsung - Enforcement of UMTS standards essential patents*, IP/12/1448 (Commission sends Statement of Objections to Samsung on potential misuse of mobile phone standard-essential patents), 21 Dec. 2012.
15. See Joint response submitted to the FTC by Cisco Systems, Inc. (for Cisco, HP, IBM, and RIM), 8 Jan. 2011 p. 21. As previously stated the term "RAND" is the US-equivalent of "FRAND". The joint response, as well as a number of other responses by industry players, was submitted to the FTC following a request for public comments related to the FTC workshop, Tools to prevent "Patent Hold-Up", project number P11-1204, 21 Jun. 2011. The comments submitted to the FTC are available at: http://www.ftc.gov/os/comments/patentstandardsworkshop/ (last checked 30 May 2014).
16. See response submitted to the FTC by Telefonaktiebolaget LM Ericsson, 8 May 2011 p. 7 where it is stated that "*[a]s there is a (F)RAND commitment, injunctions should not be allowed as a first means; i.e., without even engaging in bona fide licensing discussions. The whole purpose of the (F)RAND commitment is that standard adoption should not be blocked (unless a user is unreasonably refusing to take a necessary license)*" (spelling error corrected).
17. See response submitted to the FTC by Verizon Communications Inc., 8 May 2011 p. 18 (in particular) where it stated that "*[d]amages, not injunctive relief, generally should be the remedy when an injunction would prevent compliance with a widely adopted industry standard*".
18. See response submitted to the FTC by Broadcom corp., 5 Aug. 2011 p. 6 (in particular) where it is stated that "*[p]art of the content of RAND, then, is the absence of injunctive relief*" and that "*[a]llowing a holder* Guide on Intellectual Property *of essential rights to a standard to wield the threat of injunctive relief over other players during royalty negotiations deprives the "reasonable" term of any meaning*".
19. The statements made by Microsoft and Apple were reported in Department of Justice News Release, Statement of Department of Justice's Antitrust Division on its decision to close its

The statements issued by industry players underline that enforcement of SEPs to block competitors is not only perceived as a potential problem by regulators and legal scholars, but by industry (at least parts hereof) itself. Although the statements made by the above referenced companies may be indicative of their individual strategic interest – not necessarily reflecting the approach which best promotes effective competition – they are nonetheless important in the sense that they express the opinions of major industry players active in a field where standardization is prevalent. In this respect it is worth noticing that some of the companies referenced above are known to own large patent portfolios and to contribute technologies to SSOs, i.e., they are not 'pure implementers' without any interest in licensing revenues.[20]

While the above statements represent the position taken by part of the ITC industry other companies seem to favour a more non-interventionist approach arguing that competition law should not be used to limit what they see as a completely legitimate exercise of their IPR. Qualcomm in a submission to the FTC for instance emphasizes that a RAND (similar to the European FRAND concept) commitment is nothing more than a voluntary contract which does not preclude rights owners from seeking injunctive relief against *unwilling* licensees, i.e., recognizing that the commitment entails a contractual obligation to offer implementers of the standard to which their SEPs relate a license on RAND terms, but not a "*no injunctions, ever*" regime.[21] Underlining a similar reluctance to abstain from the use of injunctions Google in a letter to IEEE (SDO) dated 8 February 2012 explicitly states that it "*reserves its rights to use any and all judicial remedies against counterparties that refuse a RAND license*".[22] Indeed, as mentioned in Chapter 13 section §13.02[C][2] the aggressive assertion of FRAND-encumbered patents by Motorola Mobility (owned by Google) caught the attention of the Commission which on basis of formal investigations stated its preliminary view that the company's conduct may have breached Article 102 TFEU.

As mentioned in Chapter 9 section §9.03[E][3] above the vague nature of most IPR policies can be seen as a testimony to the fact that SSO participants have not been able to reach common ground as to the meaning of FRAND and the limitations inherent in a FRAND commitment. In reducing the risk of patent-holdup it is important that such discrepancy is minimized. If SSO participants cannot agree on the overall implications of FRAND commitments the risk of conflict and litigation increases. Moreover, the legal uncertainty concerning the FRAND concept may result in a distortion of licensing

investigation of Google Inc.'s acquisition of Motorola Mobility Holdings, Inc. and the acquisitions of certain patents by Apple Inc., Microsoft Corp. and Research in Motion limited, 13 Feb. 2012. Also see http://www.microsoft.com/en-us/legal/intellectualproperty/IPLicensing/ip2.aspx (last checked 30 May 2014).

20. IBM for instance claims to have "*...topped the annual list of U.S. patent recipients for the 20th consecutive year*". See http://www.research.ibm.com/articles/patents.shtml (checked 30 May 2014).
21. See response submitted to the FTC by Qualcomm Incorporated, 13 Jun. 2011, pp. 39–43. Overall Qualcomm finds that a RAND commitment does not entail a "*no injunctions, ever*" regime arguing that such regime would be detrimental to innovation.
22. The letter has to this authors knowledge not been published by the IEEE itself, but it is publicly available on the internet. See for instance http://www.scribd.com/doc/80976133/12-02-08-Google-to-IEEE-on-MMI-Patents (last checked 30 May 2014).

negotiations and impede standardization efforts. The luring threat of injunctions may prompt would-be licensees of SEPs to accept unreasonable license terms or to abstain from participating in standard setting activities. There is also a risk that patentees will be discouraged from contributing their technologies to SSOs fearing that it will result in the value of their important intangible assets being eroded.

Competition authorities in this respect hold a key role as they may guide market participants as to which conduct is acceptable from a competition law perspective and hereby contribute to the establishment of an overall framework guiding the understanding of the FRAND concept. However, the fragmented interests of industry itself represent a significant challenge to the Commission and other competition authorities who needs to strike the right balance between the interests of right holders (pure innovators and vertically integrated firms) and pure implementers alike. A too interventionist approach may limit the incentives of right holders to participate in standard setting activities while on the other hand abstaining from intervention risks transforming SEPs into strategic weapons which may be used as a means to monopolize industry sectors and halt innovation. In this respect it is important to remember that intellectual property protection entails at its very core a prerogative for the right holder to exclude third parties from practicing the protected subject matter. Thus, companies advocating in favour of less interventionist approach are not per se to be seen as proponents of effective competition which after all must be assessed taken into consideration a given conducts effect on innovation – however, in light of a FRAND commitment there is much to suggest that injunctions should be reserved for use against infringers who are unwilling to negotiate a license in good faith.

A view consistent with this reasoning seems to have been adopted by the Commission (section §13.02[C][2]) and while the approach taken by national courts deviates (section §13.02[D]) there seems to be consensus at least that SEPs should not be used as a basis for obtaining injunctions against third parties willing to take a license of FRAND terms. The obstacle to a meaningful application of such overall rule is however posed by the fact that the concept of a 'willing' or 'good faith' licensee is in dire need of clarification. Moreover, any rule relying on the assessment of whether a royalty offer is FRAND has a built in 'weakness' necessitating careful consideration as to whether the patentee or the potential license should bear the risk of the royalty rate offered being considered non-FRAND by the court handling the injunction case. Patent disputes involving SEPs clearly underline this problem of legal uncertainty. In the European Union Samsung and Motorola for instance have intensively been pursuing alleged infringers of their SEPs notwithstanding that a FRAND commitment was issued in the course of their SSO participation – claiming that the defendants were not willing to accept a FRAND license. Had a clear message as to the legality of such practices been sent *ex ante* such behaviour might have been avoided.

[B] Admissibility

Obviously the first step towards a successful competition law defence is to convince the court handling the infringement proceedings to take into account a competition law counter-claim based on Article 102 TFEU. Even though procedural law has not been harmonized there is, as argued below, basis for concluding that such defence must be accepted to ensure the efficiency of EU competition law. This arguably holds true regardless of whether the defence is raised in a case on the merits or in a case dealing with a request for a preliminary injunction.

With regard to an infringement case being decided on the merits there can be little doubt that the judge cannot dismiss a competition law defence as inadmissible.[23] Doing so would deprive the defendant an effective remedy against anti-competitive conduct, hence run counter to the principle of *effect utile* as enshrined in Article 47 of the Charter of Fundamental Rights of the European Union which dictates that "*[e]veryone whose rights and freedoms guaranteed by the law of the Union are violated has the right to an effective remedy before a tribunal...*".[24] As already explained the action for an injunction may amount to abuse of a dominant position, hence must be dismissed, provided that the defendant has a legitimate claim to a license under competition law. Moreover, the patentee cannot be entitled to damages exceeding the FRAND royalty rate which, pursuant to Article 102 TFEU, it would have been entitled to claim had a license agreement been concluded. In *Standard-Spundfass* the German Federal Supreme Court in an action for damages for instance found that:

> [if] the defendant is entitled to use the patent, compensation for damages to the plaintiff resulting from the use the defendant has made can in any case only be demanded for the amount to which the plaintiff would have been entitled if it had not refused (illegally) to grant the defendant or its parent company a licence for the disputed patent.[25]

With regard to interim injunctions it may be argued that dismissing the competition law defence is warranted, because the court may simply direct the defendant to raise its competition law claim in separate proceedings or before a competition authority.[26] More specifically, it has been argued that the purpose of interim injunctions – to provide quick remedies to IPR owners who would otherwise suffer irreparable harm – would be undermined if preliminary relief judges were forced to handle complex competition law matters, which anyway they often lack the necessary competences to deal with.[27] However, although the court handling the request for an interim injunction may not be well equipped to decide on every detail of complex competition law matters this does not entail that a competition law defence should be dismissed as inadmissible. A proper balancing of interests does not require a preliminary relief judge to

23. Cf. also Hoppner, Thomas, *Competition Law in Intellectual Property Litigation – the Case for a Compulsory License Defense Under Article 102 TFEU*, in European Competition Journal, Vol. 7(2), 2011 p. 297.
24. Charter of Fundamental Rights of the European Union, 2000 O.J. C 364/1, 18 Dec. 2000, Art. 47.
25. Case KZR 40/02, *Standard Tight-Head Drum (Standard-Spundfass)*, German Federal Supreme Court, 13 Jul. 2004. See translation in International Review of Intellectual Property and Competition law (IIC), Vol. 36(6), 2005 pp. 741–752 (p. 748).
26. See for instance Hoppner, Thomas, *Competition Law in Intellectual Property Litigation – the Case for a Compulsory License Defence Under Article 102 TFEU*, in European Competition Journal, Vol. 7(2), 2011 p. 298.
27. *Ibid.*

provide a final decision on whether competition law has in fact been violated. The court merely has to decide whether the defendant has rendered probable that the plaintiff has violated competition law by refusing to grant a license on FRAND terms in which case the request for an injunction arguably must be dismissed.[28] Moreover, the assessment does not need to be overly complex insofar as a FRAND commitment has been issued by the plaintiff – as argued below such commitment arguably entails that injunctions can only be invoked as a last resort and should be dismissed if filed for against 'willing licensees'. Focusing solely one the harm which may come to the patentee fails to achieve a proper balancing of interests and prejudices the efficiency of competition law. Once an injunction is granted and enforced it may be too late remedy the anti-competitive impact conferred upon the infringer as a result of the injunction.

It follows from the above that dismissing a competition law defence as inadmissible runs counter to Article 47 of the Charter of Fundamental Rights of the European Union (see above) as well as the principle of proportionality as set out in *Scarlet Extended* and Article 3(2) of Directive 2004/48 (see Chapter 13 section §13.02[C][1]).

[C] Competition Law Defence under Article 102 TFEU

The CJEU have not yet passed any judgments regarding the extent to which enforcing SEPs may amount to abuse of a dominant position, cf. Article 102 TFEU. However, it is possible to extract some general principles and criteria from EU case law on the extent to which European competition law limits the prerogative of right holders to assert their IPR against third parties. Bearing in mind that SEPs warrants special (and arguably stricter) treatment under EU competition law, the general principles set out by the CJEU are nonetheless useful in establishing the threshold for finding abuse and in interpreting the statements of the Commission specifically concerning such patents. The reasoning set out by the CJEU with regard to so-called vexatious litigation establishes the overall framework within which it must be determined whether the assertion of SEPs amounts to abuse.

[1] General Framework: Vexatious Litigation

For obvious reasons the enforcement of IPR can only amount to abuse in very limited circumstances. Thus, as already noted the prerogative of right holders to exclude competitors by means of litigation is an inherent characteristic of patent law which is respected by competition law. Article 102 TFEU merely imposes upon dominant undertaking a "*...special responsibility not to impair, by using methods other than those which come within the scope of competition on the merits, genuine undistorted*

28. The German courts have taken the opposite view that "*...the review can be limited to the question of whether the rejection of the offer constituted an obvious violation of antitrust law*", cf. Case 7 O 122/11, *Motorola Mobility v. Apple*, Mannheim Regional Court (Landgericht Mannheim), 9 Dec. 2011 (unofficial translation available at: http://www.scribd.com/doc/94523005/Translation-of-Mannheim-2O240-Ruling-Motorola-v-Microsoft).

competition in the common market".[29] IPR are part of the 'toolbox' upon which such undertakings may rely when engaging in 'competition on the merits' - regardless of the fact that the aim may be to eliminate or weaken a competitor. Thus, as is the case with any type of legal rights such are established in expectation that they are enforceable in court, hence actually doing so is as a main rule not abusive. The Commission and the CJEU have adopted an approach which is consistent with this reasoning - finding that the assertion of IPR will only amount to abuse in exceptional circumstances.

International treaties as well as EU legislation explicitly aim at ensuring that holders of IPR are able to achieve effective remedies, including preliminary injunctions, against infringement. The TRIPS agreement (as ratified by all Member States) for instance sets out a number of obligations in this respect as does Directive 2004/48 on the enforcement of IPR.[30] The right to obtain an effective remedy before the courts has even been enshrined in Article 6 of the European Convention on Human Rights (ECHR)[31] which states that anyone (including IPR owners) *"whose rights and freedoms as set forth in this Convention are violated shall have an effective remedy before a national authority"*.[32] Moreover, Article 47 of the Charter of fundamental rights of the European Union (as noted above) similarly aims to guarantee everyone a right to an effective remedy before a court. On the outset it is therefore clear that competition law should only be relied upon to prevent a patentee from obtaining a remedy - legally provided for under patent law - in case such remedy is clearly used as a means to promote anti-competitive conduct to the detriment of community interest.

As noted immediately below the fundamental right of access to a court was taken into consideration by the Commission and the General Court in *ITT Promedia* which concerned the possible abusive exercise of the right to bring legal proceedings against a competitor.[33] While *Microsoft Corp v. Commission*[34] (and prior case law concerning refusals to license) set out the general principle that exercise of IPR may only amount to abuse in exceptional circumstances the legal test to be applied in order to determine whether the initiation of legal action in itself amounts to abuse was established in *ITT Promedia*.

29. See for instance Case T-321/05, *AstraZeneca v. Commission*, 1 Jul. 2010, § 671 (with references).
30. World Trade Organisation, *Agreement on Trade Related Aspects of Intellectual Property Rights*, (TRIPS Agreement) and Directive 2004/48/EC of the European Parliament and of the Council on the enforcement of intellectual property rights, 29 Apr. 2004.
31. The Convention for the Protection of Human Rights and Fundamental Freedoms, 1950 (better known as the ECHR).
32. Intellectual property rights have been held to fall within the scope of the ECHR as it constitutes "possessions" within the meaning of ECHR Protocol 1, Art. 1. See for instance Coban, Ali Rize, *Protection of Property Rights within the European Convention on Human Rights*, Ashgate Publishing, 2004 p. 149 (with references to case law of the European Commission of Human Rights) and Torremans, Poul, *Intellectual Property and Human Rights*, Kluwer Law International, 2008 p. 37.
33. In its 2009 inquiry into the pharmaceutical sector, the Commission notes that "*...enforcing patent rights in court is legitimate and a fundamental right guaranteed by the European Convention on Human Rights: it is an effective means of ensuring that patents are respected*". See Commission, *Pharmaceutical Sector Inquiry*, Final report, 8 Jul. 2009, p. 238.
34. Case T-201/04, *Microsoft Corp v. Commission*, 17 Sep. 2007. The case is discussed in more detail in Ch. 12 s. §12.01.

[a] ITT Promedia: Abuse of Rights

In *ITT Promedia*[35] the General Court (then, The Court of First Instance) reviewed a Commission decision concerning the application of Article 102 TFEU (then, Article 86) to so-called vexatious litigation, i.e., baseless litigation serving only to promote an anti-competitive goal. The applicant had filed a complaint with the Commission that Belgacom SA, a provider of certain telephone directory data, had abused its dominant position by *inter alia* initiating vexatious litigation before the Belgian courts in a dispute concerning the publication of directories.[36] The Commission stated that the initiation of legal proceedings will only constitute abuse if the action:

> (i) cannot reasonably be considered as an attempt to establish the rights of the undertaking concerned and can therefore only serve to harass the opposite party and (ii) it is conceived in the framework of a plan whose goal is to eliminate competition[37]

The criteria established by the Commission are cumulative, i.e., the action must, based on an objective view, be manifestly unfounded *and* aimed at eliminating competition.[38] Accordingly, the Commission made clear that that the initiation of sham litigation does amount to abuse within the meaning of Article 102 TFEU, unless the purpose is to eliminate competition. This obviously makes sense. Thus, the objective of competition law is not to protect individual undertakings against unfair practices, but to safeguard public interest as a whole by promoting effective competition. Moreover, the first criteria makes clear that asserting rights *vis-à-vis* competitors, even if aimed at eliminating them, cannot be considered abusive as such.

The Commission did not find the cumulative criteria to be fulfilled and accordingly dismissed the applicant's complaint.[39] Thus, according to the Commission Belgacom SA had asserted what it had reasonable believed to be its rights (although the rights turned out to be void) and had done so in defence – in the form of a counter-claim – when facing litigation initiated by the Applicant. There was therefore no evidence that a court action had been initiated to harass the applicant and eliminate it as a competitor. The General Court upheld the decision on appeal.[40]

The Court agreed with the Commission that the initiation of legal proceedings is only capable of constituting abuse within the meaning of Article 102 TFEU in "*wholly exceptional circumstances*" as the ability to assert ones rights is a both a general

35. Case T-111/96, *ITT Promedia v. Commission*, 17 Jul. 1998.
36. Commission decision in Case IV/35.268, *Promedia v. Belgacom*, 21 May 1996. Referred to in appeal Case T-111/96, *ITT Promedia v. Commission*, 17 Jul. 1998, § 23.
37. Case T-111/96, *ITT Promedia v. Commission*, 17 Jul. 1998, § 30 (citing point 11 in the Commission's decision) and § 55. It seems likely that the Commission was inspired by the approach taken by the US Supreme Court in Case 91-1043, *Professional Real Estate Investors, Inc. v. Columbia Pictures Industries, Inc.*, 508 U.S. 49, 3 May 1993, where a similar two-tier test was adopted.
38. Case T-111/96, *ITT Promedia v. Commission*, 17 Jul. 1998, § 56.
39. *Ibid.*, §§ 41–42.
40. *Ibid.*, § 93.

principle of law and a fundamental right codified in Articles 6 and 13 of the ECHR.[41] Accordingly the cumulative criteria should be construed and applied strictly.[42] With regard to the first criterion the court stressed that it is immaterial whether the rights asserted actually exists or whether the action is well founded. Insofar as an undertaking asserts what it "*at that moment, reasonably consider to be its rights*" there can be no abuse within the meaning of Article 102 TFEU as the aim cannot be solely to harass the opposing party.[43]

As the applicant only challenged the specific application of the criteria the General Court on appeal did not rule on whether the two-tier test itself was in conformity with EU competition law.[44] Accordingly it was at the time somehow unclear whether the test, if eventually challenged before the CJEU, would be accepted. However, in ruling on the applicability of the criteria and assessing the reasoning underlying the test, the court confirmed the validity of the test implicitly.[45] This was confirmed in *Protégé International* where the General Court found that the Commission was right to dismiss a complaint on grounds that the criteria of the *ITT Promedia*-test were not fulfilled.[46]

[b] ITT Promedia and Standard-Essential Patents

While the *ITT Promedia* case did not specifically concern the assertion of IPR it highlighted that competition law as a main rule cannot be relied upon to prevent undertakings from enforcing their rights before the courts. This general rule arguably applies all the more with respect to the enforcement of IPR.[47] Thus, using competition law to limit the scope of intellectual property protection may not only jeopardize the fundamental rights referred to by the Commission, but also risks undermining the incentive for undertakings to innovate – hence may counteract the very goal of effective competition as promoted by competition law.[48] The necessity of safeguarding

41. *Ibid.*, § 60.Case T-111/96, *ITT Promedia v. Commission*, 17 Jul. 1998, § 60. As noted above a similar right has since been codified in Art. 47 of the Charter of Fundamental Rights of the European Union, 2000 O.J. C 364/1, 18 Dec. 2000.
42. Case T-111/96, *ITT Promedia v. Commission*, 17 Jul. 1998, § 61.
43. *Ibid.*, § 73.
44. *Ibid.*, §§ 57–58.
45. See along the same lines Jones, Alison & Sufrin, Brenda, *EC Competition Law- Text, Cases and Materials*, 3rd ed., Oxford University Press, 2008 p. 582 and Østerud, Erik, *Identifying Exclusionary Abuses By Dominant Undertakings under EU Competition Law: the Spectrum of Tests*, Kluwer Law International (International Competition Law Series, 45), 2010 p. 137.
46. Case T-119/09, *Protégé International v. Commission*, 13 Sep. 2012, §§ 51–68 (in particular). Also see Vesterdorf, Bo, *IP Rights and Competition Law Enforcement Questions*, in Journal of European Competition Law & Practice, Vol. 4(2), 2013 pp. 109–111.
47. See along the same lines Hull, David, *The EC's Investigation into the Pharmaceutical Sector: Trouble Ahead at the IP/Competition Intersection?*, In Competition Policy International, Vol. 11(1), 2008 p. 5.
48. As noted in Chapter 4 s. §4.02 EU competition law in promoting 'effective competition' does not only seek to safeguard effective price competition, but also innovation.

the incentives for undertakings to invest in research, development and innovation has been firmly recognized by the Commission and the CJEU.[49]

That said, the risk of damage to innovation is less evident in case competition law is applied to prevent or sanction the assertion of SEPs, insofar as the patentee has voluntarily committed itself to license the patents on FRAND terms to all third parties in accordance with the IPR policy of an SSO. By doing so a patentee knowingly decides to trade off (absolute) exclusivity in order to reap the monetary upside associated with having patented technology embodied in the standard set – hence clarifying that the right to exclude is not a prerequisite for maintaining its incentive to innovate.[50] Moreover, having accepted 'merely' a right to remuneration *vis-à-vis* third parties by virtue of a FRAND commitment the patentee will, as a main rule, have no objective justification for requesting injunctive relief – monetary compensation in the form of damages will be sufficient to safeguard the patentee's legitimate interest. This is not to say that a FRAND commitment should be construed as an unconditional statement that the issuer will not enforce the rights affected against any third party, but there is much to suggest that doing so will (and should) be considered legitimate only when the alleged infringer has not been genuinely willing to take a license on FRAND terms. In other words, the assertion of SEPs (or threat hereof) against a good faith potential licensee should be considered one of the "*wholly exceptional circumstances*" (referred to be the Commission and the General Court in the *Promedia* case) in which the reliance on statutory rights may constitute abuse, because in light of a FRAND commitment doing so serves only to harass the defendant and eliminate competition.[51]

As stated by EU competition commissioner Joaquin Almunia "*[t]he protection of intellectual property is a cornerstone of innovation and growth. But so is competition*".[52] The statement was made in a press release concerning the Commission's preliminary finding that Motorola Mobility, now owned by Google, has breached Article 102 TFEU by enforcing its SEPs against despite the alleged infringer (Apple) having confirmed its willingness to obtain a license on FRAND terms. The case is discussed in Chapter 13 section §13.02[C][2], but at this point is illustrative of the fact that the Commission is of the opinion that a balancing of interests must be made in determining whether Article 102 TFEU is violated. This is in accordance with *Scarlet Extended* in which it was established that the protection of intellectual property is not absolute, but must be

49. See for instance Case T-201/04, *Microsoft Corp v. Commission*, 17 Sep. 2010, §§ 704–719 (in particular).

50. Also see Commission decision C(2014) 2891 final in Case COMP/39.939, *Samsung – Enforcement of UMTS standard essential patents*, 29 Apr. 2014, § 62, where it was found that a SEP holder having issued a FRAND commitment "*... expects to obtain remuneration for its SEPs by means of licensing revenue rather than using these patents to seek to exclude others*".

51. The communication carried out between the parties in the course of their licensing negotiations is likely to be of prime importance in determining whether the alleged infringer has acted in good faith.

52. Commission press release in Case COMP/39.985, *Motorola – Enforcement of GPRS standard essential patents*, MEMO/13/403 (Commission sends Statement of Objections to Motorola Mobility on potential misuse of mobile phone standard-essential patents- Questions and Answers), 6 May 2013.

balanced against the fundamental rights of the defendant, including the right to conduct business – the case is analysed immediately below.

[c] Scarlet Extended: The Principle of Proportionality

In *Scarlet Extended*[53] the European CJEU in a preliminary ruling touched upon a different, but nonetheless related issue; the requirement that the measures imposed in court must adhere to the general principle of proportionality. Although the case did not concern competition law, it nonetheless highlights a general principle of EU law which constrains national courts handling injunction cases, including those in which SEPs are at the core.

The court was asked whether EU law, in light of the ECHR, allows national courts to grant injunctions against Internet service providers insofar as they are required to adopt certain technical (and intrusive) measures aimed at preventing copyright infringement. Having confirmed that IPR are indeed protected by Article 17(2) of the Charter of Fundamental Rights of the European Union, the Court stressed that neither the wording of that provision nor the CJEU's case law suggests that such rights are "*...inviolable and must for that reason be absolutely protected*".[54] The court went on stating that "*the protection of the fundamental right to property, which includes the rights linked to intellectual property, must be balanced against the protection of other fundamental rights*", including the freedom to conduct business.[55] Against this background the court found that requiring an Internet service provider to actively monitor all data handled as a preventive measure against potential copyright infringement would not be considered proportionate.

If follows from the *Scarlet Extended* judgment that injunctions should not be granted if the proposed measures go beyond what is necessary to strike a fair balance between the rights owner and the defendant. This reasoning is in accordance with Article 3(2) of Directive 2004/48 on the enforcement of IPR stating that remedies shall "*... be effective, proportionate and dissuasive and shall be applied in such a manner as to avoid the creation of barriers to legitimate trade and to provide for safeguards against their abuse*".[56] These objectives are obviously shared by competition law. Thus, although the principle of proportionality does not relate specifically to competition law it is a general principle of EU law of importance in establishing under what circumstances the assertion of legal rights, including patents, constitutes abuse under the *ITT Promedia*-test mentioned above. In other words, while not sufficient to establish abuse, the fact that the granting of an injunction (or other remedies) would contradict the principle of proportionality may be able to substantiate a finding that requesting the injunction was anti-competitive, because the plaintiff cannot be deemed to assert what

53. Case C-70/10, *Scarlet Extended SA v. SABAM*, 24 Nov. 2011.
54. Case C-70/10, *Scarlet Extended SA v. SABAM*, 24 Nov. 2011, § 43.
55. *Ibid.*, §§ 44–46. Reference is made to Art. 16 of the Charter of Fundamental Rights of the European Union.
56. Directive 2004/48/EC of 29 Apr. 2004 of the European Parliament and of the Council on the enforcement of intellectual property rights, Art. 3(2).

it "*at that moment, reasonably consider to be its rights*" – as noted above this is decisive in determining whether the first criteria of the *ITT Promedia*-test is fulfilled.

As explained below the Commission in its *Google/Motorola* merger decision and its subsequent *Motorola Mobiliy* and *Samsung Electronics* decisions adopted the reasoning underpinning both the *Promedia* and *Scarlet Extended* judgments in support of its position, being that Article 102 TFEU as main rule prevents injunctions being granted on the basis of SEPs.

[2] The Commission's Approach to SEP Injunctions

In 2012, the Commission adopted a decision[57] in which it approved Google's acquisition of Motorola Mobility pursuant to the EC Merger Regulation.[58] Although the decision did not concern the abuse of SEPs it nonetheless touches upon the potential anti-competitive exercise of such rights to seek injunctions – hence provides some important insight into the Commission's reasoning in this regard. Thus, Google would, as a result of the intended transaction, obtain control of a significant portfolio of SEPs.[59] This prompted certain third parties to voice their concern that the merged entity would seek recourse to injunctions against competitors based on these patents as a means to impose onerous licensing terms, in particular by demanding cross-licenses to non-SEPs.[60]

The Commission acknowledged that the assessment under Article 102 TFEU must take place within the general framework established by *ITT Promedia* and *Scarlet Extended* discussed in Chapter 13 section §13.02[C][1]. Thus, the Commission recapped that according to *ITT Promedia* it is only in 'wholly exceptional circumstances' that bringing legal proceedings is capable of constituting abuse within the meaning of Article 102 TFEU, but at the same time noted that the Court in *Scarlet Extended* held that the right to property, including intellectual property, is not absolutely protected.[61] As explained below a careful reading of the decision indicates that the Commission expects owners of SEPs to adhere to a rather strict legal standard – at least in comparison with the so-called 'Orange Book'-criteria established by the German Federal Supreme Court as discussed in Chapter 13 section §13.02[D].

In response to the concerns expressed the Commission investigated whether the merged entity would have incentives to impair effective competition by having recourse to injunctions against "*good faith potential licensees*" with the aim of imposing onerous license terms (excessive royalties or cross-license demands) and/or excluding competitors from the market.[62] The Commission clarified that "*[d]epending on the circumstances, it may be that the threat of injunction, the seeking of an injunction*

57. Case COMP/M.6381, *Google/Motorola Mobility*, 13 Feb. 2012 (Merger procedure).
58. Council Regulation (EC) No. 139/2004 of 20 Jan. 2004 on the control of concentrations between undertakings (the EC Merger Regulation).
59. Case COMP/M.6381, *Google/Motorola Mobility*, 13 Feb. 2012, § 7 (Merger procedure).
60. *Ibid.*, § 108.
61. Case COMP/M.6381, *Google/Motorola Mobility*, 13 Feb. 2012, § 106, footnote 55 (Merger procedure).
62. *Ibid.*, § 109.

or indeed the actual enforcement of an injunction granted against a good faith potential licensee, may significantly impede effective competition…".[63] Similar concerns have been raised on the other side of the Atlantic. Thus, as noted by the US Federal Trade Commission "*[s]eeking and threatening injunctions against willing licensees of FRAND-encumbered SEPs undermines the integrity and efficiency of the standard-setting process and decreases the incentives to participate in the process and implement published standards*".[64]

Interestingly, it is, according to the Commission, not a prerequisite for finding abuse within the meaning of Article 102 TFEU that the patentee actually seeks or enforces an injunction on basis of FRAND-pledged patents – the mere threat of doing so is sufficient.[65] In this respect the Commission (rightly) reasoned that the prospect of becoming victim of an injunction may prompt the acceptance of onerous license terms which otherwise would have been rejected, i.e., such threat may potentially give rise to the same anti-competitive effect as actually seeking or enforcing an injunction. However, arguably threating an injunction can still only be considered abusive within the meaning of Article 102 TFEU if the threat is accompanied by a non-FRAND demand, e.g., a request for excessive royalties or the provision of cross-licenses to non-essential IPR. Thus, absent such demand the threat itself cannot be established to have as its purpose the attainment of an anti-competitive objective to the detriment of consumers.

On the other hand actually enforcing an injunction against a 'willing' licensee in order to exclude standard complaint products from the market undoubtedly has the potential of causing harm to consumers by limiting intra-technology competition. As noted by the Commission this holds true regardless of whether the injunction is temporary as irreparable harm may come to any company forced to withdraw its products from the market – especially if (as is often the case) the injunction concerns rapidly developing markets where profits must be made within a rather short time span.[66] This observation highlights the necessity of ensuring the availability of the competition law defence in preliminary relief proceedings.

[a] The 'Good Faith' Requirement

An action aimed at excluding a company unwilling to take a license cannot be considered an unreasonable attempt to establish ones rights, cf. *ITT Promedia*, hence cannot be considered abusive – quite to the contrary. As noted the very purpose of granting a patent is to promote innovation by allowing for the exclusion of unlicensed 'free riders'. Therefore, any attempt to deprive SEP holders their statutory right to exclude companies unwilling to negotiate a license would arguably be detrimental to

---

63. *Ibid.*, § 107.
64. Federal Trade Commission, Motorola Mobility LLC and Google Inc.; Analysis of Proposed Consent Order to Aid Public Comment, File No. 121-0120, 3 Jan. 2013.
65. Also see § 113 of the decision where it is stated that "*…despite the limitations imposed by courts and other bodies, it is likely that a SEP holder retains some ability to use its SEPs to significantly impede effective completion. For example, a SEP holder can certainly threaten to seek or seek injunctions at any time*".
66. Case COMP/M.6381, *Google/Motorola Mobility*, 13 Feb. 2012, § 57 (Merger procedure).

effective competition, including innovation. It would essentially render the exclusivity granted under patent law illusory and deprive companies the incentive to participate in standard setting activities out of fear that they will effectively be deprived the right to harvest the fruits of the innovative technologies they contribute to SSOs and pledge to license on FRAND terms.

This was acknowledged by the Commission. Thus, the notion of a *'good faith'* or '*willing*' potential licensee is, according to the Commission, an anchor point in assessing whether the assertion of SEPs in infringement proceedings amounts to abuse under Article 102 TFEU. If the potential licensee, against whom an injunction is threatened, sought or obtained, has not been genuinely willing to take a license on FRAND terms the conduct of the patentee cannot be deemed abusive, because it merely serves to force the potential licensee to respect a right legitimately conferred under patent law. As noted by the Commission "*... the seeking or enforcement of injunctions on the basis of SEPs is...not, of itself, anti-competitive ...depending on the circumstances, it may be legitimate for the holder of SEPs to seek an injunction against a potential licensee which is not willing to negotiate in good faith on FRAND terms*".[67] In other words, it was clarified that a FRAND commitment does not constitute a permit to infringe upon the underlying patent rights, but an entitlement to license them following good faith license negotiations.[68]

On the outset it is therefore clear that the Commission (rightly) does not intend to apply a 'no-injunctions ever' regime in the context of FRAND-pledged patents. However, that being said it is equally clear that the Commission favours a rather strict legal standard leaving holders of such patents with limited room to 'manoeuvre'. Thus, by stating "*[i]n the event licensing discussions fail, the SEP holder may ultimately take its counterparty to court and seek an injunction*" the Commission arguably hinted that such action is only warranted as a last resort if the potential licensee is not genuinely willing to take a license.[69] To a similar effect the Commission stated that owners of FRAND-pledged patents are obliged to provide a license on FRAND terms, but "*have the right to conduct negotiations with interested parties concerning the exact terms and conditions of the licence, including the exact level of royalties and the right to enforce such agreements by means of litigation*" – hereby stressing that injunctions are off the table as a main rule.[70]

[b] Recent Developments: Another Step towards a 'Good Faith' Regime

At the time of writing the Commission has passed two decisions relating to the assertion of SEPs. The two cases were initated closely on the heels of each other and the final decisions were both rendered 29 April 2014 where the CJEU's judgment in the

67. *Ibid.*, § 126.
68. This seems in line with the reasoning of the District court of the Hague in *SK Kasetten* and *Samsung v. Apple* – see Ch. 13 s. §13.02[D].
69. Case COMP/M.6381, *Google/Motorola Mobility*, 13 Feb. 2012, § 106 (Merger procedure).
70. *Ibid.*, § 55.

Huawei[71] case, which concerns the same overall issue, was still pending.[72] Thus, whether the CJEU agrees with the Commission remains to be seen.

The Commission found that Samsung Electronics and Motorola Mobility, respectively, had acted in contravention of Article 102 TFEU by relying on their SEPs to seek and enforce injunctions against Apple which was deemed a 'willing' licensee. In its Statement of Objections the Commission had made a preliminary finding that the seeking and enforcing of injunctions on basis of SEPs, in light of the specific and exceptional circumstances of the cases concerned and in the absence of any objective justification, amounted to abuse – the exceptional circumstances being the companies' participation in the standard-setting process within an SSO (ETSI) and their commitment to license on FRAND terms.[73] In this respect the Commission recalled that the list of exceptional circumstances previously set out in the *Microsoft*[74] judgment (and prior case law) was not exhaustive.[75] Moreover, the Commission whilst referring to *Scarlet Extended* and *ITT Promedia,* according to which the enforcement of rights may amount to abuse only in exceptional circumstances (see Chapter 13 section §13.02[C][1]), found that its finding of abuse was consistent with the public interest in maintaining effective competetion and:

> fully respect the requirement that a fair balance be struck between the fundamental rights and freedoms at stake, namely the rights linked to intellectual property enshrined in Article 17(2) of the Charter of Fundamental Rights of the European Union ('the Charter'); the right of access to a tribunal, enshrined in Article 47 of the Charter; and the freedom to conduct a business, enshrined in Article 16 of the Charter.[76]

Although essentially seeking recourse to injunctions amounts to a de facto refusal to license, the Commission therefore does not intend to assess whether the 'exceptional circumstances' set out in *Microsoft* are fulfilled, but rather seems to presuppose this to be the case in light of a FRAND commitment. The Commission relies on the *ITT Promedia* and *Scarlet Extended* judgments (discussed in Chapter 13 section §13.02[C][1]) as an overall framework for determining whether the enforcement of FRAND-pledged patents constitute abuse under Article 102 TFEU and as noted above equates the threat of doing so with actual enforcement. Indeed, the Commission

71. Case C-170/13, *Huawei Technologies v. ZTE*, 5 Apr. 2013.
72. Cases COMP/39.939, *Samsung – Enforcement of UMTS standard essential patents*, and COMP/39.985, *Motorola – Enforcement of GPRS standard essential patents*. The first Statement of Objections was sent to Samsung Electronics 21 Dec. 2012 and the second one to Motorola Mobility 6 May 2013. See Commission's press releases IP/12/1448 of 21 Dec. 2012 (regarding Samsung) and IP 13/406 of 6 May 2013 (regarding Motorola Mobility).
73. Commission's memo MEMO/12/1021 of 21 Dec. 2012 in Case COMP/39.939, *Samsung – Enforcement of UMTS standard essential patents*, and MEMO/13/403 of 06 May 2013 in Case COMP/39.985, *Motorola – Enforcement of GPRS standard essential patents*. Also see Commission Decision C(2014) 2891 final in Case COMP/39.939, *Samsung – Enforcement of UMTS standard essential patents*, 29 Apr. 2014, Chapter 4 s. §4.04[A].
74. Case T-201/04. *Microsoft Corp v. Commission*, 17 Sep. 2007. This case was discussed in Chapter 12 s. §12.01.
75. Also see Commission decision C(2014) 2891 final in Case COMP/39.939, *Samsung – Enforcement of UMTS standard essential patents*, 29 Apr. 2014, § 56.
76. *Ibid.*, § 72.

referred to Article 51(1) of the EU Charter of Fundamental rights and along the lines of *Scarlet Extended* noted that the right of access to a tribunal does not constitute an unfettered prerogative, but a fundamental right which may be restricted if such a restriction is (i) in alignment with objectives of general public interest, (ii) is proportionate and (iii) does not infringe upon the very substance of the right.[77]

In the Motorola Mobility decision the abuse was found to consist in seeking and enforcing injunctions against Apple in Germany on the basis of FRAND-pledged patents essential to the GPRS standard (as adopted by ETSI) when "*...Apple had agreed to take a licence and be bound by a determination of the FRAND royalties by the relevant German court*".[78] Moreover, the Commission found Motorola to have committed a separate abuse by threating to enforce an injunction if Apple did not give up its rights to challenge the validity or infringement of Motorola's SEPs. This is only logical since such a threat has as its purpose to enforce a non-challenge clause which, as discucssed in Chapter 11 section §11.01[J], in most cases this will also be considered anti-competive under Article 101(1) TFEU. As noted by the Commission "*...[i]mplementers of standards and ultimately consumers should not have to pay for invalid or non-infringed patents. Implementers should therefore be able to ascertain the validity of patents and contest alleged infringements*".[79] Notwithstanding the abuse the Commission quite surprisingly decided not to impose a fine due to lack of EU case law and the fact that national courts case law was inconsistent.[80] Having clarified its position the Commission will most likely be less lenient going forward.

The Samsung Electronics decision likewise concerned the assertion of SEPs reading on the 3G UMTS standard (again an ETSI standard) against Apple which, according to the Commission, had shown itself willing to negotiate a FRAND license for the disputed SEPs.[81] The Commission found it irrelevant to its assesment that Samsung prior to the Commissions preliminary decision in the case had announced its intend to withdraw the injunctions in question, since abuse had already been committed.[82] Moreover, the Commission (rightly) stated it to be without relevance whether a SEP holder enforces its rights in response to lawsuits brought by the defendant on the basis of patents which have not been 'encumbered' by a FRAND commitment (Apple had

77. Commission's memo in Case COMP/39.939, *Samsung – Enforcement of UMTS standards essential patents*, MEMO/12/1021 (Samsung – Enforcement of ETSI standards essential patents (SEPs) – Questions and Answers), 21 Dec. 2012.
78. Commission's press release in Case COMP/39.985, *Motorola – Enforcement of GPRS standard essential patents*, IP/14/489 (Commission finds that Motorola Mobility infringed EU competition rules by misusing standard essential patents), 29 Apr. 2014.
79. *Ibid.*
80. An overview of national case-law in the Netherlands and in Germany is provided in Ch. 13 s. §13.02[D].
81. Commission's press release in Case COMP/39.939, *Samsung – Enforcement of UMTS standard essential patents*, IP/14/489 (Commission finds that Motorola Mobility infringed EU competition rules by misusing standard essential patents), 29 Apr. 2014.
82. Case COMP/39.939, MEMO/12/1021 (Samsung – Enforcement of ETSI standards essential patents (SEPs) – Questions and Answers), 21 Dec. 2012. This is in accordance with case T-321/05, *AstraZeneca v. Commission*, 1 Jul. 2010, § 379 and §§ 602–609 from which it follows that the success of an action is not a prerequisite for finding abuse if the action has the potential of causing harm to competition.

asserted non-SEPs against Samsung in Germany). In other words, FRAND-pledged SEPs cannot be relied upon to retaliate.

In response to the concerns raised Samsung offered a series of licensing commitments which was made binding by the Commission pursuant to Article 9(1) of Regulation 1/2003. More specially, Samsung committed not to seek any injunctions within the European Economic Area (EEA) on the basis of its SEPs for a period of five years against companies which agrees to a licensing framework providing for (i) a negotiation period of up to twelve months, and (ii) in case of dispute, having a court or, if mutally agreed, an arbitrator set the FRAND terms.[83]

These decisions make clear that the Commission, as hinted by the statements made in the *Google/Motorola* merger decision, finds the assertion of SEPs to violate Article 102 TFEU if directed at companies genuinely willing to take a license on FRAND terms. Thus, as noted above, seeking an injunction – or even threating to do so – against a 'willing licensee' may be deemed abusive according to the Commission. In light hereof, and although of course an aggravating circumstance, it not a prerequisite for finding abuse that the plaintiff has abused its dominant position by requesting non-FRAND license terms prior to seeking or threating an injunction – it is sufficient that the patentee, notwithstanding such request, does so while license negotiations are on-going and at time where there is no clear indication that the would-be licensee is not willing to take a licence on FRAND terms. This was clear from the press release concerning the opening of proceedings against Motorola Mobility as the Commission clearly distinguished between two possible abuses, namely Motorola's assertion of SEPs and its offering of unfair licensing conditions.[84] In essence therefore the assertion of SEPs against 'willing' or 'good faith' licensees will be introduced as a new type of abuse under EU competition law if eventually accepted by the CJEU.

The Commission explained that it is anti-competitive to use injunctions in relation to SEPs "... *when in a standardisation context, a SEP holder has committed to license the SEP on FRAND terms and the licensee is willing to take a licence on such terms*", since doing so may distort licensing negotiations in the SEP holder's favour and harm consumer welfare.[85] On the other hand, the Commission stressed (relying on its reasoning in *Google/Motorola*[86]) that it does not in general question the availability of injunctive relief for SEP holders against 'unwilling' licensees.[87] Guidance on how to draw the line between 'willing' and 'unwilling' is therefore of essence in deciding

83. Commission decision C(2014) 2891 final in Case COMP/39.939, *Samsung – Enforcement of UMTS standard essential patents*, 29 Apr. 2014.
84. Commission's press release in Case COMP/39.985, *Motorola – Enforcement of GPRS standard essential patents*, IP 12/345 (Commission opens proceedings against Motorola), 3 Apr. 2012.
85. Cases COMP/39.939 and COMP/39.985, MEMO/14/322 (Antitrust decisions on standard essential patents (SEPs) – Motorola Mobility and Samsung Electronics – Frequently asked questions), 29 Apr. 2014.
86. See Ch. 13 s. § 13.02[C][2] for more information on Case COMP/M.6381, *Google/Motorola Mobility*, 13 Feb. 2012, § 126 (Merger procedure).
87. Cases COMP/39.939 and COMP/39.985, MEMO/14/322 (Antitrust decisions on standard essential patents (SEPs) – Motorola Mobility and Samsung Electronics – Frequently asked questions), 29 Apr. 2014.

(i) whether seeking or threating to seek an injunction will violate Article 102 TFEU and (ii) whether a competition law defence will be succesful.

The two decisions provided some much needed clarification by establishing a 'safe harbour' upon which willing liceences of FRAND-pledged SEPs can rely to avoid injunctions. According to the Commission a would-be licensee can demonstrate its willingness to take a license on FRAND terms by agreeing that a court or mutally agreed arbitrator sets the terms in case of dispute.[88] However, the decisions fail to provide adequte guidance regarding one critical aspect – the timing of the would-be licensees request for a license. The wording of the FAQ memo published by the Commission seems to indicate that standard implementers may benefit from the safe harbour even if prior to the dispute they did not proactively approach the SEP holder to obtain a license.[89] However, as argued below such legal approach does not ensure a proper balance between SEP holders and standard implementers, since it would enable the latter to simply lean back and await the SEP holders request for royalties knowing that there will be no consequences of infringement – see section§13.02[C][2][b][iii]. In this respect, it must be recalled that SSOs typically maintain a publicly accesible database of all SEPs which have been declared essential to the standards they promote and therefore there can be no objective justification for not proactively seeking a license to the patents disclosed.[90]

The Commission also did not provide any guidenace as to when a company may be considered a 'willing' licensee in cases where the safe harbour does not apply, but merely stated that this must be assesed on a case-by-case basis taking into account the specific facts.[91] Thus, while the press releases clarify that the Commission intends to apply a flexible 'good faith' standard when assessing whether enforcement of SEPs amounts to abuse they do not however set out an exhaustive set of criteria which are of relevance in applying the standard, i.e., under which it may practically be determined whether the defendant has been willing to negotiate a license in good faith. However, some guidance can be extracted from the statements made by the Commission in relation to the cases:

[i] Challenges to Validity, Essentiality or Infringement

As noted above it is in the Commission's view it is in the public interest that licensees should be able to challenge the validity, essentiality or infringement of SEPs. Therefore an action by a potential licensee in this respect does, according to the Commission, not in itself render the potential licensee 'unwilling' – at least where it "*...otherwise agrees*

88. *Ibid.*
89. *Ibid.*
90. The situation is different in case the SEP holder has failed to disclose its patents. This 'patent ambush' scenario was discussed in Chapter 10.
91. Cases COMP/39.939 and COMP/39.985, MEMO/14/322 (Antitrust decisions on standard essential patents (SEPs) – Motorola Mobility and Samsung Electronics – Frequently asked questions), 29 Apr. 2014.

to be bound by the determination of FRAND terms by a third party".[92] This is in accordance with the conclusion made in Chapter 11 section §11.01[J] that a FRAND license agreement cannot be made conditional on the licensee accepting non-challenge clauses as this would run counter to community interest in weeding out invalid IPR – or in the case of essentiality challenges; falsely classified IPR. Interestingly, the Commission explicitly stated its view that an interpretation of the German Orange-Book judgment (as discussed in Chapter 13 section §13.02[D][1]) whereby a willing licensee is deprived its right to initiate such challenges would be anti-competitive.[93]

[ii] Acceptance of Binding Third-Party Determination of FRAND

The Commission had stated its preliminary view that that "...*the acceptance of binding third party determination for the terms of a FRAND licence in the event that bilateral negotiations do not come to a fruitful conclusion is a clear indication that a potential licensee is willing to enter into a FRAND licence*" as this "...*allows for adequate remuneration of the SEP-holder so that seeking or enforcing injunctions is no longer justified...*".[94] In the final decision this view, as noted above, resulted in a safe harbour for implementers that agree to let a third party – whether a court or arbitrator – set the FRAND terms.

It follows that the Commission supports the view that the prospect of fair remuneration as a main rule renders an enforcement action unjustified in light of a FRAND commitment which is to be construed as an unconditional offer to grant a licence. However, while the statement gives one example of how 'good faith' negotiations may come to end (by the potential licensee declaring itself willing to accept a royalty rate determined by a third party) it does however not touch upon the important question of how such negotiations must be initiated in order for the infringer to be considered 'willing' – must the potential licensee request a license prior to infringement

92. See Commission memo in Case COMP/39.985, *Motorola – Enforcement of GPRS standard essential patents*, MEMO/13/403 (Commission sends Statement of Objections to Motorola Mobility on potential misuse of mobile phone standard-essential patents – Questions and Answers), 6 May 2013.

93. Cases COMP/39.939 and COMP/39.985, MEMO/14/322 (Antitrust decisions on standard essential patents (SEPs) – Motorola Mobility and Samsung Electronics – Frequently asked questions), 29 Apr. 2014. It is clear therefore that the Commission does not agree with the judgment of the Mannheim District which granted Motorola Mobility the injunction against Apple. Thus, the court held that Motorola Mobility, under the so-called Orange-Book criteria established by the German Federal Supreme Court, was not obliged to accept Apple's license offer insofar as Apple would not abstain from challenging the validity of the disputed patents and therefore did not violate competition law by dismissing Apple's license offer. See Case 7 O 122/11, *Motorola Mobility v. Apple*, Mannheim Regional Court (Landgericht Mannheim), 9 Dec. 2011 – unofficial translation available at: http://www.scribd.com/doc/94523005/Translation-of-Mannheim-20240-Ruling-Motorola-v-Microsoft (last checked 30 May 2014). The judgment was upheld by Karlsruhe Higher Regional Court (Oberlandesgericht Karlsruhe) in Case 6 U 136/11.

94. See Commission press release in Case COMP/39.985, *Motorola – Enforcement of GPRS standard essential patents*, MEMO/13/403 (Commission sends Statement of Objections to Motorola Mobility on potential misuse of mobile phone standard-essential patents- Questions and Answers), 6 May 2013.

or is it sufficient to declare such a willingness to license at the time infringement is discovered by the patentee?

In this respect see point [iii] immediately below.

[iii] Passive, Unresponsive or Employing Delaying Tactics

It seems as if the Commission focuses solely on the conduct of the infringer from the time licensing negotiations are initiated. Thus, the Commission found that a potential license "*...which remains passive and unresponsive to a request to enter into licensing negotiations or is found to employ clear delaying tactics cannot be generally considered as 'willing'*".[95] Hereby the Commission placed emphasis on the obligation of the potential licensee to respond to a license request forwarded by the patentee, but did not set out an obligation to actively approach the patentee in order to obtain a license prior to infringement.

Arguably, such approach does not sufficiently cater for the legitimate interests of SEP holders. If a would-be licensee's declared willingness to take a license on FRAND terms is to be the focal point in assessing abuse under Article 102 TFEU the infringer must at least be able to show that it forwarded a license request prior to infringement or at the very latest, at the time it became aware or ought to have become aware of its infringement. Otherwise injunctions will be deprived of their deterrent effect and implementers will have little incentive to proactively seek a license – if they don't become victim of an infringement action they get to use the patent for free, and if they do, they 'merely' risk having to pay damages which will often equate with the FRAND royalty rate they would have had to pay in case they had requested a license. In effect competition law will act to promote wilful infringement rather than seek a fair balance which ensures SEP owners adequate remuneration. Having courts to apply such a legal standard by reference to Article 16 of Regulation 1/2003[96] arguably fails to strike a fair balance between the fundemantal rights and freedoms catered for by Articles 16, 17(2) and 47 of the Charter of Fundamental Rights of the European Union and may also be detriminal to effective competition as promoted by Article 102 TFEU insofar as it damages the incentive for patentees to participate in formal standard setting activities. Put simply, an infringer who simply leans back to passively await infringement proceedings should not be considered 'willing' to genuinely take a license on FRAND terms. As follows from Chapter 13 section §13.02[D] a similar overall reasoning has been applied by the Dutch and the German courts.

[iv] Objective Justification for Seeking an Injunction

The Commission acknowledged that SEP holders are entitled to take reasonable steps to protect their commercial interests by seeking injunctions against potential licensees

95. *Ibid.*
96. Council Regulation (EC) No. 1/2003 of 16 Dec. 2002 on the implementation of the rules on competition laid down in Arts 81 and 82 of the Treaty.

if such action can be objectively justified. The Commission highlighted the following as examples of scenarioes which would provide a SEP holder with an objective justification for seeking an injunction:

(i) a potential licensee is in financial distress and unable to pay its debts;
(ii) a potential licensee's assets are located in jurisdictions that do not provide for adequate means of enforcement of damages; or
(iii) a potential licensee is unwilling to enter into a licence agreement on FRAND terms and conditions, with the result that the SEP holder will not receive FRAND compensation for the use of its SEPs.[97]

With regard to (iii) the Commission as noted above per se seems to consider a would-be licensee 'willing' if the company in question agrees to let a third party set the terms of a FRAND licence in case of dispute. However, it remains to be seen whether this also applies in cases where the would-be licensee has not proactively sought to obtain a licence in the first place – as noted in item C) above it seems reasonable to conclude that a company which does not seek a license as soon as it knew or ought to have become aware of the patent in question should not be considered a genuinly 'willing' licensee.

As neither Motorola Mobility nor Samsung Electronics was accused of carrying out a patent ambush, i.e., of deceiving SSOs in order to have their patents embodied in the standard adopted, the Commission did not take a position as to whether and to what extent such conduct impacts the 'good faith' assessment. As discussed in Chapter 10, there is no basis for concluding that the exercise of SEPs will constitute abuse merely because the patents have not been disclosed. However, if a patentee fails to honour a disclosure obligation the infringer cannot be said to have acted in 'bad faith' by not requesting a license prior to infringement. Seeking injunctions against such (good faith) infringer without first having offered a license on FRAND terms arguably will constitute abuse. Moreover, if the patentee is found to have deliberately concealed its patents and as a result the technological composition of the standard has (or is likely to have) been altered, this, as discussed in Chapter 10, will constrain the patentee to a royalty rate (or other fees) equal to the one which would have prevailed absent the patent ambush. Accordingly, a patent ambush may impact the 'good faith' assessment indirectly by limiting the royalty rate (or other fees) which the patentee can legitimately claim prior to enforcement action.

[3] Huawei Technologies versus ZTE

The Regional Court of Düsseldorf on 21 March 2013 decided to stay proceedings and make a reference for a preliminary ruling to the CJEU in connection with a patent dispute between Huawei and ZTE (two major Chinese mobile device makers).[98] The Commission may need to adjust its practice when eventually the CJEU passes its

97. Commission decision C(2014) 2891 final in Case COMP/39.939, *Samsung – Enforcement of UMTS standard essential patents*, 29 Apr. 2014, § 62.
98. Case C-170/13, *Huawei Technologies v. ZTE*, 5 Apr. 2013.

judgment; hence it is somewhat surprising that the Commission did not await the CJEU's guidance before passing final decisions in the *Samsung Electronics* and *Motorola Mobility* cases discussed in Chapter 13 section §13.02[C][2].

Noting a discrepancy between the strict criteria set out by the German Federal Supreme Court in its Orange-Book ruling (see Chapter 13 section §13.02[D][1]) the Regional Court of Düsseldorf *inter alia* asked whether a presumption of abuse under Article 102 TFEU may result merely from the infringer's willingness to negotiate and in the affirmative whether specific requirements for said willingness to negotiate in substantive and/or chronological terms must be established or whether an orally declared willingness to negotiate is sufficient.[99] Interestingly, the reffering court made its own observation that the 'good faith' standard envisaged by the Commission is too vague and leaves infringers with the tactical option of evading injunctions by merely creating the impression of being willing to negotiate in good faith while in reality having had no serious intention to obtain a license.[100] According to the court establishing specific criteria regarding quality and timing of license offers are essential in ensuring a proper balance between infringers and SEP holders as well as the companies having negotiated a license in good faith. Arguably the court is right insofar as a prerequisite for finding abuse and succeeding with a competition law defence must be that the infringer *prior* to infringement (at least when it ought to have become aware of the infringement) has forwarded a license offer to the SEP holder – see the argument above. On the other hand, the German Orange-Book criteria are too formalistic and patentee friendly. Thus, the Commission is right in adopting a flexible 'good faith' regime allowing all factors of relevance to be taken into consideration when determining whether there is reason to deviate from the main rule: seeking recourse to injunctions in light of a FRAND commitment constitutes an 'exceptional circumstance' which satisfies the criteria for competition law intervention as set out in *ITT Promedia*. While such a flexible approach may potentially result in a non-uniform national application of Article 102 TFEU contrary to the 'spirit' of Regulation 1/2003[101] the flexibility is necessary to ensure a proper balancing of interests in accordance with the principle of proportionality as set out in *Scarlet Extended*.

Obviously, limiting the power of SEPs, as suggested by the Commission, has the side effect of also limiting their value as 'bargaining chips' to obtain cross-licenses to non-SEPs, including those used by third parties in litigation against the patentee. Some authors have accordingly argued that inhibiting the strategic power of SEPs may have the perverse effect of prolonging patent disputes to the detriment of effective competition, because holders of FRAND-pledged patents will be unable to rely on their rights as a means of defence to reach settlement agreements by threating 'mutually ensured

99. *Ibid.*
100. See 4b O 104/12, *Huawei v. ZTE*, District Court Dusseldorf (Landgericht Düsseldorf), 21 Mar. 2013, §§ 39–40 (in particular). Also see Taylor Wessing, *What does it take to be FRAND*, newsletter, 8 Apr. 2013.
101. Regulation 1/2003 of 16 Dec. 2002 on the implementation of the rules on competition laid down in Arts 81 and 82 of the Treaty.

destruction'.[102] However, this argument completely ignores the fact that allowing such use of FRAND-pledged patents will de facto confer upon the patentee immunity from infringement litigation and allow for the undue extraction of valuable IPR belonging to competitors. Thus, if SEPs were allowed to be used as a basis for injunctions any company offering product in compliance with the relevant standard would effectively be discouraged from enforcing their IPR out of fear that they might be excluded from the market. This is exactly why FRAND-pledged patents, as noted in Chapter 11 section §11.01[I], must be licensed on a cash-only basis if so requested by the would-be licensee.

[D] A Look at Germany and the Netherlands

Recent years have shown that national case law dealing with the enforcement of SEPs and the competition law defence has evolved in mainly two jurisdictions, namely the Netherlands and Germany. This is hardly any coincidence. The Rotterdam port in the Netherlands is Europe's largest and therefore an injunction granted in this jurisdiction will have a profound impact on any infringer seeking to import products into Europe. Likewise an injunction banning sales in Germany – Europe's largest economy – will have a significant effect on any infringer. These jurisdictions therefore tend to attract patent litigation. However, the courts of the Netherlands and Germany, respectively, have adopted different approaches with regard to the admissibility of the competition law defence. This section does not aim to disentangle the legal approaches adopted by the national courts of these Member States in detail, but to put the EU approach discussed above into perspective.

As noted below there is a general consensus that a competition law defence is admissible, but that a mere contractual claim to a license does not suffice to succeed with such a defence. That being said the German approach however deviates significantly from the Dutch approach which seems more aligned with that of the Commission. While in Germany a successful competition law defence is conditional on the defendant fulfilling certain conditions the Dutch courts to the contrary focus on the conduct of the parties preceding the legal action to determine whether they have acted in 'good faith'.

---

102. In this regard see Dolmans, Maurits & Ilan, Daniel, *European Antitrust and Patent Acquisitions: Trolls in the Patent Thickets*, in Journal of the Antitrust Committee of the International Bar Association, Vol. 8(2), 2012 p. 5, where the authors state that preventing the grant of injunctions on basis of SEPs "*...could have the perverse effect of prolonging the patent war and hampering the goal of achieving a cross-license that would allow all platform suppliers to compete on the basis of innovation, functionality and price*".

[1] Germany

In the *Standard-Spundfaß*[103] case decided by the German Federal Supreme Court in 2004 the court ruled that the defendant – an implementer of a SSO standard relating to industrial barrels and an infringer of related patents – could succeed with a counter-claim for a compulsory license if the patent holders license demands violated competition law (in that case they were claimed to be discriminatory). However, as the case was about damages for past infringement this is hardly surprising. As noted in Chapter 13 section §13.02[B] a court deciding a case on the merits is forced to consider such competition law counter-claims, and if they are warranted, reject the right holders claim as being illegal.

In the 2009 *Orange-Book-Standard*[104] judgment, the same court acknowledged that a competition law defence is generally admissible in infringement cases, including preliminary injunction proceedings. As explained below, the legal test established by the court however imposes high burdens on alleged infringers who wish to escape a request for a preliminary injunction.[105] Moreover, there is much to suggest that the legal test applied in Germany is inconsistent with the one favoured by the Commission – see Chapter 13 section §13.02[C][2]. SEP holders should therefore be wary to exercise their rights thinking that compliance with the criteria inherent in this test will shield them from competition law scrutiny – doing so might very well result in a violation of Article 102 TFEU.

The plaintiff (Philips) was the proprietor of a patent essential to the implementation of the so-called Orange-Book de facto standard which set out technical specifications relating to recordable compact discs (CD-R and CD-RW). On basis of this patent the plaintiff had successfully obtained an injunction against the defendants – some unlicensed manufactures of standard compliant compact discs. However, the defendants appealed the judgment to the German Federal Supreme Court and reasserted their claim that the Plaintiff did not qualify for injunctive relief because it had abused

103. Case KZR 40/02, *Standard-Spundfaß*, German Federal Supreme Court (Bundesgerichtshof), 13 Jul. 2004. An unofficial translation is available in: *International Review of Intellectual Property and Competition law* (IIC), Vol. 36(6), 2005 pp. 741–752.
104. Case KZR 39/06, *Philips Electronics N.V. v. SK Kassetten*, German Federal Supreme Court (Bundesgerichtshof), 6 May 2009. An English translation is available in: *International Review of Intellectual Property and Competition Law*, Vol. 41, 2010 p. 369.
105. The case did not involve FRAND-pledged patents. However, lower courts have subsequently applied the test as a basis for determining whether alleged infringers are able to successfully raise a competition law defence against an action for injunctive relief based on FRAND-pledged patents. See for instance Case 7 O 122/11, *Motorola Mobility v. Apple*, Mannheim Regional Court (Landgericht Mannheim), 9 Dec. 2011 and the order passed in case 6 U 136/11, *Apple Sales International v. Motorola Mobility Inc.*, Karlsruhe Higher Regional Court (Oberlandsgerich Karlsruhe), 23 Jan. 2012, in which the injunction granted was upheld. In Case 7 O 122/11 the court found that "*...even though the Orange-Book-Standard decision referred to a de facto standard, the criteria established there are likewise applicable to standards that have been developed by standard-setting organizations (here: ITU) in a standardization process*". Unofficial translation available at: http://www.scribd.com/doc/94523005/Translation-of-Mannheim-
20240-Ruling-Motorola-v-Microsoft (last checked 30 May 2014).

its dominant position by requesting discriminatory royalties. The claim was based on EU competition law as well as German competition law.

The Federal Supreme Court initially held that if a dominant undertaking seeks injunctive relief, while having abused it position by refusing to conclude a license agreement in accordance with competition law, the action for injunctive relief is abusive itself – hence must be dismissed – because it serves merely to prevent the defendant from obtaining a license to which it is entitled.[106] Thus, according to the court enforcing a claim to injunctive relief is "*...just as prohibited as the refusal to conclude the license agreement that would annihilate the claim...*".[107] Overall this reasoning is in line EU case law. As noted in Chapter 13 section §13.02[C][1] the General Court in *Promedia*[108] established a two-tier test according to which the initiation of legal action by a dominant undertaking is contrary to Article 102 TFEU if it serves merely to harass the defendant and eliminate competition. Any attempt to promote illegal anti-competitive conduct before the courts, whether to expel a competitor or to force upon licensees non-FRAND license terms, must be considered baseless hence abusive according to these criteria. If the courts could be relied upon to promote abusive conduct it would further weaken the FRAND regime as the prospect of an injunction (even if only temporary) may prompt licensees to accept non-FRAND terms merely in order to avoid sustaining irreparable harm to their business.

However, despite the initial reasoning of the German Federal Supreme Court it established a number of strict conditions which are at odds with the 'good faith' standard envisaged by the Commission. The court apparently took the position that for competition law defence to prevail it is not sufficient for the defendant to show that it has been denied a license on FRAND terms to which it is entitled pursuant to competition law – this was merely seen as a prerequisite for succeeding with a competition law defence.[109] More specifically, the court held that a request for an injunction, according to the court, was only to be deemed abusive and contrary to good faith – hence should be denied – if the defendant:

(i) has made an unconditional license offer on terms which the patentee cannot reject without violating competition law; and
(ii) has acted as a 'real licensee' not only anticipating its contractual rights but also the obligations arising from the proposed license offer – this in particular entails an obligation to render accounts and pay royalties.[110]

---

106. Case KZR 39/06, *Philips Electronics N.V. v. SK Kassetten*, German Federal Supreme Court, 6 May 2009, point II(2)(a)(bb). Also see *International Review of Intellectual Property and Competition Law*, Vol. 41, 2010 p. 371, § 27 (unofficial translation).
107. *Ibid.*
108. Case T-111/96, *ITT Promedia v. Commission*, 17 Jul. 1998.
109. Cf. also Hoppner, Thomas *Competition Law in Intellectual Property Litigation – the Case for a Compulsory License Defence Under Article 102 TFEU*, in European Competition Journal, Vol. 7(2), 2011 p. 301.
110. Case KZR 39/06, *Philips Electronics N.V. v. SK Kassetten*, German Federal Supreme Court, 6 May 2009, point II(2)(b). Also see *International Review of Intellectual Property and Competition Law*, Vol. 41, 2010 p. 372, § 29 (unofficial translation). The practical consequences of these criteria have since been elaborated upon in subsequent German case law, cf. Camesasca, Peter,

The reasoning underlying these rules is that an infringer wishing to avail itself of a FRAND defence must behave as real licensee – it is not enough to have a competition law claim to a license.[111] The practical implications of these criteria will not be discussed further in this book, since they are irrelevant to the application of Article 102 TFEU.[112] It suffices to say (i) that that the legal test adopted by the German Federal Supreme Court is very formalistic and seems irreconcilable with the flexible 'good faith' norm favoured by the Commission (discussed above) and (ii) that requiring the would-be licensee to fulfil such strict conditions arguably fails to achieve a proper balancing of interests in case a FRAND commitment has been issued by the patentee, since (as already explained) such commitment indicates a willingness to trade exclusivity for remuneration.[113] This finding underlines the need for the CJEU and the Commission to take steps to promote a uniform European approach which ensures that injunctions are not granted in contravention with Article 102 TFEU. The recent reference for a preliminary ruling made by the Regional Court of Düsseldorf provides the CJEU the opportunity to do exactly that – in this respect see Case C-170/13, *Huawei Technologies v. ZTE*[114] which was discussed above.

[2] The Netherlands

As in Germany the Dutch courts seem to have taken the position that defendants may rely on a competition law defence to repel requests' for injunctions based on FRAND-pledged patents. However, as opposed to the German courts the Dutch courts have adopted a more licensee friendly approach according to which the burden of predicting what constitutes a FRAND royalty is not placed entirely on the would-be licensee. The position taken by the Dutch courts so far has been set out in a series of cases decided by the District Court of The Hague. In particular, *Philips v. SK Kasetten* and *Samsung v. Apple* are of interest to put the approach envisaged by the Commission into perspective.

In *Philips v. SK Kasetten*[115] the District Court of The Hague ruled that the defendant, SK Kasetten, had infringed several of Philips' patents essential to a de facto

et al., *Injunctions for Standard-Essential Patents: Justice is not Blind*, in Journal of Competition Law & Economics, Vol. 9(1), 2013 p. 295.

111. Cf. also Camesasca, Peter, et al., *Injunctions for Standard-Essential Patents: Justice is not Blind*, in Journal of Competition Law & Economics, Vol. 9(1), 2013 p. 296.
112. For more details see for instance Camesasca, Peter, et al., *Injunctions for Standard-Essential Patents: Justice is not Blind*, in Journal of Competition Law & Economics, Vol. 9(1), 2013, and Laakkonen, Ari, *Defences to patent infringement in a standards context*, paper presented at the Fordham IP Conference, 2011. Available at: http://fordhamipconference.com/papershistorical/ (last checked 30 May 2014).
113. See to the contrary Camesasca, Peter, et al., *Injunctions for Standard-Essential Patents: Justice is not Blind*, in Journal of Competition Law & Economics, Vol. 9(1), 2013 p. 295.
114. Case C-170/13, *Huawei Technologies v. ZTE*, 5 Apr. 2013.
115. Joint Cases No. 316533/HA ZA 08-2522 and 316535/HA ZA 08-2524, *Koninklijke Philips Electronics N.V. v. SK Kassetten GmbH & Co. KG*, District Court of The Hague, 17 Mar. 2010. The below analysis is based on information conveyed in Kuipers, Gertjan; Groenevelt, Douwe and Lamme, Oscar, *A further perspective on Apple v. Samsung: How to successfully enforce Standard Essential Patents in the Netherlands*, in berichten industriële eigendom, August 2012 p. 224,

standard regarding CD- and DVD-discs. As part of its defence the defendant claimed that it was entitled to a compulsory license on FRAND terms under competition law for which reason the injunction should be dismissed. The court disagreed. The Dutch court found that the mere entitlement to a compulsory license on FRAND terms does not constitute a permit to infringe, hence does not suffice to succeed with a competition law defence. According to the court there was in principle no basis for allowing the defendant to use the patented technology or for depriving Philips its right to enforce the disputed patents for as long as the defendant had not actually converted its alleged entitlement to a FRAND license into an actual license. Rather than passively awaiting the initiation of infringement proceedings by Philips the defendant should, according to the court, have approached Philips to obtain a license prior to producing the infringing discs or at the moment that it became aware or reasonably should have been aware that doing so infringed the disputed patents.[116] In essence, this reasoning seems to be in line with that of the Commission as discussed in Chapter 13 section §13.02[C][2] – obtaining an injunction on basis of FRAND-pledged patents is warranted if prior to using the patented technology the infringer has not sought to obtain a license in good faith.

The strict position taken by the Dutch court in *Philips v. SK Kasetten* indicated that a competition law defence was almost per se inadmissible in the Netherlands. However, the court opened a door by stating that its judgment might have been different under special circumstances and in subsequent case law found such special circumstances to exist. The *Samsung v. Apple*[117] judgment passed by the same court presents a contrasting example of the flexibility inherent in the Dutch approach in determining whether special circumstances warrant intervention. Although the court avoided ruling specifically on Apple's competition law claim the case arguably still has relevance in the context of competition law, because the focal point was whether the injunction should be dismissed on grounds that Samsung had abused its rights or acted contrary to pre-contractual good faith in light of its FRAND commitment. Thus, there is much to suggest that the court would have carried out the competition law assessment along the same lines. Indeed, the court did refer to *Philips v. SK Kasetten* which, as noted above, was decided on basis of competition law. Moreover, as noted

---

and Camesasca, Peter, et al., *Injunctions for Standard-Essential Patents: Justice is not Blind*, in Journal of Competition Law & Economics, Vol. 9(1), 2013 p. 296 (footnote 35). The information was cross-checked with miscellaneous esteemed online patent blogs. However, note that due to language barriers it has not been possible to ascertain the validity of the findings made by these authors on basis of the judgment itself.

116. Joint Cases No. 316533/HA ZA 08-2522 and 316535/HA ZA 08-2524, *Koninklijke Philips Electronics N.V. v. SK Kassetten GmbH & Co. KG*, District Court of The Hague, 17 Mar. 2010, § 6.19.

117. Cases 400367/HA, 400376/HA and 400385/HA, District Court of The Hague, 20 Jun. 2012. The below analysis is based on information conveyed in Kuipers, Gertjan; Groenevelt, Douwe and Lamme, Oscar, *A further perspective on Apple v. Samsung: How to successfully enforce Standard Essential Patents in the Netherlands*, in berichten industriële eigendom, August 2012. The information was cross-checked by having recourse to miscellaneous esteemed online patent blogs. However, note that due to language barriers it has not been possible to ascertain the validity of the findings made by these authors on basis of the judgment itself.

above, the notion of 'good faith' also seems to be essential in determining whether there has been an abuse of a dominant position under Article 102 TFEU.

The court in *Samsung v. Apple* found that although Apple had entered the market without requesting a license Samsung had been aware of this and a license was requested as soon as Apple found out that Samsung did not condone of its activities any longer. Since Samsung had issued a FRAND commitment to ETSI (accredited SDO) the court against this background the court concluded Samsung's enforcement of its SEPs "*...should be considered abusive and contrary to the principles of pre-contractual good faith, as the threat of the requested injunction puts Apple under improper pressure in these negotiations to agree to license terms that are not FRAND*".[118] As a basis for reaching this conclusion the court did not perform a detailed assessment of whether Samsung's requested license was FRAND compliant, but arrived at the conclusion that Samsung's conduct during license negotiations supported an assumption that it was not.[119] In this respect the court relied on the fact that Apple had indicated its willingness to take a license at an early stage and had engaged in good faith license negotiations while Samsung had *inter alia* failed to respond to a number of license offers made by Apple after having submitted its own 'opening offer'.

As opposed to the *Orange-Book-Standard* judgment passed by the German Federal Supreme Court the position of the Dutch courts seems to signify a much more licensee friendly approach in line with the views of the Commission: insofar as the potential licensee has requested a license in good faith and is willing to negotiate a license in good faith on FRAND terms any attempt by the SEP holder to obtain an injunction will normally run counter to Article 102 TFEU. As already mentioned the threat of an injunction may distort license negotiations, because the potential licensee may be inclined to accept what otherwise would have been rejected as non-FRAND.

§13.03 SUMMARY

A company against which an action for an injunction is filed should have the opportunity to raise a compulsory licensing defence on the basis of competition law as the denial of such defence would allow SEP holders to take advantage of the injunction 'mechanism' as a means to promote anti-competitive conduct – this applies to interim injunction proceedings as well as proceedings on the merits. In particular, a claim stating that the plaintiff has abused a dominant position contrary to Article 102 TFEU (or the national equivalent) by refusing to grant or negotiate a license on fair, reasonable and non-discriminatory terms should be admissibly (see below). If an alleged infringer of SEPs is entitled to a license on FRAND terms under competition law and is unduly forced to exit the market due to an injunction – even if only temporarily – irreparable harm to the defendant (and effective competition) may result. Moreover, the prospect of an injunction against which there is no viable defence may prompt

118. Kuipers, Gertjan; Groenevelt, Douwe and Lamme, Oscar, *A further perspective on Apple v. Samsung: How to successfully enforce Standard Essential Patents in the Netherlands*, in berichten industriële eigendom, August 2012 p. 225.
119. *Ibid.*

alleged infringers to accept excessive or discriminatory license terms, which otherwise would have been rejected, in order to avoid the consequences of such action. Dismissing the competition law defence as inadmissibly would therefore subvert the effectiveness of competition law and run counter to the objective underlying the patent system itself the purpose of which is to promote innovation.

FRAND commitments are designed as a precautionary measure to deter anti-competitive conduct – in particular by ensuring that essential IPR is made available to all third parties – whether SSO members or not – on fair, reasonable and non-discriminatory terms. It is therefore important to appreciate that a FRAND commitment from a competition law perspective is construed as a promise to grant a license to all third parties. Hence, it should be interpreted as a statement that the issuer renounces its rights to enforce the FRAND-encumbered rights against any company genuinely willing to take a license on FRAND terms.

Against this backdrop the Commission has made clear that seeking recourse to injunctions against potential licensees on the basis of FRAND-pledged patents is likely to constitute abuse within the meaning of Article 102 TFEU provided that the potential licensee is 'willing' to take license on FRAND terms. Thus, relying on the legal framework established by *ITT Promedia* with regard to vexatious litigation, and taking into consideration the principle of proportionality as set out in *Scarlet Extended*, the Commission (rightly) finds that the assertion of SEPs may constitute a 'wholly exceptional circumstance' which warrant competition law intervention. Indeed, the Commission seems to have adopted a very licensee friendly doctrine of 'good faith' under which such conduct, taking place in light of a FRAND commitment, is deemed abusive as a main rule rather than as an exception. This approach seems to be reasonable insofar as there can only be an objective justification for asserting FRAND-pledged patents against 'willing' licensees in exceptional circumstances. However, in order to preserve legal certainty and ensure a meaningful application of such 'good faith' doctrine guidance is needed. The reference for a preliminary ruling made by the Regional Court of Düsseldorf as currently pending before the CJEU will serve to clarify the scope and implications of the 'good faith' doctrine (which most likely will be upheld by the court).[120]

It seems safe to conclude that the standard of good faith as envisaged by the Commission is not as strict and formalistic as the one adopted by the German Federal Supreme Court in *Orange Book* which, as argued in Chapter 13 section §13.02[D], requires the alleged infringer to fulfil criteria which render it exceedingly difficult to succeed with a competition law defence. Rather the legal standard pursued by the Commission is a 'flexible' one, similar in 'spirit' to that adopted by the Dutch courts, according to which the specific conduct of the parties and the license offers made must be analyzed as a basis for determining whether threatening, seeking or enforcing an injunction amounts to abuse within the meaning of Article 102 TFEU. In this respect the Commission, as noted above, seems to hold SEP owners to a rather strict legal standard, finding that threatening, seeking or enforcing injunctions will be deemed

120. Case C-170/13, *Huawei Technologies v. ZTE*, 5 Apr. 2013.

abusive for as long as the potential licensee is willing to negotiate a license on FRAND terms. Thus, there are clear indications that the Commission does not consider it a prerequisite for finding abuse that the patentee can be shown to have violated its FRAND promise by refusing to license or by seeking to impose non-FRAND terms – obstructing on-going license negotiations is sufficient. In essence therefore the Commission is about to introduce a new type of abuse in EU competition law albeit within the existing legal framework established by *ITT Promedia* and *Scarlet Extended*.

It is not entirely clear how the Commission intends to assess whether the potential licensee, against whom an injunction is threatened or sought, is indeed 'willing' to take a license. The Commission seems to have set a rather low threshold for finding abuse *inter alia* by stressing that the commitment of an alleged infringer to accept a royalty rate set by an independent third party or court is sufficient evidence that the potential licensee is willing to procure a license on FRAND terms. However, such statement made by an infringer cannot per se entail that the subsequent assertion of SEPs against the infringer is to be deemed abusive, cf. Article 102 TFEU. In assessing the 'willingness' of the infringer to procure a license it is arguably necessary to take into consideration all data relating to the licensing negotiations preceding the dispute rather than a single statement in isolation. If for instance the infringer has failed to request a license in a timely manner – merely awaiting to see whether an infringement action is initiated – or has clearly obstructed or delayed licensing negotiations, the actions of the patentee should, regardless of such statement and all things being equal, not be considered a violation of Article 102 TFEU, but a legitimate action aimed at excluding a company not willing to take a license on FRAND terms.

This is not merely a policy consideration, but a necessary precondition for ensuring that Article 102 TFEU is only applied in cases where there is firm ground to believe that the conduct of the patentee is detrimental to effective competition. Thus, the Commission's interpretation of 'good faith' fails to achieve a proper balancing of interests in accordance with *Scarlet Extended* insofar as the 'good faith' regime adopted seems to focus exclusively on the obligation of the patentee to initiate licensing negotiations rather than on the obligation of the potential licensee to actively seek a license in the first place. In this respect it is also noted that Article 31(b) of the Agreement on Trade Related Aspects of Intellectual Property (TRIPS) signed by 153 members, including the European Union and the 27 Member States of the EU in their own right, states that compulsory licenses may as a general rule only be issued if "*the proposed user has made efforts to obtain authorization from the right holder on reasonable commercial terms and conditions and that such efforts have not been successful within a reasonable period of time*".[121] If FRAND commitments are construed so as to place undue burdens on innovators they might elect not to participate in standard setting activates and the pro-competitive benefits highlighted in Chapter 9 section §9.01 are therefore at stake.

121. Cf. World Trade Organisation, *Agreement on Trade Related Aspects of Intellectual Property Rights*, (TRIPS Agreement), 15 Apr. 1994.

As the right of access to a court is a fundamental right guaranteed by the Charter and the ECHR any exception hereto must, as set out in *ITT Promedia*[122] and *Protége International,*[123] be interpreted and applied restrictively. Accordingly, the application of Article 102 TFEU to enforcement actions as such or the threat hereof should (and seems to) be reserved those cases where the infringer is able to substantiate its alleged willingness to license by demonstrating:

(1) that a license request has been forwarded to the patentee in a timely manner as soon as the prospective licensee knew or ought to have become aware of the patent (which is *prior* to infringement in case the SSO provides a publicly available database of patents declared essential); and
(2) that following such request a) the patentee has outright refused to grant a license; or b_1) license negotiations have stalled without this been attributable to delaying tactics engaged in by the infringer and b_2) the final license offer, if made by the infringer, *is not* clearly non-FRAND or to the contrary, if made by the patentee, *is* clearly non-FRAND;[124] or
(3) that following such request the would-be license agreed to have a court or mutally agreed arbitrator set the FRAND terms and therefore benefits from the Commissions safe harbour set out in the Motorola Mobility and Samsung Electrioncs decisions – see section §13.02[C].

In case such evidence is presented the patentee can arguably only have an objective justification for enforcement action in a very limited number of scenarioes, e.g., if the would-be licensee is in financial distress and unable to pay its debts. As already noted seeking recourse to injunctions in light of a FRAND commitment can only be justified in exceptional circumstances where clearly the potential licensee is not willing to negotiate a license in good faith.

While an in-depth analysis of the competition law and commercial issues related to arbitration falls outside the scope of this book it seems that encouraging the use of such clauses in standardization agreements may go a long way in promoting competition law compliance by the parties hereto and avoid conflicts resulting in actions for injunctive relief. Thus, as compared to regular court proceedings arbitration ensures a swift way of resolving disputes concerning license terms and to avoid the market impact resulting from injunctions – hence the need for competition law intervention may be avoided. In particular, the use of arbitration ensures that injunctions cannot be used as a means to exclude competitors or facilitate the acceptance of non-FRAND license terms while at the same time providing holders of SEPs with the possibility of obtaining a quick and court enforceable decision as to the fairness of the license terms

122. Case T-111/96, *ITT Promedia v. Commission*, 17 Jul. 1998.
123. Case T-119/09, *Protégé International v. Commission*, 13 Sep. 2012.
124. According to Art. 2 of Regulation 1/2003, on the implementation of the rules on competition laid down in Arts 81 and 82 of the Treaty, 16 Dec. 2002, it is for the party or authority alleging the infringement to bear the burden of proof.

requested. In essence therefore the use of arbitration caters for the interests of right holders and users of SEPs alike.

As already explained there is in most cases no legitimate explanation for seeking to exclude competitors on the basis of FRAND-pledged patents, because the commitment to license all third parties means that the patentee has renounced its right to exclude for the benefit of remuneration. However, to ensure a proper balancing of interests the arbitration provision may (and arguably should) however be drafted to ensure that companies wishing to use patents reported to be essential cannot lean back and await the right holder to take action in case of infringement. The patentee should only be obliged to resort to arbitration as a dispute settlement mechanism in case the would-be licensee has forwarded a license request *prior* to any use of the patents in question. If no such request has been submitted the infringer has not fulfilled its obligation to request a license in 'good faith' and accordingly the patentee should not be barred from requesting an injunction on the basis of its FRAND-pledged patents. Such approach arguably aligns the arbitration clause with the requirements imposed by competition law, cf. above.

PART VI Concluding Remarks

CHAPTER 14
Conclusion and Perspective

While technical standards provide many benefits to consumers they also enter into the domain of patents and entail a risk that proprietors of standard-essential patents will be conferred the ability to act as gatekeepers to the markets affected. Once a market becomes 'locked-in' to a given standard switching to alternative technical solutions may be impossible or prohibitively expensive. In effect patentees may gain significant market power by having their patents embodied in technical standards. In this respect competition law acts to restrain the market power gained by standard-essential patent holders (SEP holders) and ensure that their licensing practices do not stray (too far) from the path of virtue.

The aim of this book has been to shed light on said path by exploring how Articles 101 and 102 of the Treaty of the Functioning of the European Union (TFEU) have been (or likely will be) applied to prevent, identify and sanction patent-related abuse in the context of technical standards.

§14.01 ARTICLE 101 TFEU AND STANDARDIZATION AGREEMENTS

Competition law looks favourable upon standardization agreements despite the fact that the involve collaboration between competitors and aim to neutralize competition with regard to select product features. This is so because of the many benefits that formal standardization brings. However, some standardization agreements risks creating market power. This is especially true in the field of ICT where patent activity is immense and (i) standards are often adopted to facilitate interoperability (ii) on markets characterized by strong network effects and (iii) involve rather detailed technical specifications which may include specific patented technology. Hence, these characteristics increase the likelihood that certain patents will become essential and indispensable *ex post* standardization. Indeed, in all cases where the exercise of

FRAND-pledged patents has been subject to scrutiny under Article 102 TFEU the patents read on ICT standards.[1]

The fact that standardization may create or increase the market power held by patentees is not in itself a problem from a competition law perspective. However, in order to increase the likelihood that the benefits of standardization prevail those agreements which risk creating market power are required to adhere to certain principles in order to benefit from a presumption that they do not restrict competition within the meaning of Article 101(1) TFEU. Some of these principles relate directly to IPR and aim at preventing 'patent hold-up' – a phenomenon which occurs if and when a SEP holder refuses to license or exploits its market power to impose onerous licensing terms upon prospective licensees which have become 'locked-in' to a standard. More specifically, SSOs are required to obligate their members to (i) perform good faith disclosures of IPRs potentially essential to the standard under development and (ii) provide an irrevocable commitment in writing to license their essential IPRs on fair, reasonable and non-discriminatory terms (FRAND terms) as a precondition for having them included in the standard. Compliance with these 'safe harbour' principles is not mandatory SSOs, i.e., SSOs remain free to adopt alternative rules insofar as they do not endanger the pro-competitive benefits of standardization.

All SSO policies examined as part of this book have adopted rules which are in line with, or more strict than, the IPR related 'safe harbour' principles. However, none of the SSOs attempt to specify the meaning of FRAND and absent interpretative guidance the notion remains inherently vague. Most undertakings can arguably agree that license terms must be fair, reasonable and non-discriminatory, but not what exactly that means.

§14.02 ARTICLE 102 TFEU AND THE EXERCISE OF SEPS

A FRAND commitment is in essence a contractual promise issued by a patentee to an SSO. However, reneging on a FRAND commitment does not only have potential consequences under contract law, but may also give rise to liability under Article 102 TFEU insofar as the patentee holds a dominant position. This is not surprising when considering that SSOs are required under Article 101 TFEU to request FRAND commitments as a precautionary measure aimed at ensuring that the exercise of SEPs *ex post* standardization does not lead to restrictions of competition.

In this book it was investigated whether holders of FRAND-pledged patents are subject to a special (stricter) legal norm under Article 102 TFEU than SEP holders which have not pledged to grant licenses on FRAND terms. Since the interface between competition law, patents and standards is currently in the process of maturing and due to lack of case law some uncertainty remains. However, on the basis of an analysis of (i) CJEU case law dealing with related issues, (ii) the Commission's guidelines and

1. With regard to the exercise of SEPs the Commission has so far investigated the conduct of IPCom, Qualcomm, Rambus, Samsung and Motorola and a reference for a preliminary ruling has been made in connection with a patent dispute between Huawei and ZTE in Germany. No judgments have been passed by the CJEU until date.

decisional practice and (iii) the Commission's statements made in the context of FRAND-pledged patents, two overall findings are made:

(1) The presence of a FRAND commitment does not seem to impact the assessment of whether the license terms, including royalty rates, offered by a patentee are fair, reasonable and non-discriminatory.
(2) The presence of a FRAND commitment seems to significantly constrain the patentee's ability to seek recourse to injunctions and in principle prevents the patentee from outright refusing to license.

Thus, from a competition law perspective FRAND commitments are important. They provide the basis for applying Article 102 TFEU to prevent SEP holders from withholding licences and from seeking recourse to injunctions against willing licensees even though such conduct most often will be completely legitimate in the absence of a FRAND commitment. On the other hand a FRAND commitment as such seems to have no relevance when it is to be decided under Article 102 TFEU whether or not a patentee demands non-FRAND license terms.

[A] Non-FRAND License Terms

The Article 102 TFEU prohibition against imposing unfair or discriminatory terms upon trading partners applies in general and a special legal test is not called for in the context of FRAND-pledged patents. The legal principles forming part of settled EU case law are generic in nature and apply in the context of standardization as well. There is no basis for concluding that the threshold for finding a royalty rate (or other license terms) non-FRAND is altered, merely because the patentee has issued a FRAND commitment. Since existing CJEU case law relates primarily to tangible goods and services the legal tests already developed are merely in need of slight modification to fit the licensing context.

Overall the assessment of whether the remuneration demanded by a SEP holder is unfair and unreasonable (excessive) within the meaning of Article 102(b) TFEU involves determining whether it bears a reasonable relationship to the *intrinsic value* of the licensed technology in trade. The patentee is not allowed to claim remuneration which reflects solely the *strategic value* stemming from the fact that its patents are embodied in a standard and have become indispensable to manufactures present on the market to which the standard in question relates. In this respect it has been argued that royalties must be calculated on basis of the component that practices all or substantially all of the standardized technology in order to prevent the patentee from collecting value in excess of the actual contribution made to the standard. However, there are arguably no black listed royalty bases. What matters is whether the royalty rate when applied to the royalty base obliges the licensee to pay royalties which exceeds the intrinsic value of the licensed technology.

Although distinguishing between the intrinsic and strategic value of a patent sounds appealing from a theoretical perspective there is no simple method suited to filter out strategic value in a way which does not lead to arbitrary results. Doing so requires proxies which can be relied upon to approximate the royalty rates (or other fees) which would have been charged, but for the patents inclusion in a technical standard, i.e., in a competitive environment. Accordingly, there is not only one, but a range of royalty rates which fall within the boundaries of fair and reasonable. The difficulties in establishing whether a price is excessive have been acknowledged by the Commission and are reflected in case law – so far there have been no cases where a patentee has been found to violate Article 102 TFEU by charging excessive royalties.

Generally competition authorities and courts should abstain from acting as price setters unless there is strong evidence that the remuneration charged is exorbitant. Capping royalties or otherwise engaging in detailed micro-management of license terms under Article 102 TFEU risks doing more harm than good, since it is hard to procure sufficiently strong evidence that the patentees licensing practices are exploitative of licensees and detrimental to consumer welfare. Since case law suggests that rather strict evidence is required to reach a conclusion that a price is excessive it seems most likely that Article 102 TFEU will be applied (at least successfully) to cap the remuneration rates charged in cases where a SEP holder decides to exploit the market power gained (if any) by having patents embodied in standard to impose onerous license terms after the standard is adopted. Lowering the evidentiary burden in light of a FRAND commitment risks discouraging participation in SSOs and might be harmful to innovation and consumer welfare since undertakings will need to factor in the risk of competition law intervention when deciding whether to invest resources in R&D.

While discrimination may seem a less ambiguous concept than 'unfair and unreasonable' it also raises complex issues under Article 102 TFEU. It is clear that the non-discrimination element of FRAND does not require SEP holders to offer all licensees identical terms and conditions, i.e., a FRAND commitment does not constitute a most-favoured-licensee clause. Indeed, SEP holders have an obligation under Article 102(c) TFEU to ensure that the remuneration charged reflects any dissimilarity as to the terms and conditions agreed in order to avoid distortions of competition caused by the application of similar conditions to non-equivalent transactions. On the other the patentee must also avoid applying dissimilar conditions to equivalent transactions insofar as it inflicts upon certain licensees' a competitive disadvantage *vis-à-vis* others. However, unless the rights and obligations set out in the license agreements being compared are identical it will often be very difficult to determine whether license transactions are equivalent. A valid comparison between licence agreements necessitates establishing a level 'playing field' by attaching a value to the individual license terms. Cross-licensing arrangements, indemnity undertakings and field of use or territorial restrictions for instance impact the risk and utility value associated with a license agreement and accordingly must be taken into consideration when assessing whether diverging royalty rates (or other fees) signifies discrimination. Moreover, even if licence terms are identical licences may not be similarly situated. There may room for SEP holders to differentiate between licensees on basis of objective factors related to their willingness or ability to pay even if to some extent it leads to distortions of competition, but it is unclear from case law to what extent the CJEU and the Commission will be willing to accept such line of argumentation – most likely, the scope for doing so is limited.

[B] Refusals to License and Injunctions

Absent a FRAND commitment a SEP holder is free to refuse to license any third party and to seek injunctions against any infringer – these prerogatives are inherent in a patent. According to settled EU case law such actions will only violate Article 102 TFEU in exceptional circumstances.

To the contrary a SEP holder having issued a FRAND commitment can only refuse to grant a license in exceptional circumstances. Moreover, a FRAND commitment signifies a willingness to trade absolute exclusivity for a right to remuneration, hence, in principle leaves no objective justification for seeking recourse to injunctions against companies seeking a license to manufacture standard compliant products. This does not mean that the use of injunctions should be banned, since this would leave little incentive for manufactures to actually procure a license and may be detrimental to innovation. However, holders of FRAND-pledged patents should only be allowed to seek recourse to injunctions as a last resort if the infringer has not acted as a 'willing licensee' by reaching out to the patentee to obtain a license in good faith. Concepts such as 'willing' and 'good faith' are obviously in need of clarification. Thus, more specifically the application of Article 102 TFEU to enforcement actions as such should be reserved those cases where the infringer is able to substantiate its alleged willingness to take a license by showing that two cumulative conditions are fulfilled:

(1) that a license request has been forwarded to the patentee in a timely manner as soon as the prospective licensee knew or ought to have become aware of the patent (which is *prior* to infringement in case the SSO provides a publicly available database of patents declared essential); and
(2) that following such request a) the patentee has outright refused to grant a license; or b_1) license negotiations have stalled without this been attributable to delaying tactics engaged in by the infringer and b_2) the final license offer, if made by the infringer, *is not* clearly non-FRAND or to the contrary, if made by the patentee, *is* clearly non-FRAND;[2] or
(3) that following such request the would-be license agreed to have a court or mutually agreed arbitrator set the FRAND terms and therefore benefits from the Commissions safe harbour set out in the Motorola Mobility and Samsung Electronics decisions – see Chapter 13, section §13.02[C].

Such legal test will arguably make the parties stay longer at the negotiating table and attempt to genuinely reach a compromise. Whether indeed this test will form part of the applicable law has not been determined yet. However, the Commission's statements

2. According to Art. 2 of Regulation 1/2003, on the implementation of the rules on competition laid down in Arts 81 and 82 of the Treaty, 16 Dec. 2002, it is for the party or authority alleging the infringement to bear the burden of proof.

point in the direction of a test devised along these lines and settled EU case law does not seem to present an obstacle. Since the test relies on a determination of whether the license offers made are FRAND there is however an obstacle of a more practical nature.[3] If true, as suggested in this book, that FRAND derives its meaning from settled EU case law it will seldom be possible to ascertain whether license terms are FRAND with any certainty. The parties are therefore left negotiating in 'the dark' not knowing whether they stay on the path of virtue. However, the test leaves some room for the parties to negotiate insofar as abuse requires a showing that the license terms offered by the patentee were *clearly* non-FRAND or *vice versa*. In effect some of the legal uncertainty associated with the FRAND concept is mitigated, since there is no need to determine with absolute certainty whether an offer is FRAND or not.

The test takes into account that seeking recourse to injunctions is only warranted as a last resort if the licensee has not acted in 'good faith'. It does not deprive the patentee the possibility of initiating a court case to obtain damages and get a determination whether indeed the offer made by the licensee was FRAND.

§14.03 LEGAL CERTAINTY

Legal certainty as to the interface between patents and competition law is essential to stakeholders involved in standard setting activities. If forced to tread unknown waters there is a risk that undertakings will abstain from engaging in completely legitimate business practices out of fear that they will violate Article 102 TFEU. Ignorance may also lead to unintentional breaches of competition law. This may not only be an issue to the undertakings concerned, but to society as a whole. Moreover, there is a risk that the incentive to participate in collaborative standard setting will diminish if restraints imposed by competition law in this respect are not made clear. Bearing in mind the profound pro-competitive benefits associated with standards and their importance to modern commerce this would be unfortunate.

When recognizing that the meaning of a legal concept such as FRAND is shrouded in mystery there therefore is reason to raise the red flag. Although Article 101(1) TFEU is relied upon to force SSOs to put in place preventive contractual measures one of the most important concepts – the FRAND commitment – is inherently vague and does not serve well to prevent disputes between rights holders and implementers. It is likely that legal certainty will be improved as more disputes surface, but from the perspective of 'proactive law' it is not desirable to wait for case law to infuse such notion with meaning.[4] The analyses performed in this book contribute to legal certainty by uncovering 'state of the art' and discussing how Articles 101 and 102 TFEU are likely to be applied on the basis of the principles set out in established EU case

3. Unless the patentee outright refuses to license without an objective justification, cf. Point 2(a).
4. For a brief introduction to the concept of 'proactive law' see Haapio, Helena, *Introduction to Proactive Law: A Business Lawyer's View*, in Scandinavian Studies in Law, Vol. 49, 2006. For a more detailed discussion see Sorsa, Kaisa (ed.), *Proactive Management and Proactive Business Law – A handbook, Course material from Turko University of applied sciences*, 2011. Available at: http://julkaisumyynti.turkuamk.fi/PublishedService?pageID=9&itemcode=9789522162441.

law. However, due to the limited amount of case law specifically concerning standards and the fact that competition law operates on the basis of overall legal principles rather than being strictly prescriptive legal certainty remains an issue.

Does this mean that FRAND is broken and beyond repair? No. Although FRAND commitments as such may not be well suited to prevent disputes they establish the basis for limiting the use of injunctions and, hence, may indirectly encourage patentees from using their SEPs as strategic weapons against implementers. It will therefore be interesting to see whether in years to come the patent hold-up issues arising in the aftermath of standard setting activities will increase or whether the EU courts and the Commission will be able to quickly send a warning to patentees that certain conduct is not acceptable. The recent reference for a preliminary ruling in case C-170/13, *Huawei Technologies v. ZTE,* has provided the CJEU with the opportunity to do so and the judgment will be important in shaping the future legislative landscape with regard to the enforcement of FRAND-pledged patents.[5]

It is also appreciated that a balance between legal certainty and effectiveness must be struck. In the context of competition law it is not advisable to establish very firm distinctions between 'good' and 'bad' since this may prevent courts and competition authorities from sanctioning anti-competitive conduct which does not fit the 'profile' of bad established. Conversely, it may also prevent commercial practices which are not harmful to competition. Most often a case-by-case analysis is called for to determine whether the conduct of a dominant undertaking is detrimental to effective competition. Prohibiting the use of injunctions by SEP holders will for instance tip the scale in favour of implementers which would then have little incentive to actively seek a license – a form of reverse hold-up.

§14.04 PERSPECTIVE

Competition law in tandem with SSO IPR policies undoubtedly plays an important role in bridging the gap between patented technologies reserved for private use and standards destined for common use. However, the purpose of competition law is to correct 'market failures' when they arise – not to prevent them from arising. At this point significant harm to consumers may already have materialized. If for instance a SEP is relied upon to impose excessive or discriminatory royalties it may be too late to restore competition to its previous state. Setting out a path of virtue in the form of clear legal principles will act to prevent such market failures from arising in the first place; hence, will benefit both the undertakings involved in standardization and society as whole. Arguably resources are better spent on welfare enhancing activities, such as research and development, than on raging what has been termed 'patent wars'. While there will per definition be a winner of a legal dispute decided in court even that winner might have been better off had the disputed not erupted.

Most SSO policies do not contain dispute resolution mechanisms, but leaves it to the members to settle any dispute that might arise bilaterally. As evidenced by case law

5. Case C-170/13, *Huawei Technologies v. ZTE*, 5 Apr. 2013.

this may involve litigation and result in competition law scrutiny which is both costly, time consuming and second best to actually prevent disputes. Scholars and companies alike have suggested that SSOs can aid in combating the hold-up problem and decrease litigation in the field by reforming their IPR policies.[6] These suggestions for reform have often stressed the need for adoption of dispute resolution mechanisms which can be used to adjudicate disputes concerning the meaning of FRAND in a faster and less costly way than litigation. This intuitively makes sense, but fact of the matter is that SSOs have no yet reacted to this cry for reform. In this respect it must be recalled that the interests of SSO members are not aligned and that the 'commercial tensions' which exist likely acts as a barrier to reform.[7] For as long as SSO members cannot reach consensus on the meaning of FRAND the prospect of them agreeing on a dispute resolution mechanism is arguably slim as well. Indeed, the effectiveness of a dispute resolution mechanism relies on firm principles upon which those entrusted with the task of adjudicating the dispute can base their assessment of FRAND.

It seems that future research in the field should increasingly focus on uncovering the tensions between the stakeholders involved in standardization, e.g., on basis of interviews, and highlight the obstacles to reform of IPR policies. This is the first crucial step in suggesting reforms that will actually be endorsed by SSOs. It may very well be that the reforms which are most likely to succeed are not those which from an ideal point of view are most effective in preventing patent hold-up, but any reform which acts to infuse the FRAND concept with meaning or leads to the establishment of dispute resolution mechanisms is better than passively leaning back to await further litigation. If legal disputes involving FRAND-pledged patents continues to surface and SSO members fail to reach consensus on the adoption of preventive measures competition law will likely play an increasingly prevalent role in setting the boundaries of FRAND. However, as mentioned above prevention is better than cure. Perhaps competition law can aid to facilitate consensus, since SSO members arguably cannot object to an SSO policy which seeks to establish the meaning of FRAND by reference to the principles used to determine FRAND under Article 102 TFEU. Indeed, any discussion of an IPR policy can only be undertaking bearing in mind the regulatory framework under which it operates and competition law forms part of this framework.

6. See for instance Kühn, Kai-Uwe, Morton, Fiona Scott & Shelanski, Howard, *Standard Setting Organization Can Help Solve the Standard Essential Patents Licensing Problem*, in CPI Antitrust Chronicle, March 2013 pp.1–5; Bekkers, Rudi & West, Joel, *IPR Standardization Policies and Strategic Patenting in UMTS, in Telecommunications Policy*, Vol. 33 (1-2), 2009 pp. 93–96, where former proposals for reform of ETSIs IPR policy, made by twenty of the largest stakeholders in the field of telcommunication, are outlined.

7. Also see Bekkers, Rudi & West, Joel, *IPR Standardization Policies and Strategic Patenting in UMTS, in Telecommunications Policy*, Vol. 33 (1-2), 2009 pp. 93–96, where it is noted that although several proposals for reform of ETSI's IPR policy have been made the IPR policy remains largely unchanged. According to the authors the "*[t]he difficulty of addressing what is perceived to be a major problem suggests that ETSI has difficulty achieving consensus on more specific IPR policies across the broad range of ETSI member interests*".

Annex Overview of Select IPR Policies

SSO	Patent Search Required	Patent Disclosure Required	FRAND/RF Commitment Required – By Default	FRAND/RF Commitment Required – Voluntary	Definition of FRAND	FRAND/RF Commitments Must Be Transferred Alongside Patents	Rules Aimed at Resolving or Preventing Disputes	SSO Keeps a Database of Patents Declared Essential
ETSI[1]	No	Yes[2]	No	Yes, FRAND[3]	No	Yes (bind transferee)[4]	No	Yes[5]
CEN/CENELEC[6]	No	Yes[7]	No	Yes, FRAND[8]	No	Yes (notify transferee)[9]	No	Yes[10]

SSO	Patent Search Required	Patent Disclosure Required	FRAND/RF Commitment Required – By Default	FRAND/RF Commitment Required – Voluntary	Definition of FRAND	FRAND/RF Commitments Must Be Transferred Alongside Patents	Rules Aimed at Resolving or Preventing Disputes	SSO Keeps a Database of Patents Declared Essential
ISO/EIC/ITU[11]	No	Yes[12]	No	Yes, FRAND[13]	No	Yes (bind transferee if specific SEP's have been declared essential – else reasonable efforts to do so)[14]	No	Yes[15]
DVB Project[16]	No	No	Yes, FRAND (possible to notify specific patents for exemption)[17]	No	No	Yes (but, the obligation of patentees *vis-à-vis* transferees is not specified)[18]	Yes (arbitration)[19]	Yes[20]
W3C[21]	No	Yes (upon request)[22]	Yes, RF (possible to notify specific patents for exemption)[23]	No	No	No	No	No

SSO	Patent Search Required	Patent Disclosure Required	FRAND/RF Commitment Required – By Default	FRAND/RF Commitment Required – Voluntary	Definition of FRAND	FRAND/RF Commitments Must Be Transferred Alongside Patents	Rules Aimed at Resolving or Preventing Disputes	SSO Keeps a Database of Patents Declared Essential
OASIS[24]	No	Yes[25]	Yes, RF or FRAND (with regard to patents covering own contributions to the standard)[26]	No	No	No	Yes (Certain technical committees require participants to provide a non-assertion covenant instead of FRAND/RF commitment)[27]	Yes[28]
IEEE[29]	No	Yes (upon request)[30]	No	Yes, FRAND[31]	No	Yes (bind transferee)[32]	No	Yes[33]

1 ETSI IPR Policy (Annex 6 of the Rules of Procedure) of 19 March 2014. Available at: http://www.etsi.org/about/iprs-in-etsi (last checked 30 May 2014).

2 ETSI IPR Policy (Annex 6 of the Rules of Procedure) of 19 March 2014, section 4. Members are required to use reasonable endeavours to inform ETSI on a bona fide basis of essential IPR, including applications therefor other than trademarks.

3 ETSI IPR Policy (Annex 6 of the Rules of Procedure) of 19 March 2014, section 6.1.

4 ETSI IPR Policy (Annex 6 of the Rules of Procedure) of 19 March 2014, section 6.1*bis*.

5 http://ipr.etsi.org/ (last checked 30 May 2014).

6 CEN and CENELEC have adopted the *ISO/IEC/ITU Common Patent policy* of March 2006. The patent policy is included as Annex 1 in CEN-CENELEC Guide 8, *Guidelines for Implementation of the Common IPR Policy on Patent (and other statutory intellectual property rights based on inventions)*, 3rd ed., December 2011. Available at: http://www.cencenelec.eu/ipr/Patents/Pages/default.aspx (last checked 30 May 2014).

7 CEN-CENELEC Guide 8, *Guidelines for Implementation of the Common IPR Policy on Patent (and other statutory intellectual property rights based on inventions)*, 3rd ed., December 2011, Annex 1. Members should draw the attention to any known patent or to any known pending patent application.

8 CEN-CENELEC Guide 8, *Guidelines for Implementation of the Common IPR Policy on Patent (and other statutory intellectual property rights based on inventions)*, 3rd ed., December 2011, Annex 1.

9 CEN-CENELEC Guide 8, *Guidelines for Implementation of the Common IPR Policy on Patent (and other statutory intellectual property rights based on inventions)*, 3rd ed., December 2011, section 7.3.

10 http://www.cencenelec.eu/ipr/Patents/PatentDeclaration/Pages/default.aspx (last checked 30 May 2014).

11 ISO, IEC and ITU have adopted the *ISO/IEC/ITU Common Patent policy* of March 2006 and a set of *Guidelines for Implementation of the Common Patent Policy for ITU-T/ITU-R/ISO/IEC* of 23 April 2012. Both are available at: http://www.iso.org/iso/standards_development/patents (last checked 30 May 2014).

12 *ISO/IEC/ITU Common Patent policy* of March 2006. Members should draw the attention to any known patent or to any known pending patent application.

13 *ISO/IEC/ITU Common Patent policy* of March 2006.

14 *Guidelines for Implementation of the Common Patent Policy for ITU-T/ITU-R/ISO/IEC* of 23 April 2012, section 7.

15 http://www.iec.ch/members_experts/tools/patents/patent_policy.htm (last checked 30 May 2014).

16 DVB Project, *Memorandum of Understanding*, 3 January 2014, Article 14. Available at: http://www.dvb.org/members/iprpolicy (last checked 30 May 2014).

17 DVB Project, *Memorandum of Understanding*, 3 January 2014, Articles 14.2 and 14.3.

18 DVB Project, *Memorandum of Understanding*, 3 January 2014, Article 14.8.

19 DVB Project, *Memorandum of Understanding*, 3 January 2014, Article 14.7.

20 http://www.dvb.org/members/dvb-patent-disclosure-database (last checked 30 May 2014).

21 W3C IPR Policy of 4 February 2004. Available at: http://www.w3.org/Consortium/Patent-Policy/ (last checked 30 May 2014).

22 W3C IPR Policy of 4 February 2004, section 6. Upon request members must disclose patents of which they have actual knowledge and believe to contain essential claims.

23 W3C IPR Policy of 4 February 2004, sections 3 and 4.

24 OASIS IPR policy of 2 May 2012. Available at: https://www.oasis-open.org/policies-guidelines/ipr (last checked 30 May 2014).

25 OASIS IPR policy of 2 May 2012, section 8. Members must disclose patents and/or patent applications of which they have actual knowledge and believe to contain essential claims. Disclosure obligation extends to third party patent claims and applications of which they are aware.

26 OASIS IPR policy of 2 May 2012, sections 9 and 10.

27 OASIS IPR policy of 2 May 2012, section 10.3.

28 https://www.oasis-open.org/committees/ (each technical committee keeps its own List of disclosures).

29 IEEE-SA Patent Policy of December 2013. Available at: http://standards.ieee.org/develop/policies/bylaws/sect6-7.html (last checked 30 May 2014).

30 IEEE-SA Patent Policy of December 2013, 6. 2.

31 IEEE-SA Patent Policy of December 2013, point 6.2.

32 IEEE-SA Patent Policy of December 2013, point 6.2.

33 http://standards.ieee.org/about/sasb/patcom/patents.html (last checked 30 May 2014).

References

All references below are sorted by date with the exception of the bibliography which is sorted alphabetically by the last name of the first author Listed.

Bibliography

Anderman, Steven & Ezrachi, Ariel, *Intellectual Property and Competition Law*, 2nd ed., Oxford University Press, 2011.

Anderman, Steven & Schmid, Hedvig, *EU Competition Law and Intellectual Property Rights – The Regulation of Innovation*, 2nd ed., Oxford University Press, 2011.

Appeldoorn, Jochen, *He Who Spareth his Rod, Hateth his Son*, in European Competition Law Review, Vol. 26(12), 2005 pp. 653–658.

Bekkers, Rudi & West, Joel, *IPR Standardization Policies and Strategic Patenting in UMTS*, in Telecommunications Policy, Vol. 33 (1-2), 2009 pp. 80–97.

Bekkers, Rudi et al., *Emerging Ways to Address the Reemerging Conflict between Patenting and Technological Standardization*, in Industrial & Corporate Change, Vol. 21(4), 2012 pp. 901–931.

Besen, Stanley M. & Farrell, Joseph, *Choosing How to Compete – Strategies and Tactics in Standardisation*, in the Journal of Economic Perspectives, Vol. 8(2), 1994 pp. 117–131.

Bessen, James & J. Meurer, Michael, *Patent Failure – How Judges, Bureaucrats, and Lawyers Put Innovators at Risk*, Princeton University Press, 2008.

Bessen, James E., et al., *The Private and Social Costs of Patent Trolls*, Boston Univ. School of Law, Law and Economics Research Paper No. 11-45, 2011. Available at: http://dx.doi.org/10.2139/ssrn.1930272 (last checked 30 May 2014).

Beurskens, Michael, *An Offer You Can't Refuse*, Comparative IP Academic Workshop Working Paper No. 6, 2009. Available at: http://www.law.washington.edu/Casrip/WWIP/Papers/2009/An offer you cant refuse.pdf (last checked 30 May 2014).

Biddle, Brad et al., *How Many Standards in a Laptop? (And Other Empirical Questions)*, Arizona State University (ASU) – College of Law, 2010. Available at SSRN: http://ssrn.com/abstract=1619440 (last checked 30 May 2014).

Bishop, Simon & Walker, Mike, *The Economics of EC Competition Law: Concepts, Application and Measurement*, Sweet and Maxwell 3rd ed., 2010.

Blaseby, Matthew, *Fighting Counterfeits on the European Frontline*, in Intellectual Property Counsellor, No. 176, 2011 pp. 1–4.

Blind, Knut et al., *Standard Essential Patents to Boost Financial Returns*, Paper at the 6th Annual Conference of the EPIP Association, September 8 – 9, 2011 (footnote 4). Available at: http://www.epip.eu/conferences/epip06/ (last checked 30 May 2014).

Bonadio, Enrico, *Standardization Agreements, Intellectual Property Rights and Anti-competitive Concerns*, in Queen Mary Journal of Intellectual Property, 2013 pp. 22–42. Available at: http://ssrn.com/abstract=2237426.

Botteman, Yves & Patsa, Agapi, *Towards a More Sustainable Use of Commitment Decisions*, in Article 102 TFEU cases, in Journal of Antitrust Enforcement, 2013 (not yet published). Available at: http://antitrust.oxfordjournals.org/content/early/2013/08/13/jaenfo.jnt009.full (last checked 30 May 2014).

Brooks, Roger G. & Geradin, Damien, *Interpreting and Enforcing the Voluntary FRAND Commitments*, in International Journal of IT Standards and Standardization Research, Vol. 9(1), 2011.

Brooks, Roger G., SSO Rules, *Standardization, and SEP Licensing: Economic Questions from the Trenches*, Remarks prepared for the Research Roundtable on Innovation and Technology Standards, Searle Center on Law, Regulation, and Economic Growth, Northwestern University School of Law, 2013 pp. 6–7.

Buttigieg, Eugène, *Competition Law: Safeguarding the Consumer Interest: A Comparative Analysis of US Antitrust Law and EC Competition Law*, Wolters Kluwer (International competition law series, 40), 2009.

Camesasca, Peter, et al., *Injunctions for Standard-Essential Patents: Justice Is Not Blind*, in Journal of Competition Law & Economics, Vol. 9(1), 2013 pp. 285–311.

CCIA, *Comments of the Computer & Communications Industry Association On the Public Consultation Regarding the Proposed Revised Guidelines for the Assessment of Horizontal Cooperation Agreements under EU Competition Law*, 2010 pp. 4–6. Available at: http://ec.europa.eu/competition/consultations/2010_horizontals/ (last checked 30 May 2014).

Chaffer, Chris, *Prohibiting Discriminatory Cross-Licensing*, in Information & Communications Technology Law, Vol. 21(2), 2012.

Chalmers, Damian et al., *European Union Law: Cases and Materials*, 2nd ed., Cambridge University press, 2010.

Coban, Ali Rize, *Protection of Property Rights within the European Convention on Human Rights*, Ashgate Publising, 2004.

CompTIA, *European Interoperability Framework – ICT Industry Recommendations*, white paper, Brussels, 18 February 2004.

Contreras, Jorge L. et al., *An Empirical Study of the Effects of Ex Ante Licensing Disclosure Policies on the Development of Voluntary Technical Standards*, Publication made for the National Institute of Standards and Technology, 2011. Available at SSRN: http://ssrn.com/abstract=1916743 (last checked 30 May 2014).

Contreras, Jorge L., Fixing Frand: *A Pseudo-Pool Approach To Standards-Based Patent Licensing*, Fortcoming in Antitrust Law Journal, Fall 2013. Available at SSRN: http://ssrn.com/abstract=2232515 (last checked 30 May 2014).

Contreras, Jorge L., *Rethinking RAND: SDO-Based Approaches to Patent Licensing Commitments*, American University – Washington College of Law, ITU Patent Roundtable, Geneva, 2012. Available at SSRN: http://ssrn.com/abstract=2159749 (last checked 30 May 2014).

Cook, William, *FRAND or foe*, in Managing Intellectual Property, June 2006 pp. 1–3.

Crane, Daniel A., *Patent Pools, RAND Commitments, and the Problematics of Price Discrimination*, Cardozo Legal Studies, Working Paper No. 232, 2008. Available at: SSRN: http://ssrn.com/abstract=1120071 or http://dx.doi.org/10.2139/ssrn.1120071 (last checked 30 May 2014).

Czapracka, Katarzyna, *Intellectual Property and the Limits of Antitrust: A Comparative Study of US and EU Approaches*, Edward Elgar Publishing, 2009.

David, Paul A. & Greenstein, Shane, *The Economics of Compatibility Standards: An Introduction to Recent Research*, in Econ. Innov. New Techno., Vol. 1, 1998 pp. 3–41.

DLA Piper, Universidade Nova de Lisboa & T.U. Delft, *EU Study on the Specific Policy Needs for ICT Standardization*, final report, 2007.

Dolmans, Maurits & Ilan, Daniel, *European Antitrust and Patent Acquisitions: Trolls in the Patent Thickets*, in Journal of the Antitrust Committee of the International Bar Association, Vol. 8(2), 2012 pp. 7–18.

Dolmans, Maurits, *A Tale of Two Tragedies – A plea for Open Standards*, in International Free and Open Source Software Law Review, Vol. 2(2), 2010 pp. 115–138.

Dolmans, Maurits, *Standards For Standards*, in Fordham International Law Journal, Vol. 26(1), 2002.

ECIS, *Comments in Reply to the Public Consultation on the Revised Rules for the Assessment of Horizontal Cooperation Agreements under EU Law*, 29 June 2010. Available at: http://ec.europa.eu/competition/consultations/2010_horizontals/ (last checked 30 May 2014).

EICTA, *White Paper on Standardisation and Interoperability*, 2006.

Eltzroth, Carter, *IPR Policy of the DVB Project: Negative Disclosure, FR&ND Arbitration Unless Pool Rules OK Part 1*, International Journal of IT Standards and Standardization Research, Vol. 6(2), 2008 pp. 21–47.

EPO, *Scenarios for the Future*, 2007. Available at: http://www.epo.org/news-issues/issues/scenarios.html (last checked 30 May 2014).

Farrar-Layne, Anne, *Nondiscriminatory Pricing – Is Standard Setting Different*, in Journal of Competition Law & Economics, Vol. 6(4), 2010 pp. 811–838.

Farrell, Joseph & Saloner, Garth, *Installed Base and Compatibility – Innovation*, Product Preannouncements, and predation, in The American Economic Review, Vol. 76(5), 1986 pp. 940–955.

Farrell, Joseph et al., *Standard Setting, Patents, and Hold-Up*, in Antitrust Law Journal, Vol. 74(3), 2007 pp. 603–670.

Folmer, Erwin & Verhoosel, Jack, *State of the Art on Semantic IS Standardization, Interoperability & Quality*, TNO, Universiteit Twente, NOiV, CTIT, 2011.

Frain, Tim, *Patents in Standards & Interoperability*, paper prepared for the World Intellectual Property Organisation, 2006.

Fraunhofer Institute for Communication System and Dialogic, *Study on the Interplay between Standards and Intellectual Property Rights (IPRs)*, OJEU S136 of 18/07/2009, 2011.

Geradin, Damien & Petit, Nicolas, *Price Discrimination Under EC Competition Law: Another Antitrust Doctrine in Search of Limiting Principles?*, in Journal of Competition Law and Economics, Vol. 2(3), 2006 pp. 479–531.

Geradin, Damien & Petit, Nicolas, *Price Discrimination under EC Competition Law: The Need for a Case-by-Case Approach*, GCLC Working Paper 07/05, 2005.

Geradin, Damien & Rato, Miguel, *Can Standard-Setting Lead to Exploitative Abuse? A Dissonant View on Patent Hold-Up, Royalty Stacking and the Meaning of FRAND*, in European Competition Journal. Vol. 3, 2007. Available at: SSRN: http://ssrn.com/abstract=946792 or http://dx.doi.org/10.2139/ssrn.946792 (last checked 30 May 2014).

Geradin, Damien, *Abusive Pricing in an IP Licensing Context: An EC Competition Law Analysis*, paper prepared for the 12th EU Competition Law and Policy Workshop: A Reformed Approach to Article 82 EC, European University Institute, 2007. Available at: SSRN: http://ssrn.com/abstract=996491 or http://dx.doi.org/10.2139/ssrn.996491 (last checked 30 May 2014).

Geradin, Damien, *What's Wrong with Royalties in High Technology Industries?*, TILEC Discussion Paper Series No. 2009-043, 2009. Available at SSRN: http://ssrn.com/abstract=1104315 or http://dx.doi.org/10.2139/ssrn.1104315 (last checked 30 May 2014).

Gifford, Daniel J., *Competition and Intellectual Property Law and Policy in the Knowledge-Based Economy: Standards and Intellectual Property: Licensing Terms: Some Comments*, Federal Trade Commission, 2000. Available at: http://www.ftc.gov/opp/intellect/020418danieljgifford.pdf (last checked 30 May 2014).

Gifford, Daniel J., *Developing Models for a Coherent Treatment of Standard-Setting Issues under Patent, Copyright and Antitrust Laws*, in IDEA: The Journal of Law and Technology, Vol. 43, 2003.

Gilbert, Richard, *Deal or No Deal?* Licensing Negotiations By Standard Setting Organizations, in Antitrust Law Journal, Vol. 77(3), 2011 pp. 855–888.

Haglund, Birgitte, *Erstatningsbetingende medvirkning*, Gyldendal Juridisk, 2012.

Hausman, Jerry A., *Price Discrimination and Patent Policy*, in RAND Journal of Economics, Vol. 19(2), 1988.

Hellström, Per & Kramler, Thomas, *Competition, Standards and Patents*, in CPI Antitrust Chronicle, Vol. 2, 2012. Available at: SSRN: http://ssrn.com/abstract=2156337 or http://dx.doi.org/10.2139/ssrn.2156337 (last checked 30 May 2014).

Helmers, Christian & McDonagh, Luke, *Trolls at the High Court?*, LSE Law, Society and Economy Working Papers, No. 13, 2012 pp. 12-13. Available at: http://papers.ssrn.com/sol3/papers.cfm?abstract_id=2154958 (last checked 30 May 2014).

Hockett, Christopher B. & Lipscomb, Rosanna G., *Best FRANDs forever? Standard-Setting Antitrust Enforcement in the United States and the European Union*, In Antitrust, Vol. 23(3), 2009 pp. 19–25.

Hoppner, Thomas, *Competition Law in Intellectual Property Litigation – the Case for a Compulsory License Defense Under Article 102 TFEU*, in European Competition Journal, Vol. 7(2), 2011.

Hovenkamp, Herbert, et al., *Intellectual Property and Antitrust – an Analysis of Antitrust Principles Applied to Intellectual Property Law*, 2002 (suppl. 2006).

Hovenkamp, Herbert, et al., *Unilateral Refusals to License*, in Journal of Competition Law and Economics, Vol. 2(1), 2006. Available at: SSRN: http://ssrn.com/abstract=703161 or http://dx.doi.org/10.2139/ssrn.703161(last checked 30 May 2014).

Hovenkamp, Herbert, *Standards Ownership and Competition Policy*, in Boston College Law Review, Vol. 48(1), 2007. Available at: SSRN: http://ssrn.com/abstract=889335 or http://dx.doi.org/10.2139/ssrn.889335 (last checked 30 May 2014).

Hull, David, *The EC's Investigation into the Pharmaceutical Sector: Trouble Ahead at the IP/Competition Intersection?*, in Competition Policy International, Vol. 11(1), 2008.

Iversen, Eric J., *Standardization and Intellectual Property Rights: ETSI's Controversial Search for New IPR-Procedures*, SIIT'99 Proceedings, IEEE Conference on Standardisation and Innovation, Aachen, Germany, 15-17 September 1999 pp. 1–9.

Jaffe, Adam B.; Lerner, Josh & Stern, Scott (eds.), *Innovation Policy and the Economy*, Vol. 1, MIT Press, 2001.

Jones, Alison & Sufrin, Brenda, *EC Competition Law- Text, Cases and Materials*, Oxford University Press, 3rd ed., 2008.

Jones, Alison & Sufrin, Brenda, *EC Competition Law*, 2nd ed., Oxford University Press, 2004.

Kao, Kuo-Feng & Hwang, Hong, *Input Price Discrimination and Social Welfare in the Presence of Technology Licensing*, working paper, 2013.

Katz, Michael L. & Shapiro, Carl, *Network Externalities, Competition, and Compatibility*, in The American Economic Review, Vol. 75(3), 1985 pp. 424–440.

Klink, Bart van and Taekema, Sanne (Eds.), *Law and Method. Interdisciplinary Research into Law*, Series Politika, no. 4, Mohr Siebeck, 2011.

Kühn, Kai-Uwe, Morton, Fiona Scott & Shelanski, Howard, *Standard Setting Organization Can Help Solve the Standard Essential Patents Licensing Problem*, in CPI Antitrust Chronicle, March 2013 pp.1–5.

Kuipers, Gertjan; Groenevelt, Douwe and Lamme, Oscar, *A Further Perspective on Apple v Samsung: How to Successfully Enforce Standard Essential Patents in the Netherlands*, in berichten industriële eigendom, August 2012 pp. 222–228.

Laakkonen, Ari, *Defences to Patent Infringement in a Standards Context*, paper presented at the Fordham IP Conference, 2011. Available at: http://fordhamipconference.com/wp-content/uploads/2011/04/Laakkonen.pdf (last checked 30 May 2014).

Layne-Farrar, Anne & Padilla, Jorge, *Assessing the Link between Standard Setting and Market Power*, 2010.

Layne-Farrar, Anne, *Antitrust And Intellectual Property Rights: Assessing The Link between Standards And Market Power*, in Antitrust, Vol. 21(3), 2007 pp. 42–47.

Layne-Farrar, Anne, *Be My FRAND: Standard Setting and Fair, Reasonable and Non-discriminatory Terms*, 2010 p. 5. Available at: http://www.aipla.org/learningcenter/library/papers/SM/2010-Spring-Meeting-Speaker-Materials/Documents/ED_2010_SM_Layne-Farrar_PPR.pdf (last checked 30 May 2014).

Lea, Gary & Hall, Peter, *Standards and Intellectual Property Rights: An Economic and Legal Perspective*, in Information Economics and Policy, Vol. 16, 2004 pp. 67–89.

Lemley, Mark A. & Shapiro, Carl, *Patent Holdup and Royalty Stacking*, in Texas Law Review, Vol. 85, 2007 pp. 1990–2049.

Lemley, Mark A. & Shapiro, Carl, *Ten Things to Do about Patent Holdups of Standards (and one not to)*, in Boston College Law Review, Vol. 48 pp. 149–168.

Lemley, Mark. A, *Intellectual Property and Standard Setting*, in California Law Review, Vol. 90, 2002. Available at: SSRN: http://ssrn.com/abstract=310122 or http://dx.doi.org/10.2139/ssrn.310122 (last checked 30 May 2014).

Lévêque, François & Ménière, Yann, *Technology Standards, Patents and Antitrust*, in Competition and Regulation in Network Industries, Vol. 9(1), 2008 pp. 29–47.

Lévêque, François, *Innovation, Leveraging and Essential Facilities: Interoperability Licensing in the EU Microsoft Case*, in World Competition, Vol. 28(1), 2005 pp. 71–91.

Mariniello, Mario, *European Antitrust Control and Standard Setting*, Bruegel Working Paper, 2013.

Mariniello, Mario, *Fair, Reasonable And Non-Discriminatory (Frand) Terms: A Challenge for Competition Authorities*, in Journal of Competition Law & Economics, Vol. 7(3), 2011 pp. 523–541.

Miselbach, Roger & Nicholson, Ron, *Determination of Fair and Reasonable Royalty Rates*, N&M Consultancy Limited, 2000. Available at: http://www.licensingforstandards.co.uk/docs/fairroys.pdf (last checked 30 May 2014).

Motta, Massimo, *Competition Policy – Theory and Practice*, Cambridge University Press, 2004.

Nimmer, Raymond T., *Technical Standards Setting Organizations & Competition: A Case for Deference to Markets*, in the University of Houston Public Law and Legal Theory Series, 2009-A-23. Available at: SSRN: http://ssrn.com/abstract=1473431 or http://dx.doi.org/10.2139/ssrn.1473431 (last checked 30 May 2014).

OECD, *Policy Roundtables – Excessive Prices*, DAF/COMP(2011), 2011.

Østerud, Erik, *Identifying Exclusionary Abuses By Dominant Undertakings under EU Competition Law: The Spectrum of Tests*, Kluwer Law International (International Competition Law Series, 45), 2010.

Pappalardo, Kylie & Suzor, Nicolas, *Standardisation and Patent Ambush: Potential Liability under Australian Competition Law*, Competition & Consumer Law Journal, Vol. 18, 2011 pp. 267–295.

Paradolesi, Roberto & Renda, Andrea, *The European Commission's Case against Microsoft – Kill Bill?*, in World Competition, Vol. 27(4), 2004. Available at: SSRN: http://ssrn.com/abstract=579814 or http://dx.doi.org/10.2139/ssrn.579814 (last checked 30 May 2014).

Park, Jae Hun, *Patents and Industry Standards*, Edward Elgar, 2010.

Rapp, Richard T. & Stiroh, Lauren J., *Standard Setting and Market Power*, Comments provided for Joint Hearing of the United States Department of Justice and the Federal Trade Commission, Competition and Intellectual Property Law and Policy in the Knowledge-Based Economy, 18 April 2002.

Rubin, Jonathan L., *Patents, Antitrust, and Rivalry in Standard-Setting*, in Rutgers Law Journal, Vol. 38, 2007 pp. 509–538.

Ruikka, Timo, *"FRAND" Undertakings in Standardization – A Business Perspective*, Paper presented at the Fordham IP Conference, New York City, March 28, 2008. Available at: http://fordhamipconference.com/wp-content/uploads/2010/08/T-Ruikka-paper-FRAND-from-business-perspective-Fordham.pdf (last checked 30 May 2014).

Schellingerhout, Ruben, *Standard-Setting from a Competition Law Perspective*, in Competition Policy Newsletter, no.1. 2011 pp. 3–9.

Shaprio, Carl & Varian, Hal, *Information Rules: A Strategic Guide to the Network Economy*, Harvard Business School Press, 1999.

Smith, Adam, *An Inquiry into the Nature and Causes of the Wealth of Nations*, Vol. 1, Book I, first published in 1776.

Smith, Graham, *Internet Law and Regulation*, 4th ed., Sweet & Maxwell, 2007.

Taylor Wessing, *What Does it Take to Be FRAND*, newsletter, 8 April 2013.

Spassova, Vesselina, *What Kind of Competition Policy for Highly Innovative Markets with Network Effects?*, CAE Working Papers 27, Aix-Marseille Université, CERGAM, 2005.

Stango, Victor, *The Economics of Standards Wars*, in Review of Network Economics, Vol. 3(1), 2004 pp. 1–19.

Swann, Peter, *The Economics of Standardization*, Final Report for Standards and Technical Regulations Directorate Department of Trade and Industry, 2000.

Torremans, Poul, *Intellectual Property and Human Rights*, Kluwer Law International, 2008.

UNCTAD, *Addressing the Interface between Patens and Technical Standards International Trade Discussions*, No. 3, 2009.

Van Bael & Bellis, *Competition Law of the European Community*, 5th ed., Kluwer Law International, 2010.

Vesterdorf, Bo, *IP Rights and Competition Law Enforcement Questions*, in Journal of European Competition Law & Practice, Vol. 4(2), 2013 pp. 109–111.

von Meibom, Wolfgang & Nack, Ralph, *Patents without Injunctions? – Trolls, Hold-Ups, Ambushes, and Other Patent Warfare*, in Wolrad Prinz zu Waldeck et al. (eds.), Patents and Technological Progress in a Globalized World, Springer, 2009 pp. 495–517.

Weitzel, Tim, *Economics of Standards*, in Information Networks, Physica, 2004.

Whish, Richard & Bailey, David, *Competition Law*, 7th ed., Oxford University Press, 2012.

WIPO, *Standards and Patents*, Standing committee on the law of patents, 13th Session, 2009.

Zafar, Osmann, *The Junction between Competition and IP Law*, in Intellectual Property Magazine, April 2012 pp. 52–53.

Table of Cases

Judgments of the CJEU

Non-CJEU Judgments

06-4292, Broadcom *Corp. v. Qualcomm Inc.*, 501 F.3d 297 (3d Cir. 2007), 28 June 2007, 154

07-1086, Rambus *Incorporated v. Federal Trade Commission*, United States Court of Appeals for The District Of Columbia Circuit, 22 April 2008, 104, 106

KZR 39/06, *Philips Electronics N.V. v. SK Kassetten* (Orange Book Standard), German Federal Supreme Court, 6 May 2009. English translation available in International Review of Intellectual Property and Competition Law (IIC), Vol. 41(3), 2010 p. 369, 8, 217, 218

316533/HA ZA 08-2522 and 316535/HA ZA 08-2524, *Koninklijke Philips Electronics N.V. v. SK Kassetten GmbH & Co. KG*, District Court of The Hague, 17 March 2010, 8, 219, 220

389067/KG ZA 11-269, *Sony Supply Chain solutions (Europe) v. LG Electronics*, District Court of The Hague, 10 March 2011, 8, 191, 193

7 O 122/11, *Motorola Mobility v. Apple*, Mannheim Regional Court (Landgericht Mannheim), 9 December 2011, 199, 212, 217

6 U 136/11, *Apple Sales* International *v. Motorola Mobility Inc.*, Karlsruhe Higher Regional Court (Oberlandsgerich Karlsruhe), 23 January 2012, 217

400367 / HA ZA 11-2212, 400376 / HA ZA 11-2213 and 400385 / HA ZA 11-2215 *Samsung Electronics Co. Ltd v. Apple Inc.* et al., joined cases, District Court The Hague, The Netherlands, 14 March 2012, 192

C10-1823-JLR, *Microsoft Corp. v.* Motorola *Inc.*, 20 April 2012, 4, 146

4b O 104/12, *Huawei v. ZTE*, District Court Dusseldorf (Landgericht Düsseldorf), 21 March 2013, 215

Commission Decisions and Related Documents

Commission decision in Case IV/29.151, *Video cassette recorders*, 20 December 1977, 74

Commission decision in Case IV/31.458, *X/Open Group*, 15 December 1986, 78

Commission decision in Case IV/32.736, *Moosehead/Whitbread*, 23 March 1990, 144

Commission notice in Case IV/33.667, *Philips/Matsushita-D2B*, 23 August 1991, 139

Commission notice in Case IV/35.006, *ETSI interim IPR policy*, OJ 95/C 76/05, 28 March 1995, 39, 93, 94

Commission decision in Case IV/35.268, *Promedia v. Belgacom*, 21 May 1996, 201

Commission press release in Case COMP/37.792, *Microsoft*, IP/01/1232 (Commission initiates additional proceedings against Microsoft), 30 August 2001, 155

Commission press release, *Commission welcomes changes in ETSI IPR rules to prevent 'patent ambush'*, IP/05/1565, 12 December 2002, 83

Commission decision in Case COMP/C-3/37.792, Microsoft, 24 March 2004, 35, 60, 124, 132, 183

Commission decision in Case COMP/38.096, *Clearstream (Clearing and* Settlement*)*, 2 June 2004, 174

Commission decision in Case COMP/A.36.568/D3, *Scanlines Sverige v. Port of Helsingborg*, 23 July 2004, 121, 155

Commission Communications and Notices

EU Legislation

International Conventions and Agreements

Other Documents

ISO/IEC Guide 2:2004, *Standardization and related activities*, 3 November 2004, 29

W3C Patent Policy of 5 February 2005. Available at: http://www.w3.org/Consortium/Patent-Policy-20040205/ (last checked 30 May 2014), 83

ISO/IEC/ITU Common Patent policy of March 2006. Available at: http://www.iso.org/iso/standards_development/patents (last checked 30 May 2014), 101, 240

Cleary Gottlieb Steen & Hamilton LLP, *European Commission Consultation* Draft *Guidelines On Horizontal Co-Operation Agreements-Standardization Section*, June 25 2010, 90

Joint response submitted to the FTC by Cisco Systems, Inc. (for Cisco, HP, IBM, and RIM), 8 January 2011, 195

ETSI, *Guidelines for Antitrust Compliance*, 27 January 2011, Point C.4.2. Available at: http://www.etsi.org/about/iprs-in-etsi (last checked 30 May 2014), 96

Response submitted to the FTC by Telefonaktiebolaget LM Ericsson, 8 May 2011. Available at: www.ftc.gov/opp/workshops/standards/index.shtml (last checked 30 May 2014), 195

Response submitted to the FTC by Verizon Communications Inc. 8 May 2011. Available at: www.ftc.gov/opp/workshops/standards/index.shtml (last checked 30 May 2014), 195

Response submitted to the FTC by Qualcomm Incorporated, 13 June 2011. Available at: www.ftc.gov/opp/workshops/standards/index.shtml (last checked 30 May 2014), 196

Response submitted to the FTC by Broadcom corp, 5 August 2011. Available at: www.ftc.gov/opp/workshops/standards/index.shtml (last checked 30 May 2014), 195

DVB Project, *Memorandum of Understanding*, 3 January 2014, Article 14. Available at: http://www.dvb.org/members/iprpolicy (last checked 30 May 2014), 240

ETSI Guide on IPRs, 19 September 2013. Available at: http://www.etsi.org/about/iprs-in-etsi (last checked 30 May 2014), 83, 84, 87

CEN-CENELEC Guide 8, *Guidelines for Implementation of the Common IPR Policy on Patent (and other statutory intellectual property rights based on inventions*, 3rd ed., December 2011. Available at: http://www.cencenelec.eu/ipr/Patents/Pages/default.aspx (last checked 30 May 2014), 101, 240

ISO/IEC/ITU, *Guidelines for Implementation of the Common Patent Policy for ITU-T/* ITU-*R/ISO/IEC,* 23 April 2012. Available at: http://www.iso.org/iso/standards_development/patents (last checked 30 May 2014), 240

IEEE-SA Patent Policy of December 2013. Available at: http://standards.ieee.org/develop/policies/bylaws/sect6-7.html (last checked 30 May 2014) , 241

Federal Trade Commission, Motorola Mobility LLC and Google Inc.; *Analysis of* Proposed *Consent Order to Aid Public Comment*, File No. 121-0120, 3 January 2013. Available at: http://www.ftc.gov/os/caselist/1210120/ (last checked 30 May 2014), 206

Index

INTERNATIONAL COMPETITION LAW SERIES

1. Ignacio De Leon, *Latin American Competition Law and Policy: A Policy in Search of Identity*, 2001 (ISBN 90-411-1542-0).
2. Wim Dejonghe & Wouter Van de Voorde (eds), *M & A in Belgium*, 2001 (ISBN 90-411-1594-3).
3. Yang-Ching Chao, Gee San, Changfa Lo & Jiming Ho (eds), *International and Comparative Competition Law and Policies*, 2001 (ISBN 90-411-1643-5).
4. Martin Mendelsohn & Stephen Rose, *Guide to the EC Block Exemption for Vertical Agreements*, 2002 (ISBN 90-411-9813-X).
5. Clifford A. Jones & Mitsuo Matsushita (eds), *Competition Policy in the Global Trading System: Perspectives from the EU, Japan and the USA*, 2002 (ISBN 90-411-1758-X).
6. Christian Koenig, Andreas Bartosch, Jens-Daniel Braun & Marion Romes (eds), *EC Competition and Telecommunications Law*. Second Edition, 2009 (ISBN 978-90-411-2564-4).
7. Jürgen Basedow (ed.), *Limits and Control of Competition with a View to International Harmonization*, 2002 (ISBN 90-411-1967-1).
8. Maureen Brunt, Economic Essays on Australian and New Zealand Competition Law, 2003 (ISBN 90-411-1991-4).
9. Ky P. Ewing, Jr., *Competition Rules for the 21st Century: Principles from America's Experience*, Second Edition, 2006 (ISBN 90-411-2477-2).
10. Joseph Wilson, *Globalization and the Limits of National Merger Control Laws*, 2003 (ISBN 90-411-1996-5).
11. Peter Verloop & Valérie Landes (eds), *Merger Control in Europe: EU, Member States and Accession States*, Fourth Edition, 2003 (ISBN 90-411-2056-4).
12. Themistoklis K. Giannakopoulos, *Safeguarding Companies' Rights in Competition and Anti-dumping/Anti-subsidies Proceedings*, Second Edition, 2011 (ISBN 978-90-411-3404-2).
13. Marjorie Holmes & Lesley Davey (eds), *A Practical Guide to National Competition Rules across Europe*, Second Edition, 2007 (ISBN 978-90- 411-2607-8).
14. Sigrid Stroux, *US and EU Oligopoly Control*, 2004 (ISBN 90-411-2296-6).
15. Tzong-Leh Hwang and Chiyuan Chen (eds), *The Future Development of Competition Framework*, 2004 (ISBN 90-411-2305-9).

16. Phedon Nicolaides, Mihalis Kekelekis and Maria Kleis, *State Aid Policy in the European Community: Principles and Practice*, Second Edition, 2008 (ISBN 978-90-411-2754-9).
17. Doris Hildebrand, *Economic Analyses of Vertical Agreements: A Self- Assessment*, 2005 (ISBN 90-411-2328-8).
18. Frauke Henning-Bodewig, *Unfair Competition Law: European Union and Member States*, 2005 (ISBN 90-411-2329-6).
19. Duarte Brito & Margarida Catalão-Lopes, *Mergers and Acquisitions: The Industrial Organization Perspective*, 2006 (ISBN 90-411-2451-9).
20. Nikos Th. Nikolinakos, *EU Competition Law and Regulation in the Converging Telecommunications, Media and IT Sectors*, 2006 (ISBN 90-411- 2469-1).
21. Mihalis Kekelekis, *The EC Merger Control Regulation: Rights of Defence. A Critical Analysis of DG COMP Practice and Community Courts' Jurisprudence*, 2006 (ISBN 90-411-2553-1).
22. Mark R. Joelson, *An International Antitrust Primer: A Guide to the Operation of United States, European Union and Other Key Competition Laws in the Global Economy*, Third Edition, 2006 (ISBN 90-411-2468-3).
23. Themistoklis K. Giannakopoulos, *A Concise Guide to the EU Anti-dumping/ Anti-subsidies Procedures*, 2006 (ISBN 90-411-2464-0).
24. George Cumming, Brad Spitz & Ruth Janal, *Civil Procedure Used for Enforcement of EC Competition Law by the English, French and German Civil Courts*, 2007 (ISBN 978-90-411-2471-5).
25. Jürgen Basedow (ed.), *Private Enforcement of EC Competition Law*, 2007 (ISBN 978-90-411-2613-9).
26. Jung Wook Cho, *Innovation and Competition in the Digital Network Economy: A Legal and Economic Assessment on Multi-tying Practices and Network Effects*, 2007 (ISBN 978-90-411-2574-3).
27. Akira Inoue, *Japanese Antitrust Law Manual: Law, Cases and Interpretation of the Japanese Antimonopoly Act*, 2007 (ISBN 978-90-411-2627-6).
28. René Barents, *Directory of EC Case Law on Competition*, 2007 (ISBN 978-90-411-2656-6).
29. Paul F. Nemitz (ed.), *The Effective Application of EU State Aid Procedures: The Role of National Law and Practice*, 2007 (ISBN 978-90-411-2657-3).
30. Jurian Langer, *Tying and Bundling as a Leveraging Concern under EC Competition Law*, 2007 (ISBN 978-90-411-2575-0).
31. Abel M. Mateus & Teresa Moreira (eds), *Competition Law and Economics – Advances in Competition Policy and Antitrust Enforcement*, 2007 (ISBN 978-90-411-2632-0).
32. Alberto Santa Maria, *Competition and State Aid: An Analysis of the EC Practice*, 2007 (ISBN 978-90-411-2617-7).
33. Barry J. Rodger (ed.), *Article 234 and Competition Law: An Analysis*, 2007 (ISBN 978-90-411-2605-4).
34. Alla Pozdnakova, *Liner Shipping and EU Competition Law*, 2008 (ISBN 978-90-411-2717-4).

35. Milena Stoyanova, *Competition Problems in Liberalized Telecommunications: Regulatory Solutions to Promote Effective Competition*, 2008 (ISBN 978-90-411-2736-5).
36. *EC State Aid Law/Le Droit des Aides d'Etat dans la CE. Liber Amicorum Francisco Santaolalla Gadea*, 2008 (ISBN 978-90-411-2774-7).
37. René Barents, *Directory of EC Case Law on State Aids*, 2008 (ISBN 978- 90-411-2732-7).
38. Ignacio De Leon, *An Institutional Assessment of Antitrust Policy: The Latin American Experience*, 2009 (ISBN 978-90-411-2478-4).
39. Doris Hildebrand, *The Role of Economic Analysis in the EC Competition Rules*, Third Edition, 2009 (ISBN 978-90-411-2513-2).
40. Eugène Buttigieg, *Competition Law: Safeguarding the Consumer Interest. A Comparative Analysis of US Antitrust Law and EC Competition Law*, 2009 (ISBN 978-90-411-3119-5).
41. Ioannis Lianos & Ioannis Kokkoris (eds), *The Reform of EC Competition Law: New Challenges*, 2010 (ISBN 978-90-411-2692-4).
42. George Cumming & Mirjam Freudenthal, *Civil Procedure in EU Competition Cases before the English and Dutch Courts*, 2010 (ISBN 978-90-411-3192-8).
43. A.E. Rodriguez & Ashok Menon, *The Limits of Competition Policy: The Shortcomings of Antitrust in Developing and Reforming Economies*, 2010 (ISBN 978-90-411-3177-5).
44. Mika Oinonen, *Does EU Merger Control Discriminate against Small Market Companies? Diagnosing the Argument with Conclusions*, 2010 (ISBN 978-90-411-3261-1).
45. Eirik Østerud, *Identifying Exclusionary Abuses by Dominant Undertakings under EU Competition Law: The Spectrum of Tests*, 2010 (ISBN 978-90-411-3271-0).
46. Marco Botta, *Merger Control Regimes in Emerging Economies: A Case Study on Brazil and Argentina*, 2011 (ISBN 978-90-411-3402-8).
47. Jürgen Basedow & Wolfgang Wurmnest (eds), *Structure and Effects in EU Competition Law: Studies on Exclusionary Conduct and State Aid*, 2011 (ISBN 978-90-411-3174-4).
48. George Cumming (ed.), *Merger Decisions and the Rules of Procedure of the European Community Courts*, 2012 (ISBN 978-90-411-3671-8).
49. Eduardo Molan Gaban & Juliana Oliveira Domingues (eds), *Antitrust Law in Brazil: Fighting Cartels*, 2012 (ISBN 978-90-411-3670-1).
50. Giandonato Caggiano, Gabriella Muscolo & Marina Tavassi (eds), *Competition Law and Intellectual Property: A European Perspective*, 2012 (ISBN 978-90-411-3447-9).
51. Ben Van Rompuy, *Economic Efficiency: The Sole Concern of Modern Antitrust Policy? Non-efficiency Considerations under Article 101 TFEU*, 2012 (ISBN 978-90-411-3870-5).
52. Liyang Hou, *Competition Law and Regulation of the EU Electronic Communications Sector: A Comparative Legal Approach*, 2012 (ISBN 978-90-411-4047-0).

53. Barry Rodger, *Landmark Cases in Competition Law: Around the World in Fourteen Stories*, 2012 (ISBN 978-90-411-3843-9).
54. Andreas Scordamaglia-Tousis, *EU Cartel Enforcement: Reconciling Effective Public Enforcement with Fundamental Rights*, 2013 (ISBN 978-90-411-4758-5).
55. Bernardo Cortese (ed.), *EU Competition Law: Between Public and Private Enforcement*, 2014 (ISBN 978-90-411-4677-9).
56. Barry Rodger (ed.), *Competition Law: Comparative Private Enforcement and Collective Redress across the EU*, 2014 (ISBN 978-90-411-4559-8).
57. Nada Ina Pauer, *The Single Economic Entity Doctrine and Corporate Group Responsibility in European Antitrust Law*, 2014 (ISBN 978-90-411-5262-6).
58. Urška Petrovčič, *Competition Law and Standard Essential Patents: A Transatlantic Perspective*, 2014 (ISBN 978-90-411-4960-2).
59. David Telyas, *The Interface between Competition Law, Patents and Technical Standards*, 2014 (ISBN 978-90-411-5418-7).